So You Want to Start a Nursery

So You Want to Start a Nursery

Tony Avent

Timber Press
Portland • Cambridge

Published in 2003 by
Timber Press, Inc.
The Haseltine Building
133 S.W. Second Avenue, Suite 450
Portland, Oregon 97204, U.S.A.

Timber Press
2 Station Road
Swavesey
Cambridge CB4 5QJ, U.K.

Printed in Hong Kong

Library of Congress Cataloging-in-Publication Data

Avent, Tony.
    So you want to start a nursery / Tony Avent.
        p. cm.
    Includes bibliographical references and index.
    ISBN 0-88192-584-5
        1. Nurseries (Horticulture)—Management. 2. Nursery stock—Management. 3. New business enterprises—Vocational guidance. 4. Self-employed. I. Title.

SB118.5.A83 2003
635.9'152'068—dc21
                                                                2002045401

To
my wife, Michelle
("We're going to start a what?")

whose decades of hard work, wonderful ideas, patient tolerance, and support have made the great adventure of running a nursery possible. Her endurance, encouragement, and assistance with this book earned her a really nice vacation—this year. I promise not to proofread during our vacation at a romantic getaway.

and to
the late J. C. Raulston

I hope you're watching.

Contents

Preface: *Why Ask Why?*

There are certainly several books that address the different aspects of the nursery in great detail. Most focus on the intricate technical details of the nursery business, others detail soil mixes, and still others summarize studies of pest control. What I have attempted to write, however, is a thought-provoking book that touches on the broad range of issues that you will encounter as a nursery owner.

The issues to be covered here are less technical in nature, and I address rarely discussed topics from selecting land to writing a catalog to the effect of the nursery business on family relationships to marketing your plants. When you get under way with your nursery you will still need plenty of generally available technical information that is not covered here, but you will now know what questions to ask.

People often want to know which group or groups I am targeting with this book, and the answer is simply anyone who wants to know more about the nursery business. This group is incredibly varied and includes students with a great deal of curiosity, nursery workers contemplating going it alone, unfulfilled workers in other fields considering a career change, backyard hobbyists with excessively large plant collections, landowners looking for an income opportunity, farmers wanting to change commodities, micronurseries looking to expand, and even retirees exploring the possibility of a second career.

The nursery business is truly among the most rewarding careers for anyone with a fondness for ornamental plants. Admittedly, it can be a difficult career if you start down the long and often treacherous road without a good map alerting you to potential hazards. Although nursery owners do their share of complaining, you would be hard-pressed to find even one who would trade careers for a more lucrative or less stressful occupation. One local nurseryman I know turned down several multimillion-dollar offers for his nursery, all the while aware that he will never realize the same financial freedom by continuing to operate the nursery himself. This dedication and love of the business speaks to the soulful attachment of nursery owners to their business. If, after reading this book, you are still determined to start or continue in the nursery business, you have both my best wishes and condolences. At least you will be going forward with your eyes wide open.

Acknowledgments

A special thanks to plantsman Barry Yinger of Hines Nurseries, Carolyn Williams, a noted psychologist and plant lover, Petra Schmidt, our research manager, Wayne Mezitt, president of Weston Nursery and president of ANLA, and especially my wife, Michelle, all of whom took time out of their very busy schedules to read the manuscript and offer their frank and detailed comments.

Also thanks to Neal Maillet of Timber Press for his patience in dealing with a nursery owner who is juggling far too many projects.

A final heartfelt thank-you to the late J. C. Raulston for being such a great leader, a true inspiration, a generous plantsman, and an avid personal supporter.

Introduction

I still recall the look of horror expressed by the late J. C. Raulston when I told him that I had left my secure state job of 16 years to run our small nursery full-time. "There is no way a specialty nursery can possibly make a profit without doing something illegal," he said. "Please consider keeping your full-time job." One thing immediately hit me: Raulston had only spent time around poorly run nurseries, a fact that, if nothing else, indicated the need for a better role model. The very idea that one of the top horticulture professors in the country didn't think a specialty nursery could make money was appalling and frightening—but it was also challenging. I had never considered the possibility that such a nursery could not make money. The more I pondered his comments, the clearer it became that those in the nursery business must do a better job of helping those wanting to become a part of it.

I confess that the idea of a nursery operation with an illegal side to it was fascinating, especially since the top agricultural commodity in my state is an illegal one, *Cannabis sativa*. The only problem was that the thought of running a nursery from jail wasn't very appealing. I quickly thought about what else we could do "illegally" to generate funds, and the next time Raulston visited the nursery, he noticed we had hung a coat hanger on a clothesline near the office. On the coat hanger were several clothespins, each one clipping a dollar bill. Raulston stared at the coat hanger for a few minutes before admitting, "Ok, I don't get it." I told him that we had indeed taken his advice and that this was the money-laundering part of our operation.

By now some of you are probably wondering why a plant nerd didn't write a book about plants, and I must admit that was my original intent when I first considered writing a book. Perhaps it was Raulston's comments on top of the many calls I received about starting a nursery that first planted the seed for this book, but it was a conversation with Mike Dirr that sealed the idea. On a visit to Georgia in the mid-1990s, I was discussing many plant-related topics with Mike when I asked him which textbook he used to teach nursery management. "There isn't a good one," he replied. I couldn't get this out of my mind, and when I remembered the nursery management course taught by Raulston, I realized that his textbook was nothing more than a series of articles reprinted from various nursery magazines assembled into a packet.

I do not mean to imply that there are no books on nursery management, as nothing is farther from the truth. There is a wide assortment of books on propagation, soils, fertilization, and greenhouse construction, including tomes on virtually all the technical aspects of having a greenhouse. Amazingly, however, there were no usable, commonsense books addressing the thought processes involved in starting a nursery.

I am fortunate to have spent the better part of my life visiting and studying nurseries, from the largest in the country to the smallest. In so doing, I have concluded that defining "success" is difficult as it is measured in different ways by every nursery owner. What would be a meager income to some is entirely satisfactory to others. For some nursery owners, selling 100 plants out of a pickup truck at the local market is success; to others, sales of less than 100,000 plants is a failure. The ideas and rules that you read about here will not apply to every nursery because nursery owners all want different things from their business. Some nursery owners start their business based on a desire for a particular quality of life. Others like the independence it offers or they enjoy working outdoors. You will have to decide what you view as success in your nursery operation and which path will get you there.

As I travel around the country visiting nurseries, I find it quite easy, based solely on sound business standards, to figure out why a nursery is succeeding or failing financially. With this book I have attempted to offer a wide range of information that, if heeded, will virtually assure a successful nursery operation, regardless of your idea of success. An additional source of information that will help ensure success is Plant Delights Nursery's Web site, Start a Nursery.com (www.startanursery.com).

I have also been asked if the intent of the book is to encourage or discourage folks from starting a nursery, and the answer is neither. I want only to give a realistic view of everything that is involved in getting into the nursery business. Some ideas are pertinent for small backyard nurseries, while others are more suited to large-scale nurseries. Homeowners will enjoy a peek behind the scenes of the nursery business, while owners of backyard nurseries may gain some insights and develop some ideas into how to make their businesses grow. While the nursery business can be among the most fun and rewarding careers for anyone who likes plants, I hope the book will be a reality check for anyone wanting to start a nursery.

Chapter 1

The Roswell Factor:
Examining Nursery Myths

I really feel I've heard it all: "It looks like so much fun," or "I love plants, so I think I should start a nursery," or "I've got some spare land that's just sitting there," or "I spend so much time and money on plants that I'm thinking of starting a nursery to help recoup some of my expenses." I always chuckle when I hear people who want to start a family say they are looking for a career that will allow them to have more spare time and so are considering the nursery business. Unfortunately, plants don't have the ability to wait until it is convenient to be attended to. A former employee once mentioned starting a nursery so she would have time for long vacations, nights off to see plays and eat out, and weekends off to travel. Reality came as quite a shock after the greenhouses were built.

A common myth is that those with vacant land will get rich quickly if they start a nursery. A nearby neighbor had some vacant land and wanted to do something that would bring in lots of money with minimal effort and so he started a tree farm. It's a shame that they didn't anticipate the six-week drought that followed planting. Irrigation; nobody mentioned irrigation! Many dead plants and several years later (which included hours of mowing, pruning, watering, and spraying, as well as the purchase of a tree spade), the remaining live plants were ready to be harvested. Oh gee—marketing. A sign was stuck up beside the road and yes, I'm still driving by those 40-foot-tall river birches grown on 5-foot spacing. (Seven years later a bulldozer was rented to push over the trees. I wonder how river birch burns as firewood?) Some people want to get into the nursery business because they are too stressed out in their current job. They view the nursery business as a laid-back pastoral-like career. Imagine for a moment a late freeze that is about to kill or severely injure your newly leafed out crop. (Of course it is a presold crop, the money for which has already been spent on a load of potting soil.) Or imagine opening for a fall open house with a hurricane bearing down on the nursery that will drown thousands of dollars of plant material and leave customers with little desire to garden in the foreseeable future. Or what about the spider mites you discover in the large order a landscaper has just arrived to pick up (they weren't there last week when you checked, of course) or the foliar nematodes that have infested most of your crop soon after your catalog has been mailed. Imagine trying to ship orders that, when charged, will just meet a tight payroll, and the international shipping company that you use goes on strike. Oh no, there isn't any stress in the nursery business!

The nursery experience was best summed up by a clerk at a local farming supply store who, having seen my purchases, said I must be in the farming business. I explained I was a nurseryman, and she replied, "That's much harder than being a farmer. We tried having a nursery but it was too much work so we quit and went back to farming." Unlike farm crops, which are in and out in a few months, nursery crops often remain for one or more seasons before being ready for sale. This allows little time off during the "down season," and consequently there is more time for things to go wrong with the crop.

The first thing to realize about the nursery business is that you are dealing with living beings. Plants are not like widgets in old country stores that can just sit around for 50 years or more gathering dust until they are finally sold. Every day you keep a plant increases the chance that it will die, contract a disease, become infested with insects, grow too large, or become unsellable in some other way. What on the surface seems to be an industry of high profit—stick a cutting and sell it two months later for several dollars—doesn't actually materialize when you include mysterious factors such as overhead costs. Also, unlike some animals that can fend for themselves during your absence, plants are essentially stuck in one place waiting for either you or Mother Nature to take care of them. Just because you are on a vacation doesn't mean they will oblige by magically reducing their need for water.

The stresses of running your own nursery as a business and not as a hobby are truly unimaginable by those who have never taken the plunge. Let me simply say that if you have a low tolerance for stress then owning a nursery business is truly a bad idea. I'm not implying that nursery owners never get a day off or can't ever relax—I can distinctly remember taking one a few years back, although my wife disputes my recollection—but time off to a nursery owner usually means watering plants or pulling weeds.

I'm sure you have met some retired nursery owners who have plenty of money and travel and live a life of luxury. With rare exception, that money didn't come from growing plants. Raulston often remarked that the only way a nursery ever makes money is to sell its land for development. In the case of most smaller nurseries, no truer words have ever been spoken, but as is evidenced by the proliferation of nurseries, this does not have to be the case. With an understanding of the business and the proper combination of skills, you will indeed find it possible to make a comfortable living. Just don't enter the fray as so many folks do—with your eyes wide shut.

Chapter 2

Getting Started:
The Thought Process

The nursery business is among the few that often begin as a lark or at least without much thought about the future—or without much of a business plan. This lack of planning has resulted in most nursery operations evolving into a haphazard logistical nightmare of nearly dysfunctional, or at best overly labor intensive, growing areas. Common mistakes range from poor vehicular access that impedes the maintenance and transportation of crops to no logical plan for expansion to no mission statement to inadequate funding. According to business analysts, the most common reasons that businesses fail are a lack of adequate planning, an unfeasible business concept, poor management, or a lack of sufficient funding. Each of these needs must be carefully addressed before embarking on the road of nursery ownership.

A garden center in my area has been owned by five different operators since 1992, each lasting about two years before going bankrupt. It has been a great study in all four reasons for business failure: inadequate understanding of the customer base, poor business concept (in terms of the nursery's location), weak management, and a lack of proper financial management, all of which spelled doom for each of these business incarnations.

Undoubtedly some business concepts are doomed from the start. I'll never forget the fellow who stopped by my nursery to announce that he had started his own wholesale nursery by growing acres of agaves (century plants) in Zone 7 North Carolina. Granted, a few agaves grow successfully if sited correctly, but with the limited local agave demand, he could probably count on selling fewer than 100 plants per year. Obviously, this was an unrealistic nursery concept.

Poor management skills are something that this book will probably not be able to rectify unless you are introspective enough to know when to hire a good manager and turn over the reins. The book will, however, address some of the issues you should consider in putting together a well thought-out management plan.

The most prevalent problem in the nursery industry seems to be a lack of planning. Most people simply don't have a realistic view of everything that is involved in running a nursery, a problem I hope will be remedied with this book. A good business plan not only ensures a more realistic way to look into and plan for the future, but it also forces you to convince others to help, and not just in financial ways. Factors to consider in a business plan include your potential market, your type of business, what crops you will grow and sell, your location, and how to secure financing. The rest of the book deals with the questions that you will need to address in preparing such a plan. Additional resources you can take advantage of include classes for potential small business owners that are offered by community colleges or other comparable institutions, which are quite valuable, and the Small Business Administration (SBA), an awesome resource for help in asking the right questions and in learning where to look for answers. I also recommend visiting SBA's Web site.

Among the first issues faced by a prospective nursery owner is the question of financing. There are basically four ways of starting a nursery: you can borrow money, have your own money or savings, marry money, or start with no money. In reality, most nurseries start with no money, although this is usually not by choice. (I discuss this topic in greater depth in chapter 17.) You may wonder how you can start a business without financing, but the nursery business is one that lends itself to that mode of beginning. If you have access to seed or cuttings, you will have a product to sell with very little investment. Granted, you may not have top quality potting soil or new pots, but there is a customer for nearly every plant that can be produced. Most who start in this manner usually market their wares at local farmers markets, flea markets, garage sales, or church bazaars. Although not the fastest way to start, you will eventually stash away a nice bit of cash—if

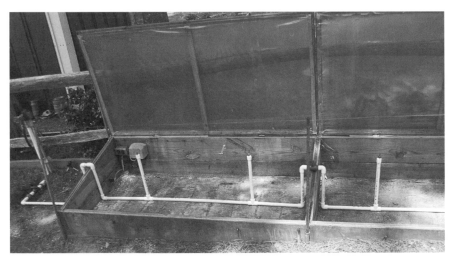

Ingenuity is enough to get you started. This homemade misting system or cold frame was constructed for a few dollars as part of a small backyard nursery. J. C. Taylor's garden, North Carolina.

you don't pay yourself a salary, that is. In all likelihood you could probably have saved more money flipping burgers, but there is something to be said for making nursery contacts by being involved in the gardening world.

The best option for those who face the difficulty of starting a nursery business without the benefit of financing is to continue working in another career while saving money. This is probably the second most common way that nursery careers begin. Nursery owners usually opt for two different strategies within this framework. The first is to choose more financially rewarding careers, such as those in the medical or legal profession. I certainly know more former doctors

Presentation is everything. A local professor's front-yard hobby turned retirement project. Holly Hill Daylily Nursery, North Carolina.

who are now nursery owners than probably any other profession—except perhaps landscapers. While this option allows for more financial savings, it often restricts industry contact to hobby gardening groups.

The second strategy for getting started in the nursery business while still working, and the one that most agree is the best, is to work in a related career that will provide not only a bit of savings but also regular contact within the industry. An additional benefit of this strategy is that it allows a prospective nursery owner to learn many of the skills needed to survive in the nursery business. For example, nursery owners who don't have at least a peripheral knowledge of carpentry, electricity, plumbing, grading, basic mechanical repair, and of course office work (which includes using a computer) are going to find themselves in some very expensive and stressful situations when the inevitable Murphy's law (if anything can go wrong, it will) comes to call.

When you make an error in judgment in your own business it is called a mistake. When you make the same error while working for someone else, it is called a "learning experience." Trust me, it is much better to have learning experiences! Mistakes are indeed a necessary part of the learning process, but they can be very costly.

After finishing school, I was fortunate enough to land a secure government job, which included overseeing the operation of a landscape, a greenhouse and nursery, and a crew of employees. This experience was invaluable in learning many tricks of the trade, which paid off many times over once we embarked on our own business. Since we had run our nursery on the side for several years and had a good stock of plants already produced, we decided that it should be my wife who left her job first. We felt that her skills in catalog preparation, shipping, computers, and office organization would be the most critical in getting the business off and running. This may sound illogical to some, but the production of plants is far from being the most important part of running a nursery business. In reality it is often the behind-the-scenes processes and work flow systems that make or break this or any business.

The toughest aspect of starting with another career before switching to the nursery full-time is knowing when to give up the security of having an outside job. By holding on to an old career too long while running the nursery on the side, you will quickly establish a reputation of spreading yourself too thin and not doing anything very well. The old adage that you can't sink or swim with one foot on the boat and the other on dry ground is certainly true in this case. If you cannot take the leap of faith that is required to make the shift from working for someone else to working for yourself you will also not have the nerve it takes to make the day-to-day gambles required in the nursery business.

The question of when to commit full-time to the nursery is nevertheless a difficult one. I recommend sitting down with your family to closely examine your financial obligations. Keep in mind that the costs incurred in commuting to and from work and in buying clothing, lunches, and other job-related things will be cut dramatically with a home-based nursery. There is no rule of thumb as to how much more money you could make by devoting more time to your business, but expecting revenues to double or triple in the first year of full-time work is certainly reasonable.

The question to ask is whether you need a salary and, if so, how much. If you do need one, you will need to take a close look at the budget and see how much money the business will have to produce in order for you to make the salary you require. There is no doubt that you and your family will have to make financial sacrifices during the first few years of getting a business started. (Few nursery owners have missed out on eating peanut butter and jelly sandwiches or pork and beans.) What you and your family must determine is this: how long are you willing to sacrifice? two years? five years? ten years? One way to keep the lean times to a minimum is to learn how to appropriately price your plants. I am always amazed that some who have been in business for years still don't understand pricing for profit. Be patient: I'll get into that in a later chapter.

So how much money should you expect to generate from your nursery? Based on personal conversations with nursery owners across the country, I have discovered that a small full-time nursery with no employees can probably generate gross sales of at least $50,000. With one or two part-time employees, the $150,000 mark is certainly reachable, depending on the value of your products of course. To go beyond this amount you will probably require some full-time employees, which will create its own headaches. Ask yourself where you want to go with this business and how quickly you want to get there. It is certainly reasonable that a well-run nursery, without start-up financing, could go from zero to one million dollars in sales within ten to fifteen years, and I discuss how to achieve such sales figures in chapter 13.

Another issue to discuss openly prior to embarking on a nursery career is that of family responsibility. Unlike many jobs, the nursery business is a way of life, not a nine-to-five job. As you can imagine, starting a nursery without remaining keenly aware of the balance between business and family will not have a beneficial effect on family relationships. Vacations will become few and far between, as will days off. The ideal situation for most people is that all members of the immediate family participate in the business together (although this may be disputed by some therapists). For a nursery to survive, both spouses must work together toward a common vision and goal.

Chapter 3

The Essential Skills

I'm going to start this chapter on essential skills by skipping right over plant skills! Horticultural skills are obviously important, but most readers of this book will already have a modicum of these. Folks mistakenly assume that horticultural skills are the only ones needed, but by now you probably realize that this is simply another myth. Most people looking to start a nursery are well characterized in Michael Gerber's book *The E-myth* (1986) as "technicians having an entrepreneurial seizure." In other words, a mastery of horticulture does not by itself qualify a person to run a nursery business.

Some prospective nursery owners forget that a large part of the nursery business involves much more than just plants. Plants are our commodity, not our business. Nurseries are a lifestyle business, but like all businesses they are multidimensional. While you can start and run a nursery without the essential skills that I will discuss, your job will certainly be much easier, less stressful, and far more financially rewarding if you have all these skills. It is crucial that you assess your own strengths and weaknesses honestly.

Entrepreneurial and visionary skills

I strongly believe that entrepreneurial and visionary skills are a natural gift. Some people are born with one or the other, but rarely with both. Visionaries see the future and know where they want to go but often lack the skills to get there. Entrepreneurs are the ones with the mind-set, energy, and risk tolerance to actually make the vision become reality. It is the combination of these personality traits that creates the nursery owner who can truly take a nursery to the top level. Of course you can run a nursery with only one of these traits, but such nurseries tend to be smaller and last for a shorter time.

The key in business is seeing the big picture. Then, having seen it, you must be able to plot the details of a workable path to get to your goal. You will need to assess your entrepreneurial skills honestly. Are you a naturally energetic self-starter who thrives on challenge and change? Can you respond to crises with maximum effort and then turn back to the daily mundane tasks? Are you an enthusiastic leader who creates confidence in others? These skills can certainly be enhanced and honed, but they are essentially innate components of a personality.

Systems skills

Systems are the processes through which work flows and tasks are accomplished. No matter how much vision or plant knowledge you have, your business will be no better than your business systems. Systems are continually being modified as the business grows. Each system will only work within a given set of parameters, especially those of size and volume. For example, a plant-potting system may work well until you reach a critical number of plants, at which point your system is no longer efficient. Similarly, a system for shipping orders works well until the number of orders received outstrips its capacity. You will find that as your business grows, a systems coordinator will become one of the most important members of your staff. If you take on the role of systems coordinator, be aware that a common mistake of many "hands on" business owners is that they are too busy with the day-to-day details to pay attention to the critical development of workflow systems. The result is a nursery that muddles along with too much time spent putting out fires each day instead of attending to issues of growth and increased efficiency. A downward spiral of profits often follows, a pattern common in fast-growing but poorly managed nurseries.

Administrative skills

Good office skills are vital for any nursery to succeed and continue. More than one nursery has failed not because of a lack of business but rather because of poor financial management. Office skills include seemingly simple tasks such as filing, bookkeeping, developing workflow systems, and communicating with others in the office (both verbally and in writing), each of which can make or break a business. I have often seen nurseries fail because of something simple like a poor filing system—if a customer calls about a shipment but the nursery staff can't find the paperwork, how long will it be before the customer goes elsewhere?

To properly manage a nursery, you must not only have good information but also good access to that information. The adage that "knowledge is power" is as true in the nursery business as in any business, and it is up to your administrative or office staff to provide this information. Nevertheless, as important as it is to capture information, it is of no value unless that information is in an easy-to-use and easy-to-access format. When a potential customer calls with a question, do you consistently have to call back after a time-consuming search for the information they have requested? If you can't accommodate information requests in a timely manner, you should consider this a red flag that your information storage and retrieval systems are not working properly.

Possibly the most important administrative skill is the ability to use and understand the basics of a computer. Today, everything comes to a screeching halt when there is a computer problem, so having access to someone with a good basic understanding of computing is essential. Whether you choose to make your own computer decisions (these include selecting hardware and software and troubleshooting problems) or assign a staff member to converse with a computer consultant, reliable computer know-how is critical.

Computers allow us to store, manage, and retrieve the data that we have assembled. Without the ability to keep track of information, we cannot make good decisions. Is it possible to run a business without a computer today? Possibly—if the business is quite small, but as the nursery grows, the need for a computer system becomes unavoidable. Without a system in place to provide you with current, useful information, you will quickly be left behind. Too many nursery owners have waited too long to enter the computer age, and this task, so long put off, has become so daunting that they opt to close up shop instead. I will tackle more administrative details in chapter 18.

Communication skills

Among the most overlooked skills is that of interpersonal communication. No matter how much of a visionary you are or how many technical skills you possess, you will not stay in business long if you don't have the ability to communicate well with your employees, your suppliers, and, most importantly, your customers. Many who go into the nursery business are introverts who want to communicate with their plants and avoid people. What these types of nursery owners usually fail to realize is that plants are just the commodity and that interaction with people is necessary as those people are their customers.

As your business grows, you will have to hire more people for it to thrive. If you lack good interpersonal communication skills, you will find it difficult to keep your employees and customers, and the business will quickly go downhill. Those of you who have trouble communicating clearly with people in a business setting should perhaps consider another career, such as programming computers or, at the very least, a nursery business in which you custom grow for a very limited base of customers.

Supervisory skills

Although supervisory skills come more naturally to some than to others, it is one skill that is absolutely necessary in maintaining an efficient workforce. There are more seminars on honing supervisory skills than on almost any other part of business, with the possible exception of computers. Business owners who overlook supervisory skills will never be able to obtain and keep high-quality employees. I will discuss supervisory skills in more detail in chapter 21.

Technical skills

It is a rare individual who combines technical skills with the visionary, entrepreneurial, administrative, or systems skills that move a business to the highest level. I am certainly not trying to minimize the need for technical skills (for without them the business would likely not survive for very long), but realistically, these are the least important skills while your business gets larger. They are, however, the most important while your business is still small.

Technical skills are usually the most common skills possessed by those hoping to start a nursery. Unfortunately, nurseries with owners who possess only these types of skills will never grow very large or be very successful by typical business standards. If you examine the nursery business from a purely technical perspective, you will discover that it probably requires an understanding of extremely diverse technical skills. How many do you possess? For example, do you know how to assemble a greenhouse? You will, with luck, be able to hire a carpenter to perform this and other related chores one day, but if you don't know how it should be done, you may be at the mercy of unscrupulous contractors. Unnecessary work could cause costs to skyrocket, but cheap and shoddy work might result in the greenhouse being decimated by a weather event. While most nursery owners install their first few greenhouses themselves, they soon find their time is better spent operating their business and that it is cheaper to pay a contractor for such specialty tasks.

Moving water correctly around a nursery site is so important that you should be able to do the grading yourself or at least understand how it is done. Too much water draining to the wrong areas could easily drown or wash away a crop. Do you know which is the right type of gravel for your road base, or will you have to redo that project? To avoid ruining the nearby environment (not to mention subjecting your business to fines and penalties), you must also know how to manage water-carrying nutrients and pesticide residues.

Plumbing skills are truly the lifeline of your nursery, and you will have to manage the water that is applied to your crops if you want to stay in business You will quickly discover that most commercial plumbing firms have little or no knowledge of crop irrigation, so if you don't understand it or know what questions to ask, you will likely wind up with an irrigation system that doesn't meet your crops' needs. Since your crop is alive, each day is critical, and irrigation systems must be monitored daily. If you have the impression that nothing ever goes wrong with water systems once they are installed, it will not take long for this myth to be shattered. When a container operation's water goes out on a sunny day, you may have only three to four hours before it starts to incur losses. Are you willing to risk trying to find a plumber who can be there instantly and at any time?

Knowing how to make electrical repairs is almost as important as having plumbing skills, especially when greenhouses are wired for power. Power problems in a nursery with covered greenhouses mean that plants can die from either excessive cold or heat within a couple of hours. An ability to diagnose and troubleshoot electrical problems and to correct minor problems is essential for saving crops.

Having the skills necessary to make mechanical repairs may not be as critical in saving crops but it does save money! Most mechanical problems in small nurseries are not major in scope and can be fixed if the nursery owner has some basic understanding of mechanics. Mechanical ability could include putting a tire on a wheelbarrow, installing a battery in a truck's engine, or making small repairs to a gas heater when the heat goes off in the middle of a snowstorm.

Horticultural education and training

Assuming for a moment that you want to become more knowledgeable in the field of horticulture, let's consider your options. You could attend several types of schools, from two-year technical schools to four-year bachelor degree programs. When choosing a school, be sure to ask whether the school's emphasis is technical or scientific in nature. A science background, which is usually more theoretically based and geared toward research or teaching, is usually less important to starting a nursery than practical or technical knowledge.

Four-year institutions often provide more opportunities to make industry contacts, so if you choose this route, be sure to take full advantage of these opportunities. Technical schools are generally more concentrated in their offerings and can move you through the programs much more quickly. Some two-year technical schools offer high-quality programs, but be sure to ask for recommendations from knowledgeable nursery owners in your area. I would also consult with nursery owners in your area to find out which school programs consistently produce the best quality graduates. Whichever school you choose to attend, be sure you take courses in business, computers, communication, economics, and accounting in addition to your horticulture courses. Often these other courses will turn out to be the most important of your career in the long haul.

Those of you who are employed in other fields but are considering a career change should look at the many night courses offered by local community colleges. In many communities, extension services offer training in a generalized horticulture arena, such as the Cooperative Extension Service Master Gardener Program. This service, like other garden volunteer programs, is an invaluable educational activity. For eight years prior to my nursery reincarnation, I was fortunate enough to be a volunteer with our county Master Gardener program. Not only did I learn from their educational programs, but I also received great training when I dealt with questions from customers who came to the plant clinics.

Local botanic gardens, arboretums, and plant societies, with their speakers and volunteer opportunities, are also wonderful places to continue learning. You can easily keep up with these local events via local papers, libraries, newsletters, and so on. Some of the best knowledge I have gained over the years has come from such venues.

With the advent of the Internet, as well as the ever-expanding horticultural print medium, the access to good information is unparalleled. The amount of horticultural information available from these improved methods of mass communication is truly mind-boggling. In fact, the amount of information is so voluminous that you will need to stay particularly focused to extract only the information that you truly need.

Professional trade organizations

In the professional realm, nursery associations, whether they are regional, state, or national, are invaluable for exchanging information and ideas. There is no better single source for learning the ins and outs of the nursery business than these associations. Although there are far too few regional or county-based associations, the ones that do exist provide excellent information about problems encountered and solutions discovered in your region. State nursery associations also offer trade shows and educational seminars, and you can do plenty of networking with other growers as you exchange information and products.

An independent national organization, the American Nursery and Landscape Association (ANLA), serves as a coordination point and clearinghouse for information related to all nursery and landscape issues. ANLA prints a series of publications on everything from nursery standards to pertinent government regulations to helpful business ideas. It also serves as your voice to Congress in pushing for new laws that will benefit the industry as well as in keeping poorly conceived legislation from adversely impacting your business. If you plan to grow your nursery beyond a backyard entity, membership in ANLA is a must. You can reach ANLA at their Web site.

Chapter 4

Formation of the Business

First, some business statistics. In 1997, the SBA reported that 885,416 new businesses that had employees were formed. Based on their statistics, 34 percent of these will not last until the end of the second year. Fifty percent will be out of business within the first five years, and 60 percent will be out of business within six years. This means that only 40 percent of all new small businesses will be in business six years after they are begun. The figures for the next few years of a business's life are too glum to reprint. The degree of planning and thought that goes into starting a business has a direct correlation on whether—and to what degree—a business succeeds. If these statistics don't sober you into paying close attention to good business practices, then stop now, do not pass go, save your money!

Your biggest challenge to beating the SBA's statistics will probably not be one of crop demand. This point is best illustrated by the 1998 census of horticultural crops published by the United States Department of Agriculture (USDA), which shows that nursery plants accounted for more than 29 billion dollars in sales and were the top horticultural commodity in the United States. Compared to other agricultural crops, nursery and greenhouse crops were the fourth largest agricultural commodity produced in the United States, accounting for 11.2 percent of agricultural sales, a pretty amazing number! Despite these good numbers, you must begin by taking a serious look at the feasibility of your business concept. Ask yourself tough questions, such as why customers will come to you instead of other similar businesses? Who will your customers be, and what products will you sell? How will you get customers to know about your products, and how will your products be distributed?

Missions and mission statements

The first step in starting a business is to develop a mission statement. A mission statement should concisely state the focus and goals of your nursery. Although owners often know what they want from their nursery and see no need to write it down, I recommend putting the mission in writing not only for your own benefit but also for the benefit of your employees and customers. Without knowing your ultimate goals, employees cannot be expected to make decisions to accomplish the mission of the business. Mission statements should not, however, be so restrictive that they do not allow for minor changes in response to market situations.

Nurseries without mission statements often drift aimlessly through the horticulture world from one focus to another, rarely doing anything very well. This is not to say that your mission statement will never change, but if you spend a lot of time and thought developing one, you will, I hope, invest the same amount of time and thought before you decide to change it. At the very least, any changes you make will be conscious and well thought-out.

Our mission statement, which is prominently printed in the front of each of our catalogs, is as follows: "Started in 1988, the goal of Plant Delights Nursery Inc. is to change the way America gardens by offering the best, the newest, and the strangest in fun, garden-worthy perennials to gardeners around the world." We go further to expand on our goals in each catalog. "Our retail nursery division is a 2.5 acre adjunct funding facility for our research/development/educational arm, Juniper Level Botanic Gardens. Income from the Nursery Division allows us to continue our research and breeding, maintain our display gardens, and expand our outreach programs." Such a mission statement allows everyone to know our priorities and our focus, and people often get involved because they agree with our mission.

Nurseries that drift from their mission statements sometimes do so because of the comments of a few customers. Customers might beg a wholesale nursery to sell retail or ask a perennial nursery to carry a few trees. This is where trouble begins because the original focus can easily be lost. Instead of doing one thing well, a nursery winds up doing several things not as well. You must realize that you cannot serve every type of customer and also have a successful business.

Other nurseries that lose sight of their stated mission do so because of the need for immediate cash during certain parts of the season. Believing that you must sacrifice the nursery mission for cash flow should be a red flag that you aren't doing something right. It's always an easy out to blame the market, but in almost all cases, a close, introspective look at your management skills and priorities is usually what is needed. If a nursery is to establish a good reputation for being consistent and true to its mission, it must focus all its energies on its stated mission.

Nursery focus and niche markets
When people who want to get into the nursery business ask me what to grow, I regard that as a certain tip-off that they are not ready to be in the nursery business. If you have done your homework, you will have studied the industry to find the gaps or market niches that are not being filled. Be careful of falling into this trap: a prospective grower canvasses nursery owners to find what plants are in short supply in the industry and then begins to produce them, little realizing

that, in most cases, others are doing exactly the same thing. Consequently, when the production period ends and the crops are ready for harvest, there is usually a glut of the plant that they have spent months producing.

The "contrarian" philosophy in the nursery business is, of course, similar to that of an investor who mistakenly buys when the market is high and sells out of fear when it drops. To make money you should do the opposite, and some nursery owners position themselves well as they watch plant market trends. As particular plants gain in popularity their production increases, often to the point that supply outstrips the growing demand. Nursery owners who have over-produced will then begin to push the crop to customers, but if they still have a surplus of plants, they will likely discard the crop altogether.

One contrarian way of exploiting a gap in the nursery business is to watch for overproduced crops that are being destroyed by other nurseries in a particular region. If a high demand has been created by those nurseries pushing their over-supply, there will still be a high demand as soon as the plants are gone, this time coupled with a low supply. Being able to quickly adjust your nursery's production and step into opening niches can be financially advantageous. I recall one example from the 1980s when there was a severe glut of *Myrica cerifera* (wax myrtle) in the southeastern United States. Overproduction had left some nurseries with tens of thousands of unsold plants. Despite using deep discounting and encouraging every visiting landscaper to use wax myrtles, nurseries still had to compost large numbers of wax myrtles to make room for other plants that sold better. Within two years there were virtually no wax myrtles to be found in the entire Southeast. It seems that the industry had been successful in creating an enormous demand among landscapers—but at a time when virtually all nurseries had scaled back their wax myrtle production. If a nursery had carefully watched this trend and scaled up production when others were dumping plants, it would have been well positioned to take financial advantage of this newly created market.

Another potential focus for inclusion in your mission statement is the niche market. Niche markets are those that focus on a specialized segment of the industry, such as plants native to a particular region, plants from a particular country, aquatic plants, and so on. These types of markets take more effort to find and develop, and often the plants require more exacting growing conditions. Such markets, however, are often less competitive, both in terms of supply and pricing pressures. You will still need to make sure that the niche you choose can support the size of your nursery and generate the amount of income you desire.

I had been intimately involved in the world of specialty collector plants for more than two decades. I studied several gaps that existed in the market, including those between the botanical and horticultural world, and between specialty collectors and mainstream nurseries. Both the botanists and the specialty collectors communicated only within their tight networks, and they rarely made contact with larger, more commercial nurseries. To fill this niche we pulled from both the collector market and the botanical world and then made these plants available to a wider, more commercial audience. You can still look in a flora of a particular state or region and find hundreds of plants with commercial potential that have never entered the horticultural market. Once you have an intimate knowledge of the entire industry, you will be able to see the niches that need to be filled.

Unfortunately, the niche that most people choose to fill is not a horticultural niche but a financial one. The most common way in which nursery owners plan to distinguish their nurseries is by selling plants more cheaply than their competitors. What they fail to realize is that their actual production costs, which I will discuss in more detail later, are far greater than they anticipate. These are the folks who, when you look at the return per hour of actual work, would make more money flipping hamburgers. It is quite sad that they do not understand that everyone wins when nurseries compete on selection and quality but that no one wins when they compete solely with low prices.

Structure of the business

A critical first step in setting up your business is to decide how you will form its organizational structure. This involves deciding who will make the business decisions, from those about financial matters to those about who will be responsible for acting under the auspices of the business. It is critical that you enlist the services of an attorney who specializes in setting up corporations. This is not an optional step; it is a necessity if you want to remain in business.

There are many ways to legally structure your business. The most common structures include the sole proprietorship, partnership, limited liability company (LLC), and corporation (both S and C types). Each organizational structure has certain advantages and disadvantages, which change regularly as the laws change. Typically, S corporations and LLCs are favored by small businesses, but most small, backyard nurseries are started as sole proprietorships. This simply means that the business is solely owned by one person, who is entirely responsible for all the debts, taxes, and liabilities of the business. This is the least expensive way to begin, as it requires no setup costs. The sole proprietorship is rarely the best option from a financial point of view, as most nursery owners discover when tax season arrives.

When businesses begin to grow, it is usually a good idea to incorporate them. Incorporation accomplishes several goals. First, it usually reduces the tax liability of the business owners, though this reduction varies as tax laws change. Second, it gives the owners limited liability protection in the event of a lawsuit, which means that if someone sues the business and wins, the only damages that can be recovered are those in an amount equal to the assets of the business, which would include cash, equipment, plants, and production inventory. Most accountants recommend that the corporation itself own very few assets and that the business owner personally own assets such as land, vehicles, and equipment that can be leased to the corporation. The amount paid by the corporation for leasing then becomes tax deductible to the corporation and taxable income for the owners. Most importantly, personally owned assets are not likely to be awarded in the case of a lost lawsuit by the business.

Many businesses start as partnerships, simply because one owner doesn't have all the talents, skills, or money required to run a business alone. Some partnerships are 50/50 financial splits, while others are a combination of 100 percent financial and 100 percent work equity contributions. In other words, one partner provides all the funding, while the other partner does all the physical work. The partner providing the finances often functions as a silent partner. Under this arrangement, the silent partner usually backs the business financially and then is rewarded financially if and when it turns a profit. It is important to specify in your partnership agreements how and within what time frame profits will be distributed, as well as in what amount or percentage.

I recommend you have partnerships drawn up by an attorney, as you cannot always anticipate all the situations that must be taken into account. Remember that business partners are responsible for one another's actions as they pertain to the business and be sure to set forth what will happen in the case of problems. For example, what will happen if one partner becomes unable to fulfill his or her role? Or imagine there is a dispute over the business and the business ceases to operate, how will the assets be distributed? It is obvious that you must be very careful when going into business with a partner. I can't begin to count the instances of business partnerships, marriages, and friendships that have dissolved along with the business. Compatibility in business is one of those things that matters most but is considered least. All partners must be aware that the nursery business involves a great deal of risk, and although they must be willing to work to minimize it, they must also remain conscious that risk will always exist.

Many human resource firms or psychological consultants offer to test one's personality, decision-making ability, reaction to stressful situations, and work style. Such a consultation can help you and a potential partner address your compatibility before you formalize any business partnership arrangements. Consultations can also help those partnerships involving spouses, especially as statistics show that the number of spouses who remain married to each other when they work together is frighteningly low. I doubt, however, that a personality compatibility check for a married couple wanting to start a nursery would be a good idea, though at the very least there should be a good, two-way line of communication between a couple.

The only thing worse than a partnership is a business that is run by a board of directors. While it may be tempting to accept investments from many people whose interests will be served by being members of a board of directors, I do not advise this kind of structure. While a board of directors may be standard practice in other businesses, it is usually a recipe for disaster in the nursery business. Decisions within the nursery business must often be made instantaneously, and each decision-maker must have a great understanding of the peculiar nature of a nursery. It is rare that quick, effective, and expert decisions can be made when there is a group involved.

An S corporation gives the owners limited liability protection but taxes the owners in ways similar to a partnership rather than a corporation. In other words, taxes on profits as well as losses from the business are the financial obligation of the owners according to the percentage of shares that each owner controls. The business corporation itself does not pay taxes. An S corporation must have regular board of directors' (who are the owners) meetings with recorded minutes. If these are not on record, the S corporation loses its legal liability protection.

An LLC is essentially a hybrid between a partnership and an S corporation. While not actually a corporation, it gives the owners the limited liability protection of an S corporation without the need for board of directors' meetings and minutes. In addition, an LLC allows for more flexibility and less restriction with regard to tax liabilities of the owners. While S corporations were the structure of choice during the 1980s, LLCs have since become the overwhelming choice.

Is this you? Do you have an image of the nursery and owner from the sign?

Naming your nursery

The naming of your nursery is among the least costly and greatest marketing opportunities you will ever have for your business. Nurseries have been notoriously uncreative in naming their businesses probably because they were started as small backyard operations without much consideration toward the future. I'm certainly not saying that a nursery with the name of Joe's Nursery or Bill's Nursery could never prosper, but it would be better not to have to overcome the hurdle of a poorly named business in the first place. In other industries where businesses were actually planned, it is quite rare to see "Joe's Pharmaceutical Company" or "Joe's Airlines." The other commonly used naming procedure in the nursery business is to name it after its location. If you are selling only to local markets or if you have a generic-sounding location name, such a name may not be an obstacle to widespread name recognition.

I recommend selecting a nursery name that describes your nursery or that, at the very least, engages your customer. Names should give customers a good or upbeat feeling about your business or convey a positive portrayal of your wares. Decide on the impression you want to create and find words that do that. For example, if you want to give your nursery an earthy feel, then use earthy terms, but if you are aiming for a high-tech feel, use related terms. Don't be afraid to ask friends and family to submit and critique potential names. The more input you have, the better your chance will be of coming up with a good, marketable name. We chose our nursery name after more than a year of careful thought. We looked for a name that would be both positive and upbeat and also summarize what we were about in a couple of words. We felt that the name "Plant Delights Nursery" said it all, since it captured our two-fold focus on plants and on delighting our customers.

When you have arrived at the perfect name, be sure to check with your Secretary of State's office to ensure that the name you chose has not been taken. If you plan to do business nationwide, you might want to check all 50 states. You can find a state homepage directory at the SBA Web site.

Identifying your customers and markets

What type of nursery business do you want: wholesale, liners, retail, or mail order? The overwhelming answer is wholesale or mail order, and for one simple reason: most nursery owners get into this business because they want to grow plants and not deal with people. Retail has an additional drawback in that it involves interacting with customers on a far more regular basis than a wholesale or mail-order business. As I mentioned earlier, the common fallacy is that plants are our business when in fact they are only our commodity.

If you choose the wholesale over the retail market, you are reducing your number of customers. Wholesale customers include other nurseries (both retail and wholesale), landscapers, public gardens, and garden centers. You will need to choose which of these customers will be your primary target. Garden centers may like one size of plant, while landscapers may prefer plants of a different size. You will also need to schedule production and delivery around your customers' needs. It is also customary that most wholesalers extend credit to their customers on what is known as a net 30 basis, meaning that full payment without any discount is due within 30 days of the invoice. I discuss payment methods further in chapter 13.

If you opt to become a liner grower (one who produces small plants to later sell), then your market will primarily be other nurseries. More than likely, these nurseries will not be the same as those who purchase a finished crop, since their missions would be quite different.

If you plan to open a retail nursery, be aware of the needs of your customers. You must have a location that is easily accessible to customers and you must maintain a customer-friendly shopping environment. Nurseries often pop up far out of town, which necessitates a long drive. Since retail nurseries must rely on high traffic to make a typically more expensive location pay off, you will need to determine which hours of operation will maximize your customer interaction without chaining you to the nursery. Remember that if the nursery is open, it will have to be staffed. Will you be able to find adequate employees to work the hours you decide on? By not attending to customers, you will exit the retail business very quickly.

A mail-order nursery is an interesting variant on the business. It combines the best of both worlds: less personal, face-to-face contact with customers and the higher prices of retail. Mail order, however, requires a much greater understanding of order processing, shipping, and marketing than wholesale, liner, or retail nurseries. When competing on the same items as local nurseries, mail-order nurseries cannot outdo the garden center when it comes to plant sizes because of the difficulty and expense of shipping large plants. If you plan to also have a local retail outlet, you will have to either focus on plants that do not have good local availability or offer materials that are not available from most local garden centers.

Just as you should invest in the stock of a company with which you are intimately familiar, you should also choose the type of nursery business you want based on your areas of expertise. My long history as a nursery mail-order customer made a mail-order business the logical choice for our nursery. Since we were opting to specialize in rare and little-known plants, it was obvious that a local market was not going to be enough to sustain either our desired pricing structure or our growth projections. We therefore chose to target an international market while simultaneously trying to build the knowledge base and market in our local region.

Instead of operating a retail site we decided to have a few open houses during the year. We settled on three seasons, spring, summer, and fall, and opened for six days during each season. By creating special event days, we gave customers more of a reason to visit us and not other nurseries that are open during regular hours. This arrangement also allowed us not to have to maintain a sales staff during the days we were not open. To our amazement, gardeners began to plan their vacations and bus tours around our open-house dates, and despite being open for only 18 retail days per year, these open houses generate an amazing 40 percent of our yearly sales.

Keep in mind that the type of nursery business you start will be affected in different ways by the state of the economy. As a general rule, good economies result in more construction, which in turn leads to the purchase of many common utilitarian landscape plants on a wholesale level. During economic upswings, specialty nurseries also seem to hold their own, but in periods of economic downturn, those same wholesale nurseries often suffer as new home construction declines. While I am certainly not an economist, I have noticed that during minor economic downturns, specialty nurseries and garden centers really seem to flourish, probably because people stay home and enjoy their gardens more. In 2002 following the terrorist attacks on the United States, nurseries catering to home gardeners saw a tremendous boom in their business. Wholesalers that target garden centers therefore appear less likely to feel the recessionary crunches that impact new construction projects.

There is always the temptation to try to serve more than one market, which can cause problems. For example, when a nursery tries to be both a wholesale and retail marketer, it doesn't take long to upset wholesale customers by directly competing with them. In general, however, a retail establishment and mail-order nursery would be more compatible, as long as plants purchased by mail-order customers for later shipment can be isolated from retail customers. Of course this isn't to say that there aren't rare exceptions to any rule, and one good friend successfully operates both a wholesale and retail nursery. When I mentioned to him that some of us felt it was a problem with him undercutting us in his position as a retailer and then selling to us as a wholesaler, he replied that he had many wholesale customers and no one else had ever complained. Unbeknownst to him, however, many of his former wholesale customers had complained to me. They had not expressed their concerns to him because they said it was easier to stop buying or offer another excuse if they were questioned. We are all pretty good at convincing ourselves of anything that we want to believe.

Once you have identified the market you are willing to serve, you will need to address its scope. If you become a wholesale nursery, how far are you willing to ship? If your focus is native plants, do you perhaps want to consider plants that are specific to a particular region?

You will next need to profile your desired customer base within your chosen market. Even within a narrow market, such as a retail mail-order, native-plants nursery for a particular region, you will have to determine which group of potential customers to target. Will your focus be more on the customers who order one or two plants, or would you rather have those who are ordering hundreds of plants? Very small hobby nurseries with low overhead may decide to target small volume customers, while others who are trying to be self-sustaining would rather discourage the less profitable orders. Discouragement can be accomplished by setting a high minimum number of orders or by using high shipping charges. We often have customers who want to order only one $10 plant and can't understand why we won't ship them just the one plant. The reason we don't is that we can't make money on such a small order.

How sophisticated are the clients you are hoping to attract? If you plan to compete on commonly marketed items, what will set you apart from the discount stores or established garden outlets? Do you want to appeal to wealthier gardeners who would rather purchase larger, higher quality items regardless of

Presence and stature! An entrance sign for a large wholesale operation. Iseli Nursery, Oregon.

price, or do you want to appeal to the collector who has a limited budget? These questions should be answered and summarized in your mission statement, particularly as the presentation and marketing of your business is closely linked to who your target customer will be.

No matter which type of nursery you decide to operate, you must have a hook (or several hooks) that makes your nursery stand out. So many nursery owners miss out on this critical opportunity in setting up their business. We have already discussed how important it is to decide on the focus of your business, but there is a lot more to consider too. What makes your nursery stand out in the midst of others? Are you known for your catalog? Does it offer so much information that your customers use your nursery as a point of reference? Do you focus on customer service, new plants, a higher quality product, faster delivery, a wider range of products, or other services? Whatever you decide will be your hook, you must at least have one.

Chapter 5

Selecting Your Land

Selecting the proper land is critical to the start of a successful nursery. The land you choose has an impact on virtually everything you do, from the plants you can grow to the customers you will have, the labor you can hire, the irrigation you can use, the winter protection you will need, and the cost of producing your plants. Let's talk first about how the land you choose will impact your customers. A location that is close to a large customer base is not as critical for mail-order nurseries, as shipping is usually done through mainstream commercial carriers. For a wholesaler, by contrast, the proximity to your customers is key. Similarly, if you are a retail nursery, a highly visible, easy to access location means everything to your success. No matter what type of nursery you have, if you ship across a large area, look for land with good access to major highways. If you sell primarily to landscapers, choose a location that will be nearby and easily accessible to the regions in which most of the landscape work occurs.

In deciding which piece of land to select, you will have to answer the key question of what size you want your nursery to become. It is always good to have an idea of any self-imposed constraints that need to be considered in developing your nursery. If you never want to exceed an acre in size nor hire any help, it would be ludicrous to become a wholesale nursery, but if you do want to become a wholesale nursery, you want a location where you can acquire a large amount of inexpensive acreage. Conversely, if you would rather run a small nursery that sells high-dollar items, you may find it more economical to acquire a small piece of more expensively priced real estate.

Don't forget to consider matters of zoning or land use planning. Most communities control all land under their jurisdiction through zoning. Land is usually zoned as industrial, residential, commercial, or agricultural, although other classifications exist in some communities. The issue of zoning can be a major headache in any nursery start-up or expansion and, where possible, should be addressed in advance of any purchase. You should always check with your county zoning board or real estate tax office to determine the zoning laws governing your potential property. If the land falls within a city's jurisdiction, be sure to check on their regulations regarding things such as signage.

Nurseries are still considered an agricultural business in most regions, but as governments put less emphasis on agricultural businesses, this could, unfort nately, change at any time. Each branch of government views various parts of the agricultural community differently, which creates big headaches for those trying to plan where to locate their nursery. In some counties and states, farming is farming, whether you grow edible or ornamental crops, but other counties treat ornamental crops as store merchandise rather than a product of farming. Where possible, try to obtain agricultural zoning on the land you use for nursery production. Not only will this classification save on the purchase price in some jurisdictions, but it will usually also qualify you for a break in property taxes. An equally important benefit is that agricultural businesses can often be located in areas that other businesses cannot. Businesses zoned as agricultural may enjoy other benefits, such as exemption from building permits or protection from certain legal actions and lawsuits. In most communities, however, agricultural activities are permitted on land with other zoning, but I recommend you investigate this thoroughly to be sure.

A common zoning quirk is that a particular area may allow for wholesale but not retail nurseries. The terms "wholesale" and "retail" as used in these areas are confusing and refer to the amount of walk-in traffic, not the prices charged. Additionally, an agricultural zoning does not automatically allow plant sales on the property where they are produced. A mail-order nursery should qualify in most areas as "wholesale," even though the prices are strictly retail. Zoning issues can be confusing, so if you have zoning questions I recommend you hire a good attorney who specializes in these matters. Also ask other business owners for their suggestions, and don't be afraid to ask your local municipality's zoning staff for names of attorneys with whom they have a good working relationship. You really can catch more flies with honey.

Once you have decided where to locate your nursery, you next need to decide how much land you need. Have you done realistic planning? In most cases the answer is no. In the first two to three years of a full-time nursery's existence, sales often double every year. After the third year, a well-run nursery can figure on a 30 to 40 percent increase for the next five to ten years. Then expect a growth of 15 to 20 percent for the next five to ten years, and thereafter a leveling off at 5 to 10 percent per year. These figures are only guidelines, but they are useful to think about as you project the need for future expansion.

To convert these growth figures into actual numbers, imagine that your nursery grosses $20,000 in year one and doubles for the next two years; that puts the sales figures at $80,000 in year three. If you figure a 35 percent increase for the next seven years, the sales will be $654,000. In the next three years, the yearly increase in growth drops to 15 percent, which means you should hit the one million dollar mark in sales by year 13. If the same 15 percent increase continues for the next ten years, your sales would be in excess of four million dollars by year

23. Two questions immediately arise: are you ready for each of these projected sales levels, and can your systems and land accommodate these numbers? To answer these questions you will need to know the dollar value of plant inventory that you can fit on the property you select. If you are growing commonly available shrubs and selling them at wholesale prices, an acre of land may have the potential to generate sales of only $50,000 per year. If, however, you choose to retail rare plants, that same acre will generate more than one million dollars. Your choice of crops and market obviously has a tremendous impact on the type and amount of land you will need.

Remember to always allow for the possibility of expansion. Like most nursery owners, you probably can't buy all the land you need up front, so work to develop optional plans for the future. Such plans could include acquiring options on surrounding land. Having a first option on a piece of property gives you the right of first refusal when your neighbor decides to sell. Try to choose land where there is a possibility of expansion.

Among the factors to consider when planning for expansion is whether or not the land is suitable for a septic system or systems. You may not need these systems while your land is used only for production, but when in the future you construct office buildings or employee housing, you will need to have an area of land that is suitable. You should also take into account future construction needs, such as shipping buildings and potting sheds. You do have a crystal ball, don't you?

Before you buy the land for your nursery you should also carefully examine all the long-term options for the property. Will it be worth more for development purposes at some time in the future? In a rapidly growing area where housing is encroaching, the land may become so valuable that high property taxes make it difficult for you to grow nursery crops economically. If you can project this eventuality, you might decide to stay away from incurring the expense of building greenhouses and use only ground beds. In addition, you must consider if the prospect of nearby housing makes for more customers as you create a potential retail client base or simply more headaches for you as a wholesale grower. Taking an even longer view of the future, did you think to check with your state highway department for future construction projects near your property? States often plan projects 15 to 25 years in advance, and land purchasers are often unaware of these plans until their business is already established. You should also look into whether your land could be annexed into a city that may have regulations that adversely affect your business. I have posed just a few of the questions you must consider, but there are obviously many more.

Where to locate your business is certainly an important decision, not only in terms of how much the land will cost but also in terms of how your neighbors will react. Establishing and maintaining good relationships with your neighbors should not be overlooked; a disgruntled neighbor can add many unneeded headaches to an already stressful business. Doing a few small things such as sharing plants, giving free advice, communicating well and regularly, and being active in community affairs can go a long way to establishing good relationships.

Another decision you will inevitably have to make involves whether you should live on the nursery property or not. While the advantages outweigh the disadvantages, don't enter into this situation without a good understanding of the potential problems. As the owner of the business, you will probably be the one who has to take care of the emergencies created by waterline breaks, bad weather, late deliveries, and all the other unforeseen problems that will arise despite all your efforts to prevent them. Your privacy will also be severely compromised. Even if you install chains, signs, and other warnings, you will still have visitors approaching during hours when the nursery is closed. Most nurseries, as a matter of economics, will have their offices located in their homes. I strongly urge nursery owners to move their offices out of their homes as soon as is economically possible. Home offices work well until you would like a day off or until the fax begins ringing all night with growers sending their availability lists and customers sending their orders.

One additional factor to keep in mind when you decide on where to site your nursery is what impact your nursery's location will have on the number and quality of potential employees. If you need to hire highly educated people, your nursery's remote location may make it difficult to find suitable employees who

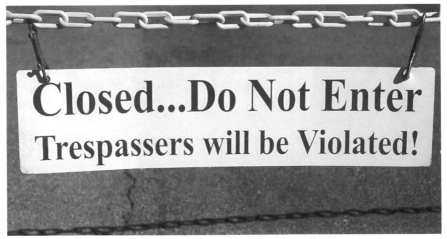

What part of "no" didn't you understand? The nursery gate sign at Plant Delights Nursery, North Carolina.

are willing to live far from a cultural center. There is no question that the educational quality of employees increases the closer you are to a region with good technical schools and colleges and more cultural activities. Do not, however, make the mistake of assuming that educated employees are necessarily better workers. Generally, wages in nurseries are lower than in other professions, so employees who live nearby can often afford to work for a bit less since their travel costs are lower. If you choose to locate in a remote area, you may need to consider employee housing, especially if you plan to use seasonal or migrant labor.

Where you locate your nursery will also influence your ability to grow the plants you want to produce. Obviously, the colder the climate the more costly it will be to operate a greenhouse during the winter months and the more likely the chance of winter weather disasters. Conversely, if you locate in a climate that is too warm, many of the plants that you want to grow may simply not survive the summer heat. If you locate too close to a hurricane or tornado corridor, you will also have to take that risk into account by purchasing extra insurance.

Once you have decided on the region in which you want to locate, you will need to match your choice of land to the crops you plan to grow. If you grow shade plants, making use of a lightly wooded lot will save you the cost of building shade structures. However, although such a growing situation will work, the overall consistency and quality of the plants will not be as good as if they were being grown in a more uniform growing shade structure or shaded greenhouse frame, which could more easily be installed in a cleared field. Conversely, if you plan to grow full-sun crops, you wouldn't purchase a wooded lot.

Other property-related quirks must be considered when locating your nursery. Microclimates often vary dramatically within very short distances. In a mountainous region, one side of peak may receive 80 inches of rain a year while the other side receives only 20 inches. One piece of land in a valley may be a frost pocket that could damage crops in spring while another may stay cold for a long time, so delaying spring plant emergence and also shipping. Does your land drain into a watershed or basin that is nutrient sensitive? If so, you will have to consider the numerous regulations governing runoff into streams.

Even if you aren't planning to field grow your crops, you should check the county soil survey maps for potential problems or quirks of the property. Are you purchasing land in the midst of an alkaline limestone outcrop while planning to field grow acid-loving plants? How does the land drain? If you are growing field stock, poor drainage can be devastating when the seasonal rains arrive. If you consider buying land in a rural area, take advantage of the marvelous insights from nearby farmers who may know the history of the land: "Old Joe used to get his tractor stuck out there" or "That sure was some poor quality land in that field; Joe never could grow a decent crop in it."

Just because your land drains well, doesn't mean you are completely safe. Make sure the land that you are purchasing isn't located within a 100- or 500-year flood plain. Granted, you aren't going to find many neighbors that have actually witnessed a 500-year flood, and consequently many nursery owners don't take this threat seriously. In 1999 I witnessed a nearby 500-year flood brought about by a hurricane that dumped a record 29 inches of rain in one night, and I can assure you that it is almost impossible to imagine the devastation that flooding can cause to unsuspecting nurseries. Picture the owners of a 100-acre nursery who awoke to find that nearly all their nursery stock was under 20 feet of water and that underground main water lines were ripped from the ground and swept away. So are you going to check that flood data now?

What was the land use in the preceding five, ten, twenty, or thirty years? Many farmlands are either nutrient poor or chemical rich, depending on the farming practices that were employed. It's far easier to check on potential problems involving past chemical or pesticide misuse on the property before you complete the purchase than to try investigating problems you are having growing a crop. Costs to clean up most pesticide residues are exorbitant and far exceed what the average nursery business can absorb.

Growing plants successfully depends on one factor above all others and that is an adequate water supply. While everything we have discussed in this chapter

It hadn't flooded this badly before! Hurricane Floyd versus Fairview Nursery, North Carolina. (Photo by Ted Bilderback.)

about your nursery's location is important, nothing is as critical as having a good water supply. I am amazed that most nursery owners purchase their property first and then later hope they find water. It is critical that you establish a reliable water supply before you get started, whether that supply is in the form of ponds, wells, or streams.

As you can imagine, streams are the least reliable source of water, and in some parts of the country it is illegal to use streams for irrigation. Surprisingly often, the stream that no one ever remembers running dry quickly evaporates when you depend on it for your livelihood. My first attempt at an outdoor nursery was in a friend's backyard where, according to his repeated assurances, the stream never went dry. We started the nursery, only to have the stream run dry during the hottest part of the first summer we were in operation. Despite spending many weekends and nights digging the streambed deeper and constructing holding ponds, we still could not get enough water. Trust me when I tell you that buying tanks of water from the local fire department is not the best solution.

Many nurseries that choose to use wells are hiring consulting hydrologists to help them detect water. Hydrologists can use several water locating techniques, including exploring for underground fossil fuel deposits to find veins of water. This ever-improving science can take a lot of the guesswork out of finding what is an essential ingredient in a successful nursery. In many western and southwestern states, water rights have become a serious issue. As the rights to limited underground aquifers are often transferred with the sale of the land, it is illegal to pump more water than what was allowed at the time the land was purchased. In most states, any user of groundwater over a certain quantity must register with the state in which the business operate, so be sure to carefully examine your potential and future access to water before getting started.

If you are considering irrigation ponds, you will need extra land on which to dig these ponds. If the property is a small one, you may find that ponds that are large enough to provide an adequate supply of water are competing with crop space.

Chapter 6

The Wholesale Nursery and the Re-Wholesaler

The Wholesale Nursery

Once you have made the decision to operate as a wholesale nursery, you will have a new round of decisions to make. Beyond deciding who your customers will be, what you will sell them, and what kind of presentation you will use, you must come up with a strategy for your wholesale nursery to avoid some of the more common pitfalls. You should also pay special attention to how you plan to deliver plants to your customers, as this is an especially tricky aspect of the wholesale business.

Customers and products
When you decide who your customers will be you will also be deciding on the size and type of plants to grow and whether to grow plants in the field or in containers. Landscape customers usually prefer field-grown plants but will need container-grown plants for summer transplanting projects since they are more widely available during the summer and transplant better during the growing season. Garden center customers, of course, prefer year-round availability, which necessitates using containers. Keep in mind that the cost of producing a container plant is usually far greater than that of a field-grown plant. Digging plants from a field nursery is not without costs, however, as it is a seasonal job that requires a large quantity of skilled labor, despite the modern convenience of tree spades. An additional factor to consider is that container-grown plants provide an income stream during most of the year, whereas field-grown harvesting produces a very limited season of positive cash flow.

Your customer base also determines what quality of product presentation is required. An upmarket garden center would need to have a high level of plant perfection as well as bar-coded labels and signs. A nursery that sells to customers that are more cost conscious, however, would be able to offer lower quality plants without labels.

Landscapers usually require much larger plants for their jobs, whereas garden centers require both large and small specimens that have a near perfect quality. A key ingredient in developing a good wholesale nursery is the maintenance of a continuous supply of plants. If customers depend on your nursery for their source of plants, they must be assured that you will have what they require. A nursery that is always out of stock will soon begin to lose customers. For most landscapers, plant labels are a drawback since they must spend time removing the labels after planting.

Most wholesale nurseries choose to grow what are known as commodity plants. Commodity plants are those that are most commonly used by builders, primarily for utilitarian purposes. Builders are certainly the largest market—and for good reason—but they also represent the more difficult market in which to compete.

Most container growers produce plants in pot sizes from 1 quart to 10 gallons, which are the sizes most customers request. Nurseries generally prefer to sell larger plants that can be produced with only a slightly longer growing time, as this method results in a larger profit margin. As the public desire for instant gratification grows, so the market for larger material increases, as does the public's willingness to pay premium prices.

The most profitable crops are those that can be produced and sold in the shortest period of time and for the most money. Fast-growing plants that can be sold in large sizes are usually the most profitable. For example, if it takes 12 months to produce a gallon-sized plant, it may only take two more months to produce the same plant in a 5-gallon pot. You can believe that the price the 5-gallon plant commands is far more than double the price for the 1-gallon plant. While the larger plants command a much higher price, they also take more time to produce and have greater space requirements (also known as residency costs). These production and residency costs must be accounted for when you compute the true costs of production. Keep in mind, too, that cash flow is more difficult to manage with large specimens because there is a longer recovery time for up-front investments. Another difficulty in producing large plants is the self-control required to say no to customers who beg for your growing-on stock before it is ready. Saying no is a lot more difficult than you think, especially when cash flow is tight—perhaps the nursery industry needs one of those Just Say No programs.

Most wholesale customers have long been resistant to increases in pricing, especially on the more common commodity items. Fortunately a few of the more progressive-thinking customers have realized the advantage of purchasing a better selection of a particular plant for a higher price and then selling it at a higher profit margin. In other words, purchasing a $10 liner and selling it for $20 as opposed to buying a $1 liner and selling it for $2 can yield much higher profits, provided the production numbers for the better plant bring in the same or greater amount of sales dollars as does the commodity plant. We will continue this discussion in chapter 13.

Strategy and pitfalls

Whichever type of crops you choose, remember that the best way to make a living in the wholesale nursery business is to deal with large numbers of a limited number of items. Wholesale growing is not very profitable when small numbers of many different items are handled. Unless plants can be produced on a very large scale, the cost to a small wholesale grower and a small retail grower producing the same plant is virtually identical. The difference comes when the small retail grower charges three times what the wholesale grower does for the same plant.

To be more profitable, a wholesale grower must produce (and sell) large quantities of every plant. The economics of wholesale production come down to this: the ability to handle most plants in a similar production schedule and regimen. Such efficiency results in a lower cost of production and a higher volume of sales, and to this end, wholesale growers usually opt to specialize in only one type of crop, such as perennials, shrubs, or trees. Since each of these types requires rather different care, it is difficult or nearly impossible to manage more than one of these crops very economically.

Wholesale nurseries operate both by purchasing small plants and growing them to sell as larger specimens and by propagating plants for their own use. Since there are only a limited number of liner or plug producers (plugs are one type of liner), the wholesaler will have to grow and sell much larger quantities to compete with retailers, who may purchase from the same sources. The wholesaler must buy stock in large enough quantities to get a price discount over a retailer, who will typically purchase in smaller numbers. The same is true for pots, soil, and other supplies.

If you opt to become a wholesale grower, you will need much more land to produce the larger numbers of plants required to make wholesale economics work. This expansion will, of course, require a correspondingly larger labor force or increased mechanization to produce more plants. The catch-22 is that the farther away from a town you move to acquire affordable land, the more difficult it is to lure away quality help from the population centers. The nature of the wholesale business is such that it can afford to attract only the lesser skilled workers (who will then be lower paid) simply because there is less money to be made per item and lower profit margins. Another quirk in the wholesale business is that the larger a nursery becomes, the more inefficient it becomes. It is critical that you as an owner work to maintain peak efficiency as the business expands.

Other complex problems that are associated with the large tracts of land on which wholesale production takes place are those of irrigation and chemical runoff. As communities become more concerned with water quality and water availability, these two issues grow in importance. Acquiring large tracts of land is increasingly difficult, so nurseries are opting for smaller tracts within a given community or region. Multiple growing sites for a single wholesale nursery have become quite common, and they present more issues for the nursery owner to consider. For example, the owner will have to work out methods of transportation and communication between the various sites, as well as how to secure both the crops and equipment at each site. All these solutions could increase the cost of crop production.

If you opt to run a nursery with a long-term initial payoff (for example, one that produces large trees), you may wish to consider growing nurse crops, especially if several years of initial capital investment are not easily accessible. Nurse crops such as annual bedding plants are quick-money crops that can be produced inexpensively and provide a flow of cash that may keep the nursery afloat in the early lean years.

The idea of growing nurse crops is not a new one, and there are both upsides and downsides to implementing it. Growers who choose an initial crop with a long-term pay off will usually need to realize some cash flow before the first crop is harvested. These growers often opt to produce more quickly maturing crops (such as seed-grown annual bedding plants) with turnaround times as short as four to six weeks. Even fast maturing perennials or woody plants (these

Mama mia, that's a bigga nursery! A large wholesale operation at Hines Nursery, California.

are plants that mature quickly and provide you with an inexpensive or free source of propagation stock) can be used to produce quick cash while you wait for your first crop of trees.

I offer a few additional cautions about growing nurse crops. It may take some time to establish the market for the nurse crops you are growing, and you will need to be careful that the nurse crops don't interfere with the long-term mission of your nursery. Also, the facilities required for the nurse crop are many times quite different from those you need for the longer-term crop. The best scenario involves a nursery owner who contract-grows a particular crop for another grower during this initial phase of a slow cash flow.

Delivery

Among the most difficult aspects of operating a wholesale nursery is the delivery of your plants to your customers. You will have to match not only the type of delivery to the needs of your customers but also the schedule. Some nurseries purchase their own delivery trucks, while others find it cheaper to lease vans during the delivery season. Still other nurseries own box trailers and contract with tractor-trailer companies (called common carriers) for delivery. The ideal situation is to have your customers pick up their plants at the nursery. However, while this arrangement may work for a few customers, it is simply not feasible for most others.

To make the economics of a wholesale nursery work, the nursery must be able to deliver large quantities of plants at a fair price, which means it needs to count on large orders in each transaction. Consequently, nurseries will usually impose a rather large minimum dollar purchase before shipping plants or plant materials. The best nurseries look for the least expensive method of shipment to save the customer money, and this usually involves combining several shipments on the same truck.

You will find that coordinating delivery schedules is enough to give gray hair to a bald nursery owner. Garden centers prefer that trucks arrive when customers are not around and they are not busy. However, this is often not the optimum time for the delivery trucks. Landscapers may not be on site when deliveries are scheduled, and small nurseries often don't have enough help to speed the unloading process. Unloading delays, combined with traffic-related delays, often create logistical nightmares. It is essential that you take these factors into account when you quote a shipping price to a customer as accurate scheduling and good planning is of utmost importance if you are going to keep control of shipping costs. Modern communication devices have, at least, made unexpected problems easier to resolve than in the past.

When the shipments are delivered, make sure that the plants are inspected, counted, and signed for by both the customer and driver. There is nothing like returning to the nursery after delivering plants only to find a message waiting for you that several plants were missing or damaged. This type of problem is much easier to solve if the delivery driver is an employee and not an independent hauler.

Most growers choose to charge a separate delivery fee instead of having it included in the cost of the product. Delivery charges are usually computed as a cost per loaded mile but deliveries within a close radius of the nursery or that are large enough are often made at no extra charge. Many nursery shippers have found it necessary to impose a time limit on the customer getting the truck unloaded; for any time after that a "slow unload" surcharge is added. Some nurseries have switched to delivery on racking systems. These systems are moved about through the nursery growing area, loaded with the orders, then rolled onto the truck using hydraulic truck lifts or forklifts. Racks can be off-loaded at the delivery site and left for the customer to unload at a later time, then picked up when making a future delivery. Disposable racking systems that the customer pays for as a part of delivery costs are sometimes used. Although these disposable racks can occasionally be reused by the customer, they are often a liability as they present disposal problems.

The wholesale nursery's ability to increase sales volume is often restricted by its delivery system. Obviously, the more plants that can be delivered in a day the greater the potential sales. A wholesale nursery's customers, like those in all the nursery businesses, usually want their plants delivered during the short window of spring. You will quickly find that your ability to load trailers depends on the amount of labor and docking space you have or on something as simple as a good plant-flow system. Being able to ship large amounts of plants has

Easy come, easier go. A rack delivery system used by wholesalers, Blooming Nursery, Oregon.

become a source of bragging rights to wholesalers, often reminiscent of the fish tales that one hears in other professions. When wholesale nursery owners get together over a drink, they compare sales volume by comparing the number of tractor-trailers loaded on a typical spring day.

The Re-Wholesaler

An increasing number of "nurseries" known as re-wholesalers exist simply to transfer plants from one location to another. Typically, re-wholesalers house plants at their own sites and sell from there, whereas plant brokers simply arrange for the plants to be delivered from the original grower and so are not real nurseries. If you possess more business than plant skills, the re-wholesaler business may be a good option since it allows you a way to get into the nursery business without actually having to be a plant grower.

Customers and products

Re-wholesalers cater primarily to landscapers and so are most prevalent in areas where the landscape industry is booming. They actually purchase plant material and have it delivered to their site, which is set up as a nursery. Re-wholesalers depend on being able to order large quantities of material, which they then make available to landscapers who could not otherwise justify such a large order.

Strategy and pitfalls

There is far more risk involved in being a re-wholesaler, which is why so few of these businesses exist. Re-wholesalers buy large wholesale lots on speculation and hold them until they are sold. The re-wholesaler therefore has the worries of the producing nursery owner because the plants must be maintained in good condition until they are sold. The stock is obviously subject to the same insects, diseases, water stresses, and weather peculiarities as those of the producing nursery owner—just not, with any luck, for as long.

Another obvious risk for the re-wholesaler is that the plants may not sell quickly. Re-wholesalers often have to pay up front for large quantities of inventory prior to having negotiated any re-sale, all while working to keep the plants alive and in sellable condition.

Delivery

Re-wholesalers usually require that customers pick up their orders, as this is the entire function of the re-wholesaler. Holding nurseries are usually located in areas of the most landscape activity as this keeps the travel time for landscapers to a minimum.

Chapter 7

The Liner Nursery

What exactly is a liner? In the old days liners were small plants, usually tree seedlings that were lined out in field nurseries, then dug and sold as dormant plants at the end of the season. Nowadays, the term "liner" encompasses virtually everything that is sold as a small starter plant, so any plant that is sold and then grown on to a larger size by the purchasing nursery is a liner. Liners may be in the form of rooted cuttings, tissue cultured plants, seedlings, or plants produced by a variety of other means. To a grower of one-quart plants, a small cutting or seedling is a liner. To a grower of 10-gallon trees, a 1-gallon or 3-gallon tree is a liner.

Customers and products

As long as there are nurseries, there will always be a need for liner producers. Liner nurseries fit into an interesting niche in the market, as they often sell to both wholesalers and retailers who grow their own plants. Producing liners offers a great chance for a nursery to specialize in one particular part of production without having to deal with large container plants or field-grown specimens.

A liner nursery can be developed in a variety of ways. Most liners are still produced from seed, as seed is often easy to acquire and production costs (with the possible exception of land costs) are low. If you want to sell tree liners, you will need a cooler or similar storage facility so you can harvest the plants in the fall, grade and ship them in the winter, and hold any unsold plants, even for a short time, until they can be sold.

The next most popular type of liner is that which has been vegetatively propagated. The trend in the liner industry is toward growing larger quantities of improved, asexual clones, and this type of liner is taking over more of the market each season. The desire for uniformity and specified traits as opposed to the variability that occurs in seed-grown plants is driving this trend. Vegetatively propagated material is reproduced by cuttings, tissue culture, or grafting. Such propagation techniques allow for the offspring to be genetically identical to the parent plant, thus preserving the selected traits.

Cutting propagation still dominates the vegetatively propagated liner market as it can be performed without needing overly specialized facilities. Grafting must be carried out by someone with good technique but it can also be done relatively inexpensively. The main expense in grafting is the cost of the understock material on which to do the grafting. The new kid on the block with regard to vegetative liner production is tissue culture. In this type of propagation, plants are reproduced in a laboratory-type setting. Plants are divided with small scalpel-like knives and grown in sterile conditions inside test tubes using agar or a similar material for the medium. Large numbers of plants can be obtained in a short time using this method, and it is not uncommon for quickly multiplying plants to go from a single plant to 10,000 and even 100,000 plants in one year.

Plants in nurseries can usually grow in the same soil mix, but each group of tissue culture plants seems to prefer a uniquely formulated medium that is com-

Mo' woodies, mo' better. Typical woody liner production with an array of crops at Panther Creek Nursery, North Carolina.

posed of various plant hormones in different concentrations and ratios. Culturing the tissue of plants presents another opportunity to either grow a wide range of plants or specialize in a particular group. The best protocols or hormone balances for the more commonly tissue-cultured crops have already been researched, but the newer crops, for which the demand is highest, are usually the least researched. While the newer crops may offer more profit potential, you will have to weigh that potential against the time and money that it will take to research and develop your own production protocols.

Before you start your own tissue culture lab, be aware that they are far more expensive to build than greenhouses. The cost of maintaining a sterile and fully

Ready for the potting crew. Liner production in cell packs at Plant Delights Nursery.

heated environment is not insignificant. Since sterility is key, you will need to purchase expensive, specialized equipment designed to maintain sterile conditions. Tissue culture labs must be isolated from all other parts of your nursery to avoid contamination, and it will be necessary to hire a special person who is able to do repetitive work in these antiseptic conditions. In addition, someone will have to research which media protocols are necessary for each different plant. As you can see, unless you have an experienced lab manager and are able

That's pretty cool! Tissue culture with black mondo grass at the test tube stage. B & B Labs, Washington.

Bifocals anyone? Tissue culture, division stage of production. Terra Nova Nurseries, Oregon.

to produce a large number of plants, the three to five years it takes to pay back your initial investment is usually longer than with a conventional nursery. I recommend that you do not embark on this type of propagation for your liner nursery without doing plenty of preliminary research.

Tissue culture plants are sold when they are either stage three or stage four plants. Stage three plants are essentially small balls of callus (undifferentiated plant parts) with a few tiny leaves and no roots. Unfortunately, most nurseries are not equipped to handle plants at this stage without some specialized help in handling sterilized cultivars. The more common tissue culture plants are stage four plants, which are callused plants that the tissue culture lab has rooted into cell packs. The shipped plants are similar to seed or cutting grown liners. It is possible for some plants to root directly in the test tubes but this ability varies with the crop. A tissue culture lab that tries to operate without a growing facility other than the lab itself will not be able to grow the plants in cell packs.

You will not only have to decide what type of liner to produce but also the size. Your customers' needs are key in determining what size liner to grow, and if you decide on smaller cell-pack liners, you have the choice of 16s, 32s, 48s, 72s, 96s, 128s, and so on. These numbers refer to the numbers of plants or cells in each tray. Whichever size liner you grow, you will have to cater your production facilities to that size.

Regardless of the type of liner to be grown, the liner producer will have to carefully coordinate production times, plant quantities, and customer needs or else be faced with the problem of having either too many or too few plants. Once they have determined the production times, many liner growers are able to predict plant availability schedules that can be published in advance for customers. Keeping customers requires maintaining a consistent product supply and providing that supply when you promised you would.

Strategy and pitfalls

Most nurseries tend to purchase liners in the fall and early spring. Spring is peak time for purchasing container-grown liners, especially herbaceous perennials, while fall and winter are the seasons for purchasing bare-root woody liners (bare-root plants have no soil on their roots). Probably the trickiest part of producing container-grown liners is maintaining them until they are sold. The more plants per tray (for example, a tray of 128s), the smaller the individual plants and the more difficult it is to maintain them at that size for any length of time. It is much easier to hold onto an unsold tray of 16s than an unsold tray of 128s because of the difficulty of keeping the soil moist when a plant becomes too large for its container. Similarly, growing areas that have liners in different stages of readiness are also difficult to maintain. You may find it cheaper to simply discard unsold liners, as the cost of each liner increases the longer it remains unsold and in need of upkeep.

A major drawback of a vegetative liner business is that you must first establish sufficient cutting stock. If you want to produce your own cuttings, you will need large stock blocks far in advance of when you want the cuttings. Perennial liners are easier to produce, and the cutting stock typically produces more than one crop each season, unlike most woody plants. Even when you have vigorous cutting stock, you will have to replace stock plants every few years. Stock blocks often become weak when too many cuttings are taken every year, and they may also become diseased over time. Many producers of perennial liners have stock plants tissue-cultured every year or two to clean up pathogens that may have infected the stock.

Producing vegetative liners offers the nursery owner the opportunity of establishing a good relationship with the owners of nearby container or field nurs-

Mass production at its finest. Perennial liner production done on a large scale at Blooming Nursery, Oregon.

eries who may want their plants pruned. In return, you could form an agreement to sell the rooted cuttings back to the cutting supplier. Your decision on the type of liners to produce will largely depend on the needs of nurseries in a specific region that are not being met or that can be met more economically. If you are starting a liner nursery in the Southeast and woody plant growers in your area are purchasing liners from the West Coast, you will have found a niche

Uh oh! Liners can quickly overgrow not only their containers but also the cold frame. Nursery name withheld.

to fill. There is a wealth of possibilities in this arena as liner growers who are closer to their customers can save on delivery costs.

Seed-grown liners present other potential pitfalls. For example, dogwoods from West Virginia will likely not fare well in a Florida climate, so you must know the provenance of your seed, especially with woody plants. You should also establish stock seed blocks and cutting propagation blocks for clonal plants; at the very least, form a relationship with someone who will provide you with a consistent seed source. The genetic variability in the growth rate of seed-grown plants means that you will need to do more grading and culling with seedlings than you would with vegetatively propagated plants to ensure uniformity.

Foreign countries with more conducive climates and lower labor costs may produce liners more quickly than liner nurseries in the United States. It is therefore critical that you study the market availability of the crops you think you might want to produce so that you know how to be competitive. Remember that you will be competing on price, quality, trueness to name, and, of course, customer service. If you understand your stock well you stand a better chance of producing plants not only more quickly but also more cheaply.

Delivery

Many of the delivery problems faced by other types of wholesale nurseries are the same as or similar to those faced by liner businesses. Since liners are much more perishable than larger plants, it is critical to your success that you not only keep your customers informed about the availability of your current liner products but that you also accurately predict future availability dates.

The biggest difference between the liner business and traditional wholesale nurseries is the system of delivery. Unless you are growing only for local growers, which is quite rare, you will have to become a mail-order nursery when it comes to delivering the plants. Although you will probably not be dealing with delivery trucks, you will likely use national shipping firms that ship boxed materials. The number one problem with national shippers is that they use inadequate packing, and so liners do not always remain liners as they are delivered to customers. When a customer receives a box of liners and finds them broken and strewn throughout the box, tangled with the packing, and without any soil on the roots, you can be assured that the customer will not be excited—at least not in a positive manner.

Some nurseries also sell liners in containers of soil. A few that I buy from ship liners in 1-gallon pots through the mail. My costs for postage end up being many times higher than for the actual plants. I purchase quite a few liners and am truly amazed at how little thought and care goes into delivering a satisfactory product.

Chapter 8

The Retail Nursery and Garden Center

Both retail nurseries and garden centers have the same end goal, which is to sell plants at retail prices to consumers. The basic difference between the two is that the retail nursery usually grows some or all of its own plant material while most garden centers strictly purchase and resell plants. Other than semantics, there is also a big difference with regard to tax status and adherence to many government regulations. As a general rule, a nursery that grows 50 percent or more of its own plants is considered an agricultural farm, whereas one that grows less than that amount is considered a retail shop. Again, go back to your mission statement to determine what type of products you will carry and whether you will be a grower or strictly a retailer.

Customers and products

As always, you will need to determine your product mix, which market you would like to address, and how you will make your retail nursery or garden center stand out in that market. Perhaps you are the only retail establishment in your area, but if not, you will need to develop a niche as we discussed earlier. Effective niches include a better selection of plants, a better range of sizes, a good selection of plant accessories, and solid horticultural advice. If you are located in a region featuring lots of new construction, perhaps common utilitarian plants will be a large part of your mix. If you are located in an older neighborhood, perhaps unique perennials for shadier yards might be more popular. The key is to match the products that you carry to both your mission statement and your clientele.

As I've discussed earlier, it is the larger plants that offer the most potential profit in a retail setting. Other high profit items include new and unique items such as the mythical Blue Velvet Elvis Birdbath, or other such items that are not offered by your competitors and therefore are not subject to price pressures. Nurseries have also realized that added value can be obtained simply by linking the plants to a decorative container or, in many cases, actually preplanting the plants in the container. Along the same lines, preplanted combination pots are, since the 1990s, prepared by the nursery. Profits can skyrocket if you sell a combination of several, low profit items in a single decorative container rather than sell those same items individually. For example, a nursery may take four $1.50 plants and plant them together into a $2 container. What would normally retail for $8 will now sell for $24.95—that's added value.

Many nurseries sell accessory items in addition to plants. These items are known as "pull-through" sales items. They can be profitable if they are high-profit items and if they are used to complement plant sales. Production nurseries, however, may find it easier to do a good job with the task at hand—growing plants—than to carry hard goods as well. If, however, you purchase rather than grow most of your plants, then you might as well carry some items that are not as perishable.

While price pressures on books are much greater than they once were, meaning that profits are limited, books are easy to manage as inventory and are not subject to spoilage if they don't sell immediately. The right books will help increase the knowledge level of your customer, which in turn creates a better consumer. Many retail nurseries carry an array of other items, including clothing (especially those featuring your nursery logo), sculptures, gift items, garden furniture, tools, chemicals, fertilizers, and soil amendments. In general, the highest profit non-plant items are garden furniture and pieces of sculpture, while soil amendments and fertilizers are among the lowest.

Gotta spray! Plant accessory items on a pesticide shelf at Rake and Hoe Garden Center, North Carolina.

It is only by understanding your customer base that you can pinpoint the most effective marketing strategies and choose your inventory. In 1992, Charles Safley of North Carolina State University examined the customers of garden centers within the state by doing on-site surveys. The results were quite fascinating. The findings indicated that 44 percent of the customers were female, 61 percent of all customers had moved into the area from out of state, and that most drove an average of 12.8 miles to reach the nursery. Of those surveyed, 44 percent were between 25 and 44 years old and had a household income of between $35,000 and $80,000. Of the respondents, 81.5 percent worked 40 or more hours per week. More than 92 percent owned their own home, 44 percent of which had done so for less than five years, and most owned homes valued between $100,000 and $150,000.

When the same respondents were asked why they decided to shop at that particular garden center, 52 percent said they were regular customers, 24 percent cited convenience, and 9 percent cited referrals. At the bottom of the list of reasons given were television ads (1 percent), radio ads (2 percent), and newspaper ads (4 percent). When asked for the most important factors in selecting a garden center, 66 percent said good quality plants, 11 percent cited a good plant selection, and 7 percent said that a knowledgeable sales staff topped their list. Convenient location checked in at 5 percent and low prices at 3.9 percent. At the

What else can we sell 'em? Cart and spreader as garden center accessory items. Rake and Hoe Garden Center, North Carolina.

bottom of the list were quick service (0.3 percent), convenient hours (0.5 percent), and friendly service (1.3).

Although customer service was not at the top of the list, that doesn't mean it is unimportant. In fact, it was probably not at the top of the list because the surveys were taken at garden centers that already had a high level of attention to the customer. Like other industries, nurseries are in the business of serving customers, and nursery owners must be sure to keep their customers comfortable. Without facilities such as restrooms, refreshments, and entertainment for nongardening spouses and children, you will not be able to maximize the potential income from your customers. Many nurseries seem to have completely forgotten about customer service. If customers are kept waiting in line only to have a rude person greet them at the checkout area, they will likely not come back, no matter how good your plant materials are. You need to work to establish a relationship with your customers. On my travels around the country, I have written off more than one retailer because of its poorly trained workers.

In addition to serving customers, we nursery owners must also work to educate them. I think most retail nurseries do a better job of confusing customers than educating them. A nursery that carries 50 different types of fertilizers when one or two would be more than adequate is doing more to confuse than to educate a customer. Similarly, why have 62 cultivars of Japanese maples, some priced at $29.95 and others at $3,000? Such discrepancies in price and ranges in products for sale are classic causes of a customer's confusion. To see your nursery from the perspective of an uneducated customer, you should solicit the advice from someone outside the industry. Think about providing your new, arriving customers with a printed sheet of nursery instructions that explains about the nursery and how your sales, pricing, checkout, and so on will be handled. Often, we nursery owners are so close to the situation that we miss seeing those simple ideas that will help our customers navigate what to them is a confusing process. For example, you could either print or post a map of your nursery's layout that lets customers know where and on what row they will find the plants they want.

Another valuable study you may want to make use of is the 2000 Grapevine Study, sponsored by ANLA, that examined the gardening preferences of 1,600 households. This study is a valuable tool in understanding your customer base. For example, it found that 70 percent of those responsible for gardening purchases in a home were women, while the average age of all gardeners was 51. When asked what independent garden centers could do to improve, 27 percent wanted lower prices, 22 percent suggested more knowledgeable staff, and 18 percent requested a larger selection of live plants. If you are thinking about getting into the retail nursery business or expanding an existing one, you will find this study an eye-opener.

Strategy and pitfalls

A garden center operates using the same strategy as the re-wholesaler: purchase inventory, then try to "turn over" that inventory as quickly as possible. This system means the inventory must be kept alive and healthy during the period when the plants remain in the nursery. As I mentioned, a few retailers do grow their own plants, but coordinating both the growing and retailing is a very difficult situation to manage well. Too often, the growing of plants takes precedence over waiting on customers.

The location of a retail establishment, unlike that of mail-order or wholesale nurseries, is absolutely critical. A top quality retail nursery or garden center can certainly draw people from great distances, but your chance for success is diminished without a location that is convenient for the majority of your customers. When you are deciding on the location of your nursery, you will want to weigh the increased cost of prime land against the anticipated profitability of the well-positioned nursery. Be sure to talk with other retailers in the area, and don't be afraid to ask—at least in general terms—for sales volume figures.

Remember that, in retail, appearance sells. How your facilities look can dramatically increase (or decrease) your sales. Every business speaks to customers before they even enter the premises. What does your nursery say to people who drive by? How does it look from the nearby highway—inviting, or a place to stay away from? Nurseries, with their piles of containers, potting soils, and partially covered cold frames, naturally look junky or cluttered, so if you want to give a good impression, be aware that you will have to expend some effort. This effort includes not only attractive plantings and screened-off production areas but also good-looking signs. Almost all nurseries seem to have old, tattered signs, which are at best unflattering. On visits to nurseries with such signs, I am often concerned that the one I am looking for has gone out of business. If you want the chance of keeping your customers, you must first get them into your business.

Before you decide what and how much product to stock, you will need to determine your level of sales. According to Bill Pearson (2000) of Retail Management and Analysis Company, a well-planned and well-run garden center in its first year can expect to gross about $500,000. Most retailers can figure that about 12 percent of this amount will be spent on labor. Rent usually consumes about 12 percent of gross, and purchasing inventory is about 52 percent. Assorted other expenses will typically be around 15 percent, leaving a gross profit margin of 9 percent.

While the above figures make the retail garden center business look quite profitable, they are ideal numbers. Purchasing mistakes, where too many or not enough plants are ordered, are commonplace, as the ordering of plants is a lot like playing Russian roulette. If you order too many plants and the weather turns bad, you will be hard-pressed to pay the bills. Conversely, if you order too few plants, customers will go elsewhere for a better selection. Further complicating your purchasing efforts is that suppliers tend to sell out of popular items quickly in spring, so your supplemental shipment may not be as good in either quality or quantity.

Many publications deal with the subject of plant displays and on-site merchandising, but their message, simply put, is that the number of plants you sell is directly proportional to the quality of your displays. You can have the best plants in the world but without good, on-site marketing, a retail establishment will not realize its full potential. So how should you display your plants? Some nurseries prefer to group like plants together, such as shrubs, trees, perennials, or annuals, whereas other nurseries assemble plants as they might appear in the landscape, using color or texture to determine combinations. For example, you could group plants with similar moisture or sun requirements, or arrange a grouping based on similar flower color. Perhaps you want to try something new—how about grouping flowering plants according to the Zodiac signs under which they flower? As you can see, the list of possibilities is almost endless.

A "wow" display! Retail display at Waterloo Garden Center, Pennsylvania.

Be sure that sale plants are clearly visible and easily accessible to customers. I am amazed that nurseries expect to sell plants that are hard to reach or even securely rooted in the bed in which they are displayed. Display tables, often called "benches," are always a good idea because they make smaller plants more visible and easier to examine. The closer the plant is to the customer's hands, the better the sales.

Something as simple as signage on each plant or among a group of plants makes a big difference to on-site sales. While some customers will ask questions, most prefer to shop without intrusion from staff. These types of customers rely solely on your signage to learn a plant's name, its mature characteristics, and the cultural requirements, as well as the price. Inadequate signs in a retail nursery will result in a large number of missed sales. I have lost count of the number of retail nurseries I have walked out of empty-handed when something as simple as a sign with pricing or minimal plant information would have been all that was required for me to make a purchase.

The best signs for a nursery are those with color photos of the plant. You must realize that we are a very visual generation, and nothing increases sales like a

Some folks have the art of display down to a science. Retail display at Waterloo Garden Center, Pennsylvania.

color photo. A sign may be the only way a customer can envision a plant's potential. Every plant will not be flowering when your customers are in the nursery, so you must help them visualize what the plants will look like when they are at their best. I encourage retailers to try a simple experiment: include photos of mature plants with some plants in a particular genus but not with others. I am convinced you will find that the plants with the color photo signs will sell out first.

When we started doing retail weekend open houses, we looked for an inexpensive way to produce quality display signs. After several failed attempts, we decided to export the text-only information from our catalog file directly into a printed format that fit the widely available garden center sign holders. We opted for the metal sign holders that are 5 inches tall by 7 inches wide. We then placed the paper on which the sign was printed into the copier and copied the information onto a Xerox paper product called Never-Tear. The sheets, which measure 8.5 inches by 11 inches, are printed two per page and then cut to fit the sign holders. This plasticlike paper product is waterproof, stainproof, and ultraviolet resistant. Not only are these signs inexpensive but they can also be produced in-house in a matter of minutes. Most major sign companies offer similar products.

Another good sales tool that seems to be gaining in popularity is "point of purchase" or POP signage. For example, if you are selling plants that attract butterflies, use an attractive sign with a picture of a butterfly on it to lure customers. Even butterfly-shaped tags attached to each plant will help in this effort.

While color signs in a nursery used to be prohibitively expensive for smaller nurseries, many CD-ROMS have downloadable photos that make attractive sales signs. These photos can also be printed onto the same Never-Tear paper if you have the appropriate model of color printer. If this sounds like too much work, consider contacting the several horticultural label companies that have similar products already prepared.

Simple by design. Signage label made with Never-Tear paper in metal sign holder. Plant Delights Nursery.

Display gardens are among the best sales tools available to a retail establishment. I had better qualify that statement by saying that display gardens that are well designed, properly labeled, and attractively maintained are a good sales tool. At worst, poorly maintained display gardens remind the homeowner how awful their own home gardens may look, and at best they do not encourage sales. Most people have more than their share of poorly designed, very dry, weed-infested beds waiting at home for them. It is difficult to quantify the effect of good display gardens on sales, but virtually all nurseries that have tried them seem very pleased with the results. How much to spend on display gardens is a tough question, but I recommend that any such expenditure be part of your advertising budget. While Plant Delights has a dedicated garden staff, many retail establishments use nursery workers to maintain the display gardens, which also creates a better and more educated staff. There is no substitute for firsthand experience with a particular plant.

There are pros and cons to having plants in display gardens that are not for sale. Some customers may be frustrated that they cannot buy the plant; however, this could be an opportunity to lure regular customers back for a future

Pretty as a picture. Display area, H&H Botanicals, Michigan.

visit when the plant will be in stock. Another advantage of having display gardens that contain plants you don't sell is that you can send customers to a nursery whose offerings complement your own. Overall, I would argue that having well-grown plant specimens on display helps to educate your customers.

I believe so strongly in the benefits of display gardens that we have designed our entire nursery around them. Of Plant Delights's developed property, 70 percent is covered by display gardens. We use the gardens as a place to observe all the plants that we grow under actual garden conditions and to see their mature size. Our display gardens also double as a trial area for new plants that will be produced in upcoming seasons. I believe this has helped to spread the word about new plants before they actually hit the market, which ties in perfectly with our mission statement. Our display beds integrate trees, shrubs, groundcovers, perennials, and bulbs, just as they would at a customer's home. Although we sell only perennials, we direct visitors to local garden centers for the rest of their purchases. These local garden centers tell us that they can always expect an increase in their business during one of our open garden days. It is our goal to inspire open-house visitors in a way that they take away at least one idea—and, we hope, several plants—that they can use in their own gardens.

Make them forget the weeds at home. A display garden at Plant Delights Nursery.

Often retail nurseries develop a landscape division through a partnership with a complementary landscape company. By doing this, nurseries sell not only a few plants but also the entire landscape, including the installation of those plants and the products needed for their maintenance. Nurseries with such partnerships also achieve the desirable result of increasing the sales per customer. An alternative to this kind of partnership involves the referral of customers to landscape designers. At Plant Delights we recommend designers who we believe do high-quality work and who use the types of plants we offer. Of course there is no obligation for either the landscape designers or the customers to purchase their plants from our nursery.

Spring is the primary sales season for retailers, though for some it is the fall. Many retailers turn to some type of Christmas sales season to help with winter's low cash flow. Without the high profitability of the Christmas season, many nurseries would go out of business or, at the very least, find it difficult to keep paying the salaries of good staff during the winter months.

Delivery

Have you thought about delivering items to your customers? While many retail nursery owners don't consider this possibility, keep in mind that the larger, more profitable items are often those that are difficult for the typical homeowners to transport. Large balled and burlapped trees, loads of mulch or sod, or even statuary are difficult for most customers to transport. You will probably need to make arrangements for delivery of these items if they form a key component of your business.

Chapter 9

The Mail-Order Nursery

Most mail-order nurseries started as backyard operations that evolved into mail-order businesses without a real business plan. These nurseries are typically those that grow their own plants. The larger mail-order nurseries, by contrast, purchase plants that they then offer for resale. One disadvantage to this latter strategy is that nurseries without a retail component to dispose of unsold inventory must get rid of it at the season's end even though so much money is tied up in those unsold items. While nurseries that grow their own plants may suffer this same fate, the costs involved are usually much less.

Customers and products

Starting a mail-order nursery requires that you ask many of the same basic questions you would if you were starting a retail nursery. Will you grow or purchase your plants? Will you sell potted or bare-root plants? What types of plants will you handle and in what sizes? Of course, answers to most of these questions should form part of your mission statement.

Nurseries in the South tend to lean toward container plants, whereas those in the northern zones offer more bare-root plants. The higher cost of overwintering plants in containers often prevents the more northern nursery from competing on price with those in the South where overwintering costs are much lower because of the milder winters. Although containerized crops can be much more easily accommodated into an extended shipping schedule, it is often more expensive and difficult to maintain them in containers during the growing season.

Plants that will be shipped bare root must be dug in the fall and stored in cool conditions, usually in refrigerated coolers. Many deciduous woody plants and perennials are handled in this manner. Storing plants in coolers is anything but an exact science, and you should expect high losses with certain crops. No matter where your nursery is located, coolers will be a necessity if you are handling bare-root materials.

You will need to carefully examine your target customer base before jumping into the mail-order business. Typically, nurseries that grow unusual or specialty plants fare best as they are able to reach plant collectors across the country, even across the world. Plant collectors are often willing to pay higher prices for a specialty plant than what the local market will bear. For example, a nursery that specializes in spider-type daylilies could charge $200 for a new introduction by targeting a specialized, national or international audience. Locally, however, the same plant might fetch little more than a run-of-the-mill daylily.

Similarly, difficulties exist for mail-order nurseries that are trying to compete with local retailers or garden centers. Local nurseries should always be able to offer a larger plant at a similar cost to that offered by a mail-order nursery. The size of a plant that a mail-order nursery can ship is limited by the high cost of shipping and the difficulty of packaging large plants. It is rarely feasible to ship a plant that grows in anything larger than a 1-gallon pot, though obviously there are exceptions with very expensive plants.

Strategy and pitfalls

Plant geeks looking to start a nursery tend to prefer mail-order nurseries. These often anti-social types feel they can avoid customer contact by locating a mail-order nursery in an out-of-the-way location. While mail order does allow for more privacy, you will likely have plenty of visitors if you do a good job of running your business. It is inevitable that customers, out of pure curiosity, will search out and find your nursery, so you will have to decide whether to prohibit all visitors or schedule visits in a way that allows you to maintain your privacy.

Since you are operating a remote business where customers cannot regularly drop by, the need for prompt responses to customer queries is even more critical than with a typical retail operation. Communication can, of course, occur using faxes, e-mail, phone, and, to a lesser degree, regular mail. I have found that some who start a mail-order business are often poorly prepared for the actual handling of orders. There is simply no excuse, however, for being blindsided by orders when that is precisely how the business has chosen to operate. Doing a poor job of satisfying customers in your start-up years creates a bad impression that is difficult to overcome, so start out well prepared.

Delivery

You have no doubt heard the phrase "follow the money." In the nursery business, the equally pertinent phrase is "follow the paper trail." In an ideal world, every order could be filled completely, would arrive at your nursery with the proper payment, and would incur consistent shipping charges. As you will soon realize, this scenario is unfortunately not reality. Of all the types of nurseries discussed, it is the mail-order business that has the most complex process of getting plants to customers, and if you do not have a good paper trail, confusion will reign.

At the outset, let me offer one simple procedural rule that can help you avoid disaster. Let's imagine a nursery worker who takes a stack of original orders into the nursery to pull plants. Along comes a thunderstorm and all the orders are destroyed. Does this sound unrealistic? I can assure you that it is not! I have firsthand experience of the need to always protect the original order in case of unforeseen problems or later confusion. I recommend generating your own separate set of paperwork from which you process orders. Original paperwork should never be allowed to stray from the security of your office.

Customers rarely visit mail-order businesses; instead, you deliver the product to them, and this makes your shipping operation of paramount importance. There are many shipping options for your plants. Be sure to thoroughly investigate each one and choose the one or ones that best fit your needs. Carrier rules, regulations, and prices change so often that you will need to make a special effort just to keep up with this facet of the business. Also, be aware of the possibility of labor strikes. If you depend on a shipper whose employees go on strike, you will be prevented from delivering your product to your customer. I will never forget the year our shipping carrier went on strike during a time when cash flow was particularly low and when we had a large number of orders ready for shipping. I learned never to rely completely on one shipper and to keep my options open.

When choosing a shipping service, keep in mind that a shipper's published rates are not necessarily what you will pay—providing you take time to negoti-

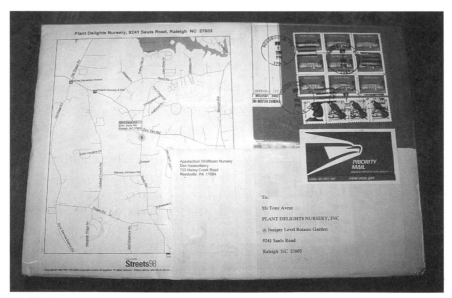

Thinking "outside" the box. A neat idea for shipping labels if your shippers keep losing packages.

ate. You should contact the local or regional representative for each potential shipping service and request a quotation of their rates. Be sure to ask about the shipper's ability to track packages that become lost or that are not delivered on time. Find out about the types of delivery options: overnight, two-day delivery, three-day delivery, or delivery whenever the item arrives, the latter usually being the cheapest option. Also ask about hidden surcharges, which are increases over normal rates. Surcharges such as those for dimensional weight kick in when a package is too long for a specific set of existing parameters. Even if the box fits all other criteria for a particular shipment charge, if it is slightly too long the shipping price can go up as much as threefold, so be very careful of this charge.

The shipping company will ask you for information on how many boxes per week you will ship, the sizes of those boxes, and other related questions. Shipping rates are based on volume, so the more you ship, the better your rates will be. Another factor that impacts shipping rates is location. If your nursery is in a very remote location, it will be very expensive for the delivery service to visit your business so you will be less likely to receive a discount. On the other hand, if the shipper wants to build up business in a particular location or has a competitor business nearby, it may find it cost effective to give you a much larger discount than any it would give a customer in an established service area.

A number of computer-based shipping systems are available to choose from, their versatility increasing with the number of packages you ship. Some systems provide the package's weight, print a shipping label directly from your database, track packages, and even compare the cost of various shipping companies. Contact the various shippers for information on their systems, but also check the phone book for shipping systems that are manufactured by independent companies. If you ship a large enough volume with a particular shipper, you will usually be provided with a shipping computer and system at no charge; at the very least you should receive a label printer and software. Be sure and ask the shipper to help you integrate its system with your own database so that order information does not have to be reentered into the new shipping system.

Several states have imposed agricultural restrictions on bringing soil or potting mix across state lines unless the soil or mix has been treated with an array of chemicals. While these restrictions certainly make it difficult to ship plants during growing seasons, it is not impossible (although many nurseries refuse to ship into those restricted states). If you decide to ship into these states, you should first determine the time it takes to wash the soil from the roots or to treat each plant and then calculate a standard charge (possibly as a percentage of the order) that will cover the extra cost of shipping to these states. Be aware that there is a big difference among plants in terms of how easy they are to bare root and that their survivability also varies with each species.

Regulations involved in shipping to other countries can also be overwhelming to a small nursery, and for that reason many nurseries opt out of that market. The advantages of shipping overseas generally include the large size of orders (orders need to be large to make the high shipping costs worthwhile) and the customers who help you connect with overseas suppliers of new and different plants.

While regulations constantly change, most overseas shipping requires that the plant be soil-free. Each country has a department or ministry of agriculture that sets and administers these rules. Your state's department of agriculture should have copies of the rules and regulations for each country to which you plan to ship. Usually, shipments outside the country of origin will need to be accompanied by a certificate of compliance, known as a phytosanitary certificate. This certificate, issued by the USDA or a designated state agriculture representative, certifies that the plants you are shipping meet the requirements imposed by the country of destination. The general procedure involves state or federal inspectors (each country specifies which to use) performing an on-site inspection of the plants you want to ship. Once the inspection is completed, the inspector issues the phytosanitary certificate for each shipment.

The restrictions on shipping certain plants are based both on plant material that is itself prohibited and on diseases and insects that are often found on the culprit plants or in the country of origin. Your local department of agriculture should be able to provide you with such lists. Often an entire shipment can be rejected if one prohibited plant is included. Your nursery can get into pretty serious trouble if it ships plants that are prohibited in certain regions.

The USDA has a Federal Noxious Weed List, and while some of the plants on the list are often grown as ornamentals, it is illegal to own or ship them. Many people are unfamiliar with this list until federal agents come calling at their door. Several states are developing their own lists of prohibited plants based on more localized problems, so you should contact your state department of agriculture for help. As more and more states form Exotic Pest Plant Councils (EPPC), there will no doubt be more and more regulations regarding which plants can be shipped into which states and regions. It is the function of these councils or groups to develop a list of plants that are invasive in their state or region.

While it is true that plenty of nursery plants are bad for the environment (and I believe growers will do themselves a service by making sure that they are not contributing another weed to the environment), it is nevertheless unfortunate that much of the information on invasive plants is published without good scientific data regarding a plant's true effect on the ecosystem of a region. Furthermore, most of those charged with developing such a list do not distinguish between species, and even more fail to acknowledge that there is a difference between cultivars.

Overseas shipments rarely arrive at their destination without complications, despite the efforts you have made to comply with all the regulations. Misinterpretations of different governments' regulations will destroy as many shipments as will incompetent governmental employees. I quit keeping track of the number of times that government officials in a foreign country didn't have a good grasp of their own regulations, though it's possible they just wanted to display their authority. Often it is not even the particular plants that inspectors have problems with but the way the forms are filled in. For example, a plant may be prohibited if it is listed as a plant on the form but will be permitted if it is listed as a bulb, corm, or rhizome. Rarely will an inspector offer this helpful information, however. In our experience, most agricultural inspectors would rather avoid work or flaunt their authority than try to help an importer solve a problem.

Even if everything goes right with your overseas shipment, be aware that the shipping costs by themselves are quite high. Add to that the costs of inspection and permits, plant preparation time (remember that the cost for this is much higher than it is with local shipments because of the greater amount of labor required), and the costs of carriage, which is what the shipper charges to deliver the plants to the customer.

Something else to consider is the kind of box you will use for shipping. When getting started, most small nurseries opt for recycled boxes, and many of their owners can recall staking out Dumpsters at the grocery store or the local recycling center. While we are confessing, I will admit that during the early years I spent far more time than I care to remember waking up drunks or being terrorized by wild-eyed cats while prowling through restaurant Dumpsters for the perfect shipping box. I had a very hard time getting used to the concept of purchasing boxes.

I will also admit that I have seen the error of my early ways, an error that was no better pointed out to me than when a local mail-order nursery reused a frozen food box for shipping a plant. The customer, upon receiving the box, paid attention only to its printed instruction to "freeze immediately." Only after several weeks did it occur to the customer that the box might contain the plant order, but by then it was several weeks too late. At some point, you too will decide that hunting for used boxes is no longer cost effective and that your own or your employees' time is worth more doing other jobs in the nursery.

Once you make this leap from wanting only free boxes to being willing to pay for them, you may still want to consider box overruns. Most box companies offer these "seconds" at a greatly reduced rate. When you require large numbers of boxes, however, it may become economical to purchase new boxes with your nursery logo and name printed on them. Alternatively, you could purchase rolls of tape (they are usually 3 inches wide) with your name and logo printed on the tape. You could also have "fragile," "living plants," and so on printed on the tape. With tape wrapped around the box, its identity is very clear to the recipient.

I recommend that you use only a few standard box sizes, as not only is having too many sizes quite confusing to packers but it is also uneconomical. By choosing a limited number of box sizes and noting how many plants will fit in each, you will save lots of time by being able to match box size to the order size. You must also consider the weight of your shipment: you want to make the box manageable for your customer while at the same time ensuring that you avoid shipping surcharges for sending out overweight boxes.

Now that you have your boxes picked out, think about the packing material you will use. As much as we in the nursery business wish for it, there is no such thing as the perfect packing material. If you are into recycling, you could try commonly used products such as shredded paper. Unfortunately, shredded paper has two drawbacks: its supply is spotty and it packs down in shipping, allowing the plants to move around in the box. Probably the best packing materials are still the dreaded Styrofoam peanuts. This material is very lightweight and does not pack down during shipping. While biodegradable peanuts have been used, they tend to degrade if there is any moisture in the box and so do not provide the needed cushioning for the plants. Another favorable material is wood fiber.

Regardless of which packing material you choose, it is critical that it keep the plants from being tossed around in the box and not be so heavy as to increase shipping costs. While you may take great care in handling and packing the or-

So many boxes, so few ordered plants. If you use standard box sizes, you'll find it easier to match boxes to orders. Plant Delights Nursery.

der, rest assured that this level of care will not be given during the rest of the journey. I always recommend packing a test box that your staff tosses around for a couple of days to determine if your shipping material and packaging methods are sound.

When plants are shipped with bare roots, some form of media must be used to keep the roots from becoming excessively dry. Although plants are most often lost during shipping because they were packed too wet, it can be just as damaging at the other extreme. Root-protecting materials include peat or sphagnum moss and sawdust. Be sure to check with your state's department of agriculture for any special regulations pertaining to some recipient states and almost all foreign countries. These regulations are sometimes a nightmare even when they are followed. We had several shipments rejected by a state inspector who didn't even know his own state regulations!

My favorite packing material has always been the universally accepted shredded sphagnum, which is soaked and then squeezed free of all excess moisture before use. Materials used to hold the root protective media around the roots include aluminum foil, plastic, and of course the containers themselves. If you ship plants in containers, it is critical that the soil media remain in the pots during the shipping process. There is nothing worse that receiving a box of plants with all the soil in the bottom of the box and the plants at the top. Good packing can keep the soil in the containers but it is more typical to use some type of breathable seal over the soil surface of the pot.

Remember that plant foliage should be allowed to breathe during shipping but not be sealed or kept moist. I recommend you experiment with various preparation methods to find one that produces the best-shipped product at the lowest price and with the least labor.

While shipping in containers is a boon for the customer who likes to receive larger plants that don't need to be planted immediately, the increased shipping weight often drives the costs too high. Nurseries that ship plants in large containers with heavy soil mixes must devise some way to hold the

Wrap . . . the old fashioned kind. Packing can be the weakest link in the mail-order business. It's not how the plants looked when they were packed that matters but how they look when they arrive. Plant Delights Nursery.

heavy pot of soil steady in the box. Common packing materials will not work; the pot must be secured to the side of the box by some means of attachment, such as strapping.

You must also decide which time of the year to ship. Several different ideas about shipping schedules can be considered. Some nurseries ship from fall to early spring, while others ship from spring through fall. Most commonly, perennials are shipped in spring and fall and woody plants are shipped in winter. While this schedule may be the easiest for you, it doesn't allow your customers to get plants when they want them. If you really want to service your customers, you will have to make accommodations to ship during the entire season. More and more nurseries are experimenting with year-round shipping, and doing so with surprising success.

Other factors must also be considered when choosing a shipping season. For example, the climate in your area will have an impact on your decision. If your plants are frozen solid in the winter, shipping them during that season will be difficult. How you grow your plants, too, will play a role. Plants grown in the ground cannot be shipped year-round, whereas plants grown in containers can be. In fact, more and more nurseries are opting for container growing as it greatly extends the shipping season.

In determining your shipping schedule, keep in mind the efforts required to maintain the plants—watering, fertilizing, and pruning—during your non-shipping season. A long delay in shipping may be an economic disaster. If you lengthen the turnover time of a crop, the cost of production, which is based on the cost per square foot per day of the growing area, will skyrocket, often beyond what you could sell the plant for.

It is often difficult to ship plants from one climatic region to another. A nursery in the deep South that is experiencing early spring (at least in comparison to the North) will have trouble shipping to northern gardens that thaw only in late May. Likewise, shipping to or from warmer climates has to be restricted to the summer. Plants should not be shipped when temperatures go above 95°F, particularly since gardeners don't like receiving plants when it is that hot. I always liked to ship and receive plants when they are in active growth. Opening a mail-order box of high-quality plants is like opening a birthday present, and it should be a thrilling experience. When a box is opened to reveal dormant or bare-root plants, some of that thrill will be missing, even if the plants go on to grow very well. Additionally, many homeowners are ill equipped to deal with bare-root plant and so feel uncomfortable dealing with them.

You will need to be careful if you grow container plants in cold frames or greenhouses, as these plants will start growing earlier in the season than plants that are growing outdoors. Shipping plants that are in tender, new growth to colder zones can be disastrous; as a rule, plants should not be shipped when young as the new growth can be easily damaged or broken.

Once you have gotten the preparation work out of the way, the plants must be assembled or "pulled" for shipping. Most nurseries will start by printing a pull ticket that indicates which items should be pulled. The ticket will also state which items are out of stock or back ordered, assuming of course, that you have a workable inventory. The pulling is usually done in one of two ways, either by individual order or in bulk by plant variety. The plants are then staged (meaning they are gathered temporarily and arranged prior to shipment) in the area from which they are to be shipped.

Figure 1. Sample Pull Slip

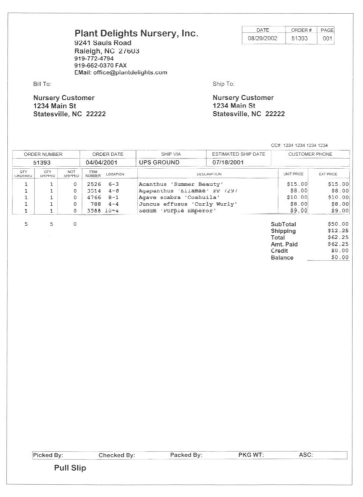

On shipping day, the plants are prepped (they are bare rooted if necessary) and bad foliage and weeds are removed. The plants are then boxed for shipment. You will always come across plants at the last minute that cannot be shipped for one reason or another (because they are too small, for example, or because there are problems with insects or disease), but the seriousness of this situation can be minimized if the staff pulling orders understands and adheres to the quality standards you have put in place. Having last-minute delays means that you are then faced with more paperwork in the form of back orders, credits, or refunds, depending on how your nursery is organized. All these back orders, credits, and refunds must in turn be recorded in your shipping records. Once the order is filled, the boxes are packed and readied for shipment.

I am always astounded when I learn that most nurseries don't have a clue as to how much it costs to ship a plant. All nurseries generally see is the actual shipping or carriage costs, and while nursery owners may not actually incur all the costs I outline below, they should always charge the customer as though these costs really were incurred, for one day they may be. The cost to ship an order be-

Get outta that kitchen and scrub those roots and fans! A shipping and packing facility for bare-root mail order. Klehm Nursery, Illinois.

gins with paying someone to open the mail and should include the cost of fax paper, even of Internet service. The order must next be processed, which will in most cases include entering it in some sort of computer system or database. You now have to include the cost of the time spent entering that data, as well as the costs of both computer software and hardware.

Even at the pulling stage there are a number of costs that should be figured into the cost of shipping. Costs that pile on here include time spent assembling the plants to fill an order, any clerical time spent issuing refunds or credits, and the money itself that is being refunded. Last but not least is the cost of storing the paperwork for each order. You should store that paperwork for a minimum of three years, not only because of tax-related reasons but also because you will need it to answer the questions that customers will surprise you with years after the orders have been filled. Keep in mind that every time you touch an order, the cost of processing it increases.

Figure 2. Cost of Processing a Mail Order

TASK	TIME REQUIRED
Time spent on each order:	
Opening mail orders and recording check numbers	1 minute/order
Phone orders	6 minutes/order
Data entry	3 minutes/order
Payment processing	2 minutes/order
Filing of order by order number	2 minutes/order
Pulling and staging orders	10 minutes/order
Checking orders	3 minutes/order
Packing orders	10 minutes/order
Processing shipping information	2 minutes/order
Customer communication about orders	1 minute/order
Issuing refunds or credits	2 minutes/order
Obtain order confirmations	2 minutes/order
Average time to process an order	**44 minutes**

ITEM	AMOUNT
Additional charges per order:	
Phone charges	$0.10/minute in phone charges
Packaging costs (includes packing products and tape)	$0.08/order
Cost of boxes	$0.75/order
Average cost per order	**$1.43**

If you are paying your workers an average of $11 per hour, your actual labor burden rate or cost for the employee is probably closer to $14.49 per hour, depending on the benefits you provide. Multiply this more realistic number by the number of minutes per order: $14.49 an hour × 44 minutes (0.73 of an hour) to get a much closer idea of your true processing cost, which is $10.58 per order. This figure assumes that all employees work at peak efficiency at all times, which is obviously not realistic. If you add $10.58 to your additional supplies figure of $1.43, you will see that your average cost of shipping an order is $12.01. How many of these costs did you figure into your shipping charges? And remember that the $12.01 amount does not include the actual shipping cost.

I like to break down each of these operations into how many minutes it takes to complete each task. This gives me a much better idea of how to break even on the shipping charges. Once I know the costs I can determine how small an order I can afford to ship and still make money. The industry standard for minimum mail orders ranges from $20 to $40, but in reality it's hard to make a profit at the lower end of this range.

Chapter 10

Preparation for Growing Plants: *The Technical Stuff*

Many nurseries I have visited that started out without any land use plan suffer the consequences in the form of lowered efficiency, poor traffic flow, and inadequate facilities. I have also found that virtually all nursery owners, when asked if they would lay out their nursery differently if they were to start again from scratch, answer with a resounding "yes." So why did they not do it right in the first place? I presume that they did not realistically anticipate their nursery's growth even as the nursery was taking on a life of its own.

The land plan

The first step in setting up your nursery is developing a land use plan. While you could formulate your own plan, I strongly recommend you hire a landscape architect, preferably one who has experience with nurseries. The best nurseries are laid out using the combined skills of a competent landscape architect and a prospective nursery owner who understands the industry, has visited other successful nursery operations, and has a realistic expectation of growth. Plenty of nursery business consultants can also help with sketching out a plan. If your nursery is small, there is no need for a fancy, all-color plan; a simple ink sketch will often do the trick.

What you are trying to capture in your land use plan are good flow patterns. Flow patterns include the movement of workers, the movement of plants, and even the movement of water. Chart what will happen from the time the plant first enters your nursery until it is delivered to the customer. Where will the plants be started or placed when they arrive? Where will they be maintained until they are sold? From where will they depart? Use the figures that I mentioned in chapter 5 regarding growth projections to get an idea of how much larger the space must become each year to accommodate your needs. No matter what size your nursery is, production should always flow in a steady stream from young starter plants to plants that are ready to ship. Remember that the fewer times a plant must be touched or moved, the lower your cost of production.

A common error in designing a nursery is that not enough room is left for vehicular movement. While you may be picking up potting soil in a pick-up now, what happens when you upgrade to a tandem truck and then a tractor-trailer? It is truly astounding how much room it takes to maneuver a tractor-trailer around on a piece of land. Do you have a centralized potting location that is easily accessible to all your production and growing areas? If you grow your plants in the field, does your digging and transportation equipment have good access to get the plants out of the field and onto waiting trucks? In addition, all production areas should be easily accessible to large vehicles.

If you are going to put up greenhouses or grow sun-loving plants, you will need to consider the cost of clearing the land. Land clearing costs often far exceed the actual cost of the land, so I advise you accurately figure out this cost before you purchase the land. Local grading companies can give you a rough, per acre cost to clear the land, and if the land is covered with large trees, perhaps a timber consultant can save you some money by selling off the timber. Clearing land can become very complicated if you don't ask enough questions. Are you in an ecologically sensitive area or near a stream? In many communities, it is illegal to alter the runoff into streams. Even in areas where it is not required by law, I recommend you allow a 20- to 50-foot-wide grass strip (or similar vegetation buffer) near streams to prevent silt infiltration and nutrient runoff. Be sure to check with your soil and water conservation office for more details before closing the deal on what looks like the ideal piece of land.

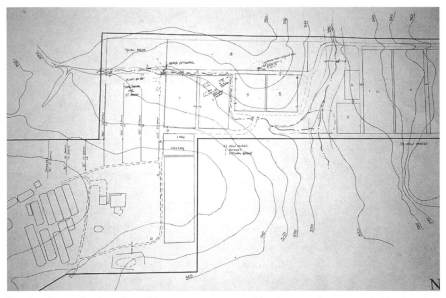

De plan, boss, de plan. Everything goes more smoothly when you have a workable plan that is prepared by a competent landscape architect. Plant Delights Nursery.

If your land is cleared, how are the wind-flow patterns? If there is no wind-break, strong winter breezes can wreak havoc by routinely blowing plastic off greenhouses. From firsthand experience, I can tell you that there is no foolproof method of keeping plastic on greenhouses in overly windy sites, so you should develop windbreaks early on in the planning process. I can also tell you that no chore is more difficult than replacing plastic that has broken free from a green-house while you are also battling strong winds.

Nursery grading and set up

Before you begin grading and preparing the property for use as a nursery, you will need to plan the water flow on your property. Where is the water coming from, and where do you want it to go? If you haven't had experience in grading or planning water flow, you may wish to engage the services of a landscape ar-chitect. In fact, most zoning laws require that a grading permit be issued, before major grading over a certain square footage can begin. Also, be aware that most zoning regulations do not allow any additional water to be channeled onto a neighbor's property. You may need to install drainage systems and piping to handle runoff, especially as nursery surfaces are often impermeable because of the roads and covered greenhouses.

People are always surprised when they realize how much water is actually running off their property. If you have ten greenhouses that are 20 feet wide by 100 feet long, you have approximately 30,000 square feet of impermeable sur-faces when you account for the arch of the greenhouses. A 1-inch rainfall will create a runoff of 30,000 inches or 2,500 cubic feet of water. Each cubic foot of water is approximately 7.5 gallons, making the runoff 18,750 gallons for each measured inch of rain. Therefore, a 5-inch rainfall would produce a staggering runoff amount of 93,750 gallons. Keep in mind this figure takes into account only the covered greenhouse surfaces; you would have to add the runoff amount that results from other impermeable surfaces, such as building roofs and paved roads.

Incorporated into drainage systems at almost all nurseries (except the back-yard type, of course) are nutrient retention ponds. Not only do these ponds catch contaminated water but they also serve as irrigation ponds once the con-taminants have been filtered out. It is essential that no nutrients or chemical residues leave nursery property. Most nutrients and other contaminants can be filtered out by the proper use of aquatic or wetland plants in the nutrient reten-tion pond. Progressive nursery owners can easily find a way to turn a potential runoff problem such as this into a money-making opportunity by producing the aquatic or wetland plants for sale.

If it looks like a retention pond and acts like a retention pond, guess what it is? Panther Creek Nursery, North Carolina.

Functional and attractive—would Martha approve? A nutrient retention pond that collects runoff and makes use of an ornamental bog plant filter. Plant Delights Nursery.

Ground preparation

You simply place container plants on the ground and they're fine, right? It would be nice if things were that simple but they're not. The first thing roots in container plantings do is head right out of those containers and into the ground, where they come into contact with every detrimental fungus, nematode, and other soil-borne pathogen that is nearby. Try selling a plant after you've mustered the strength to extricate it from the growing area but have left most of its root system in the ground. You can imagine what the plant will look like a few minutes later, and there isn't enough water in your irrigation system to keep it from wilting, trust me.

Containers must never sit directly on the ground for another very important reason, namely drainage. Have you ever noticed that the drainage holes on many pots are on the bottom? If the pot sits on a hard, impervious surface, the water will not escape the plant's root system fast enough, and before you know it, the plant will have drowned.

It is generally advisable to put down a layer of washed gravel (the kind that does not contain the fine particles used for packing), usually a 3- to 4-inch-deep layer to make a good growing surface. These gravel surfaces are usually used in addition to a material called ground fabric. Ground fabric, a polymer-based ma-

Been there, done that. Containers produced on a layer of plastic during the early days of Plant Delights Nursery.

terial that comes in large rolls, allows water to filter through into the ground but prevents weeds, mud, and subsurface particles from coming through. Growers have varying opinions on whether ground fabric works best under or on top of the gravel layer. I have observed both arrangements in successful growing situations, and each seems to work well. I prefer the ground fabric on top of the gravel because it's easier to clean up debris that way, though constant traffic can wear holes in the ground fabric as it rubs against the gravel underneath.

Much better than our earlier method! Containers growing on ground fabric. Plant Delights Nursery.

Rocky: The Sequel. You've heard it before, but don't skimp on the use of drainage-improving gravel for container growing areas. McLamb Nursery, North Carolina.

If you will be moving vehicles and carts around in a large greenhouse situation, you should consider making the floor surface solid. Some situations call for a concrete walkway or possibly a porous concrete surface that covers the entire growing area. Porous concrete formulations are more often seen in the floriculture industry, where a different concrete mix (one that has less sand) is used to allow water to drain through the concrete. Rarely is this economical for standard nursery crops, however, but it could be an option for specialty high-dollar crops.

Growing structures

The first question to answer is whether or not you actually need growing structures. If you strictly produce crops in the field, for example, a greenhouse is unnecessary. Greenhouse structures are primarily used to protect the crop (and workers) from the weather. Propagation is typically done inside greenhouses to allow for better control of humidity and, to a lesser extent, temperatures. Most growers of general nursery crops use greenhouse structures exclusively for overwintering purposes. These structures are left open during the growing season and covered during only the winter months. Such unheated structures or greenhouses are called cold frames. Unlike typical greenhouses, which are high enough for workers to walk around inside, cold frames are much lower, with some barely exceeding crop height. A less expensive option for very winter hardy crops is to "winterize" the crops by bunching them closely together and covering them with a crop blanket. If you need access to your crops during the winter months, however, a greenhouse or tall cold frame may be a better option.

You will need to quickly develop a great deal of understanding about the hardiness of the crops you are growing, as plant hardiness will determine your need for investing in growing structures. Typically, plants grown in above-ground containers are noticeably less hardy than the same plant would be if it were growing in the ground. This difference in hardiness results from the plant roots being far less hardy and less adaptable to rapid temperature fluctuations than the crown or other parts of an above-ground woody plant. The ground provides insulation that a container cannot, and the roots of a plant in a container can be more than 25 degrees less hardy than those in the ground (Steponkus et al. 1976). Although cold temperatures play a role in killing plants, it is often the length of time that the roots remain frozen that is critical in determining the plants' survivability.

Another problem with inadequate winter protection is that root-damaged plants may actually leaf out and look well enough to be sold just before they collapse and die. The shipping season is often half over before you are able to truly assess your losses. In deciding if it is economical to invest in greenhouses, you should determine the acceptable or "normal" losses during the winter using either growing method. Assume that leaving the plants outdoors with no winter protection incurs losses of 25 percent, that using winter protection blankets results in a 10 percent loss, and that greenhouses see only a 5 percent loss. By calculating the value of your crop, you can easily determine if it is economical to build greenhouses or to change your methods of overwintering instead. Granted, getting an accurate handle on losses is a long-term proposition, especially if you are growing new and different crops, so you might consider checking past climatic data for your region. While losses may not have been a problem in four out of five winters, would the temperatures in that fifth year have been enough to wipe out your entire crop?

The decision about using growing structures may be a fairly straightforward one. If your business requires that a crop be ready earlier than is normally possible by growing it outdoors (for example, you may need to supply plants to garden centers south of your area or mail order them to other parts of the country), then climate-controlled greenhouses may be your only option. Greenhouses with minimal heat can produce some astonishing growth in a number of cool-growing crops. Many growers can plant these types of crops in the fall, heat a greenhouse to between 32° and 40°F at night, and finish a crop by spring.

The type of nursery business you plan to start may require that you have a greenhouse or series of greenhouses that you keep at warmer temperatures, simulating a floriculture environment. Keep in mind the costs of keeping these greenhouses heated during the winter months, and make sure the crop you are producing will still be profitable. Sometimes it may be more economical to have the crop grown by someone else for later resale.

The array of growing structures to choose from is truly mind-boggling. The most important consideration in selecting a greenhouse is how to fit the structure to your crop without going overboard. Considering the cost and amount of disruption involved in replacing growing structures, you should begin by purchasing the best quality structure you can afford.

Nursery owners argue constantly about what size of greenhouse is the most efficient. The key fact to remember is that greenhouses that are not the right size are inefficient. Those that are too narrow or short are obviously problematic, and those that are excessively wide may require extra heating and may adversely affect efficient bench-to-walkway ratios. Only when you switch to greenhouses that are connected with gutters (which are known as gutter-connected houses and consist of more than one set of hoop greenhouses under the same roof) that vehicles or large carts can traverse does a larger greenhouse become efficient. If you are installing these large, gutter-connected greenhouses, consider the importance and economics of automation by using rail transport systems and other laborsaving technologies.

Most overwintering houses are constructed from noncorroding bent metal pipe. Houses below 6 feet in height are usually built with a pipe diameter of between 0.75 inches and 1 inch. Houses that are taller than 6 feet usually use pipe that is between 1.5 inches and 2 inches in diameter. Some nurseries create their own houses by simulating these bow or arch arrangements using PVC pipe. While these constructions are not going to tolerate severe winter weather conditions or last forever (they have brittle weathering properties and an inherent lack of strength), they may be a viable way to save money when you are just

All under one roof. High-quality, gutter-connected greenhouse. Blooming Nursery, Oregon.

The owner of this nursery saved money, but a PVC overwintering structure is not a great idea when snow arrives. Shadybrook Nursery, North Carolina.

starting out. However, the desire to save money at the outset must be offset by a plan of action for a worst-case, winter-weather disaster.

When looking to purchase a greenhouse frame, be aware that not all greenhouses are created equal. Some greenhouse frames come with predrilled holes so that bows can simply be bolted together and stood upright. Quality greenhouses with predrilled holes actually match up with the corresponding pieces, whereas cheaper houses tend to arrive with severely mismatched holes. Some lower-priced greenhouses may not come with predrilled holes, which can add a time-consuming and often aggravating step to the greenhouse construction process.

The quality of metal used to build greenhouses will also vary from one manufacturer to another. Generally, the thicker the pipe the better quality the greenhouse. Some manufacturers price their greenhouses based on bows being placed every 4 feet, but others recommend distances of up to every 6 feet. This spacing difference can result in significant differences in your initial cost comparisons.

Every greenhouse should be rated as to snow load, which is the amount of weight that the structure can support without collapsing. Bow spacing is only one factor affecting the snow load that each greenhouse can withstand; good design and accompanying cross braces allow some houses with a 6-foot bow spacing to actually support more snow load than those with a 4-foot bow spacing. The style of greenhouse should withstand the worst weather recorded in the area in which it will be located.

If you decide to erect a greenhouse, remember that the actual price of the greenhouse frame is the smallest part of your cost. Even the cost of constructing the greenhouse is a significant factor; just the framing lumber for the ends and base of the sidewalls can sometimes equal the purchase price of the base frame. You can generally figure on spending three to four times the cost of the frame to make a greenhouse fully functional.

While some nurseries like to assemble their own greenhouses—some even bend their own metal hoops—be sure to take a close look at actual costs of doing this. Sure, you are already paying your staff, but are there other jobs that your employees could be doing that would produce a sellable product? Would it not be cheaper to hire an outside contractor who might be more efficient in the assembly process? Don't automatically assume that doing it yourself saves money.

From the simple, plastic-covered greenhouses known as Quonset greenhouses, the range of greenhouses expands to include as many options as there are for cars. Coverings can range from simple polyethylene and glass to many of the new artificial Plexiglas or polycarbonate-like materials. If you choose the common polyethylene-covered houses, you will notice that all plastic film used in a greenhouse covering is rated by a unit referred to as "mil." Mil is a measurement of thickness equivalent to 0.025 millimeters or 0.001 inches. The industry standard for year-round covered greenhouses is 6 mil plastic, while the standard for overwintering houses is 3 or 4 mil plastic. Overwintering plastic is relatively inexpensive and is not designed to last for a long period, usually about six months.

Completely different types of plastic are needed for greenhouses that are going to be covered during the growing season. In fact, you should use clear plastic that has been treated to resist ultraviolet light breakdown for anything other than overwintering houses. Ultraviolet resistance is the most important factor in the breakdown of polyethylene films, regardless of the thickness of the covering. Most films are rated according to the number of years they will last before they begin to breakdown, which is usually three to five years. While estimates are probably on the conservative side, it is best not to gamble on this as the plastic could break down at an inopportune time during the winter.

If you grow crops that are very light sensitive, you may still need to change the greenhouse cover before it begins to degrade. Even with ultraviolet films, light transmission begins to diminish after the first season. Your greenhouse supplier should be able to give you light transmission charts for the type of coverings you use.

It is standard practice to cover heated greenhouses with a double layer of polyethylene plastic as that provides a dramatic 30 to 40 percent energy savings over using just a single layer (Short 2001). A small inflation fan placed between

Got cramped? A Jaderloon Quonset greenhouse during construction. Plant Delights Nursery.

the two layers of plastic produces the insulating air pocket between the plastic sheets, but two common mistakes keep this system from working properly. The first is that the outside layer of plastic is not loose enough. There must be enough give to provide a 2- to 4-inch inflation layer between the outside and inside sheets of plastic. The second and most common mistake in using a double layer of plastic is that the insulating air is pulled from inside the greenhouse, the idea being that the warm air will reduce heat loss. As a result, hot, humid air from inside the greenhouse meets cold air on the outside layer, and that in turn produces a dramatic increase in condensation that will very nearly simulate a rainforest climate inside your greenhouse. While it may seem backward, always pull the less humid air you plan to use for inflation from outside the greenhouse. I have seen growers lose major portions of their crop simply because of improper installation of the inflation fan.

While the proper installation of an inflation fan works wonders in a dual layer greenhouse, you will still be faced with major condensation problems in a single layer overwintering house. The best solution I have found is a clear liquid (I use Sunclear) that is sprayed on the inside of the plastic. The liquid causes the water droplets to disperse into tiny particles that adhere to the plastic and run down the sides of the greenhouse without dripping onto the plants and enhancing conditions for diseases. Better quality anticondensate plastics are also hitting the market.

Most growers using overwintering houses opt for a white polyethylene film or plastic. The white film keeps temperatures more consistent and reduces the dramatic fluctuations that would occur if clear plastic were used. White plastic is usually recommended, as light transmission is not as critical with crops that are simply overwintering in a dormant or semidormant state. White film is not recommended, however, for crops that are actively growing during the winter, as the reduced light levels causes plants to stretch and produce spindly growth.

You are now ready to order your plastic. But wait: how large a piece of plastic do you need to cover a 20-foot by 96-foot greenhouse? If you order a 20-foot by 100-foot piece of plastic, you will be sadly disappointed. It's easy to forget about the ends, and although some growers use end wall materials other than polyethylene, these end walls must be taken into account when you are calculating how much plastic covering to order. First add the length of the house to the height of both ends, then add on a few more feet to allow for fastening. If your greenhouse is 10 feet tall, add 96 feet to 20 feet for the greenhouse itself and then add an extra 2 feet for fastening. That means you will need a roll of plastic that is 118 feet long. Most rolls of polyethylene come in increments 25 feet long, so you will probably need to order a roll that is 125 feet long.

The width of the plastic you will buy is another matter to consider. A 20-foot roll will not nearly cover a 20-foot-wide greenhouse. In most cases, a 32-foot-wide or longer roll will be needed for a standard greenhouse. If you have a tall greenhouse with vertical sidewalls, you may require a 48-foot-wide sheet of plastic. The width of plastic you need is based on the height of your greenhouse and the angle of arch in the bows. Don't fret—your greenhouse manufacturer will have information on the width of plastic needed for their greenhouses. Don't make the mistake of ordering a roll that is far too wide because if you leave the excess hanging, you will have created a way for the wind to get a grip on the cover and begin removing it, probably long before you are ready.

Most greenhouse and plastic manufacturers offer early order programs for overwintering film. The majority of nurseries actually order their greenhouse film during the late spring or early summer for fall installation. Overwintering film is critically important so it is a good idea to have it on site much in advance of the dates that you will actually be covering your greenhouses.

If the greenhouse is to be heated during the winter months, it will probably be covered long before the first frost. If, however, the crop is to be unheated, it is best to allow the plants to go through at least one hard frost to first put them into a dormant condition. Covering nondormant, unheated crops means they stay "soft" and risk being severely damaged by the first hard freeze later in the winter.

Covering a greenhouse is—or should be—a fairly simple chore for either two or three people. I have, however, seen some people turn this into a far more

All bundled up and no place to go. Overwintering Quonset houses made of metal and covered with plastic. Yadkin Valley Nursery, North Carolina.

complicated process than is necessary. I recommend that you visit other growers and learn a technique that you like firsthand as there seems to be no consistency on how to cover a greenhouse. Typically it should take between one and two hours for two to three people to completely cover a 20-foot by 96-foot greenhouse. No matter which technique you use, the first rule to follow is to cover the greenhouse on a day when the wind is calm. It is difficult to truly appreciate the strength of wind until you have tried to install plastic on a greenhouse. I have seen plastic ripped from the hands of greenhouse workers trying to do this installation, but even more impressive is the sight of an entire crew of workers literally lifted off the ground by a strong wind gust while trying to hold onto a piece of polyethylene.

Another equally important tip is to install the polyethylene cover on a warm day. If the cover is installed tightly when it is warm, it will subsequently shrink and fit even more tightly when the weather cools. If the plastic is too cold when it is installed, it will become loose on warm days and thus much more subject to damage from strong winds.

The best technique I have seen is for two people to first unroll the plastic parallel to the greenhouse, to each take hold of one corner of the long end of the plastic, and then for one person to stand by the front door of the greenhouse while the other walks down its side. This method causes the plastic to ride up on one edge of the front wall of the greenhouse. Once the plastic has worked its way up to the roofline, the second person walks down the opposite side from the first. The two people then work their way to the back of the greenhouse, pulling the plastic as they walk. The plastic is then fastened all the way along one baseboard (someone will have made sure that the edge length of the plastic is parallel along the entire baseboard). Next, the plastic is fastened tightly to the opposite baseboard so that all the wrinkles and creases are pulled out. Before any of this work begins, of course, you should ensure that the plastic will not get caught on any loose boards, metal pieces, staples, or other sharp objects.

What is the best way to go about attaching the plastic to the greenhouse baseboard? Again, there is no consistent method in the nursery industry but most of the experienced growers choose some form of clipping system. In such a system, a metal base plate that is attached to the wood foundation is in turn bolted to the base of the greenhouse bows. Once the plastic is draped over the side of the base plate, a top plate is installed (it can be pressed on) that holds the plastic secure. A good fastening system should be quick and easy to install and remove. Some nurseries put this locking system only on both sides of the bows, but others put it on the front and back of the houses as well.

Other equally common and initially less expensive methods of attaching plastic to the wood base plate include stapling or nailing strips to the wood. The strips must be secured tightly against the greenhouse base otherwise a stiff breeze will remove the covers. Growers with greenhouses that are located in open windy areas often install a security strapping that crisscrosses across the top of the plastic to help prevent its unwanted removal.

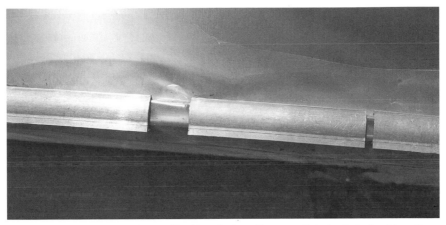

Polly wants a clip. The initial cost of locking devices (these are Poly-Lock devices) is quite high but they are reusable and are most effective in holding down the plastic in the case of high winds. Plant Delights Nursery.

Cold frame with white poly that is reinforced for windy conditions with shade-cloth strips. Plant Delights Nursery.

Shade structures

All plants have a particular light requirement for optimum growth, and the shade-loving plants in your nursery will require some type of light-reducing cover. Too much shade is almost as bad as not enough and will result in specimens with reduced growth rates and an unattractive leggy appearance. Many growers purchase a wooded site for the production of woodland plants, and while this method will certainly work, the quality and consistency of the plants will not be as high as if they had been grown under an artificially engineered environment. Most growers of shade plants opt for some type of shade structure. A variety of shade cloths can be used to cover either production greenhouses or specially built shade structures, where the cloth is removed in the fall and reinstalled in the spring. The shade structure may be perfect in areas where the plants can be overwintered outdoors, but in colder climates where winter protection is needed, it may be more economical to simply cover production houses with shade cloths in the summer and overwintering plastic in the winter.

Shade cloths come in black, green, or white, black being the favorite among most growers. Although they come in several standard sizes, most are made to order by greenhouse distributors. When you order a shade cloth you will be asked several questions: what size you want, whether or not you need grommets and, if so, how many, and the percentage of shade you need.

With regard to the amount of cloth you should order, a 20-foot by 96-foot greenhouse that will not have its ends covered will probably require a piece of

Snow in the forecast? A shade house with its shade cloth removed to prevent it from collapsing under a heavy snowfall. Buds and Blooms Nursery, North Carolina.

cloth 98 feet long. The width required varies with the height of the particular greenhouse; often a piece 30 feet or 32 feet wide is sufficient, but check with the greenhouse manufacturer. If you still have questions, go outside and measure. Keep in mind that shade cloths will shrink slightly in the sun, so allow a foot or so of cloth for each side and use grommets where the shade cloth will be tied onto the greenhouse instead of stapled or clipped.

Determining the exact percentage of shade will require some practice. In most parts of the country 63 percent shade is standard, although some growers prefer 57 percent if they can apply enough water to shade plants to keep them from burning. Some crops require 75 percent shade, even in more northerly climates. The farther south you are, the higher the percentage of shade your greenhouses will need. Obviously the converse is true as you move farther north into areas with cooler summers.

If you are using a shade structure other than a Quonset greenhouse or cold frame, don't forget to cover the sides as well as the top. I have seen plenty of shade structures with adequately covered tops but with unshaded sides, and as you can imagine the crops were scorched. The exception is the north side of a shade structure; that side can remain uncovered since light will not enter the greenhouse from this direction. You can save a small amount of money by not buying shade cloth for the north side and by improving air circulation inside the house.

Equipment systems

Now that the greenhouses are covered, let's examine some of the other costs involved in making them operational. Greenhouses must have ventilation; a greenhouse without ventilation is a disaster waiting to happen. Losses in plants and plant growth in an unventilated greenhouse will inevitably surpass the cost of ventilation, usually in a single season. Plants, even while dormant,

Sunburn prevention for plants. A shade cloth structure over a cutting propagation area. Hines Nursery, California.

must have air circulation. As plants grow they use carbon dioxide (CO_2) and release water vapor, which increases humidity. As the CO_2 levels drop, so does the rate of plant growth (Both 2000). There is nothing like moist, damp conditions to kill crops or cause plant diseases to spread like wildfire through a greenhouse.

Greenhouses can be equipped with side vents, top vents, walls that move, retractable ceilings, and many other devices that create ventilation. The cheapest way to create quick venting is to install a knee-wall along each side. This is simply a 2-inch by 6-inch (or similar) board that is attached to the greenhouse bows at a point, usually about 3 feet above the ground. When the weather warms, the plastic is unfastened from the base of the greenhouse, rolled upwards, and then refastened to the new knee-wall. Knee-walls allow for good cross ventilation while permitting the cover to be quickly dropped to the base in case of inclement weather. If you live in an area where the cover will have to be raised and lowered many times, you should use a thermostatically controlled, mechanical side or roof vent that can eliminate the manual part of this operation. Since heat rises, roof vents are the most effective.

The point of mechanized ventilation is to pull air in the greenhouse across the crops. The standard recommendation is to move 10 cubic feet per minute of air. To achieve this amount of air movement, locate one or more fans at one end of the house and one or more ventilation shutters at the other end. You can refer to formulas that will determine the size and number of fans and shutters you will need based on the cubic feet of air in your greenhouse (Acme 2001). Your greenhouse manufacturer can also help with this information. Both the fan and the shutter vents should be attached to a thermostat that will open at a prescribed temperature. You want the ventilation shutter to open just before the fan (a couple of degrees difference is all that is needed) since a simultaneous opening would create air suction that would prevent the vents from opening fully. I have seen such a miscalculation suck the plastic loose from a greenhouse end wall.

I prefer to set the ventilation thermostat as low as possible so that the air is pulled across the plants for the longest possible time. Most growers will allow a ten-degree differential between the settings of a ventilating fan and shutter system and a heater. If the heater is set to come on at 35°F, the ventilation system would close at 45°F.

Another means of circulating air in a greenhouse is through the use of poly-tubes. Large plastic tubes 1 feet to 2 feet in diameter run the length of the greenhouse and hang from the ceiling. A fan mounted at one end pushes air through the tubes and out through a series of holes spaced along the length of the tube. Air that is pushed through the poly-tubes can come either from outside the greenhouse or from air recirculating on the inside. Poly-tubes are often ceiling mounted, so the inflation fan will be positioned just in front of hot-air heaters.

In this arrangement, the poly-tubes aid in distributing heat to the far ends of a long greenhouse.

If you grow crops that are more disease sensitive, consider adding recirculating fans. A total of three to four fans per 100 feet of length of greenhouse is usually recommended. These fans simply hang from the ceiling and keep the air

It's limp now, but a little puff of air and it's ready to work. An uninflated poly-tube hanging from the greenhouse. Gilbert's Nursery, South Carolina.

Air-rumba . . . let's move. An air recirculation fan hangs from the greenhouse ceiling. Blooming Nursery, Oregon.

moving. They are not thermostatically controlled and are allowed to run without interruption. The standard setup is for two fans, equally spaced on each side of the center aisle, to blow lengthwise in opposite directions. Recirculating fans are most effective when there is no cross-ventilation.

If you produce high-dollar crops where the greenhouse covers are not removed during the summer months, you may need the additional cooling that evaporative cooling systems provide. These systems work by pulling warm outside air through wet cell pads that cool the air. In small greenhouses, evaporative cooling systems can be installed as single, self-enclosed, duct-fed units, which are known as arctic or swamp coolers. In larger greenhouses, an entire greenhouse end wall would be replaced with pads that have water dripping through them, while the wall on the opposite end is equipped with a fan. Operating on the same principle, this setup is known as a pad and fan system. The dimension of pad area you will need, as with fan and vent size, is based on a standard formula that pertains to your climate.

We should also consider heating the greenhouse in winter. Heat for greenhouses basically comes from four sources: solar radiation, hot water or steam, fossil fuels, and hot air. Although electric heaters may be fine for a small, hobbyist's greenhouse, they are simply not economical for commercial nurseries.

Few greenhouses still use solar radiation as a sole means of heat. Most of the solar collectors have proved too bulky, and more than a day of cloudy weather rendered most of these unreliable. Many greenhouse growers take advantage unknowingly of passive solar radiation during sunny days when sunlight warms a greenhouse to a toasty level, and a few maintain water barrels that have been painted black to absorb heat during the day and release it at night.

It's one of those love-hate relationships. These are propane-powered, forced air heaters for inside the greenhouse. Plant Delights Nursery.

Most greenhouses originally operated on steam heat. Steam was created by large boilers, which in turn were fired by wood, coal, or a petroleum product. The cost of boilers was quite high, so steam heat was not an option in most smaller greenhouses. Where boilers are still used, steam heat is distributed throughout the greenhouses via radiant fin systems. As long as the boiler remains operational, steam heat is among the most economical and reliable forms of greenhouse heating for large nurseries.

A spin-off from steam-heat technology is the specialized hot water system that is used for heating in greenhouses, especially localized crop heating and propagation. (Localized heating means that only the air near the crop is heated, thus saving the cost of heating all the air in the greenhouse.) In most of these systems, water is heated in a standard water heater common in most households and then piped into the greenhouses. The water is run through a large pipe header in the greenhouse and then into a smaller, spaghetti-like tubing system. These heated tubes are laid out on benches or even embedded in ground beds and the crops are then placed on top of the tubes. By implementing this sort of hot water system, you provide the crop with the heat that it needs for optimum growth but without having to use the extra energy to heat the air space in the greenhouse.

Hot bottoms and cool tops. No, we are not at the beach but inside a propagation greenhouse where hot water is being circulated through a tube system to keep the heat where it's needed. McLamb Nursery, North Carolina.

Crops are placed on top of a hot-water tube system. McLamb Nursery, North Carolina.

All greenhouse heaters are sized based on their heat output in BTUs (British thermal units). Typically, heaters are manufactured in increments of 25,000 BTUs. The amount of BTUs that it will take to keep a greenhouse at a desired temperature is based on a formula that accounts for the minimum outdoor temperatures in winter, the heat loss factor of the greenhouse covering, and the size of the area to be heated.

If, for example, you have a single-layer, plastic-covered Quonset greenhouse that is 100 feet long by 22 feet wide, you will need a piece of plastic that is 34 feet wide (it needs to be wider than the actual width of the greenhouse because of the arch). According to the heat loss calculation construction chart (see figure 3), the BTU loss would be 298,000, 269,000 of which are lost from the top of the greenhouse and 29,000 from the side. The next chart to look at is the heat loss calculation construction factor chart (see figure 4).

Figure 3. Heat Loss Calculation Construction Quonset BTU Loss Chart

HEAT LOSS CALCULATION CONSTRUCTION QUONSET BTU LOSS CHART												
COVERING WIDTH—FEET												
18'	20'	22'	24'	26'	28'	30'	32'	34'	36'	38'	40'	48'
END LOSS (BOTH) MBTUH												
8	10	12	15	17	20	23	26	29	33	36	40	60
COVERING LOSS MBTUH												
7	8	9	9	10	11	12	13	13	14	15	16	18
14	16	17	19	21	22	24	25	27	28	30	32	38
28	32	35	38	41	44	47	51	54	57	60	63	76
43	47	52	57	62	66	71	76	81	85	90	95	114
57	63	70	76	82	89	95	101	108	114	120	127	152
71	79	87	95	103	111	119	127	134	142	150	158	190
85	95	104	114	123	133	142	152	161	171	180	190	228
100	111	122	133	144	155	166	177	188	199	211	222	266
114	127	139	152	164	177	190	202	215	228	240	253	304
128	142	157	171	185	199	214	228	242	256	271	285	342
142	158	174	190	206	221	237	253	269	285	301	316	380
285	316	348	380	411	443	475	506	538	570	601	633	760
427	475	522	569	617	664	712	759	807	854	902	949	1138
570	633	696	759	822	886	949	1012	1075	1139	1202	1265	1518
712	791	870	949	1028	1107	1187	1265	1345	1424	1503	1582	1898

ROOF LENGTH FEET:
5, 10, 20, 30, 40, 50, 60, 70, 80, 90, 100, 200, 300, 400, 500

(Reprinted with permission. Acme Engineering & Manufacturing Corporation.)

Figure 4. Heat Loss Calculation Construction Factor Chart

HEAT LOSS CALCULATION CONSTRUCTION FACTOR CHART	
All metal (good tight glass house—20 or 24 in. glass spacing)	1.08
Wood & steel (good tight glass house—16 or 20 in. glass spacing) Metal gutters, vents, headers, etc.	1.05
Wood houses (glass houses with wood bars, gutters, vents, etc.—up to and including 20 in. glass spacing	
Good tight houses	1.00
Fairly tight houses	1.13
Loose houses	1.25
Corrugated Fiberglass covered wood houses	1.06
Corrugated Fiberglass covered metal houses	1.09
Double glazing with 1 air space	0.70
Plastic covered metal houses (single thickness)	1.08
Plastic covered metal houses (double thickness)	0.70
Plastic structured sheet metal frame (16mm thick)	0.51
Plastic structured sheet metal frame (8mm thick)	0.60
Plastic structured sheet metal frame (6mm thick)	0.67

(Reprinted with permission. Acme Engineering & Manufacturing Corporation.)

A single plastic layer has a heat loss factor of 1.08, which you multiply by your BTU: $1.08 \times 298,000$, which equals 321,840 BTUs. Finally, look at the heat loss calculation climate chart (figure 5). Determine the temperature difference that you have to maintain between the outside and inside temperatures. If you need to maintain 60°F indoors, and if the outside temperature can drop to −20°F, then your temperature differential is 80°F. Still looking at this last chart, you will find what the worst case outside wind speed will be when the temperatures are at their coldest. If you expect 25mph winds, then the chart shows the climate factor to be 1.26. Multiply this factor by what you calculated the BTUs had to be: $1.26 \times 321,840$, which totals 405,518 BTUs. This total is the amount of BTUs your heater will have to produce to maintain your desired inside temperature.

Your greenhouse manufacturer or supplier should have charts to help you select the appropriate heater. A heater that is too small will run without a rest period while also not maintaining the desired temperature. Conversely, an oversized heater will result in excessive on-off cycling, which will also prematurely wear out the heater.

Figure 5. Heat Loss Calculation Climate Chart

HEAT LOSS CALCULATION CLIMATE CHART					
INSIDE/OUTSIDE TEMPERATURE DIFFERENTIAL	WIND VELOCITY—MPH				
	15	20	25	30	35
30	.41	.43	.46	.48	.50
35	.48	.50	.53	.55	.57
40	.55	.57	.60	.62	.64
45	.62	.65	.67	.70	.72
50	.69	.72	.74	.77	.80
55	.77	.80	.83	.86	.89
60	.84	.88	.91	.94	.98
65	.92	.96	.99	1.03	1.07
70	1.00	1.04	1.08	1.12	1.16
75	1.08	1.12	1.17	1.21	1.25
80	1.16	1.21	1.26	1.30	1.35
85	1.25	1.30	1.35	1.40	1.45
90	1.33	1.38	1.44	1.49	1.54

(Reprinted with permission. Acme Engineering & Manufacturing Corporation.)

Forced air heaters that operate on fossil fuels are the most common form of heat sources found in greenhouses today. They are a great cause of stress, but like many other things in life, you can't live with them or without them. The heaters you select should be designed for greenhouse conditions, meaning they can take the humidity, moisture, and salts present in a greenhouse environment. Even the best-selling brands of greenhouse heaters have a ridiculously short life span with parts needing to be replaced usually in the second season. By the fourth or fifth season, you have normally rebuilt the entire heater or replaced it. Forced air heaters must be wired into your electrical system. While they derive their heat from fossil fuels, the gas pilot and the heater fan run off electricity. Without power, the heater will overheat since the fan cannot keep the heater controls cool enough and the emergency shutoff switch will stop the heater. Consequently, when you lose power you will have no heat.

It can be quite a chore to hang forced air heaters from the bows of the greenhouse since they can weigh several hundred pounds. Be sure to follow the installation directions exactly—better yet, hire the technician from your fuel company to help you as so much can go wrong in what seems like an easy process. However, if you decide to go it alone, here are some words of advice. Always make sure that the heater is hung at the proper height: you don't want to set the benches or greenhouse plastic on fire. Forced air heaters are located near one end wall and then vented to the outside so that potentially harmful fuel byproducts are carried away from the plants.

As part of the venting process, a metal exhaust pipe is attached to the back of the heater and extended outside through the end wall of the greenhouse. At the point where the pipe passes through the end wall, you will need to frame out a small square box (about 18 inches square is usually adequate) for the pipe to pass through. Attached to this box is a piece of sheet metal in which a hole is cut for the pipe to extend through. The idea is to prevent the hot exhaust pipe from touching either wood or plastic.

Once the exhaust pipe is extended far enough outside the end wall, an upright section of pipe is attached to pull the exhaust fumes upward and out. At the top of the vertical stack is a cap that allows gases to escape while keeping water from entering the exhaust system and flowing back into the heater. Also be sure to install a screen on the exhaust and other parts of the heater; you would be amazed at how many bird nests have to be dislodged from heaters and exhaust pipes.

It is also critical that you follow the height-to-length ratio of the exhaust pipe in the heater instructions exactly. It is usually recommended that the vertical height of the exhaust stack be twice the length of the horizontal pipe. If the horizontal pipe is too long or the vertical stack is too short, the exhaust will not draw correctly and the heater will overheat. This will result either in the internal safety switch shutting off the heater or the heater itself giving out, neither of which is desirable.

An arctic cooler unit pad system for a small greenhouse. Pretty cool, huh? Plant Delights Nursery.

It is amazing that virtually no one keeps spare heater parts on hand, so don't expect your gas company to have any. Greenhouse heater manufacturers and distributors are also notorious for being unable to promptly supply replacement parts, probably because there is a lack of adequate competition. You can see that it is critical for you to keep spare heater parts on hand, especially those that fail most often. For a start, include thermocouples, fan motors, gas valves, burners, and transformers in your collection. If all your heaters are the same size, you may consider keeping an entire spare heater for backup. Some greenhouse growers have even gone to the expense of using two smaller heaters in one house instead of one large enough to heat the entire house. The theory behind this practice is that although one heater will probably fail, the second heater will, if nothing else, keep a tender crop from completely freezing.

Of course you will need to know if and when a heater fails. Failure can occur with something as simple as a gust of wind blowing out the pilot light or as complex as a burner failure. Most nursery owners with heated greenhouses don't get a lot of sleep in the winter months. One owner said he was almost unable to sleep at all during cold nights, while another described his ritual of setting his alarm clock to wake him at 90-minute intervals throughout the night so he could go outside and check greenhouse temperatures. As you can imagine, this ritual will not put you in great shape to make good decisions during the daylight hours, nor will it be without an impact on your family life.

A number of alarm systems are available that will help with this problem of inadequate or interrupted sleep. One simple option is a low voltage wire that runs from a greenhouse-mounted thermostatic control to a transformer-rung bell in your home. Plant Delights uses a more complex system in which the Wilbur irrigation controller computer is notified of any failure by the same greenhouse-mounted thermostatic control. The computer program then systematically dials a series of pre-programmed phone numbers to let someone know of a heat failure with a prerecorded message. We have programmed the computer to call our nursery, home, cell phone, facilities manager, and nursery manager, in that order. Nothing beats having several backups! While this system does have some initial installation costs, those costs are moderate, and avoiding the loss of even one crop or preventing greenhouse checks at midnight makes it a worthwhile investment.

My not-so-subtle mention of the unreliability of greenhouse heaters leads me next to a discussion of backup heating systems. While having spare parts and spare heaters will help if there is electrical power, what will you do in the case of a power failure? A nursery that has any crop of significant value in a heated greenhouse must have a backup generator. Backup generators can be small enough to operate the fan on a single greenhouse heater or large enough to run several greenhouses as well as office systems. Generators are usually gas-powered engines that generate electricity. Work with a licensed electrician to evaluate your needs and to select the proper equipment. Remember that having a generator is like buying health insurance: you are gambling that you will not need it but are prepared in case you do.

Before we leave heaters, we should talk a little more about fuel. The primary fossil fuels are heating oil, bottled propane gas (which is liquefied petroleum or LP gas), and natural gas. Natural gas is usually preferable, not only because of cost but also because there is an uninterrupted supply. The key to having natural gas is locating your nursery in an area that has access to natural gas lines. The comparison costs of other fuels must be closely monitored as the most cost-effective fuel varies with fuel efficiency, market fuel costs, and heater efficiencies (Short 2001). Your greenhouse or heater manufacturer can provide cost comparisons to help you decide on the best and most economical fuel for your nursery.

The amount of fuel you need varies with the type of covering on the greenhouse as each covering is rated with a heat loss factor. The amount of fuel consumed is also directly related to outside temperatures, and there will be a tremendous difference in fuel usage depending on the amount of sunlight hitting the greenhouse. Even if outdoor temperatures are in the 20s, the inside of a greenhouse can be quite warm if sunlight is striking the greenhouse. Some parts of the country get plenty of sun in the winter months, while others get virtually none. If you plan to heat your greenhouses in the winter, contact your regional weather service to see how many sunny days your area typically enjoys as they will go a long way toward reducing your heating bills. In setting your minimum acceptable night temperature, keep in mind another rule-of-thumb: for every one degree that you can reduce your night time temperature, you will see a 3 percent savings on your fuel bill (Short 2001).

Choosing a good fuel supplier is another critical decision you will have to make. Not only should you shop around for prices, which can vary widely for fossil fuels, but you should also choose a firm with which you can establish a reliable working relationship. You will be relying on fuel delivery as well as on service when heaters fail. When a heater fails in the middle of a cold night with an entire crop on the line, you will want to know the home phone number of a person who is willing to help. Consult with other local nurseries to get a good start in choosing a reliable supplier.

If you use either propane gas or oil for your fuel supply, your fuel vendor will usually supply a fuel tank. The tank size is based on the number of greenhouses to be heated and the length of time that the tank of fuel will last under a worst-case weather situation. Gas companies frequently don't understand the rate at which gas is consumed in a greenhouse and tend to undersize tanks. Be sure to demand a large size tank as you cannot afford to run out of gas. You will need to do some planning before your tank arrives, as their are rules that dictate how close the tank may be to structures such as buildings, greenhouses, and driveways.

Most oil and propane gas companies offer to keep the tanks continuously filled. While this service is highly recommended, do not trust that it will always happen without checking it yourself. You or a staff member should regularly check the fuel pressure or level in your tanks. Be aware that on cold nights, it is possible for a 1000-gallon fuel tank to drop 20 to 30 percent in gas pressure depending on how many greenhouses are being served. I recommend that the gas level never drop below 25 percent.

Fuel prices can fluctuate wildly, and more than one nursery has gone out of business as a result. Growers who monitor their cost of production usually base their budgets on fuel prices that fall within a predicted range. All of a sudden there is a winter where an increased demand of fuel is coupled with a short supply—you can imagine what happens. During one winter our fuel prices tripled over the course of three months. The best way to avoid having to pay ongoing, increased prices is to prepay your gas bill based on your expected usage. Many growers prepay in spring or summer when prices are usually much lower. If you use this option, you will often find that you are paying less for fuel than your supplier is paying for it wholesale.

Benches

Greenhouse benches are basically platforms used to support the plant at some level above the ground. In selecting benches, be sure to look at how the greenhouse will be used, whether the benches need to be portable, and the economics of choosing material with either a long or short life expectancy. You will have to carefully consider the cost of the benches, their life expectancy, and the value of the crops that will be grown.

In wholesale growing areas, benches are used to make plants more accessible to workers, to create dual layers for plants in a production setting, to help with disease control, and to allow better drainage for plants that are particularly sensitive. I've seen growers lose entire greenhouses full of expensive plants simply because the plants were not elevated on benches and the water could not escape the pots fast enough to prevent root damage.

Benches in retail nurseries have the benefit of making plants more accessible to customers and of allowing them to be displayed in a more aesthetically pleasing fashion. Many nurseries have realized that attractive benches result in the improved display of plants, which in turn can translate into increased sales.

The choice of benching fabric is quite vast, ranging from treated wood lathe to metal panels to rigid plastics. Treated metal and plastic will not rot, rust, or harbor diseases but it is more expensive. Treated wood, on the other hand, will rot and can harbor diseases but it is less expensive. The material you choose will obviously depend on which factors are more important to you at the time of purchase.

Smaller growers are renowned for being inventive when it comes to rigging up makeshift benches. The standard supports are concrete blocks, but they have the disadvantage of moving when attacked by a passing water hose. Some growers make wooden legs that are attached to wood-framed benches but they are less mobile and must be braced well.

Tool time. Examples of simple, homemade greenhouse benches. H&H Botanicals, Michigan.

Simple elegance. Homemade benches using concrete blocks and treated wood. Plant Delights Nursery.

Beginning in the 1970s, many larger commercial growers realized that aisles were taking up an average of 40 percent of usable space in each greenhouse. To maximize the amount of usable space, many growers began using movable or rolling benches. These expanded metal benches sit on raised, horizontal pipes that are fastened to raised bench frames in such a way that the bench can be rolled along them. Rolling benches are used primarily in large gutter-connected greenhouses and form the only aisle in the entire greenhouse or at least in a large section of one. The position of the aisle can be shifted as needed simply by rolling the benches from side to side.

Rolling benches, when properly used, can increase usable bench space to 80 percent (Bartok 2000). If you increase the usable production space in a 2,000 square foot greenhouse from 60 to 80 percent, you gain 400 extra square feet. If your greenhouse generates an average of $20 per square foot, the rolling benches can generate an extra $8,000 of income per greenhouse. By comparing increased production figures to the cost of the bench, you can determine the economics of switching to this bench design. Rolling benches have two disadvantages: two workers cannot be working in different aisles at the same time, and if these benches are very long or not precisely installed, they become very difficult for employees to move.

Labeling plants

I admit that I am a bit compulsive about labels but with a varied plant collection as large as ours, I quickly learned that a plant without a label can lose much of its value and result in an array of other problems as well. Don't underestimate the need for accurate labels, as labeling is important for the wholesale producer, the retailer, and, in time, the customer. Given that labels are not optional extras, you will also need to find a good, economical means of producing them.

Labels become a critical part of a production nursery's record-keeping process. They are used to track the progress of crops and they help ensure that the correct plants are identified as they move through the production and sales process. In the production phase, labels not only include information such as the name of the crop but they also track the source of the stock and the date it was potted, fertilized, sprayed, and otherwise treated. Imagine that you purchased a particular plant from three sources, and as you grew the plants on, you found that some were either not the same as the others or were diseased. How would you separate out which plants came from which grower without a good labeling system?

Potting and fertilizer dates recorded on the labels will similarly allow you to track problems that may occur with bad batches of fertilizer or potting soil. On several occasions a problem at the soil mixing plant has resulted in us buying bad batches of soil. The nutritional problems didn't begin to show for a month or two after the plants had been potted, but fortunately we were able to track down the affected plants because we had good labeling in place. The same holds true for fertilizer; there is little worse than having used a contaminated batch that results in a dead or severely distorted crop.

Labels allow you to monitor the effectiveness of pesticide applications or other treatments while you are in the growing area. This information should be recorded elsewhere in your nursery records too, but during nursery scouting there is no better substitute for keeping the information posted on a crop label. I like to have labels in each block of plants and to have them indicate potting dates as well. Knowing the potting dates allows me to track the progress of a crop as I walk past, particularly if I know that a plant ought to be ready for sale a certain number of weeks after it was potted.

As far as plant identification is concerned, the value of signage labels should be pretty obvious. I went to a nursery many years ago to buy azaleas prior to flowering time, but because its labeling system was so shoddy, it took much longer than it should have to choose the plants because we were attempting to match winter leaf types. It was virtually impossible to make our selections with 100 percent accuracy; in fact, the nursery owner realized too late that he had mistakenly sold us all of a new, rare variety that had been mixed into the more common stock. While some nursery crops such as azaleas can be separated by color each spring, other plants may not show their distinguishing characteristics until they are five to ten years old. You do not want to discover that lost tags caused so much confusion in your nursery that you accidentally sold a new variety of birch at a much lower price than you could have sold it for had you known it was the one that produced much better bark at maturity.

How do you create labels for your plants? Production labels can be as simple as a handwritten tag or as complex as a computer-driven, thermally printed tag. Again, your decision of which kind of labeling system to use depends on the costs involved. If your nursery is small or you use only a few labels, handwritten labels are the answer. Affordable label options here are wooden or plastic, with the plastic labels being far more expensive. While wooden labels, even those that are treated, are very prone to rot, plastic labels will eventually become brittle. Both plastic and wooden labels come in a variety of lengths and thicknesses. If you are using the label for a very short time, a thinner, less expensive label is suitable, but if it will be used for a longer duration, then select the thicker label. I strongly believe that you should always use the best labels that you can afford, which for me has meant using a good, thick plastic.

There is actually a standard procedure for labeling, which is that all flats, pots, and rows are labeled from the back to the front and from the left to the right. In other words, in a flat of pots or cell packs, the first label is always at the back left.

With everyone adhering to this convention, no one has to worry that one grower will choose a different standard that could lead to confusion. It may seem like common sense, but if you start the writing at the top of the label and restrict it to that part of the label that sticks out of the soil, you will make the reading of labels much easier. Quite a bit of the labor cost in a nursery is spent looking for particular plants, so remember that more labels means less labor.

Another determination to be made is how many labels are needed in a production setting. My preference is to never rely on a single label as it is always subject to an early death, disappearance, or other mishap. I prefer no fewer than two labels per single flat of plants. The same is true with a block of plants: never rely on one label but determine the number needed by the particular label's death rate and the proximity of similar-looking plants.

If you are handwriting labels, be careful about what type of pens and pencils you use. While many people use waterproof marking pens, most are not ultraviolet resistant. After a short while you will be able to read only the writing that was hidden beneath the soil. An artist's paint pen, wax pencils, or regular pencils seem to work the best and last the longest. The softer the lead, the easier it is to write on plastic surfaces. Be sure to test your labels, as some of the plastic ones have a side on which pencil lead will not adhere.

Hands getting cramped? Consider a thermal label printer that works off your computer database to rapidly print pot tags.

We potted it when? Two pot tags, one with potting information (the date and source) that is later replaced with a "sales tag." Plant Delights Nursery.

If you or your staff spend far too much time handwriting labels, perhaps it is time to move to a thermal printer. Thermal printers are computer-driven printers that use a heat process to permanently print on roll-fed plastic labels. These thermal printers can be tied into your computer database and, assuming that the two programs are compatible, plant names and other information can be selected on the screen and transferred directly to the label. The advantages of a thermal printer are twofold: the lightning speed of printing whereby hundreds of tags are ready in mere seconds and the durability of the printing.

The thermal printing technology for labels gained widespread acceptance in the 1990s but is not without more than its share of headaches. Even a tiny speck of dust around these machines will cause printing to distort, and the absurdly expensive printer heads are prone to nothing but problems. However, even given these problems (which will be solved as more companies compete in the market), thermal printers still beat handwriting, especially for large label runs.

Another, perhaps less obvious, advantage of good labels is how they can be used to enhance the marketing and sales of your plants. Most of the better nurseries offer labels that include helpful information such as plant photos, planting and care advice, and bar codes. It is obvious to envision how the photos, together with good plant information, can assist in sales, but the bar codes are a great tool as well. Not only are they useful when the customer purchases the plant but they are also being used more and more often by production nurseries to track plant flow and monitor inventory numbers. Many wholesalers offer to provide color picture tags when you purchase liners and it is your choice to use them or not. If you purchase a patented plant, however, you will usually be required to use their official patent tag because this is how the wholesaler monitors that you are selling only those plants you are authorized to sell.

If you are printing labels for marketing purposes, some good computer-labeling packages as well as several national nursery-sign companies will do a fine job of printing these for you. Regardless of whether you print your own labels or hire this work out to others, make sure that each tag promotes your nursery. Have your name, address, phone number, Web site, and other relevant information preprinted either on the front or the back of each tag. The additional cost of having this preprinted is minimal compared to the return that you will get when customers wonder where such attractive-looking plants came from.

Nursery transportation systems
We touched on the topic of transporting plants from area to area in the context of a nursery's land use plan. Remember that every time a plant is touched and the longer a labor-related task takes, the more the cost of production increases and profits decrease.

Some wonderful, large-tire nursery carts are able to move plants short distances, and many of them have multiple shelving racks. The more plants you can move per trip, the fewer trips you will have to make, so improving your efficiency and reducing your costs. Consequently, it makes sense that the larger the trailer that will access your growing area, the greater the reduction in transportation costs.

All aboard! An overhead, pulley-based, racking transportation system for moving plants through greenhouses. Blooming Nursery, Oregon.

Some industry standards will help you keep an eye on labor costs. Based on a real-life example in which plants are moved from the potting area to the growing area via a hand-pushed rolling cart, the typical ground speed of a nursery worker is 4 feet per second or slightly slower when actually pushing the cart. Lifting or setting down a flat takes about 1.5 seconds each time. Most nurseries find square pots to be far more economical in terms of reduced labor costs than round ones because a flat can contain 18 square quart pots compared to only 11 round ones.

In this real life example, 100 flats of pots will be moved from the potting area to the greenhouse, a distance of 400 feet via a cart that holds four flats. At the rate of 4 feet per second, the worker will take 100 seconds to take the plants to the greenhouse and 100 seconds to return, a total of 200 seconds or 3 minutes and 20 seconds. To move 100 flats on a cart that carries four flats per trip will take 25 trips. Multiplying 25 trips × 200 seconds each, we arrive at a total time for the task of 5000 seconds or 83.3 minutes. I am not including the time to lift and place each flat, since this will be the same regardless of the size of the cart on which the plants are to be hauled. Now, let's compare how long it would take to do the same job using a tractor-pulled, flatbed trailer, which can carry 50 flats per load. If the tractor averages 10 miles per hour (146 feet per second), the 800-foot round-trip would take 5.5 seconds. It would take only two trips or 11 seconds to move the same 100 flats with the trailer compared to 5000 seconds with a smaller cart. This example clearly shows how efficiency around a nursery can be dramatically improved when the correct transportation equipment is used.

You should continue to evaluate your plant transportation scheme as your business grows. It's not only plant hauling that can improve efficiency but "people hauling" as well. Employees who have to walk long distances or whose tasks are delayed waiting for transportation cost you a staggering amount in terms of lost productivity. Having a vehicle move employees more quickly from one place to another may seem like a luxury but could actually improve the bottom line.

I encourage each nursery to take its own real-life time and distance measurements to determine its particular costs in each phase of the transportation scheme. These measurements can then be used to determine if a larger cart or a more mechanized system of plant transportation will result in a decreased cost of production.

Chapter 11

Growing Plants:
The Nuts and Bolts

What a relief—you've done all the preparation work and now it's time to get ready to grow plants. Plant growing is usually the fun part of running a nursery and is what brought people into the business in the first place, so let's get started. The next set of concerns you will have to deal with includes choosing appropriate potting soils, selecting the right container, knowing how to make the best of the potting operation, identifying irrigation sources and establishing a reliable irrigation system, figuring out how much to irrigate, deciding how you will fertilize your crops, establishing field-growing operations, establishing a suitable pruning schedule, adopting a plan for winterizing crops, determining whether to propagate or purchase plants, and dealing with the agricultural inspection that precedes licensure. Whew!

Potting soils

A good potting soil is the first requirement for growing a quality container plant. There are many places to cut corners, but potting soil is not one that makes good economic sense. Price is often a good indication of the quality of a potting soil: you get what you pay for. Choosing a good potting soil depends primarily on your maintenance techniques, the crops that you grow, and the weight of the soil when you ship the plant. The choice of which soil to use is as varied as the nurseries that use them.

Most crops require a potting soil that holds adequate moisture but that also drains well. While this may seem paradoxical, several nursery soils fit the bill. Your watering techniques dictate which soil will work best in your nursery; a potting soil that works well for a nursery that waters frequently would be disastrous for a nursery that waters less often. One difficulty in purchasing plants from several different growers is that each of them probably uses a different mix, making it virtually impossible for you to irrigate them all under a standard regimen.

In most parts of the country, drainage is the key to growing a container crop. If you live in a high rainfall area, it is even more critical that you use a fast draining mix. Although this means you will have to apply more water, you will quickly find that it's a lot easier to correct underwatering than overwatering. Only in very drought-prone areas should a mix be used that will actually hold moisture. When choosing a potting mix, plan for the worst rainfall scenarios you can imagine, both too much and too little. Will your soil mix hold enough water during the worst drought, and will it drain fast enough during the heaviest rainfalls?

Most commercial mixes are formulated with a composted bark base, although more and more alternative products are being studied for use as amendments. Other commonly used components in potting mixes include peat moss, sand, perlite, and vermiculite. Properly sized bark increases drainage, whereas peat moss holds additional moisture and nutrition. Sand, perlite, and vermiculite are used to make the mix drain better. Sand also adds weight and stability to the mix. The properties and performance of a potting mix can vary widely depending on the proportions of each of these components.

Another factor to consider is the weight of the mix. While a heavy soil mix has its advantages (containerized plants are less easily blown over in the wind), extra weight in handling and shipping the plants can cause major problems and added expenses. Although virtually all nursery soils are based on organic materials, the degree to which each mix is composted when you buy it varies dramatically. The longer the mixes are composted, the more stable the mix will be, and consequently the higher the cost per unit of mix. A load of 20 cubic yards of an undecomposed potting soil may soon be 15 yards of soil after sitting in your potting area for a short while. What may have seemed like a bargain at first often turns out not to be.

After determining your crops' particular requirements, you may need to add amendments to the potting soil, such as micronutrients, lime, pesticides, and some biological disease-suppressing organisms. Any supplier of high quality potting soil can, during the mixing process, either supplement the soil mix with particular amendments or adjust the water-holding capacity of the soil.

You will also need to determine if you can best handle your mix in bags or as a bulk delivery. Typically, bulk

Potting soils are like personalities—there's a time and place for all of them. One is a fine mix for seed (Metro Mix 360), the other a coarse, well-drained mix for use in larger containers (Bio Comp 5). Plant Delights Nursery.

mix is cheaper, but if it will be stored on your property for a long time, bags may indeed be the better choice. Soil mixes that are exposed to the elements can undergo physical changes, ranging from a drop in pH to a loss of fertilizer activity. In addition, exposed mixes may become contaminated with both weed seeds and disease pathogens. I once attended a talk by a college professor who had been requested by a grower to prove that soil mix manufacturers were shipping soil that was infested with weed seed to growers. What the professor found was that the opposite was true: in all cases, the weed seeds were blown into the mix after it was delivered to the nursery.

Commercial bagged mixes are often a better choice when smaller amounts will be used at one time or when the mixes have to be transported to distant work sites without the benefit of loading equipment. Although bagged mixes may appear to be protected from weeds, most are actually formulated to "breathe," meaning they will need to be protected from the rain otherwise they become so waterlogged that they are virtually impossible for mere mortals to move. They will also suffer from the same changes in chemical properties as do piles of bulk soil mix. Some bagged mixes are formulated primarily for use inside a controlled greenhouse and hold far too much water to be used outdoors. Be sure to ask questions—better yet, put each mix to the test.

New mixes seem to appear on the scene every year, and you will be pressured by salesmen to switch brands. I always recommend a trial period with a free sample of any new mix that you are considering. My rule of thumb is to use the

A good kind of segregation. Soil bins are used to contain different mixes and components. Champion Nursery, North Carolina.

new mix on the crop you are having the most trouble growing with your existing mix as any improvements will be easy to notice. Do not be afraid to ask for free samples and perform your own comparison trials.

I recommend that you also ask a potential media supplier plenty of questions, including how fast can they turn around your order. Other inquiries include the size of the supplier's delivery trucks, their willingness to make custom-formulated mixes, and the quality of the monitoring of a mix's consistency. Check out the references of long-term clients to see how happy they are with that particular supplier's mix as well as their service.

You always have the option of mixing your own potting soil. I strongly question the wisdom of this practice in all but the largest nurseries. If you have access to the ingredients you prefer to include in your potting mix at a good price, as well as access to the mixing equipment, then doing it yourself may indeed be economical. Small growers use a cement mixer, while large growers choose either commercial soil mixers or, more commonly, a tractor with a front-mounted scoop bucket. The tractor-mounted bucket will certainly work, although the two most frequently encountered challenges when using this machine are finding a clean, disease- and weed-free surface and producing a mix that is both well blended and consistent.

The advantages of mixing your own potting soil can include a cost savings, but more often it is the greater reliability of supply. There is a clear benefit in being able to produce potting soil as it is needed instead of trying to plan its delivery in advance and having to rely on your supplier to get the mix to you when you need it for potting. If you decide to mix your own soil, check with your county's Cooperative Extension Office to determine what mix is most commonly used in your climate. In most areas you can create inexpensive mixes either with straight bark or a bark and sand combination, usually somewhere between a 10:1 and a 3:1 ratio. Adding more sand would speed drainage from the mix.

If you assumed that once the plant is potted you no longer need to pay attention to the soil in the containers, I can tell you that noth-

I told you nursery people are a creative bunch. A small nursery mixes soil in an old boat. Paulson Nursery, Virginia.

ing is farther from the truth. As we discussed, the quality of composted mixes varies widely and will therefore require different levels of monitoring. The longer the mixes are composted, the more stable the mix will be in the container and the less you have to worry about them. Cheap mixes that have not been decomposed well will shrink in the pots, leaving the pot only half full of mix after a season. While the mix may have been cheaper at the time of purchase, the cost of refilling the containers as the mix decomposes will more than offset the higher initial cost of a good, well-composted mix. The water- and air-holding capacity of decomposing mix also changes over time. In general, decomposing mixes will hold far more water than the crop needs because of the reduced air space in the soil. As you can imagine, this will result in rotted roots that, at least in our experience, have far less value than the crop we actually intended to produce.

Container selection

After you select the soil mix for your containers, you will need to select the containers for your plants. Most novice nursery owners don't have a true appreciation of the quality of nursery containers that are available today. As recently as the 1970s, virtually all nursery containers were recycled food cans, usually scrounged from nearby schools and restaurants. Punching drainage holes in the cans was a despised job that took weeks, and manually hauling these plants around the nursery was an equally daunting task. The highlight of those "good

You can't keep a good plant down. Large pots ranging from 5 to 25 gallons are used for growing woody plants. Panther Creek Nursery, North Carolina.

old days," however, was trying to remove a root-bound plant from a sharp-lipped can for planting or transplanting. This task was usually reserved for those needing to expel some aggression on an inanimate object.

Selecting containers in today's world is very different. Container size primarily depends on the market that you have decided to target. Standard sizes for smaller pots usually increase by the inch, so there are pots with 2-inch diameters, 3-inch diameters, 4-inch diameters, and so on. Larger outdoor nursery containers are usually offered in the following sizes: 1 quart, 2 quart, 3 quart (known as a trade gallon), and 4 quart (called a full gallon), and 2 gallon, 3 gallon, 5 gallon, 7 gallon, 10 gallon, and so forth. Among the true quirks in the nursery container business is that pot sizes usually do not conform to actual amounts that they contain. The classic example is that a 1-gallon nursery pot is actually closer to a non-nursery 3-quart measure than to a true gallon. While many manufacturers actually make a "true" gallon pot, the 3-quart pot remains the "one gallon" standard in the industry. The ANLA standards for nursery stock help clarify any pot size definitions.

If you sell primarily to landscapers, you will probably choose larger pot sizes since larger plants make more of an immediate impact in the landscape. Conversely, if your primary business is mail order, you'll likely use 1-quart pots. Retailers or wholesalers that sell to garden centers will probably offer a wide array of sizes. It is important that you match the size of container to the plant, the customer, and your costs per square foot to produce that container plant.

How big can you go? These giant tree containers can be assembled and disassembled to make transplanting easier. Panther Creek Nursery, North Carolina.

The proper container for your operation depends on how long the plant will be in the container and whether the pots will be reused. If you plan to reuse the pot or keep it for a long time, you should opt for a higher quality pot, but if you are selling items with a fast turnaround and a low profit margin, then use a cheaper pot. The two most common types of pots are those that are injection molded and blow molded. Injection-molded pots are the type most often seen in a greenhouse and they have less durability; obviously their price follows suit. Blow-molded pots are generally used for outdoor nursery operations, as they are formulated to last longer under outdoor weather conditions. Keep in mind, however, that there are many different qualities of blow molding, from thin molding, which is cheap, to thick molding, which is more costly.

As nursery crop specialties increase, the variation in pots increases proportionally. You can find deep pots, very deep pots, pots with virtually no bottom (called tree bands), hexagonal pots—the list goes on and on. If you are growing your plants without spacing between containers (pot to pot), then square pots are certainly the most efficient. Although square pots often cost slightly more, that increase is more than offset by what you save on fertilizer, preemergent herbicides, and water that is lost through the cracks between round pots. As I mentioned earlier, more square pots fit into a flat, so your transportation costs are also reduced. Round pots have been the standard for many years, however, and they work well if plants are spaced out and if the number of plants per flat is not your most important concern.

Who says don't be a square? Three sizes of square pots, 1 quart, 2 quart, and 3 quart, at Plant Delights Nursery.

Space, the final frontier. Notice the difference in the space required by both round and square pots, especially in flats. Plant Delights Nursery.

Some pot manufactures have different pot designs based on how the pot improves the root structure of the plant. For example, pots with ribbed sides or bottoms are believed to help roots from becoming such a tangled mess. Each pot manufacturer has its own theories and research, and you should ask to see this. Some manufactures have produced shorter or "squat" pots to save money. While this does save in the amount of potting soil used, which makes squat pots especially popular for low profit-margin plants such as garden mums, they also hold much more water than their taller counterparts. If you want pots to hold more water then squat pots are a good option, but most people mistakenly think that shorter pots drain better and hold less water. Anyone who has ever watched Mr. Wizard on TV knows that the taller the column of soil in the pot, the greater the force of gravity in pulling the water out of the soil.

The quality and design of pots also vary dramatically. If the holes are in the bottom of the pot, as they often are, and if the pots are sitting on a hard surface, then drainage will not be good as there is literally no place for the water to escape. Many pot manufacturers are putting side drainage holes near the bottom of the pot in place of or in addition to the holes in the bottom of the pot. While it's never a good idea to grow plants on top of an impermeable surface, these side drain holes are at least a good measure of protection against the plants drowning during the production cycle.

Many manufactures have tried to "capture" customers by making their own line of pots that fit only in their line of flats. Should you decide to use their pots, you must also buy flats that fit (and vice versa). If the manufacturer or distributor is out of stock on an item, they have made it impossible to find a replacement item from another manufacturer. I have shied away from manufacturers that only offer proprietary sizes of pots and flats because I don't want to be short of pots.

Purchasing pots can pose real dilemmas, especially for smaller nurseries. Probably only a few nurseries did not go the "used pot" route when starting out. An ad in the local farmers-market bulletin often brings forth plenty of folks with stacks of old pots. Be aware that how the pots were stored is an important factor in a container's degradation as ultraviolet light from the sun causes virtually all plastic containers to break down. Another big drawback with used pots is that you will get a wide range of both sizes and colors. Such a conglomeration of containers makes it difficult to manage a crop with any consistency because water and fertilizer needs vary tremendously with pot size.

A little planning at the time of purchasing pots can make life easier as well as cut costs. First, remember that all pots are not always available. A pot manufacturer doesn't always keep a stock on hand in all its sizes, which I think is inexcusable! I often hear that a particular production machine is broken or a certain mold is out of commission—the excuses are numerous. The problem is that when you need pots, you don't want to have to wait one to two months as that is often very costly. Unfortunately, being forced to wait is usually the rule instead of the exception.

By carefully monitoring your container usage and anticipating your future needs, you should be able to predict and plan your container needs far in advance. The more pots you order at a time, the cheaper they are, so be sure to ask your manufacturer or representative at what quantity the price breaks (quantity discounts) begin. The actual shipping of pots is also a large part of the cost of purchasing nursery containers. Often 1,000 pots cost the same to ship as 100,000 pots. By coordinating with other nearby nurseries, you can often arrange a split shipment whereby the nurseries save on both the cost and shipping of the pots. In addition, many of the pot manufacturers and distributors will provide free shipping when the pot order reaches a certain high volume.

Another factor to keep in mind is petroleum prices. Virtually every winter and again during the summer vacation season, petroleum prices are at their highest. Nursery containers are petroleum products so their costs are directly related to the cost of petroleum. By watching and coordinating such factors, you can often make notable savings; I have seen a pot vary as much as 30 percent in price over the course of a single year.

While the color and style of the pots may not matter to the plants, it does matter to your customers. I'm not saying that no one will buy your plants if the pots aren't consistent, but small details such as this give customers an idea of how you handle other details in your business. Customers who are looking for quality and consistency will most certainly be less than enthusiastic with a rainbow assortment of containers, while customers looking for a cheap bargain plant will probably not care.

Many larger growers have developed their own unique style of pots that sets them apart from those in the rest of the industry because of the color, shape, or name or logo on each container. Some nurseries that, in the past, priced plants by container size hit on the idea of keeping the size the same but changing the color of the pots according to price. For example, the lowest priced gallon plant could be in green pots, the next highest priced could be in silver pots, and the most expensive plants could be in gold pots. While linking price to pot color is a great strategy, you will need to do a high enough volume in each color to make the costs of manufacturing the specially colored containers economical.

If you grow plants in 1-gallon or smaller pots, you will also have to be concerned with selecting a flat. Smaller pots typically reside in flats for transportation purposes. The industry standard (if such still exists) is a 1020 flat. In other words, the flat is 10 inches wide by 20 inches long. Each flat takes up 200 square inches of space or about 1.6 square feet. Because of the difference in the number of pots that will fit a standard 1020 flat depending on pot shape, you can nearly double your growing capabilities by switching to square pots.

The quality of the flat varies with the amount and design of the plastic webbing. Some flats are very durable and can take more than a decade of regular use. Other, cheaper, lower-quality flats will often not last a single trip from the greenhouse to the truck. While you need to determine if the flats will be reused, the cheaper flat in most cases is false economy. Think about how many times you see nurseries staff having to use double- or even triple-stack flats simply because a single flat is not sturdy enough. You could easily justify paying twice as much for a higher quality flat instead of doubling up flats.

The potting operation
When it comes to the plant production side of a container nursery business, the efficiency of the potting operation has one of the greatest influences on the cost of production. This influence may not be very noticeable on a high-dollar crop, but on a crop with low profit margins, the cost of production can make or break the nursery.

Grab a trailer, pots, and soil and we're on the move! In some large operations, potting may be more efficient when done in the field. McLamb Nursery, North Carolina.

When your nursery is small, potting is a fairly simple chore that is mostly done by hand, from moving soil to filling pots to the actual potting. Improved efficiency in this scenario may come from using larger shovels to move the mix and, eventually, adding a front-end loader or tractor-mounted bucket as soon as it is feasible. Greater efficiency can also be achieved if potting is performed at a bench or trailer at a height that workers find comfortable. Bending over to pot wastes time and is also a discomfort to workers. While most people can pot for a short time at a height that is incorrect in relation to their own height, it will not only cause joint stress and back pain, but the rate of potting will also drop dramatically because of the worker's discomfort. Be aware that workers who are shorter may need a stool or elevated platform at the potting area to be more productive. You should also take into account the effects of inclement weather. Are you prepared to make workers comfortable on hot sunny days as well as during cool and rainy times? Potting cannot stop because of the weather, so be sure to make plans ahead of time.

You want it where? When? Having equipment that makes tasks more efficient becomes critical as your nursery grows. Here a forklift operator moves stacks of recently filled pots to the potting area. Blooming Nursery, Oregon.

Establishing and maintaining a good work flow at your potting station will go a long way toward improving efficiency in the production cycle. Among the most critical elements to review include the depth at which plants are planted, how the water and fertilizer are applied, how labels and other information-recording procedures are incorporated into the operation, and the speed and consistency with which the plants are potted.

Efficient procedures, such as filling flats of pots instead of individual pots, often escape employees, an oversight that ends up costing you money. Similarly, simple details, such as how full to fill your pot, need to be addressed. The standard rule of thumb is to leave about ½ inch to 1 inch below the rim of the pot. You don't want to leave too much room so that the depth of the root growing area is greatly reduced; nor do you want to leave too little room so that the soil mix and fertilizer rolls out of the pot. If your soil mix rises all the way to the lip of the pot, it will be virtually impossible to grip the lip of the pot and carry it (assuming it is not being transported in a flat).

The depth at which a plant is planted in the pot also has a tremendous bearing on how the plant will grow. The worst problem in most potting operations is that the plants are planted too deep in the pot. If planted too deep, it may drown; at the very least it will be forced to form a new set of roots higher up on the stem. The opposite is often true with perennials, however. Perennials grown from cuttings must be potted deep enough so that one or two growing points or nodes are below the soil level. Unlike woodies, perennials die to the ground each year, and if there is a root system below the ground without a growing point, you will find in spring that you have a pot of roots and no plant.

How will the plants be watered after they are potted? Most nurseries do their initial irrigation at the potting area, as the initial amount of water required to settle the soil around the roots will be quite different from what is required during the maintenance phase. I have always liked the idea of loading the plants on a trailer that, when driven away, passes under a boom that is mounted with irrigation heads. These heads are either operated manually or are connected to an electric eye that operates the water only while the plants are within a given area.

Among the most important factors in the potting process actually occurs before the potting has begun. For example, look at how moist the potting soil is. While many of the higher quality potting soils contain a wetting agent, which helps to disperse water through the mix, most commonly used mixes do not have this additive. Dry potting soils can be extremely difficult to wet initially, as they are often hydrophobic (they hate water). Often it takes a number of waterings before the mix actually absorbs water. I have seen an amazing number of smaller nurseries pot in bone-dry potting soil before irrigating, only to find that the water did not wet any part of the mix except the surface and the sides. If this problem is not detected or rectified, your loss rate will be astronomical. Potting mixes should always be thoroughly moist before they are used for potting.

If you use surface-applied, slow-release fertilizer, I recommend you use the potting time to apply fertilizer. If large blocks are potted at once, it may be easier to fertilize after the plants are placed in the growing area. If you find yourself potting smaller blocks at a time, you might be better off doing the fertilizing at the potting area.

You will need to work to develop a standard procedure for labeling each flat or group of plants to avoid confusion when the plants are unloaded in the growing area. I recommend keeping accurate records of your potting operation. These records allow you to constantly upgrade your procedures and to resolve problems when they occur. At Plant Delights we use a simple system whereby a loose-leaf binder containing a complete nursery inventory is kept at the potting area. As the plants are potted, information pertaining to them is entered into the binder. For example, an entry would read: "200 *Hosta* 'Great Expectations'; potted from cell packs into 3-qt. pots; 4/1/00; from such-and-such a nursery; placed in greenhouse or bed 16, row 2." This information is transferred into our computer database once a week.

As more and more workers are assigned to the chore of potting, the level of efficiency tends to drop dramatically, as does the consistency. To maintain quality and ensure that standards are met (in terms of plants being planted at the proper depth and at a consistent rate per hour), you will need someone to coordinate the potting phase of your operation as your crew size increases. This is why most nurseries involved in a lot of potting eventually turn to potting machines. A common intermediate step in eliminating the manual moving of soil is the use of conveyors. Often if soil needs to be moved a distance that makes shovels inefficient, it becomes feasible to use motorized conveyors on which the soil is loaded at one end and then conveyed to the potting bench.

Potting machines are designed so that soil is fed into a hopper or dumped in via a loader. They can be set up to use premixed soil or to mix the ingredients as part of the potting process. The soil is mixed (if that is necessary) and then dropped automatically into a conveyor-fed line of containers. The containers are then moved via belts to the potting crews at a rate of speed that can be set by the nursery. Not only does this system improve the quantity of plants potted but it also helps greatly with consistency.

Potting machines range from the very simply designed machines used in small- to medium-sized nurseries to large, multimillion-dollar, computerized monstrosities that only the largest nurseries would consider. As with every other decision, the economics of your business must be the determining factor in which kind of machine to use: will it reduce your labor cost in this very labor-intensive area? Keep in mind that the increased costs of a potting machine will come from its repair, upkeep, and actual operation. We'll discuss how to make these labor cost projections in chapter 16.

From deciding how to pot you should next decide what to pot. If you produce or purchase a flat of liners (whether they are cuttings or seedlings), you will notice that not all liners are created equal. The potting stage is a critical point at which to cull weak plants. If you pot all the liners and 10 percent are weaker than the others, the result will be that 90 percent of the plants in each flat or block will be ready and sellable, while the other 10 percent will not. Some growers mistakenly assume that the other 10 percent will be sellable eventually, but this is rarely true. More vigorous plants tend to shade out weaker neighbors so that in most cases the weaker plants rarely produce anything that is sellable.

If you do decide to pot weaker liners, you will not only have to later cull them prior to shipment, but you have also wasted valuable growing space and potting time on a crop that will probably not be sold, at least not at the same time as the rest of the crop. Even if the remaining smaller plants remain alive, it will take an increase in costs to maintain these plants and make them sellable. Expenses will include the cost of the growing area, fertilizers, pruning, and other general maintenance.

Sales staff, looking only at computer inventories, expect to sell all the inventory that they see in the computer. However, because plants that should have

The need for speed. A potting machine makes large potting operations much more efficient. Gilberts Nursery, South Carolina.

been culled were potted, 10 percent of the crop that your sales staff sells is not suitable for shipment. If you take a close look at what it costs to keep weak or poor plants at the potting stage, you will quickly realize that it is far more economical to discard them at the potting stage than to carry them any further through the production process.

Irrigation sources

One part of the growing operation that can make or break a nursery on any single day is irrigation. A reliable irrigation system is truly one of the backbones of any plant-related business. How many times have you visited a plant retailer and seen that all the plants were wilted or nearly deceased, making them rather unappealing? What about the wholesale grower whose plants don't achieve their maximum growth each year compared to those in other nurseries in the area? More than likely the answers to both these questions can be found by looking at how the plants are irrigated. When a plant wilts, you are losing out on its potential growth. It doesn't matter how many things you do correctly; without proper irrigation, all is lost.

Wells and ponds are the two most common sources of nursery irrigation, each of which has positive and negative aspects to consider. Ponds offer larger reserves and are easily replenished by rainwater, but during periods of drought, evaporation from a pond can be quite high. Also, ponds that will hold enough water for your irrigation needs will take up a huge chunk of land, so the size of your property and also its price become important considerations. Be sure, therefore, to consult with an irrigation specialist on the amount of water necessary to supply your needs now and in the future. Pond water almost inevitably has to be treated to remove the more damaging contaminants such as waterborne diseases that can cause disaster overnight if the crops have been irrigated. Similarly, the array of weed seed that can be spread from pond irrigation is truly amazing. Smaller nurseries could use municipal water, but not only is this usually prohibitively expensive but you will also have to research whether the crop you grow is sensitive to fluorine, which is usually present in treated water.

Wells are very reliable in areas with good groundwater. Deep wells offer a good supply of clean water as long as the water vein holds out and does not become contaminated. While well water may occasionally require a filter to remove grit particles or excessive minerals, these treatment requirements usually pale in comparison to those applied to surface water from ponds.

While digging a pond is fairly simple—dig a hole and wait for the rain—drilling for water by putting a hole in the ground requires a real leap of faith. Although drilling wells is still not an exact science, much of the technology used in oil drilling is used in locating water. It should be relatively easy for a well-drilling company to determine where water exists on your property and, within a given range, even how much flow you can expect. If your local well-drilling company doesn't have access to this technology, keep looking until you find someone who does. I'm certainly not trying to offend those who divine for water with a willow branch, but let's just say that some people like to gamble more than I.

Although it may seem expensive, I always recommend that nurseries have more than one source of irrigation water. If you plan to use a well, drill two wells. I also advocate tying the two wells together so that in the event of one well's failure a valve can be opened, allowing water to again flow via a back feed from the working well. Nurseries that use ponds often use a combination of wells and ponds, where the wells pump directly into the ponds, keeping them filled during times of drought.

It is critical to have a backup water supply. I cannot imagine a nursery without a backup well or pond for emergencies. Bilderback (2001) cites recommendations that container nurseries have "no less than 1 acre inch (approximately 27,000 gallons) of irrigation storage per acre of nursery stock per day.... Nurseries should be developed to have a storage capacity of at least a 30-day irrigation supply."

During the hot part of the growing season, a one-day loss of water could be enough to destroy an entire crop. A backup water supply is not a luxury, it is a necessity. Many nurseries in eastern North Carolina lost crops after Hurricane Fran, not because of winds or rain but because there was no power for more than a week with which to run the irrigation systems. Be sure to have some type of emergency power supply to handle your irrigation needs when emergencies arise.

Irrigation systems

It may seem there are more types of irrigation systems than there are nurseries, as each nursery tries out several systems before settling on something with which it feels comfortable. In reality, however, there are five basic types of irrigation systems: surface irrigation, subsurface irrigation, overhead sprinklers, drip or micro-irrigation, and hand irrigation. Surface irrigation is relegated to field growing where the field is flooded through a series of canals. Subsurface irrigation is a similar procedure used in greenhouses. Overhead sprinkler irrigation is the application of water overhead, while drip or micro-irrigation is the application of water only to a limited area of soil. Manual irrigation is simply that which is done by hand.

You will have to decide which of these systems is best suited to the crop you will be growing, as well as whether to water manually or automatically. In other words, are you going to drag out the water hose every day or try to develop an automated system? Let's look at a few figures. It takes an average of one minute to hand water 10 square feet of plants (McKay 2000). If you have a greenhouse or bed with 2,000 usable square feet, it will take 200 minutes or 3.33 hours to water it. Figuring an actual labor cost of $8 per hour, the cost each time of watering a greenhouse would be $27. If you have to water twice daily during the hot season, you can see costs of $378 per week per hour. Without any question, then, the most efficient use of your time is to automate this part of your operation.

Nurseries that try to irrigate manually quickly realize that watering plants correctly is a true skill not possessed by all workers. While it is tempting to make watering plants the lowest paid position at the nursery, it usually doesn't take many blocks of dead plants for nursery owners to realize the error of their ways. The person or persons in charge of irrigation is exceptionally critical to your success.

Quite a few small- to medium-sized nurseries still make use of hand watering. If this is you, try and match your equipment to the task. Hoses come in an array of shapes and sizes, and when it comes to water hoses, you get what you pay for. Typically, hoses come in a variety of diameters: ⅜ inch, ½ inch, ⅝ inch, ¾ inch, and 1 inch. For most operations, a ⅝-inch hose is the best. Hoses with smaller diameters are more apt to kink, whereas those with larger diameters are so heavy that many workers are unable to maneuver them through the nursery, at least not without turning over plants or greenhouse benches.

Water hoses are primarily made from vinyl or rubber materials. Rubber is usually much heavier than vinyl. Good quality hoses often have a support on the female end of the hose that connects to the faucet, as this is usually the first part of the hose to wear out. (If you haven't yet heard the terms *male end* and *female end*, they are plumbing terms used to refer to ends of pipe, hoses, and other items. Two pipes are always connected with the male end going inside the female end.) When siting your water hydrants or hose bibs (commonly called faucets), keep in mind that hoses come in a variety of lengths from 50 feet to 100 feet. If your water source can be located in the center of the greenhouse or bed instead of at one end, then both the length of hose you will need and the amount of effort needed to move it will be reduced.

Pulling hoses around through a nursery is a quick way to destroy crops unless some type of "stop" or hose guard is installed. It is easier to pull hoses around sturdy, round surfaces than around sharp or even flat surfaces, such as cement blocks. A number of commercially available pulley-based hose guards may help in this regard.

I always recommend having a water cutoff on the end of each hose. Having to run back out to the main water cutoff is not always feasible during the watering process. While the plastic water cutoffs are much cheaper, you will quickly see why: they break, wear out, and just don't work very well. In a commercial setting, where the end cutoffs are used more regularly, the cheaper plastic models simply don't have a long life span compared to the more costly brass cutoff nozzles.

Hand watering is rarely done without a specialized nozzle or diffuser. This is where the wide assortment of hose end nozzles comes into play. Different hose nozzles have been designed for different types of watering chores. The most common is a simple round nozzle, which usually comes in sizes ranging from 1 inch to 2 inches in diameter, depending on how much water flow is desired. Fan nozzles, which are more commonly used for large flats or ground beds, produce a watering spray that is much wider. Among the more unique nozzles is a fog nozzle. Here the water holes are very tiny, producing the effect of a high-pressure fog. This type of nozzle is most often used on cuttings or young seedlings when the foliage should remain moist but the soil does not need to stay waterlogged.

Nozzles and hose ends that are allowed to contact the ground will quickly pick up an assortment of soil-borne fungi, which will in turn quickly be applied to your crops with each watering. Nurseries often overlook the critical importance of having a clean place to hang the nozzle and male end of the hose. Watering with contaminated equipment is among the most common ways that soil-borne diseases are spread through a nursery.

Even nurseries that employ automatic watering systems will need some hand watering. Perhaps, for example, a special house with a diversity of crops may not adapt to an automatic system, or perhaps hand watering is necessary when the wind blows and sprinkler coverage is not as precise. Regardless of your irrigation system, hand watering will always be an important chore. To this end, remember that hand watering must be done by humans, and that means someone will have to attend to this chore seven days a week.

To avoid dragging hoses you could install an irrigation system that operates with valves that are turned on and off manually. While this system is a giant step forward compared to using a water hose, it too has its drawbacks. First, someone has to remember to turn the water on, and second, someone has to remember to turn it off again. The main advantage over hose watering is that irrigation systems will allow you to water large blocks of plants in a relatively short period, provided you don't get sidetracked and forget the on-and-off routine.

Before you install any type of irrigation system yourself, it is essential that you take a class on irrigation systems as there are a tremendous number of costly errors to be made when installing your first irrigation system. Most irrigation suppliers hold irrigation installation classes on an annual basis. Even before you begin you will need to know the volume and pressure of the water at your source. If you have no pumping system, you can actually work backwards and plan your source accordingly. The pressure and volume of water at your source determines not only what size but also what types of irrigation emitters you can use. Every emitter is rated for both the amount of pressure and volume needed for it to operate correctly and for the distance the water will cover when operating under those constraints.

Let's assume you have a pump that will produce a flow of 30 gallons per minute (gpm) at 60 pounds of pressure per square inch (psi). You will next need to find sprinklers that will operate efficiently at 60 psi and whose total output per zone (the number of sprinkler heads running simultaneously) will equal the volume produced of 30 gpm. Let's assume that you are trying to run a production area that contains 30 sprinkler heads, each with an output of 3 gpm. This will require 90 gpm to operate, which is more water than your pump can provide. You have two options: purchase a larger pump or switch your sprinkler nozzles. In this example, you may be able to use the same 60-psi sprinkler provided there is a 1.0-gpm nozzle available. By simply switching nozzles, the gpm output is reduced to 30 gpm, the amount produced by your pump. What this will mean, however, is that you will have to operate your sprinklers for three times longer than is necessary with a 3.0-gpm nozzle distributing the same amount of water.

Another factor to consider when planning your irrigation system is something known as pressure loss due to friction. The more water that is forced through a smaller pipe, the greater the amount of friction. As friction is produced, pressure is lost, so the greater the friction the water encounters on its way to the sprinkler heads, the less pressure will actually be available when the water reaches the sprinkler heads. It is impossible to eliminate friction loss, although losses can be substantially minimized by adequately sizing the pipes.

Plumbing supply houses can furnish you with a pipe pressure loss chart. If you find that a 2-inch PVC feeder line loses 30 psi per 100 feet of length, try switching to a 3-inch feeder line to reduce the psi loss to a mere 1 psi per 100 feet. Remember that every time water goes through a pipe, valve, or fitting it suffers a loss of pressure. Pressure loss must be accounted for at the design phase or the system will never work as desired.

Once you have an irrigation system in place, what type of sprinklers are you going to use? The most common system in outdoor nurseries is overhead impact sprinkler. Impact sprinklers are usually mounted on top of tall risers that allow them to spray above taller plants. As water is forced through the end of the sprinkler nozzle, it impacts or hits a "spoon" that is mounted on a pivot. As the spoon is forced forward, it rebounds because of the spring's pressure and the sprinkler head is forced to rotate. Since impact sprinklers are based on springs, they can wear out. I recommend monitoring the reliability of sprinklers on a regular basis; depending on the original quality, replacement at regular intervals will be necessary.

Figure 6. Irrigation Friction Loss Characteristics

Friction Loss Characteristics

PVC SCHEDULE 40 IPS PLASTIC PIPE

(1120, 1220)   C = 150
PSI Loss Per 100 Feet of Pipe (PSI/100 ft)

PVC SCHEDULE 40 IPS PLASTIC PIPE
Sizes 1/2" thru 6"   Flow 1 through 600 GPM

SIZE	1/2"	3/4"	1"	1¼"	1½"	2"	2½"	3"	4"	6"
OD	0.840	1.050	1.315	1.660	1.900	2.375	2.875	3.500	4.500	6.625
ID	0.622	0.824	1.049	1.380	1.610	2.067	2.469	3.068	4.026	6.065
Wall Thk	0.109	0.113	0.133	0.140	0.145	0.154	0.203	0.216	0.237	0.280

Flow G.P.M.	1/2" Velocity F.P.S.	1/2" P.S.I. Loss	3/4" Velocity F.P.S.	3/4" P.S.I. Loss	1" Velocity F.P.S.	1" P.S.I. Loss	1¼" Velocity F.P.S.	1¼" P.S.I. Loss	1½" Velocity F.P.S.	1½" P.S.I. Loss	2" Velocity F.P.S.	2" P.S.I. Loss	2½" Velocity F.P.S.	2½" P.S.I. Loss	3" Velocity F.P.S.	3" P.S.I. Loss	4" Velocity F.P.S.	4" P.S.I. Loss	6" Velocity F.P.S.	6" P.S.I. Loss
1	1.05	0.43	0.60	0.11	0.37	0.03	0.21	0.01	0.15	0.00										
2	2.11	1.55	1.20	0.39	0.74	0.12	0.42	0.03	0.31	0.02	0.19	0.00								
3	3.16	3.28	1.80	0.84	1.11	0.26	0.64	0.07	0.47	0.03	0.28	0.01	0.20	0.00						
4	4.22	5.60	2.40	1.42	1.48	0.44	0.85	0.12	0.62	0.05	0.38	0.02	0.26	0.01						
5	5.27	8.46	3.00	2.15	1.85	0.66	1.07	0.18	0.78	0.08	0.47	0.02	0.33	0.01	0.21	0.00				
6	6.33	11.86	3.60	3.02	2.22	0.93	1.28	0.25	0.94	0.12	0.57	0.03	0.40	0.01	0.26	0.01				
7	7.38	15.77	4.20	4.01	2.59	1.24	1.49	0.33	1.10	0.15	0.66	0.05	0.46	0.02	0.30	0.01				
8	8.44	20.20	4.80	5.14	2.96	1.59	1.71	0.42	1.25	0.20	0.76	0.06	0.53	0.02	0.34	0.01				
9	9.49	25.12	5.40	6.39	3.33	1.97	1.92	0.52	1.41	0.25	0.85	0.07	0.60	0.03	0.39	0.01				
10	10.55	30.54	6.00	7.77	3.70	2.40	2.14	0.63	1.57	0.30	0.95	0.09	0.66	0.04	0.43	0.01				
11	11.60	36.43	6.60	9.27	4.07	2.86	2.35	0.75	1.73	0.36	1.05	0.11	0.73	0.04	0.47	0.02				
12	12.65	42.80	7.21	10.89	4.44	3.36	2.57	0.89	1.88	0.42	1.14	0.12	0.80	0.05	0.52	0.02	0.30	0.00		
14	14.76	56.94	8.41	14.48	5.19	4.47	2.99	1.18	2.20	0.56	1.33	0.17	0.93	0.07	0.60	0.02	0.35	0.01		
16	16.87	72.92	9.61	18.55	5.93	5.73	3.42	1.51	2.51	0.71	1.52	0.21	1.07	0.09	0.69	0.03	0.40	0.01		
18	18.98	90.69	10.81	23.07	6.67	7.13	3.85	1.88	2.83	0.89	1.71	0.26	1.20	0.11	0.78	0.04	0.45	0.01		
20	21.09	110.23	12.01	28.04	7.41	8.66	4.28	2.28	3.14	1.08	1.90	0.32	1.33	0.13	0.86	0.05	0.50	0.01		
22			13.21	33.45	8.15	10.33	4.71	2.72	3.46	1.29	2.10	0.38	1.47	0.16	0.95	0.06	0.55	0.01		
24			14.42	39.30	8.89	12.14	5.14	3.20	3.77	1.51	2.29	0.45	1.60	0.19	1.04	0.07	0.60	0.02		
26			15.62	45.58	9.64	14.08	5.57	3.73	4.09	1.75	2.48	0.52	1.74	0.22	1.12	0.08	0.65	0.02		
28			16.82	52.28	10.38	16.15	5.99	4.25	4.40	2.01	2.67	0.60	1.87	0.25	1.21	0.09	0.70	0.02		
30			18.02	59.41	11.12	18.35	6.42	4.83	4.72	2.28	2.86	0.68	2.00	0.29	1.30	0.10	0.75	0.03		
35					12.97	24.42	7.49	6.43	5.50	3.04	3.34	0.90	2.34	0.38	1.51	0.13	0.88	0.04	0.38	0.00
40					14.83	31.27	8.56	8.23	6.29	3.89	3.81	1.15	2.67	0.49	1.73	0.17	1.00	0.04	0.44	0.01
45					16.60	39.09	9.64	10.24	7.08	4.84	4.29	1.43	3.01	0.60	1.95	0.21	1.13	0.06	0.49	0.01
50					18.53	47.27	10.71	12.45	7.87	5.88	4.77	1.74	3.34	0.73	2.16	0.26	1.25	0.07	0.55	0.01
55							11.78	14.85	8.65	7.01	5.25	2.08	3.68	0.88	2.38	0.30	1.38	0.08	0.61	0.01
60							12.85	17.45	9.44	8.24	5.72	2.44	4.01	1.03	2.60	0.36	1.51	0.10	0.66	0.01
65							13.92	20.23	10.23	9.56	6.20	2.83	4.35	1.19	2.81	0.41	1.63	0.11	0.72	0.02
70							14.99	23.21	11.01	10.96	6.68	3.25	4.68	1.37	3.03	0.48	1.76	0.13	0.77	0.02
75							16.06	26.37	11.80	12.46	7.16	3.69	5.01	1.56	3.25	0.54	1.88	0.14	0.83	0.02
80							17.13	29.72	12.59	14.04	7.63	4.16	5.35	1.75	3.46	0.61	2.01	0.16	0.88	0.02
85							18.21	33.26	13.37	15.71	8.11	4.66	5.68	1.96	3.68	0.68	2.13	0.18	0.94	0.02
90							19.28	36.97	14.16	17.46	8.59	5.18	6.02	2.18	3.90	0.76	2.26	0.20	0.99	0.03
95									14.95	19.30	9.07	5.72	6.35	2.41	4.11	0.84	2.39	0.22	1.05	0.03
100									15.74	21.22	9.54	6.29	6.69	2.65	4.33	0.92	2.51	0.25	1.10	0.03
110									17.31	25.32	10.50	7.61	7.36	3.16	4.76	1.10	2.76	0.29	1.22	0.04
120									18.88	29.75	11.45	8.82	8.03	3.72	5.20	1.29	3.02	0.34	1.33	0.05
130											12.41	10.23	8.70	4.31	5.63	1.50	3.27	0.40	1.44	0.05
140											13.36	11.74	9.37	4.94	6.06	1.72	3.52	0.46	1.55	0.06
150											14.32	13.33	10.03	5.62	6.50	1.95	3.77	0.52	1.66	0.07
160											15.27	15.03	10.70	6.33	6.93	2.20	4.02	0.59	1.77	0.08
170											16.23	16.81	11.37	7.08	7.36	2.46	4.27	0.66	1.88	0.09
180											17.18	18.69	12.04	7.87	7.80	2.74	4.53	0.73	1.99	0.10
190											18.14	20.66	12.71	8.70	8.23	3.02	4.78	0.81	2.10	0.11
200											19.09	22.72	13.38	9.57	8.66	3.33	5.03	0.89	2.21	0.12
225													15.05	11.90	9.75	4.14	5.66	1.10	2.49	0.15
250													16.73	14.47	10.83	5.03	6.29	1.34	2.77	0.18
275													18.40	17.20	11.92	5.99	6.92	1.60	3.05	0.22
300															13.00	7.05	7.55	1.88	3.32	0.26
325															14.08	8.17	8.18	2.18	3.60	0.30
350															15.17	9.38	8.81	2.50	3.88	0.34
375															16.25	10.65	9.43	2.84	4.15	0.39
400															17.33	12.01	10.06	3.20	4.43	0.44
425															18.42	13.43	10.69	3.58	4.71	0.49
450															19.50	14.93	11.32	3.98	4.99	0.54
475																	11.95	4.40	5.26	0.60
500																	12.58	4.84	5.54	0.66
550																	13.84	5.77	6.10	0.79
600																	15.10	6.78	6.65	0.92

Note: Outlined area of chart indicate velocities over 5' per second. **Use with caution.**

Velocity of flow values are computed from the general equation $V = .408 \dfrac{q}{d^2}$

Friction pressure loss values are computed from the equation: $h_f = 0.2083 \left(\dfrac{100}{C}\right)^{1.852} \dfrac{q^{1.852}}{d^{4.866}} \times .433$ for psi loss per 100' of pipe

Impact rotors are similar to impact heads. They are usually enclosed in a plastic casing, and in my experience have been a bit more precise and durable than impact heads. Shrub heads or spray stakes can be used for smaller beds. These sprinklers are generally smaller (about droplet size), making them better in areas where controlling splash is more critical and where the amount of water has to be more exact.

It may be possible to hang a sprinkler system from the ceiling in greenhouse structures or other display-type houses. Because the piping can be run on top of the cross bows or hung from the greenhouse ceiling, no trenching is required once the waterline enters the greenhouse. Be sure to investigate which types of sprinklers will actually work when hanging upside down. I am a big fan of spinners for installations that are both right side up and upside down. Spinners are nozzles that work by shooting water from two holes located opposite each other, which results in a spinning action that gives a good water distribution. As with virtually all sprinklers, many nozzles of different sizes are interchangeable; it all depends on the water rate or gpm you wish to apply.

If water conservation is critical in your nursery, you may want to consider drip or micro-irrigation emitters. Drip emitters are small nozzles that are fed from a secondary irrigation line through a series of tubes with very small diameters. Instead of spraying a large area, drip emitters apply water directly onto the root system of the targeted plant rather than its foliage. The main advantage to

Sudden impact—sounds like a movie title. Impact-irrigation heads are the most common and versatile of nursery irrigation heads. Plant Delights Nursery.

Got a big head? In large production areas, a rotor such as this Rain Bird R-50 might work. Plant Delights Nursery.

a drip emitter is that it better targets the water with rates of 90 to 95 percent efficiency compared to 25 percent for overhead sprinklers (Haman 2000). Additionally, drip irrigation is less prone to evaporation. Since drip emitters use small amounts of water in a low-pressure system, it can be used where water pressure is quite low or not adequate for overhead sprinklers.

One disadvantage to drip irrigation is the small size of the secondary feeder lines, which makes them much more susceptible to getting clogged with contaminants. If you choose a drip system, you will need to invest in several thousand dollars worth of filtering equipment, particularly if you use surface water. Additionally, the expense of purchasing a large number of emitters, coupled with the high labor cost of installation, makes drip system less economical for plants that will be sold when they are still small. For nurseries such as a pot-in-pot operation (meaning that pots are buried in the ground where they serve as holders for large container plants), drip systems are the only viable irrigation choice. Drip irrigation systems are usually economical for plants grown in sizes larger than one gallon (Childs et al. 2000).

Once the sprinklers or emitters are in place, the next step is to automate their operation. This is accomplished by replacing the manual on-off valves with automatic valves called solenoids. Solenoid-operated valves are controlled via electrical impulses (usually low voltage) that are sent by a wire that runs from the solenoid valve to a time clock. Next, determine an irrigation schedule for

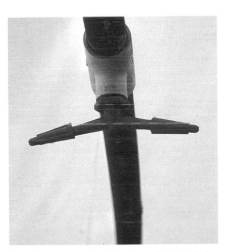

Upside down and rightly dizzy. Spinner irrigation heads, such as this Roberts spinner head, deliver a good spray whether they are right side up or upside down. Plant Delights Nursery.

Who says no one wants a drip? These drip stakes are perfect for pot-in-pot operations where overhead irrigation is impractical.

each solenoid valve, which is known as a watering zone. Even with an automated irrigation system, you must carefully and regularly monitor your crops so that they do not become too wet or too dry. Even the most reliable of watering systems will not end your potential irrigation problems.

Automatic irrigation systems are usually associated with underground piping, although some nurseries in warmer regions simply lay the piping above ground. All in all, an automatic irrigation system has a far greater up-front cost in terms of installation but the long-term savings over hand watering will be tremendous.

There is a wide selection of inexpensive timers that are especially good for small operations just getting started. Once a nursery needs more than one or two timers, however, it is probably best to centralize your irrigation control, especially if you are irrigating from one central source. Coordination of your irrigation zones is essential since your pump will only be able to handle a certain number of beds or greenhouses at one time.

An increasing number of centralized computer-based controllers allow all irrigation to be controlled from a centralized point. At Plant Delights, we located our central irrigation computer in our shipping building, where it will be secure but easy to monitor. Unlike other nursery computers that are networked, this unit stands alone. The irrigation computer is connected to satellite control

When you don't want time to stand still. Inexpensive controllers are fine for small nurseries until there are too many conflicting needs for water. Plant Delights Nursery.

Irrigation Brain Central. A centralized, computer-controlled irrigation system called Wilbur. Plant Delights Nursery.

boxes that are stationed throughout the nursery by communication wires. The satellite boxes are in turn connected with low voltage wires to each solenoid valve. The irrigation computer runs a special program for controlling irrigation functions throughout the nursery. We are then able to enter our irrigation parameters into the data fields of the program detailing our irrigation preferences. The better systems allow for programming into the future (up to a year in advance with some systems), have weather overrides based on outdoor sensing equipment, and incorporate alarms or other notification methods in case problems arise.

The latest trend in irrigation, particularly in larger greenhouse operations, is called subsurface or flood irrigation. In these systems, a giant holding pit is constructed under the greenhouse. Water is moved via huge pumps onto a greenhouse's impermeable floor. The crop actually sits in the water for a few minutes, and then the water is drained back into the pits below via holes that open up in the floor. The advantages of this system include better crop uniformity as a result of even water distribution and a reduction in foliar diseases and insect problems. This is certainly the most expensive type of irrigation system to install but it is the one that uses the least labor, if you don't consider the amount of time spent on maintenance and repair. While flood irrigation can be a wonderful system, numerous potential disasters also await, such as fertilizer salt buildup in

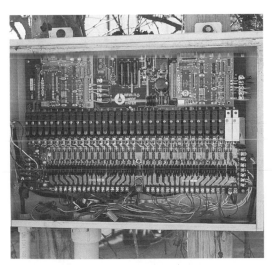

The right brain is connected to the main brain—the Wilbur system control box. An automated, satellite irrigation control box with manual override that is connected by wires to the central controller. Plant Delights Nursery.

Serious pumps! A flood floor irrigation system pumps, piping, and underground water storage. Blooming Nursery, Oregon.

containers, a disease-contaminated water supply, and pump failures. This type of system should only be installed with the help of an expert in flood irrigation.

Subsurface irrigation is a modification of the old practice of surface irrigation in field nurseries. Although it is rarely used in the United States compared to other countries, surface irrigation moves water through a series of channels through the growing fields on an as-needed schedule to soak the soil where the plants are growing. These types of systems work best in clay-based soils and in fields where the land is relatively flat. The complexities of surface irrigation systems are beyond the scope of this book.

Up it comes and down it goes. A flood irrigation floor with holes for water flow. Blooming Nursery, Oregon.

A plant wading pool. Here comes the water as the flood irrigation system begins to operate. Blooming Nursery, Oregon.

Irrigation needs

We have discussed irrigation systems, so let's now look at how to irrigate, both in terms of frequency and amount. If you have an automatic irrigation system, you should make sure that all the plants in a particular watering zone require and use the same amount of water. Ideally, they would be similar plants of similar size. Plants that are root-bound and dry out quickly should not be grown in the same house as young plants with a limited root system as one or the other will be unhappy.

You will obviously have to learn the water requirements of each of your crops. Some plants may have extensive root systems that use water at a high rate and require irrigation two to three times each day. Don't be fooled into thinking that one watering per day will keep all plants alive. The amount of water that a plant needs will be influenced by a number of factors: the amount of sun, the amount of wind, the stage of growth, the season, the size of the container, and the type of soil mix. Dormant plants, as well as those potted from bare-root stock, for example, will need to be kept on the dry side until they begin to grow, at which time watering can be increased. Overgrown plants may require three waterings per day unless they are cut back, which reduces the water requirement until they regrow. Trying to use a "one watering schedule fits all" approach in a nursery is a recipe for disaster.

Determining how much water to apply each time is also quite complex. The general thought has been to apply water until it begins to run out of the plant's container. This method helps to get all the roots moist and it leaches excess fertilizers from the containers. Using the perfect amount of water takes great skill, however, as too much leaches fertilizers from the soil mix. Excess irrigation not only deprives the plants of needed nutrients but it also moves these nutrients into nearby rivers and streams where the nutrients are actually harmful to the environment.

Bush (2001) has shown that it is possible to achieve less runoff in all cases and better growth on many species by splitting the normal watering time into two or more separate applications, each application taking a corresponding fraction of the normal daily amount of water. The obvious drawback is that plant blocks that are being watered are not accessible to workers during the irrigation cycle. Cyclic irrigation is much more difficult to accomplish in large nurseries because of how complicated the required scheduling can get.

Fertilizer needs

There seem to be as many different ways to fertilize crops as there are nurseries and it is rare to find any two growers who fertilize in the same manner. In setting up your fertilizer program, you will have to choose a fertilizer formulation, the type of nutritional release pattern, and an application method that fits your growing regimen. You will also have to know the requirements of your crops and then set up a monitoring program. Just as with irrigation, you will need to find a fertilizer that fits your growing regimen.

In selecting a fertilizer, you will first have to have a basic understanding of soil and plant nutrition. Thirteen essential elements are required for plant growth, although that number is sometimes debated. The elements that are needed in the largest quantities are called macronutrients (macro means large) and are Nitrogen (N), Phosphorus (P), Potassium (K), Calcium (Ca), and Magnesium (Mg). Eight other elements that are equally as essential but in smaller quantities are called micronutrients (micro means small). They are Iron (Fe), Manganese (Mn), Zinc (Zn), Copper (Cu), Sulfur (S), Boron (B), Sodium (Na), and Molybdenum (Mo). Since these elements are essential for plant growth, they must be included in your soil mix or fertilizer. Taking a test of your potting mix is consequently a good place to begin in selecting a fertilizer.

Your next step is determining how long the plant will remain in the container. The longer the crop stays in the pot, the more economical a long release fertilizer will become. I always like to choose a slow-release fertilizer that will release slowly enough not to burn the plants. As a general rule, the faster the nutrients in a fertilizer become available, the more potential they have to burn the plants. Additionally, the more people you have applying fertilizer, the greater the need for a consistent standard to prevent an over-fertilizing accident.

Crops with a fast turnaround such as bedding plants and other floriculture crops are usually fertilized with a water-soluble liquid fertilizer. While this type of fertilizer may work for certain crops, it is usually not the best solution for crops with a longer production time. Granular, fast-release fertilizers such as 10–10–10 are rarely used in the nursery business as they release all their nutrients over a very short time and leach quickly from the containers. Growers prefer some type of a slow-release fertilizer for most nursery crops. Slow-release fertilizers are, as the name suggests, those that are formulated to release nutrients over a longer period instead of all at once. Slow-release fertilizers may release in as little as two months or as much as twelve.

Slow-release fertilizer formulations operate by a number of different nutrient release mechanisms. Some release their nutrients according to temperature, some according to moisture, and others more according to time. The key is to match the fertilizer to your crop. If you are growing a crop that requires a full year to produce, you would probably opt for a 9- to 12-month fertilizer. If the crop goes dormant regardless of the fertility level, then it would be all right to have fertilizer remaining at the end of the season as it would provide an early season boost. If you are growing a crop that is sensitive to high levels of fertilizer salts, high fall fertility levels would pose a problem since reduced irrigation would not flush out the excess salts; be sure, therefore, to use a formulation that would be completely exhausted by fall.

Equally as critical to the growth of your crop is that the slow-release fertilizer does not "dump." Dumping is a common problem in many of the less expensive slow-release fertilizers, where the coating is not as stable and the fertilizer is subject to a number of factors that cause premature release of excessive nutrients. The result is that roots are burned; often the plant foliage does too, and occasionally the plant dies. As often happens in over-fertilization situations where foliar burning may not be evident, there is underground root damage that can cause a substantial loss of growth. Conversely, if a fertilizer that is supposed to last all season runs out of nutrition in midsummer, a tremendous amount of potential growth will be lost during the remainder of the year. Growers always try to get the maximum amount of growth on their plants each year, so insufficient fertilizer is also a major problem.

In determining the amount of fertilizer to use, you should work closely with your fertilizer representative. Virtually all major fertilizer manufacturers will have a representative in your area or available to you via phone. They will be of great help in setting up a fertilizer program, ensuring that you apply the correct amount at the correct time. Part of getting the proper amount of fertilizer to your crop is knowing its fertility requirements. While most crops have been well documented with data that are available from your state's department of agriculture, it is the little-known specialty crops that will require some experimentation. I don't know any specialty nursery that has not killed its share of crops while experimenting with fertilizers. If you are not sure, always err on the side of caution, meaning you should use less and in smaller amounts. I also recommend that you not hesitate in asking your fertilizer manufacturer or distributor to provide you with independent tests comparing their fertilizer with that of other brands under rainfall conditions that simulate those in your area.

Slow-release fertilizers are applied in one of two ways, by surface application or incorporation. If all your crops require the same amount of fertilizer and all your potting is done in a short window of time, it is far better to have the slow-release fertilizer incorporated into your soil mix when it is being blended. Virtually all manufacturers of potting soil are glad to do this. There are three benefits to this strategy: the mix is more uniform, the fertilizer is not spilled when the containers tip over, and the fertilizer is less exposed to the elements and consequently less prone to rapid breakdown. The drawback is that nutrients leach out of the container faster than surface-applied fertilizer. Incorporating fertilizers into your potting soil will not work, however, when crops requiring different amounts of fertilizer are potted from the same load or when crops are kept

longer than one season. Also, if a pile of potting soil is used for potting over a period of six months or more, there would not be the same duration of fertilizer
release in a plant potted in March as one potted in September.

We grow many different crops at Plant Delights and we are therefore locked
into using surface applications. We have developed a chart that shows which fertilizer formulation to use based on potting dates. For example, from January
through April, we use a 180-day formulation; from April to July we use a 120-
day formulation; from July through August we use a 100-day formulation; and
from September until November we use a 70-day formulation. We also use various container sizes, which again requires a chart detailing how much fertilizer
to use for each pot or flat of pots. A one-quart pot requires far less fertilizer than
a 1-gallon pot, and so forth.

Plants that were surface fertilized when potted are always fertilized again to
start the new season. A small amount of leftover nutrition is usually not a bad
thing and actually helps give the plants a little early spring boost, particularly
since many slow release fertilizers will not release until the weather warms (unless they have some quick release nitrogen added). The important thing is to get
the fertilizer to the plants before they begin growing, especially those that have
only one flush of growth per season.

Surface fertilizers can be applied to containers in a number of ways. These
methods range from guessing to using measuring scoops or spoons to using a calibrated fertilizer applicator. While the less accurate methods seem to be the most
prevalent, you will create less waste and more even growth when the fertilizer is
applied accurately. If you choose high-quality, more expensive fertilizers, it will
more than pay for the cost of calibrated fertilizer applicators in the first season.

These applicators, complete with hoppers that hold the fertilizer, are actually
fairly simple devices. A valve is set for the desired amount of fertilizer that is
then dispensed each time the trigger mechanism is depressed. While the temptation may be to use the old rotary grass seed dispensers, it is usually cost pro-
hibitive when using more expensive, quality fertilizers. The excess fertilizer that
is left on the ground to wash away and contaminate nearby streams and rivers
also makes the rotary dispenser a poor option.

Once you apply fertilizer, your work is not finished. Soil nutrition is a constantly changing process that must be monitored. You are not interested only in
the amount of nitrogen, phosphorus, and potassium (known as N-P-K) in your
fertilizer since other nutrients are not only essential for the plants but are also
essential for the plant's use of N-P-K. The uptake of N-P-K into the tissue of the
plants is greatly affected by the balance of many of these micronutrients and the
soil pH, so despite an essential element being plentiful in your soil mix, it may
still be unavailable to the plant.

So what is this pH thing that everyone keeps talking about? It is a measure of the acidity or alkalinity of the soil expressed as a measure of the percentage of hydrogen ions in the soil. In layman's terms, pH tells you how your soil ranks in terms of acidity. Using a scale of 1.0 to 14.0 with 7.0 being neutral, a pH of 6.0 is ten times as acidic as a pH of 7.0, and a pH of 5.0 is 100 times as acid as a pH of 7.0. The pH of the soil has a dramatic effect on the solubility and, consequently, on the availability of soil nutrients. If the pH is not in the proper range, the plant fertilizer in the soil may not be available to the plant. The problem with pH is that we can't see it and so many nursery owners adopt the "out of sight, out of mind" thinking.

The more water that goes through the mix, the more the pH will drop because the liming materials, such as calcium, potassium, and magnesium, are being leached from the media. You will need to know the pH of your irrigation water (is it acidic or alkaline?) to be able to predict if your soil acidity will rise or fall. I have seen the soil pH in a nursery container drop from 6.0 to 3.2 in less than

Feeding time. Fertilizer needs of smaller plants can be calculated and then applied with a cup. Plant Delights Nursery.

For larger plants that would require more bending, a fertilizer applicator is recommended. Plant Delights Nursery.

one year, a thousand-fold increase in soil acidity. As you can imagine, the plants had a less than ideal appearance as growth came to a screeching halt.

Soil mixes also change based on the formulations of particular elements that were used in the mix. Some mixes that contain slowly soluble forms of particular elements may release more of certain nutrients as time passes. Other mixes may become deficient in some elements because they may have been used in a more soluble formulation. Even the fertilizer you choose may impact the chemical properties of your soil mix, as some fertilizers cause the mix to become more acidic, while others have the opposite effect.

It is critical that you monitor soil nutrition levels in plants that have been potted longer than one season. Several fairly inexpensive monitoring meters can be used in the nursery, but they are not, however, the dime-store pH testers, which are essentially worthless. The most common procedure is to perform what is called a pour-through test. The container in which the plant is growing is watered and allowed to sit for one hour. More water is then poured through the soil (substrate) and is collected in a clean cup or tray. This water (known as leachate) is then tested with your meter for both the soluble salts level and for soil pH. Your state's department of agriculture should have charts detailing desired pH target levels for most crops that you can compare your reading against. Most state departments of agriculture will also perform this service for a small fee.

A plant "psa" test. By catching and testing leached irrigation water, you will know if your plant has adequate pH and fertilizer levels. Plant Delights Nursery.

If you encounter a nutritional problem with your crop, take a test not only of the soil in the container but also of the plant tissue (called a plant tissue analysis). This way you can compare what is available in the soil with what is actually in the plant. Problems are often caused by a lack of or imbalance in micronutrients. North Carolina State University researchers Ted Bilderback and Dick Bir have developed a chart detailing optimum nutrient levels for your irrigation water, soil (substrate), and the actual tissue of the plant (Bilderback and Bir 2001). Your fertilizer company representative can help you find the right package of micronutrients to correct deficiencies.

Figure 7. Nutrient and Chemical Capacity Factors for Water, Mid-Season Substrates, and Plant Tissue for Woody Ornamental Nursery Container Crops: Suggested Ranges and Limits.

CAPACITY FACTOR	IRRIGATION WATER	SUBSTRATE LEACHATE	PLANT TISSUE
pH	5.4–7.0	5.2–6.3	
Conductivity	.2–2.0 mmhos/cm	.5–2.0 mmhos/cm	
Dissolved Salts	<1000 ppm	<1400 ppm	
Nitrogen (N)		100–150 ppm	2.0–3.5%
Phosphorus (P)	<1–10 ppm	3–15 ppm	.2–.5%
Potassium (K)	<10 ppm	<100 ppm	1.1–2.0%
Calcium (Ca)	<60 ppm	40–200 ppm	1.0–2.0%
Magnesium (Mg)	<6 24 ppm	10–50 ppm	.3–.8%
Sulfur (S)	<24 ppm	75–125 ppm	
Iron (Fe)	.2–4 ppm	.3–3 ppm	35–250 ppm
Manganese (Mn)	<.5–2 ppm	.02–3 ppm	50–200 ppm
Zinc (Zn)	< 3 ppm	.3–3 ppm	20–200 ppm
Copper (Cu)	<.2 ppm	.01–.5 ppm	6–25 ppm
Boron (B)	<.5 ppm	.5–3 ppm	6–75 ppm
Molybdenum (Mo)	<.1 ppm	0–1 ppm	.1–2 ppm
Aluminum (Al)	<300 ppm	0–3 ppm	
Fluorine (Fl)	<1 ppm		
Sodium (Na)	<50 ppm	<50 ppm	.01–.1 ppm

(Reprinted with permission. Bilderback and Bir 2001)

Nutrition is as critical in field growing as it is in containers but field nutrition is much easier to manage. While slow-release fertilizers can also be used in field growing, you would achieve better long-term success by working to improve the soil through the use of composts and organic fertilizers. By feeding the soil instead of the plants themselves, the plants become more self-sufficient and the soil microbes much healthier. The overall result is that the plants are better able to prevent and fight off pathogens. Few people realize that every ounce of field soil contains nearly 500 billion—yes, billion—microorganisms, including bacteria, actinomycetes, fungi, protozoa, nematodes, and others. Microbes keep nature in balance and make the soil livable for plants. As a steward of the land, you should nurture these microbes as they will assist your efforts in improving your crop's growing process. Yearly soil tests are essential in the monitoring and soil improvement process.

Field-growing operations

Many nurseries, especially those with smaller labor forces, have field-growing operations. Growing plants in the field reduces the immediacy of plant mainte- nance, at least as far as watering, picking up windblown plants, and other simi- lar types of labor is concerned. Also, as a general rule, plants grow much faster in the ground because the ground allows for an unrestricted and much cooler root system compared to a container.

Figure 8. Determining Number of Plants Required Per Acre

DISTANCE BETWEEN ROWS IN FEET	DISTANCE BETWEEN PLANTS IN INCHES				
	12"	24"	36"	48"	60"
1	43,560	21,780	14,520	10,890	8,712
2	21,780	10,890	7,260	5,445	4,356
3	14,520	7.260	4,840	3,630	2,904
4	10,890	5,445	3,630	2,722	2,178
5	8,712	4,356	2,904	2,178	1,742
6	7,260	3,630	2,420	1,815	1,452
7	6,223	3,111	2,074	1,556	1,245
8	5,445	2,722	1,815	1,361	1,089
9	4,840	2,420	1,613	1,210	968
10	4,356	2,178	1,452	1,089	871

(Reprinted with permission. Bilderback 2001)

Good field production starts with the proper spacing of plants, extends through the process of maintaining plants, and ends with the digging of the plants from the field. Woody plant spacing in the field is a difficult part of the business to manage; most growers try to fit more plants on a plot of land than should be grown. The plant must have enough room to develop a good shape by harvest time without being crowded. You also have to take into account that all plants will probably not be harvested on a prearranged, carefully planned schedule. If you are unable to complete your digging because of weather or eco- nomic constraints, will your spacing allow the plants to have an extra year in the field without sacrificing their quality?

Spacing in field nurseries is important not only for the growth of your plants but also for the maneuverability of the harvesting crews and their equipment. Field-grown woody plants are incredibly heavy—larger plants can weigh a ton or more. Balled and burlapped woody plants are very difficult to move long dis- tances without some type of equipment.

There is a wide array of primarily tractor-mounted or motorized digging equipment designed to handle digging and root-pruning chores. Different equipment will produce many different sizes of balled and burlapped plants. In terms of maneuverability, the most popular types of diggers are mounted on skid-steer loaders. The ability of these machines to twist and turn in tight places means plants can be more tightly spaced than would be possible if a tractor or truck-mounted digger were used. The manufacturers of these machines can provide the turning radius that will be required to dig the desired size of root

Field of dreams. Most production of woody trees and large shrubs still takes place in the field, where costs are less. Harvesting is more time sensitive, however. McLamb Nursery, North Carolina.

balls with a particular machine. In laying out your rows, allow enough room for hauling vehicles and digging equipment to maneuver without damaging the other plants.

The key to producing a good field-grown plant and to good survivability rates after harvest directly depends on the amount of root pruning that is done during the production period. Tractor-mounted equipment should regularly cut the roots before they become large. If roots are not cut, you will not be able to harvest the entire root system when you dig a field-grown plant. This will cause the plant to suffer since the plant top is expecting a certain number of roots to help support its growth. By pruning the roots during production, you gain two advantages. First, you are better able to keep the root system from getting too large, and second, you force larger roots to branch into smaller feeder roots. It is much easier to capture all the small feeder roots that have been formed by the pruning process as unpruned roots may extend 20 feet or more from the plant's trunk, making them a lot harder to capture.

Size counts! A tree spade can be easily mounted on a skid-steer loader for smaller digging jobs but it must be sized to dig a large enough root ball if the tree is to survive. McLamb Nursery, North Carolina.

Herbaceous perennials and bulbous crops are also often field grown, especially those that do not grow and multiply rapidly in containers. Generally, these are harvested bare root in the fall and winter and are consequently quite lightweight. Herbaceous perennials and bulbous crops are usually harvested with a tractor and a modified harvesting implement.

Field-grown woody plants are usually sold using different terminology from container plants. Container sizes are not applicable for woody plants grown in the field so they are usually sold by height, by the size of the root-ball, or caliper (the width of the trunk). Shrubs are typically sold by height, such as 3–4 feet, 6–8 feet, and so on. Field-grown woody liners are usually sold by the number of times that they

Necessity is the mother of invention. A potato harvester has been converted to a canna lily harvester. Quality Gladiolus, Arkansas.

My, that's an attractive field! Field-grown daylilies. Klehm's Song Sparrow Nursery, Wisconsin.

have been transplanted. For example, "2T" would mean that the plant had been transplanted twice. This terminology is most commonly used for woodies that are sold bare root.

Trees are typically sold by caliper, which is equivalent to the diameter in inches of the trunk, measured at a designated height that is usually 6 inches to 1 foot from the ground. It is tricky to measure trees that are pruned to a multistem form

All wrapped up, but what's inside? A balled and burlapped pine. Plant Delights Nursery.

Where are the roots? A balled and burlapped pine with the burlap removed. Plant Delights Nursery.

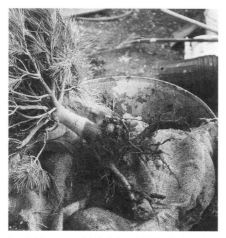

Look Mom, my birthday suit! A balled and burlapped pine with both the burlap and soil removed. Plant Delights Nursery.

Putting on too much bark? Pinch an inch and check. A caliper is used to measure the diameter of trees.

instead of a single trunked form. Some nurseries still sell all their field-grown trees by the size of the root ball, that is a 20-inch ball, 30-inch ball, 40-inch ball, and so on. Unless you know the nursery with which you are dealing or that the American Standard for Nursery Stock (ANLA 1996) standards (which give the proper ball size for each plant size) have been complied with, these terms are often meaningless. Obviously, the larger the plant, the larger the ball should be. Some nurseries unfortunately like to skimp on ball sizes, as that allows them to reduce the weight of the ball as well as the amount of soil leaving their fields. These smaller balls often translate into lower success rates for transplanted plants.

The primary downside to field growing a crop is harvesting it. The window of time for field digging is quite narrow, particularly for woody plants, compared to container-grown plants that are ready year-round. Although there is equipment from tree spades to modified tractor harrows for removing field-grown nursery stock from the ground, lots of hard manual labor is still required for the balling and burlapping process.

Most perennials are field planted in spring or early summer and are harvested in the fall. In the case of long-maturing crops, they are sometimes harvested after more than one growing season. Dormant perennials are usually stored in a cooler facility or, when possible, are shipped immediately to the customer. Considerable variability exists in the cold storage requirements of different plants, so if you are going to produce crops that will require winter storage in coolers, be sure to investigate in advance how to satisfy their storage requirements.

The harvesting and storage of woody plants is similar to perennials in that most digging is done in the fall. In some regions of the country, however, only a limited period of spring digging is possible. This lack of late spring and summer availability has led to the innovation known as pot-in-pot culture, which combines the advantages of pot culture with those of field growing.

A pot-in-pot operation consists of field rows of large containers that are sunk into the ground up to their lips. Large container-grown trees are slipped down inside these slightly larger containers. Gone are the problems with tipping, so often experienced with containerized trees, the problems of soil loss when trees are dug from the ground, and the problems of heat when the root systems of containerized plants are cooked as the sun hits the black plastic pots. Studies have indicated that soil and root-zone temperatures over 100°F, which is common in containerized plants, is very detrimental to root systems (Bilderback 2001). Ted Bilderback found that summer temperatures in above-ground containers that can reach 130°F may be reduced by as much as 25°F in a pot-in-pot container system (Bilderback 2001). Growers who operate pot-in-pot operations find that plants grow between two and three times as fast as they do in above-ground containers.

The downside to a pot-in-pot operation is the high cost of its initial setup, which includes purchasing these very expensive, large pots, burying the pots, and installing drip irrigation. Many growers also install drain lines below the buried pots to ensure that the long-term drainage remains intact. Growers I talked with cite an initial per pot cost of between $5 and $10.

As it is with all container plants, irrigation is critical in a pot-in-pot operation since the roots cannot pull moisture from the surrounding soil. The large outer pots are coated inside with chemicals, one of which is usually a copper-based product that burns off the root tips that try to reach for the soil. If the roots from the inner pot were to spread into the soil, extracting the tree would be most difficult, and the benefit of extended seasonality that pot-in-pot harvesting offers would be lost.

Beneath every good plant there's a . . . spacer? Spacers are often used in the bottom of pot-in-pot operations to ensure that roots don't clog the only drainage hole.

Pot-in-pot—the legal kind. Some nurseries have switched to a pot-in-pot operation to save growing time and permit year-round harvesting.

Pruning schedules

Once your plants are growing, you will need to keep them presentable, which means maintaining them at the proper size and in a shippable and sellable condition. A good pruning schedule is vital. While some crops that grow from a crown require little or no pruning, many spreaders, climbers, shrubs, trees, and perennials do require a considerable amount of maintenance to keep them looking good in the nursery. Proper pruning can work wonders for reinvigorating tired plants as well as keeping plants at a sellable size until they are sold.

I visited a perennial nursery several years ago in August and listened to the owner complain about how bad everything looked and then also proclaim that this was the way perennials were supposed to look during the summer. This was not at all the case but was instead the nursery owner rationalizing his lack of proper pruning practices. No wonder the nursery's sales were nonexistent for summer perennials.

Two types of pruning techniques are used in nursery production, shearing and structural pruning. Most pruning of trees and of some shrubs is for structural purposes. Structural pruning is more permanent than shearing. Shearing is performed more for temporary appearance purposes and its results are rarely permanent. Structural pruning of trees and some specialty formed shrubs is used to make the plant either a single trunked or multitrunked specimen. A simple topping of the main trunk when it is young will make a single trunked tree into a multitrunked tree. Conversely, removing all the basal shoots and low branches of the tree will result in a single trunked specimen. Another very important purpose of structural pruning is that it forms good crotch angles in young trees. Some trees naturally form weak branch angles that will split apart later in life so a good pruning as the scaffold branches are forming will create a permanent structure that the tree will maintain. Most of the better landscapers prefer to tag their own plants in the field so they can look carefully at various factors such as form and good branch structure.

Pruning of perennials and most shrubs is in the form of shearing. Shearing is used either to make the plants more dense and well branched or simply to promote new growth. In some cases, the constraints on nursery shipping sizes limit the size of plants that can fit into shipping racks or shelving, and so pruning is done. In most cases, however, pruning is performed to create an artificially dense or compact plant that will be more attractive to the consumer, as many plants simply don't show off their natural beauty in a container.

Any time you can mechanize the pruning process you will improve your bottom line. Nursery owners are a creative bunch who have manufactured all kinds of pruning apparatus, from gas hedge shears on conveyors to a dozen lawnmowers welded together atop a moving steel frame. Obviously, these contraptions only work well when large numbers of a single type of plant need to be pruned. Regardless of the pruning technique that you choose, keep in mind that the more time you spend pruning your plants the higher the cost of production. Developing a pruning plan will evolve as you learn about your crops. While many shrubs will require only one pruning each season, faster-growing perennials may need three to five prunings per season to achieve or maintain the desired appearance. When choosing the crops you grow, keep in mind that faster growing plants will usually require more pruning than slower growing plants.

Pruning also poses challenges with the scheduling and sales of crops. Because of the "morning after" pruning appearance, the plants that have just been sheared will not be sellable for a while. This is where preparing a working schedule for each crop becomes critical. While crop schedules are published for an array of commonly grown crops, be aware that most studies were performed in ideal controlled greenhouse conditions and will vary dramatically in different climates. I recommend spending the first few years experimenting with each crop you produce so that you can develop your own pruning schedules.

Winterizing plans

Among the most important nursery tips that newcomers to the nursery business learn too late is that plants are far less hardy in their containers than they are in the ground. In fact, many plants are 20 to 30 degrees less hardy in containers than in the ground. Most container plants grown in temperate climates will therefore require some type of winter protection. If you don't feel it is necessary to build a greenhouse or overwintering structure, consider using a crop protection blanket.

For years growers had to rely on burlap and plastic sheeting but beginning in the mid-1970s, new, spun polyester fabrics began to enter the market. These crop protection covers or blankets were an improvement over older materials, particularly plastic, which provided similar winter protection but magnified daylight so that the plants underneath were scorched.

New plant protection blankets are made from an assortment of materials, which provide anything from a few to several degrees of protection from cold weather. In a 1990 report from NCSU, researchers found that overwintering plastic and row covers increased temperatures ten to thirty degrees as measured by soil temperature (Warren et al. 1990). While the soil temperatures of the plants protected by overwintering plastic remained high, foliage that actually touched the protective plastic cover was damaged whereas the foliage of plants under row covers showed no damage at similar temperatures. Even consolidating containers tightly together provides a soil temperature increase of ten degrees along the outside edge of the containers.

Crop blankets are woven in a way that creates an air buffer that reduces heat loss while also allowing the crop to breathe. Many of these products on the market vary in thickness, amount of light transmission, and insulating value. Keep in mind that while the protection from cold is important, it is the heat that accumulates during the day that may cause the most problems. Plants can be flushed into early growth, which results in more damage when the night temperatures drop. The more light that passes through the cover, the warmer the air becomes underneath, so the more opaque the cover, the less heat will be generated during sunny days.

Just as timing is important with overwintering greenhouse plastics, so it is with crop protection covers. These blankets should not be installed until the plants have gone dormant after several fall frosts. They should be secured not only on top of the pots but also down the sides; they should then be secured to the ground by large, metal, ground staples or heavy objects that will not be disturbed during the first wind storm of the winter. You will need to add further protection (such as bales of straw) along the sides of the rows for further root protection in colder regions. Growers who do not do this often discover in spring that the outer two to four rows of plants are completely dead, while those on the inner rows are still fine.

Crop blankets can also delay the emergence of plants in the spring, so keep this in mind when trying to schedule your spring crops. This delay can be advantageous in spring when there is still the danger of late spring frosts damag-

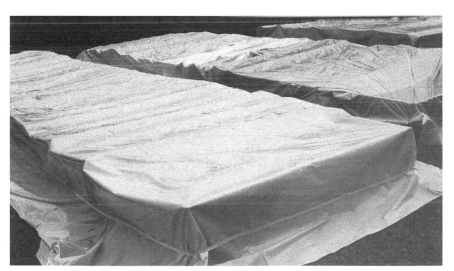

Plants nestling snugly in their beds. Crop protection blankets add several degrees of protection for roots in container grown plants, J. C. Raulston Arboretum, North Carolina.

ing or killing your early emerging plants. Even after you remove the covers, I advise you keep them where they can be quickly replaced. While some growers ice down plants with water to protect tender growth from late spring frosts, this most often results in more damage than if they had taken no action. The protection provided by water is only effective in a narrow range of temperatures in the mid- to upper 20s, and is only provided as long as water is actually being applied at a specific rate. As the water freezes, heat is produced, keeping the encased leaf tissue from freezing. Once the water application ceases or falls below the necessary application rate, plant tissues encased in ice actually super cool and drop below the outside temperature. An effective but slightly different method involves covering the plants with tightly woven shade cloth and then icing it down when dangerously cold weather approaches. The result is an insulation effect, much like an igloo, that seals off the escape of ground heat, which in turn protects the plants.

Propagating versus purchasing plants

Where will your nursery get its plants from? There are essentially three options: produce your own plants, buy liners, or buy finished stock. Of course, you can always use a combination of these options. Some nursery owners believe it is cheaper to produce their own plants, while others prefer to purchase plants for growing-on or resale. Both these methods work depending on the individual situation; the key is to determine if your nursery setup makes it economical for you to produce your own plants. Factors to consider include your mission (is it one that focuses on retail or production?), your propagation or production capacity, your labor availability during the propagation season, your familiarity with the crop, and your access to adequate numbers of stock plants from which to propagate.

If you are a producer of large field-grown plants and are not set up for propagation, it will certainly be cheaper for you to buy liners instead of doing your own propagation. If you are set up to propagate trees and shrubs but decide to add a few perennials, it will probably be easier to purchase those since the production techniques are quite different. Nurseries that produce plants primarily from cuttings may find it cheaper to buy plants that are grown from divisions. If the plants you grow are highly commercial and readily propagated from tissue culture, it is highly likely that they are already being produced in a commercial lab. In this case, it will probably not be economical for you to start your own tissue culture lab. One reason that many growers produce their own liners is because of the matter of availability. Liner growers walk a thin line between having just enough plants and too many at any one time. Unlike larger plants, liners don't remain sellable for very long, so it is virtually impossible to always find the liners you need. This uncertainty is among the most compelling reasons for producing your own stock and buying plants only when you run short. A second reason is that finding a consistent high-quality liner producer is often a problem, and you will quickly notice that the quality of the plant material you purchase varies widely.

Garden centers and landscapers, especially those located in an area where it is difficult to find a continuous supply of quality plants, often think they will produce their own plants. Most soon realize, however, that this may not be the best option since their focus should remain on their primary income-producing business, which is not growing but selling and maintaining the crop. Even when plants are produced, they are often not of the quality that could have been purchased.

Many larger garden centers and landscapers have plants contract-grown to fit their variety, size, and quality specifications. Some growers are glad to do this if the quantities ordered warrant it. As you can imagine, it is very difficult to grow small numbers of plants in a specific manner when that manner differs from the normal production scheme. The cost of having a plant contract-grown will therefore often be higher if your numbers are small and require that the grower establish new growing protocols that differ from the norm.

Agricultural inspections

Most states require some type of license for agricultural business such as nurseries. The SBA's Web site has a link to most states' business license requirements that you can follow by going to their "hotlist" and then "license" links. In most areas, nurseries are certified by the state's department of agriculture. The certification process usually consists of a cursory walk-through by an inspector followed by the nursery's payment of a license fee. Once your nursery is licensed, an inspector will usually follow up with an annual re-inspection, although this varies in some states. Unfortunately, most inspections are not much more than a formality and are often of little help in isolating potential problems. It is always good to establish an excellent working relationship with your agricultural inspector; our personal experience with agricultural inspectors has never been anything but extremely positive. Some nurseries are lucky enough to get a knowledgeable inspector, but this is sadly the exception rather than the rule.

The duty of the inspector is to look out for pest problems in your operation. These could be diseases, weeds, insects, and so forth. Both state and federal departments of agriculture list plants that are illegal to grow, and inspectors should also keep their eyes open for these. Many of the plants listed as federal noxious weeds are, surprisingly, grown as ornamentals. One local nurseryman was actually selling one of these plants, *Heracleum mantegazzianum* (giant hogweed), only to have the inspectors see it in his catalog and then pay him a visit and destroy his entire crop.

Don't be afraid to ask for help from your inspector as this is, at least in some states, one of their duties. For example, if your nursery growing area becomes part of a quarantine area for a particular pest, the agricultural inspector can work with you to develop a treatment program to certify that your nursery is free of, or is being treated for, the pest in question. Without proper certification, the inspectors can restrict movement of your plants to other states or countries. Similarly, if you purchase plants from outside your region or state that are infested with a particular pest, your agricultural inspectors should be your first phone call for help.

Chapter 12

Pests and Pesticides

Like telephone answering, pest control is a true bane of a nursery owner's existence. Pests are often among the most costly factors in the operation of a nursery, both because of plant loss and because of plants that are rendered unsellable. Pests are usually divided into the following groups: microbial organisms (diseases), insects and similar organisms, mollusks, nematodes, weeds, and animals. Solutions to a pest problem will of course depend on the type of pest that is harming your crop, but even after you have a solution, you will still have to figure out how best to deal with regulations regarding pesticide application as well as with the application itself.

Identifying the type of pest

Just as you would not think of taking medicines without determining which illness you suffer from, you should not treat a pest problem before identifying the pest. The first course of action in handling a pest problem, therefore, is to identify the pest. This can be accomplished either by examining the pest or, in many cases, by looking at the damage caused to the crop.

Diseases are probably the worst of the pest groups, as they can spread quickly and wipe out an entire crop, often in a matter of days. Diseases can consist of several unrelated organisms such as fungi, bacteria, and viruses. Each requires its own method of control, which rarely works on the others. As a typical rule, fungi and bacteria most often show up on crops as spots or as a rotting of the plant's foliage, stem, or roots. Bacterial and fungal rots are accompanied by a recognizable unpleasant odor. On the other hand, viruses usually manifest as a yellow leaf discoloration (in the form of spots or streaks) on both the leaves and the flowers.

Fungi on plants are most often associated with improper conditions—too wet, too hot, too cool, or insufficient air circulation. Most of these conditions are controllable, so both prevention and monitoring are key. If conditions are right for a particular fungus, it can spread as much as several feet a day, wiping out plants by the hundreds. The most common fungal problems are botrytis (usually attacks leaf surfaces), mildew (leaf spots), fusarium (root rot), rhizoctonia (stem rot), sclerotia (stem or crown rot), pythium (root rot), rusts (leaf spot), and anthracnose (leaf spot).

163

Fungicides are generally useful only to suppress diseases and prevent their spread, as they rarely kill off the offending pathogen completely. Fungi are virtually everywhere in our environment, and most are actually beneficial. It is therefore unrealistic and undesirable to think you will rid yourself of all fungi. Keep in mind that it is usually the unhealthy or stressed plants—and even healthy seedlings—that are the most susceptible to detrimental fungi, and that each fungal disease only occurs under a narrow range of environmental conditions.

The symptoms of bacterial diseases often appear similar to fungal diseases, but those caused by bacteria are harder to eliminate. Thank goodness bacterial diseases do not have the same ability to attack plants like fungi do. Bacteria usually do not have the ability to puncture cell walls so instead must look for a toehold on a damaged part of the plant. The chief difference that distinguishes the two diseases is that only fungi produce reproductive hyphae. (If you have ever seen mold on bread or meat then you have seen a fungal hyphae.) A good laboratory can also distinguish bacterial diseases from fungi.

There's a fungus among us. Root fungi can spread rapidly, as it does here through these pots of seedlings. Plant Delights Nursery.

The most common bacterial pathogens include *Erwinia* (bacterial rot) and *Pseudomonas* (bacterial leaf spot). Fungicides are generally ineffective on bacteria, and only bactericide or antibiotics are of any benefit on bacteria. In most cases you are better off simply discarding the infected plants. Many bacterial problems can be prevented with good sanitation of tools and working spaces.

Viruses are the most difficult of the plant pests to control. In fact, there is no control other than the removal and disposal of infected plants. Although viruses in the nursery business can be spread by plant or human contact, they are more often spread from plant to plant by insects. This ease of transmission makes controlling transmission agents or vectors even more critical when viruses are present. While viruses rarely kill the plant, they can reduce its vigor. You will often hear growers complain that a particular cultivar is no longer vigorous, and such a condition is usually the result of a virus. Visible signs of a virus infection usually include a white or yellow spotting or streaking on the leaves or flowers.

Insects are usually the most noticeable pests in a nursery setting, in part because they are the largest and most mobile of the pests. Insects do some of their worst damage as transmission agents for diseases. Of course plenty of insects do damage on their own by sucking the life out of a plant or injecting toxins inside the plant, but their role as transmission vectors is a serious secondary threat. The most common nursery pests include whiteflies, aphids, thrips, scale, fungus gnats, spider mites, mealybugs, grasshoppers, beetles and weevils, slugs and snails, and nematodes. Each has a particular mode of attack and is often easily identifiable based on when and how the insect is found on the plant.

Whiteflies are, in fact, tiny white flies that are found on the underside of the leaves where they feed and lay their eggs. They weaken the plants by sucking plant juices from the leaves and they also transmit viruses. Whiteflies are among the most mobile and also the most stubborn of insect pests to control, as they quickly develop resistance to pesticides. As their own populations explode, whiteflies cause a decline in plant vigor.

Aphids should get an award for being the most prolific of insects; it seems like there can be one or two aphids one day and hundreds the next. They congregate on the tips of young succulent growth or on flower buds, so the worst aphid problem a nursery will encounter will be in early spring when everything is young and tender. Aphids are actually quite easy to kill compared to most other insect pests, but if you miss even one, they will quickly return—and in large numbers.

Thrips are another very difficult pest to control, partly because they are so tiny (they look like miniature flies), and partly because they often attack flowers and growth buds before they unfurl. The damage is seen when the plant flowers but it was done long before it is actually visible.

Scale insects are large enough to be seen with the naked eye. They form a protective coat, which is either brown or white, that looks like a miniature Volkswagen bug. You will most often find scale on the stems of plants and more rarely on the foliage. Scale is most vulnerable when, after the protected mother has laid her eggs and those eggs have hatched, the young crawlers emerge from underneath the protective coat or scale and travel short distances to form their own home.

For years fungus gnats were thought to be of little consequence to growers, but this belief is anything but true. These tiny black flies are usually seen when plants are shaken; they rise like a little cloud from the soil's surface. Fungus gnats are born in the top one inch of moist soil, where the larvae live and consume young tender plants and roots. Germinating seedlings are often eaten even before they break ground. Not only are fungus gnats themselves bad but they may also spread several fungal pathogens as they feed. Control is usually achieved through a combination of biological control agents and cultural techniques. Allowing the soil surface in containers to remain dry, as well as reducing or eliminating moisture-holding peat moss in the soil mix, will help. There is a delicate balance between a soil surface that is dry enough to prevent fungus gnats and too dry for plant seedlings.

Two pests that are fairly readily eliminated are spider mites and mealybugs. Spider mites, which are tiny and best seen with a magnifying glass, resemble very small red spiders. They inhabit the backs of leaves, and when populations build to high levels, the leaves on the infected plants begin to turn a silvery bronze, then yellow or brown. When populations are totally out of control, the mites will form a dense webbing around the leaves and branches. Spider mites are fairly easy to control, as long as spray is directed under the leaves and repeated every seven to ten days to catch hatching eggs. Mealybugs, which are white, are cottony to the touch and are usually found in the crotches of branches instead of under the foliage. Unlike whiteflies, mealybugs do not fly. They are actually among the easiest of the plant pests to eliminate with insecticides, if you can get to them.

Grasshoppers are certainly the most visible of the major insect pests, but thankfully they are also among the easiest to kill. Grasshopper infestations are usually worse during the intense heat of summer, especially in dry areas when normal food sources are not as plentiful. Their large size allows them to wreak considerable damage quickly as they eat the leaves, starting from the outer edge. Although several sprays are effective for contact kill, the best results usually come from using biological baits.

Beetles are similar to grasshoppers, both in size and in their ability to devour leaves, and they are also quite easy to kill with an array of contact chemicals. Weevils, while related to beetles, are usually much more difficult to kill. Root weevils are a major pest in cooler parts of the country and are responsible for a great decline in the vigor of many ornamental plants.

Slugs and snails belong to a group called mollusks, and while they are not insects, the dramatic damage they cause would make any insect proud. These succulent mollusks feed primarily at night and can quickly skeletonize a leaf. Although a variety of sprays will kill slugs and snails, the best results are achieved from slug baits that are placed in dark, damp areas such as under pots, where slugs and snails hide during the daylight hours. Slug problems are generally worse when plants are kept moist and grown on ground level.

Nematodes are microscopic, wormlike creatures that come in many types, most of which are beneficial. It is the small number of harmful ones that are of great concern to nursery owners. The damaging, parasitic nematodes can also be divided into two types, root nematodes and foliar nematodes. While most people are familiar with the root types, it is the foliar nematodes that are a far worse pest for nursery crops. Root nematodes are generally found in sandy soils and they infect the plants by feeding on the plant roots, forming the well-recognized swollen root nodules. While root nematodes don't often kill the plants, the plants become weak and lose vigor. If you are growing for production or stock in soils formerly used in agricultural crop production, it is critical that you have the soil checked for nematodes prior to use. Soil-borne nematodes don't kill every plant, so your crop could be unaffected regardless of the presence of the nematodes.

There is no way of totally controlling soil-borne nematodes. While agricultural crop growers often "sterilize" a field, this only serves to suppress nematode population long enough for a fast-maturing crop to reach maturity. Root nematodes can also be a problem in container-grown plants that are grown on ground fabric, especially where benches are not used and roots grow out of the drainage holes and into the soil. Chemical control of root nematodes is of no use for most field-grown nursery crops, which remain in the soil for a much longer period than agronomic crops. The only long-term control is an organically active soil containing high populations of good soil microbes that will not allow the harmful nematode population to grow large enough to cause significant damage.

Foliar nematodes are found in both the foliage and crown of the plant but not in the roots. This leaf and crown damage is a major problem in the nursery industry, although the symptomatic browning and necrosis of the leaves in summer and fall are often excused as being the result of heat or early dormancy. Like root nematodes, foliar nematodes are very difficult to control because the chemicals available for their control are very limited. Since foliar nematodes spread rapidly by splashing water, the best control is to first discard infected plants (as well as anything within several feet of the last plant displaying symptoms). Some plants may be asymptomatic (meaning they do not display visible symptoms) carriers; only with a microscope can you determine that a plant is free of foliar nematodes. Perhaps the most frightening aspect to this pest is that they can lay dormant for decades in leaf debris or ground fabric but will actually rehydrate when moistened, coming back to life like a villain from a bad horror movie.

Monitoring for all pests is indeed critical. Someone at your nursery must know the symptoms and signs to look for as well as which plants are most susceptible to which pest. Monitoring for flying insect pests is easy to do with "sticky traps." These traps are colored cards with a sticky, adhesive coating that literally traps the insects so that they can be studied and counted. The traps are suspended at the same height level of the crop and monitored at regular intervals. Published counts for each type of insect detail the levels of infestation that are acceptable as well as levels that will require corrective action.

Good monitoring allows for better applications of pest controls if and when they are needed. Be sure to check with your local entomologist to determine which color of sticky traps to use, since different insects are attracted to different colors. For example, yellow traps are most commonly used to check for the presence of whiteflies, while blue sticky traps are most often used to detect thrips (Pasian and Lindquist 1998).

While weeds can't fly, crawl, or cause plants to rot, they are the most prolific and widespread of nursery pests. They are also easily disguised by nurseries, meaning that far too many nurseries have weed control practices that consist of pulling the weeds from the plants only as the plants are prepared for shipment. This practice allows the weed roots and seed left behind to sprout when the plants arrive at the retailer or at the customer's home. I am very offended by a nursery that sends along its weeds for my staff to pull, a practice that still happens far too often. This is a classic sign of a poorly run nursery.

Weed control is actually fairly simple: keep the weed seed from entering the nursery and eliminate the weeds that are already in the nursery. Weed control can be as simple as manual removal, which works very well if it is attended to on a regular basis, or as complex as chemical preemergent control. There are certainly more chemical choices each year and a broad spectrum of plants on which they are safe. Most chemical weed control is in the form of preemergent herbicides, which, as the name implies, are applied to growing plants before the weed seeds germinate. Preemergent herbicides are therefore applied according to the crop during the season in which the target weed sprouts. Again, know thine enemy before deciding which attack strategy to use. Also be sure to test new preemergents before getting carried away, as you can't afford to loose an entire crop over a weed problem.

Many growers in the past would spray first and ask questions later. Now, the combination of increasing restrictions on pesticides use and greater attention to employees being exposed to potentially toxic pesticides have resulted in pest control strategies changing dramatically. "IPM" (or integrated pest management) has become an accepted buzzword in most nurseries. IPM doesn't mean "don't spray"; it simply refers to using the least toxic pest management practice, which includes integrating various options such as spraying pesticides, controlling sanitation or cultural conditions, and using beneficial organisms. Pest control emphasis has shifted toward scouting (close monitoring of potential pests) and the use of biological and cultural controls as a first line of defense. By keeping a growing area clean and plants free from stress, you can dramatically reduce most pest problems.

The method still preferred in the greenhouse floriculture industry, however, is one of spraying as a preventative or precautionary measure. This preference is in part based on these crops being sold mostly for indoor use, where the level of tolerable pest damage and insect population is extremely low. By contrast, growers of outdoor crops find there is a higher tolerance for pests and the damage they cause. Growers of outdoor crops tend to spray on an as-needed basis rather than as a precautionary measure.

Precautionary pesticide applications are best when they are based on a thorough knowledge of the crop as well as on a good pest-monitoring program. For example, if you grow lantana, you know in advance that you will have problems with whiteflies, at least in most climates. In this case you will need to develop a control plan in advance. The first step in developing an IPM plan is to set tolerance levels for each pest. If the pest is a particular weed in the crop, you must determine how many weeds are acceptable before you devote time to their elimination. If your problem is a disease, how much can you allow the disease to spread before control must be implemented? Likewise, how many insects can infest each plant before control is necessary? You must also realize that there is no such thing as 100 percent control in any living crop, as nature never deals in absolutes. Remember, too, that each "pest" has a purpose in the balance of nature.

The use of cultural practices as a means of pest control is certainly not a new one, although its emphasis today seems to be at an all-time high. Many times, pests can be reduced simply by making procedural changes in your growing practices. If botrytis fungus is a problem, for example, then perhaps more air circulation or heat will solve it. Perhaps keeping the top of the soil mix drier will solve a fungus gnat problem. Using beneficial organisms as a mode of pest control gained widespread acceptance in the 1980s. The 1990s saw a clear trend toward introducing lady beetles to control aphid populations in spring, releasing an insect to control a problem weed, or applying a beneficial fungi that will colonize the plant roots and prevent dangerous pathogens. Some great books such as *The Green Methods Manual* (Cherim 1998) and *Insects and Gardens* (Grissell 2001) will help you choose the proper organism to fight your particular battle, so do not overlook the exciting possibilities that this type of control presents.

One last area of pest management involves animal control, a subject that is getting more and more attention. A number of animals can cause problems not only in home gardens but also in production nurseries. The worse pests include voles, which consume plant roots and crowns both in the ground and in containers; rabbits and deer, which eat the tops off plants; armadillos, which dig plants out of the ground; and mice, which are a terrible pest in seed beds. Be sure to check with your county's cooperative extension office for control options, since many animals are actually protected species despite their pestlike behavior.

Pesticide laws and regulations

The laws governing pesticide application and record keeping change at an almost dizzying pace, but as a nursery owner, you must keep up with them if for no other reason than to comply with the legalities of pesticide use. The primary law that regulates the registration, manufacture, sale, transportation, and use of pesticides is the Federal Insecticide, Fungicide, and Rodenticide Act (FIFRA). FIFRA, which was first enacted by Congress in 1947 and has been amended many times since, essentially establishes pesticide standards and authorizes the Environmental Protection Agency (EPA) to oversee the regulations.

The first part of the pesticide law worth studying is pesticide application licensing. It is illegal in the United States to apply a pesticide at or for a nursery without a valid pesticide license. Pesticide licenses are issued by each state after a certification test has been passed; some states also offer an optional training program. Most pesticide application licenses are good for a period of years, provided state-mandated recertification requirements are met. These recertification requirements usually involve additional training or attendance at educational seminars. While homeowners can apply most of the same chemicals (except those that are labeled "restricted use") without a license, it is imperative from a legal standpoint that anyone growing plants for commercial purposes follow the pesticide laws and regulations.

Pesticide application licensing is only one regulation in the myriad of government rules regarding pesticide use. Another important regulation is that of pesticide labeling. No pesticide in the United States may be sold without an EPA-approved label. It is also illegal to use a pesticide in any manner inconsistent with the label. Remember that pesticide labels are not suggestions for use; they are legal requirements for use.

The process by which chemical companies label pesticides has become very cumbersome and expensive; they often spend millions of dollars to satisfy the government's testing and labeling requirements. The result is that if a crop on which the pesticide is to be used is a minor one in terms of sales volume, the manufacturer will often not generate enough revenue in sales to justify the labeling expense. In such a case, the product would either be pulled from the market or labeled for use only on crops considered to have a high value. Therefore, even when a particular pesticide is the sole means of controlling a particular pest on a crop, federal laws can render the pesticide illegal for use on your crop. If a chemical is only labeled for controlling whiteflies on poinsettias in other words, it would be a federal crime to use this product to control whiteflies on Easter lilies. Needless to say, this poorly constructed legislation has created a lot of federal criminals out of people running nurseries.

One form of little-known assistance that the federal government provides is the Interregional Research Project 4 (IR-4). IR-4 was developed as a joint effort between the USDA, the Cooperative State Research, Education, and Extension Service (CSREES) and the Agricultural Research Service (ARS). This program works with state representatives to provide scientific test data for minor ornamental crops to the EPA. The data can be used to help pesticide manufacturers justify including a minor crop on their label without spending the money that would normally make such inclusion unfeasible. Anyone, with the exception of the chemical companies, may submit a request for research on a particular crop. More information regarding IR-4 research or how to submit a request can be found at IR-4's Web site.

Additional federal regulations that are important and that you should investigate are contained in the 1992 Worker Protection Standards (WPS). The WPS is administered by the EPA and is designed to protect workers in agricultural industries from pesticide exposure. The WPS includes requirements such as the prominent posting of all information regarding pesticides used and their application, as well as the posting of warning reentry signs when pesticides have been applied. Other requirements include conducting pesticide training for all employees and providing decontamination sites and emergency assistance for employees who are exposed to pesticides. I recommend you first obtain a copy of the "The Worker Protection Standard for Agricultural Pesticides—How to Comply," which is a publication prepared by the EPA regarding worker protection standards for agricultural pesticides. It is downloadable from the USDA's Web site.

Pesticide labels provide valuable information regarding the toxicity of the pesticide. All pesticides are classified either as "restricted use" or "non-restricted use." Restricted-use chemicals are those that the EPA has determined could cause harm to the environment if not used correctly and therefore cannot be used except by licensed pesticide applicators or someone under their direct supervision. Such chemicals are designated on the label with the words "Restricted Use Pesticide."

Other information found on the pesticide label includes the official "signal words." These words signal the relative toxicity of the pesticide to humans, indicating the likelihood that you will experience toxic effects if you suffer overexposure to the pesticide. All pesticides have one of four signal words: *caution, warning, danger,* or *poison.* Those pesticides labeled *caution* are the least toxic, while those marked *danger* or *poison* are the most toxic.

The toxicity of each pesticide is expressed in the term *LD50* (lethal dose 50). The LD50 is the amount of the pesticide based on body weight that is required to kill half of a population of test subjects. In other words, if a pesticide has a LD50 of 4, then it takes only 4 milligrams per kilogram of the subject's body weight to kill half of the group. Some less toxic pesticides may have an LD50 of 30,000, meaning that it takes much more of the pesticide—30,000 milligrams per kilogram of body weight—to kill half the group. Each pesticide is toxic in a different way, and therefore each product formulation has four different LD50s, one for dermal exposure (skin), ingestion (swallowing), eyes (ocular), and breathing (inhalation). In other words, some pesticides are far more toxic when inhaled, while others are most toxic when absorbed through the skin.

The pesticide label also details the active ingredient of the chemical and the type of formulation. Each formulation has initials that you will quickly learn to recognize. Some of the more common chemical formulations include EC (emulsifiable concentrate), meaning that the product is in a concentrated liquid form; L (liquid flowable), indicating it is a ready-to-mix liquid concentrate; WP (wettable powder), which is just that, a powder that dissolves when wet; D (dusts), which are products that are used directly without mixing; A (aerosol), which are pressurized-release formulations; RTU (ready to use); and G, granular products. Note that some of this information may be on the accompanying "Material Safety Data Sheet" (MSDS) rather than on the pesticide label. Each pesticide that is sold must come with an MSDS, so if you find a pesticide without the

I know you've heard it before, but read the instructions first! The front of a sample pesticide label.

The back of a sample pesticide label.

sheet, call the pesticide manufacturer immediately to get a new copy, as it is a legal requirement to keep this on hand for each pesticide that you own.

The MSDS also contains information regarding the REI (reentry interval), the minimum amount of time that must elapse before unprotected workers can

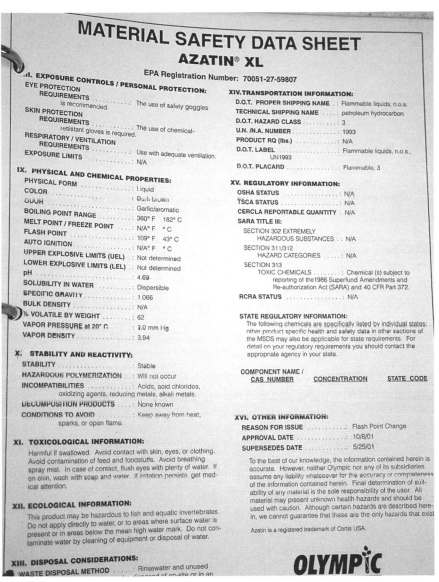

MATERIAL SAFETY DATA SHEET
AZATIN® XL
EPA Registration Number: 70051-27-59807

.II. EXPOSURE CONTROLS / PERSONAL PROTECTION:

EYE PROTECTION
REQUIREMENTS . . . .
  is recommended. . . . . : The use of safety goggles

SKIN PROTECTION
REQUIREMENTS . . . .
  resistant gloves is required. : The use of chemical-

RESPIRATORY / VENTILATION
REQUIREMENTS . . . .
EXPOSURE LIMITS . . . . : Use with adequate ventilation.
. . . . : N/A

IX. PHYSICAL AND CHEMICAL PROPERTIES:

PHYSICAL FORM	: Liquid
COLOR	: Dark brown
ODOR	: Garlic/aromatic
BOILING POINT RANGE	: 360° F 182° C
MELT POINT / FREEZE POINT	: N/A° F ° C
FLASH POINT	: 109° F 43° C
AUTO IGNITION	: N/A° F ° C
UPPER EXPLOSIVE LIMITS (UEL)	: Not determined
LOWER EXPLOSIVE LIMITS (LEL)	: Not determined
pH	: 4.69
SOLUBILITY IN WATER	: Dispersible
SPECIFIC GRAVITY	: 1.066
BULK DENSITY	: N/A
% VOLATILE BY WEIGHT	: 62
VAPOR PRESSURE at 20° C	: 2.0 mm Hg
VAPOR DENSITY	: 3.94

X. STABILITY AND REACTIVITY:

STABILITY . . . . : Stable
HAZARDOUS POLYMERIZATION . . : Will not occur
INCOMPATIBILITIES . . . . : Acids, acid chlorides,
  oxidizing agents, reducing metals, alkali metals.
DECOMPOSITION PRODUCTS . . . . : None known
CONDITIONS TO AVOID . . . . : Keep away from heat,
  sparks, or open flame.

XI. TOXICOLOGICAL INFORMATION:

Harmful if swallowed. Avoid contact with skin, eyes, or clothing. Avoid contamination of feed and foodstuffs. Avoid breathing spray mist. In case of contact, flush eyes with plenty of water. If on skin, wash with soap and water. If irritation persists, get medical attention.

XII. ECOLOGICAL INFORMATION:

This product may be hazardous to fish and aquatic invertebrates. Do not apply directly to water, or to areas where surface water is present or in areas below the mean high water mark. Do not contaminate water by cleaning of equipment or disposal of water.

XIII. DISPOSAL CONSIDERATIONS:

WASTE DISPOSAL METHOD . . . . : Rinsewater and unused
  disposed of on-site or in an

XIV. TRANSPORTATION INFORMATION:

D.O.T. PROPER SHIPPING NAME	: Flammable liquids, n.o.s.
TECHNICAL SHIPPING NAME	: petroleum hydrocarbon
D.O.T. HAZARD CLASS	: 3
U.N. /N.A. NUMBER	: 1993
PRODUCT RQ (lbs.)	: N/A
D.O.T. LABEL	: Flammable liquids, n.o.s., UN1993
D.O.T. PLACARD	: Flammable, 3

XV. REGULATORY INFORMATION:

OSHA STATUS	: N/A
TSCA STATUS	: N/A
CERCLA REPORTABLE QUANTITY	: N/A

SARA TITLE III:
  SECTION 302 EXTREMELY
    HAZARDOUS SUBSTANCES . . : N/A
  SECTION 311/312
    HAZARD CATEGORIES . . . . . : N/A
  SECTION 313
    TOXIC CHEMICALS . . . . : Chemical (s) subject to reporting of the1986 Superfund Amendments and Re-authorization Act (SARA) and 40 CFR Part 372.
RCRA STATUS . . . . : N/A

STATE REGULATORY INFORMATION:
The following chemicals are specifically listed by individual states; other product specific health and safety data in other sections of the MSDS may also be applicable for state requirements. For detail on your regulatory requirements you should contact the appropriate agency in your state.

COMPONENT NAME / CAS NUMBER	CONCENTRATION	STATE CODE

XVI. OTHER INFORMATION:

REASON FOR ISSUE	: Flash Point Change
APPROVAL DATE	: 10/8/01
SUPERSEDES DATE	: 5/25/01

To the best of our knowledge, the information contained herein is accurate. However, neither Olympic nor any of its subsidiaries assume any liability whatsoever for the accuracy or completeness of the information contained herein. Final determination of suitability of any material is the sole responsibility of the user. All material may present unknown health hazards and should be used with caution. Although certain hazards are described herein, we cannot guarantee that these are the only hazards that exist

Azatin is a registered trademark of Certis USA.

OLYMPIC

MSDS . . . Anyone seen a vowel? If you use pesticides, you will need to become very familiar with a Material Safety Data Sheet or MSDS.

reenter a treated area. All pesticides are required to have a reentry interval. If constant access to crops is critical, you should choose the pesticide with the lowest REI. Reentry intervals can be as short as a couple of hours or as long as several days.

The required PPE (personal protective equipment) detailing what type of protective gear the pesticide applicator must use must also appear on the label or MSDS. Protective gear includes chemical resistant gloves, protective goggles or other eyewear, respirators with the proper filtration cartridges, a protective spray suit, protective boots, and protective headgear. To be safe while applying a pesticide, you will have to wear some type of protective clothing. This information is not to be taken lightly and should be adhered to at all costs, not only because it is the law but also because ongoing exposure to and misuse of pesticides does not usually create immediately noticeable damage to the body but instead has a cumulative detrimental effect. In other words, you will often not realize the damage from pesticide exposure until years later, when it is too late.

After chemicals have been applied to the crops at your nursery, you are required to post an approved "pesticide application" sign that details which pesticide was applied and the reentry time. These signs must be posted at all possible access points to the treated area. Signs should be promptly removed after the REI expires or workers will begin to disregard them.

Nursery owners must also plan for accidents by having procedures in place to handle an accident. A "decontamination site" is required for any nursery using pesticides. Essentially, this consists of a place for workers to wash pesticides off their bodies. The law sets forth requirements as to how many of these sites are required in a particular area and what these sites must contain, such as soap, eyewash, and other similar items.

There are also stringent recording requirements for all pesticides that are applied at your nursery. Growers must keep a log, listing all chemicals that were applied, the rate and date of application, and the crops that were treated. By law, this information must be readily available to all employees. Additionally, the WPS requires that every nursery employee be trained by a certified trainer. The training is simply an overview of pesticide procedures used at the nursery, including what to do in the event of a disaster.

The storing of chemicals is another highly regulated area. Pesticides, as you can imagine, can only be stored in approved cabinets whose locations are restricted. Obviously, you would not store chemicals near the employee lunchroom or in an area where workers would regularly breathe chemical fumes. You will also need to consider the types of pesticides that you will be storing together. A sure recipe for disaster would be the storing of herbicides in the same cabinet with insecticides. This dangerous practice has occurred on more than one occasion, the insecticide becoming contaminated with fumes from the nearby herbicide. When the infected insecticide was later applied, it caused major crop damage. While this is certainly not a problem with all herbicide or insecticide combinations, a storage situation like this must absolutely be avoided.

Pesticide formulations can change over time based on the length of time they are stored and the conditions in which they are stored. Many chemicals undergo a change in their physical properties if they are stored at temperatures that are either too hot or too cold. Often information such as "do not store this pesticide at temperatures below 32°F" is found on the MSDS but if it is not, do not hesitate to call the product manufacturer. Any change in the chemical property of a pesticide may cause a normally good chemical to become deadly to the crop it was designed to protect.

Have you seen any aliens? These suits, though silly looking, are critical to fully protect employees from pesticide exposure. Plant Delights Nursery.

Warning, warning, warning! Pesticide warning signs are a legal requirement for pesticide application and reentry intervals, so don't take their use lightly. Plant Delights Nursery.

Just as the milk we drink has a shelf life, so does every pesticide. Some pesticides have a long shelf life, while others degrade quite rapidly. When I purchase a pesticide I immediately write the date of purchase on the container itself, not the paper label, and I use a waterproof pen. This allows me to monitor the age of each pesticide against the manufacturer's shelf life recommendations.

The other storage requirement for pesticides involves the notification of your local fire department. If a fire were to occur at your nursery, the toxic nature of many pesticides would change the way firefighters address the fire. If your storage of pesticides grows past a level set by your local fire department, you are required to submit a list of products in your inventory. In addition, you may be required to post a sign on one of your buildings indicating that flammable pesticides are stored inside.

Selecting and applying pesticides

Once you determine that you will need to apply a pesticide, you next have to decide which pesticide to use as well as the rate, timing, and mode of its application. Both national and state publications detail which pesticides are labeled for controlling which pests, and they detail rates and other application information. Most of these publications are updated annually as pesticide registrations change quite often. The state manuals are usually the best, as they are more specific for the region in which your crops are growing.

Pesticides are selected based on their efficacy, reentry intervals, lack of phytotoxicity (the undesirable damage caused to crops), and labeling for the crops that need spraying. Many pesticides are toxic to certain crops as well as certain pests. Jim Baker (1996) explains, "The word phytotoxicity is derived from two Greek words, phyton, meaning plant, and toxikon, a poison into which arrows were dipped." He goes on to say that while dimethoate (Cygon) is very useful for controlling insects and mites on azaleas, camellias, boxwood, and a few other plants, it "can cause all the leaves to drop from Chinese holly and elaeagnus if applied in the spring. The true ferns, English ivy, palms, and the bracts of poinsettias are extremely sensitive to pesticides."

With anything other than a closed greenhouse, weather is among the most important factors in setting a spray schedule. Each weather-related factor from wind to temperature affects the efficacy of the pesticide application. Many chemicals cannot be applied when the temperatures get too high, often above 85°F. Above a certain temperature, the plant's reaction to the chemical may change, and in the case of pesticides with high levels of volatility, the pesticide itself may change. The temperature regimen under which application is safe is indicated on the label or MSDS. No pesticide should be applied when wind is significantly strong, as drift to nontarget species is an obvious no-no. I once saw more herbicide damage than I care to recollect when, despite the great care that was taken during the application, weed killers were sprayed on a day that was far too windy.

A very important consideration when deciding what pesticide to apply and when to apply it is the REI, information contained either on the pesticide label or on the MSDS. From an economic point of view, the most effective chemicals with the lowest REI will usually be the first choice. Chemicals with a 12-hour REI can be sprayed late in the day, often after most employees have left, without losing any worker-access time in that particular part of the nursery.

In determining a pesticide's application rate, which is the next step in the process, look at the range of application rates provided on each label or MSDS. Usually the lower rate is for lesser infestations while the higher rate is for severe infestations and more difficult-to-control pests. Determining application rates is a frustrating part of pesticide use because, for some bizarre reason, chemical companies provide application rates in pounds of chemical per acre rather than in a more usable rate of ounces per square foot. I understand that many products are also used for large-scale applications, but why these companies cannot also give rates for smaller nursery use is incomprehensible. Are you companies out there listening?

Figure 9. Pesticide/Fertilizer Dilution Chart

RATE PER 100 GALLONS	RATE PER 10 GALLONS	RATE PER 5 GALLONS	RATE PER 1 GALLON
2 gallons (fluid)	25½ ounces	12⅞ ounces	2½ ounces
1 gallon (fluid)	12¾ ounces	6½ ounces	1¼ ounces
1 quart (fluid)	3³⁄₁₆ ounces	1⁹⁄₁₆ ounces	⁵⁄₁₆ ounce
1 pint (fluid)	1⁹⁄₁₆ ounces	⅞ ounce	³⁄₁₆ ounce
8 ounces (fluid)	¹³⁄₁₆ ounce	⁷⁄₁₆ ounce	½ teaspoon
4 ounces (fluid)	⅜ ounce	¼ ounce	¼ teaspoon
5 pounds (dry)	8 ounces	4 ounces	4⅘ teaspoons
4 pounds (dry)	6⅜ ounces	3¼ ounces	3⅘ teaspoons
3 pounds (dry)	4¹³⁄₁₆ ounces	2⅜ ounces	2⅖ teaspoons
2 pounds (dry)	3³⁄₁₆ ounces	1¾ ounces	2 teaspoons
1 pound (dry)	1⁹⁄₁₆ ounces	⅞ ounce	1 teaspoon
8 ounces (dry)	¹³⁄₁₆ ounce	⅜ ounce	½ teaspoon
4 ounces (dry)	⅜ ounce	³⁄₁₆ ounce	¼ teaspoon

(Reprinted with permission. Bilderback 2001)

You will need to have a good conversion chart as well as an understanding of sprayer calibration (see figure 10). If the pesticide application rates are given for a particular square footage of coverage instead of per gallon of spray, you will need to know the amount of chemical that will cover that area. For example, if the directions state that 10 ounces of concentrate should be applied to each acre sprayed, your first step would be to convert the acres to square feet, which is 43,560 square feet. Then divide that number by ten to work out how many ounces of pesticide should be applied to each square foot. In our example, one ounce of pesticide per 4,356 square feet should be applied.

Figure 10. Application Rates Conversion Table

RATE PER ACRE	RATE PER 1000 SQUARE FEET	RATE PER 100 SQUARE FEET
100 pounds	2 pounds, 4 ounces	3½ ounces
200 pounds	4 pounds, 8 ounces	7¼ ounces
300 pounds	6 pounds, 14 ounces	11 ounces
500 pounds	11 pounds, 8 ounces	1 pound, 2 ounces
700 pounds	16 pounds	1 pound, 9 ounces
900 pounds	20 pounds, 9 ounces	2 pounds, 1 ounce
1,000 pounds	23 pounds	2 pounds, 5 ounces
2,000 pounds	46 pounds	4 pounds, 9 ounces
1 gallon	3 ounces (fluid)	⅓ ounce (fluid)
5 gallons	14½ ounces (fluid)	1½ ounces (fluid)
100 gallons	2⅓ ounces (fluid)	29⅓ ounces (fluid)

(Reprinted with permission. Bilderback 2001)

Next, use a spray tank of water to see how much area a gallon of spray will cover. Let's say that with 1 gallon of water you can cover an area that is 43 feet long by 10 feet wide, or 430 square feet. It will therefore take 10 gallons of water to cover 4,356 square feet, so you should use one ounce of pesticide per 10 gallons of water. If you only want to use one gallon of spray, divide one ounce by ten. To do this, refer back to your chart to find that each ounce equals 2 tablespoons or 6 teaspoons. Therefore, 0.6 or ⁶⁄₁₀ of a teaspoon (just over half) will be required in each gallon of water.

Many pesticides have restrictions as to how many times the chemical can be used on a particular crop, both because of the possible damage done to the crop and because of the resistance that insects may develop. Many insects produce new generations so quickly that the few insects that survive in each generation become a little more resistant to the chemical with each spray. Where the same sprays are used again and again, insects will actually evolve to the point that a particular pesticide has little or no effect on the target pest. This ability to build up resistance is why pesticides, particularly insecticides, must be rotated.

The different formulations of pesticides will determine the application method you will use to apply pesticides. The most common formulations are drenches, sprays, granular applications, or aerosols. Drenches control soil-borne pests, both insect and disease. Sprays are normally the choice for controlling foliar diseases and pests. Granular applications are usually used for controlling weeds and for applying systemic insecticides, and aerosols are best in controlling insects in a closed greenhouse environment.

Drenches are usually applied with an injector. An injector is a siphon device that, in smaller jobs, is attached to a water hose, or in larger operations, can be a free-standing unit. Water pressure creates the suction that pulls along the concentrated pesticide at a rate preset by the injector and then mixes it with the water. Among the most important things to do before using an injector is to install a backflow preventer to keep the mixed pesticide from flowing back into your feeder waterline, which often is used as drinking water at some earlier point in the line. If you use injectors, be sure to label each water source through which pesticides are applied as "non-potable water."

Suck it up. Siphoning devices (this is a Dosatron) allow pesticide drenches to be easily and accurately applied. Plant Delights Nursery.

Absolute power covers absolutely. To get good spray coverage in a timely manner, use a properly sized power sprayer.

Sprays are applied with a sprayer that matches the task and the crop. For small jobs, most growers use backpack sprayers. In fact, backpack sprayers have become the industry standard for most spot spraying. These sprayers are strapped to your back and an extended handle is pumped with a rocking arm motion to build pressure in the spray tank. Backpack sprayers cannot generate very high pressure or hold spray quantities much larger than three or four gallons.

Consider power sprayers for larger spraying jobs. These larger sprayers are battery-, electric-, or gasoline-powered and come in either hand-pulled or trailer-mounted models. They can generate hundreds of pounds of pressure per square inch (PSI). Be sure to match the sprayer's size and capabilities to the size of your task. A small, trailer-mounted sprayer that generates between 100 and 200 PSI is perfect for most nurseries.

Sprayers usually come with a choice of nozzles and spray hoses. I recommend purchasing a hose that far exceeds the pressure than can be generated by the sprayer to avoid the hose bursting too soon. Nozzles vary depending on the type of pesticide applied, but most nurseries use an adjustable cone-type nozzle. You may need to experiment with several nozzle types to find one that fits your needs. Tractor-mounted hose sprayers or boom sprayers that get power from the power take off (PTO) on the tractor are great for field-grown or container row crops. With a little modification, many farm tractors adapt well to nursery use.

Once you finish spraying, you will need to rinse the sprayer. It is critical that pesticides are never dumped on the ground. Many old nurseries that practiced dumping have left behind soil that will remain toxic for many generations to come. In some areas, leaching or runoff from slowly deteriorating pesticides has even seeped into groundwater and contaminated nearby wells. Rinse-water must always be sprayed back onto the crops until the tank is clean.

Old pesticide containers should also be rinsed well and then rendered unusable for other purposes. The standard for rinsing both sprayers and old pesticide containers is to triple rinse. Once containers are triple-rinsed, the integrity of the containers should be compromised, either by ripping apart old pesticide bags or puncturing cans or jugs. Most jurisdictions allow compromised containers to be disposed of in the regular trash. If you find yourself with leftover chemicals, contact your county's cooperative extension office for help with disposal. Old pesticides cannot simply be discarded but must instead be disposed of only in an approved hazardous waste facility.

Just as it is important to keep rinse water from being dumped on the ground, so must pesticide spills be correctly handled. Spills must be cleaned up immediately, and care must be taken so that spilled pesticides do not seep into the soils or make their way into nearby water sources. Soil that is contaminated with pesticides must be removed and treated as hazardous waste. Once the contaminated soil and spilled chemicals are removed, you should dispose of them in a hazard waste disposal facility. I also recommend keeping a supply of activated charcoal on hand, as this is usually the preferred method of absorbing spills. Other absorbent materials include vermiculite, sawdust, and kitty litter.

The transportation of pesticides is another area where great care must be taken. Pesticides that are being transported should be placed only where they can be made secure; they should never be transported in the passenger area of a vehicle in case of a spill or accident. A nurseryman I know was carrying a box of canisters containing methyl bromide fumigant in the cab of his truck when one exploded. While he was not killed, he was disabled for life. Not only should pesticides be tightly secured when you are traveling with them, but they should also never be hauled at the same time as other persons, clothes, pets, and so on are being transported. While I hope that you will never experience any damage caused by exposure to a pesticide, let me assure you that hindsight is indeed 20 20.

Chapter 13

Running the Business

The intricacies of running the business will make or break your nursery. You must plan your growth at a manageable and steady level, price your plants using figures that account for your costs, and then make sales happen. When you combine all that with great plants, you will be well on your way to a successful business.

Nursery growth—too much versus too little

When you own a nursery, you want it to grow as fast as it can, right? Wrong! While small nurseries can handle a large percentage of growth without missing a beat, it is the larger nurseries that find it more difficult to handle the same percentage increases in growth. If your nursery is small and grossing $5,000 per year, the jump to $10,000 per year would represent a 100 percent increase, but if the nursery is grossing $500,000 per year, the same percentage of increase would find sales at the one million dollar level. Handling a 100 percent increase in sales at this level would obviously be difficult and would also pose an array of production, order processing, and delivery problems.

The inherent problem with rapid nursery growth is that the systems you have set up for a smaller operation no longer work for a larger operation. For example, if one person is responsible for potting, pulling, and shipping, a dramatic increase in business will mean that some part of these duties will go lacking until new staff is hired and trained. The part of the business that is typically neglected during dramatic growth spurts is customer service. Unfortunately, this is the worst part of the business to neglect, since negative word-of-mouth and customer disappointment can take years to overcome.

Rapid expansion of a business causes even more problems, especially when funds are not available. This is a problem of undercapitalization. If your nursery has the potential to double sales by building more greenhouses, how will you afford more greenhouses in order to produce more revenue? Greenhouse growers who can find willing lenders often end up deeply in debt because of poor cash-flow management or other unexpected sales downturns. The year 2001 was a classic example of the latter, when a slowing economy and the terrorist acts caused most nursery sales for the year to drop drastically. Nurseries that had been too aggressive in expansion found themselves bankrupt or in a dire cash-flow problem. The key thing to remember is that you are growing a living crop. Plenty of things can go wrong with the plants or the market, but the lenders will still want their money.

A too-rapid expansion program with inadequate planning can be a pitfall for other reasons as well. Some owners keep adding to their nursery facilities a little bit at a time to get by each year instead of making the financial arrangements necessary to expand their facilities in a more efficient manner. I have seen more than a few nurseries continue to expand their offices one room at a time, and in virtually all cases they would have been better off borrowing the money and constructing a more efficient office building, a conclusion they would agree with if they had to do it over again. Granted, you may not be able to furnish your office or production building with all the luxuries that you would like initially, but do not skimp on size. Plan construction projects so that these additional upgrade features can be added at a later date without major inconvenience or cost.

We have discussed reasons for limiting or managing growth, but let's also look at how to accommodate that growth. Before embarking on a quest for growth, I recommend you develop a master plan using realistic revenue projections. If, based on past growth figures, you can predict that your business will double in five years, don't waste time slightly enlarging your production space or office area; go ahead and build for five to ten years into the future. Increasing your facilities and changing your work processes just to manage for the next year is simply not cost efficient in the long-term. Even though all the equipment in an expansion project may not be purchased at the outset or all the offices not finished at once, it is essential that they be incorporated into the plan so that when the time comes to add them, it does not disrupt what you have already built.

The nursery industry is plagued by the erroneous assumption (usually made by us men) that bigger is always better. In the nursery industry, bigger can indeed be better, but it can also be worse. I have seen plenty of nurseries with gross sales that ranged from $30,000 to $100,000, whose owners were quite content to remain within that range for a long time. The larger a nursery becomes, the more efficient it can become, if and when size allows operations to be more efficiently mechanized. Conversely, as the size of a nursery increases, many of its operations and processes can't be efficiently mechanized and so become less efficient. The larger a nursery becomes, the more critical it is to have good management and staff to facilitate the process of team building.

We nursery owners are all interested in maximizing our profit or bottom line. As your nursery grows past certain set-points or stair-steps in sales volume, profitability will actually decline. The nursery industry seems to have a number of these set-points. A one-person operation can usually generate up to $50,000 in sales without much problem and without a lot of expenses. A single person with some part-time help can probably reach the $100,000 barrier but will probably need the help of a full-time staffer as sales get to the upper end of that range. It is when a nursery passes the $100,000 mark in sales that things start getting complicated. Most nursery owners agree that once sales go beyond $100,000, the next most profitable point is when the nursery does between one and three million dollars in gross sales (Greenridge 2000). As a result, there are many years in which nurseries struggle to maintain profitability.

These sales levels of $50,000, $100,000, and one to three million are the result of what we call the stair-step effect. Although sales volume may increase in a smoothly rising curve, cost of production rises in more of a stair-step fashion. The differences between sales volume and costs of production create periodic reductions in profitability. For example, if sales rise $20,000, you may have to invest in a potting machine that costs $50,000 or in two more employees to accommodate even that small amount of growth. In other words, for a year or two your profit may actually go down until you maximize the production capability of the new employees or machinery. This is where good financial planning helps to keep the lines of increased cost and increased sales at least close to parallel with each other.

Another cause of declining profits during expanding growth is the lack of human cloning. Yes, there is only one of you, and as a smaller business, you could maintain a hands-on approach to make sure things were being done correctly and at an optimum speed. However, when you get above the one-million-dollar sales level, you must begin to hire managers and to rely on them more. No matter how good your managers or supervisors are, they will not manage money and time as well as you, certainly not without a vested interest in the business. As owner you will have to set standards with regard to each phase of your nursery operation and then hold your managers accountable.

So how do you control this growth that is going to cause you so many problems? There is no single answer. The inherent problem in business is a classic catch-22 scenario: The better job you do with your nursery, the faster it will grow. If you do a poor job, your business will decline. Unfortunately, it is not possible for a business to stay the same size, despite this feat being attempted by the majority of small nursery owners.

Even if you produce the same number of plants each year, your nursery will not stay the same size but will instead begin to decline. Imagine a small wholesale nursery with ten customers, each of whom buys your plants and likes your operation. Their businesses will also probably grow each year, and as they grow, they will need more plants. If you are unable to meet their needs because you have chosen not to expand, they will probably have no choice but to take their business elsewhere—to a nursery supplier with a larger supply of plants.

Few businesses realize that often the best way to limit growth is to raise prices. Every consumer item, especially mass-produced "commodity items," has a point at which sales will decrease as the price increases. As a nursery owner, you will have to find these points. If you cannot keep up with demand for your plants at your current price, what effect will a 10 percent price increase have on your sales? How about a 25 percent increase? Will the quantity of items that you sell remain the same, decrease, or continue to increase? A decrease in sales volume may in fact be a good thing, as you will be making more profit with less production. It is still hard for many nursery owners to understand that gross sales is less important than net profit.

Something interesting that good marketers have discovered is that price increases often cause the consumer to perceive the product as having a higher value. Dramatic price increases have occasionally caused sales to soar. As we will discuss later, marketing has a tremendous impact on the price that can be demanded for your plants, especially those that are not yet commonplace in the trade.

Have you ever looked at a giant garden center, or one that has several locations, and wondered how they do it when you can barely handle one location? The answers lie in their ability to delegate to competent employees and in their good organizational systems. No matter how competent you are as the owner, you can only handle so much business being under your direct, personal control. Growth of a business is directly related to the ability of the nursery owner or manager to hire competent staff and delegate responsibility to those who will allow the business to grow and expand, topics we will discuss later.

You are probably wondering about where most nurseries stand in terms of size and sales. According to the 1998 USDA Census of Horticultural Specialties, nurseries and nursery-related businesses had gross sales according to the following figures:

Sales over $1,000,000	8.4%
Sales between $500,000 and $999,999	6.7%
Sales between $250,000 and $499,999	10.0%
Sales between $100,000 and $249,000	19.5%
Sales between $50,000 and $99,999	16.9%
Sales between $10,000 and $49,999	38.4%

These figures reflect not only the size that owners have chosen for their businesses but also the difficulty in moving a nursery business past each financial set-point. At each level, major changes in your business must occur for you to be able to function at the next higher level. This data is simply another piece of the puzzle in trying to select your niche in the nursery industry.

Establishing work standards

As your business grows and you find yourself unable to personally handle or even supervise all the tasks directly, it becomes critical that you establish work standards. Such standards give your supervisors a level of productivity that they need to achieve. Additionally, you can implement incentive programs for increased productivity but only if you have a base standard from which to start.

Standards are actually quite easy to establish if you keep good records. First, let's look at the task of sticking cuttings. Begin by delving into your records for the past year to create a chart that starts with a monthly breakdown of how many cuttings were stuck and how many hours were spent on the job. For each month, divide the number of labor hours spent by the number of cuttings stuck. This figure represents the time per cutting stuck. Multiply this number by your actual cost of labor (known as your burden rate) to get the cost per stuck cutting. Finally, divide this number by the success rate to give you your net cost per cutting. This calculation can be summarized as follows:

Labor hours divided by number of cuttings stuck   = time per cutting
Time per cutting × burden rate   = cost per stuck cutting
Cost per stuck cutting divided by success rate   = net cost per cutting

It is apparent from figure 11 that cuttings cost more in some months and less in others. The best month economically in which to stick cuttings is May, when the net cost is $0.023 per cutting. The worst month is December, when cuttings cost us $0.216 each. It's a shock to most nursery owners when they prepare such a chart and find that the same task is costing up to ten times as much in one month as it is in another. Over the course of the year we stuck a total of 114,250 cuttings at an average cost per cutting of $0.051 each for a total of $5,827. If we had been able to maintain our standard rate of $0.023 for all the cuttings we stuck, our labor bill for the same job would have been $2,628, a savings of $3,199. You see why developing labor standards for each repetitive task is so critical.

Having seen these figures, you likely realize you have one of two options: change your production schedule so that all cuttings are taken in the months when they cost less, or set a standard and work to meet that standard during the entire year. You will find that employees and supervisors are better able to achieve the standard you set once they know what it is. I recommend setting your initial standard at the lowest rate that you have already achieved, say $0.023 per cutting. If your managers or employees are able to achieve a better rate, then they can share in the savings. By offering the employees 20 percent of the savings in the example above, you would see a savings of $3,199 and the employees would share a bonus of $639.

Figure 11. Cutting Production Standard

MONTH	NUMBER STUCK	LABOR HOURS	TIME EACH	BURDEN RATE	COST TO STICK	SUCCESS RATE	NET COST
January	10000	40	.004hr	$10.75	$.043	80%	$.054
February	9000	30	.003hr	$10.75	$.032	70	$.046
March	6000	20	.003hr	$10.75	$.032	70	$.046
April	9000	40	.004hr	$10.75	$.043	90	$.048
May	35000	80	.002hr	$10.75	$.022	95	$.023
June	25000	80	.003hr	$10.75	$.032	85	$.038
July	9000	50	.006hr	$10.75	$.065	85	$.076
August	5000	20	.004hr	$10.75	$.043	75	$.057
September	2000	10	.005hr	$10.75	$.053	70	$.076
October	1750	10	.006	$10.75	$.065	65	$.100
November	1500	10	.007	$10.75	$.075	60	$.125
December	1000	10	.010	$10.75	$.108	50	$.216
Total	114,250	400	.0035	$10.75	$.038	75	$.051

In the example regarding the cost of sticking cuttings, I used the term "labor burden." This is an important term to understand in any computation of production cost as it is the actual cost to the company of each employee. Figuring the labor burden rate starts with an employee's base pay rate, which is usually only about ⅔ of the cost to your business. Using the employee burden rate chart, you will notice that each position is broken down by yearly salary, which is divided by 2080 hours (40-hour work-weeks multiplied by 52 weeks). The first position of nursery grower has a base salary of $27,498 or $13.22 per hour. (In this example the employee was salaried and therefore did not earn any overtime.)

Continuing down the chart we find entries for Social Security (FICA), Workers' Compensation (W/C), State Unemployment Tax (SUTA), and Federal Unemployment Tax (FUTA). By adding these totals to the original base salary, the original salary of $27,498 becomes $30,691. In the next couple of blocks, add any extra benefits that the nursery gives to the employees, such as uniforms or bonuses. This brings the total cost for our first employee to $31,462.

The next step in our calculations is to take the number of hours worked during the year (which is 2080 hours if no overtime has been worked) and subtract the nonwork hours. Nonwork hours are times that you are paying an employee not to work and include public holidays, vacation, sick and personal leave, and daily breaks. In our example, the first employee has been paid for 281 hours of nonwork time. When you subtract this amount from 2080, you are left with 1799 hours that are actually worked. To determine the per hour actual cost of this employee, divide the total employee cost of $31,462 by the actual hours worked. The result is an actual cost of $17.49. Since you pay an hourly rate of $13.22, the burden rate is $4.25 or 32.16 percent per hour. Part-time employees will have slightly less burden rate since they usually don't receive the same extent of benefits as full-time employees.

Figure 12. Employee Burden Rate Chart

A	B	C	D	E	F	G	H
NAME							
DEPARTMENT	Nursery	Nursery	Nursery	Nursery	Shipping/ Nursery	Office	Shipping
POSITION	Grower	Worker	Manager	Worker	Worker	Customer Service	Manager
CLASSIFICATION	Full Time	Full Time	Full Time	Seasonal Part Time	Seasonal Part Time	Full Time	Full Time
Base Hourly Rate	$13.22	$11.00	$13.94	$8.00	$8.50	$12.73	$18.03
Yearly Base Salary	$27,498	$22,880	$28,995	$16,640	$17,680	$26,478	$37,502
Overtime Pay	0	$908	$1,150	$660	$701	$1,050	0
Total Pay	$27,498	$23,788	$30,145	$17,300	$8,381	$7,529	$37,502
FICA	$2,104	$1,750	$2,218	$1,273	$1,353	$2,026	$2,869
Workers' Compensation	$902	$780	$989	$567	$603	$77	$1,230
SUTA	$132	$132	$132	$132	$132	$132	$132
FUTA	$56	$56	$56	$56	$56	$56	$56
Total Pay Cost	$30,691	$26,506	$33,540	$19,328	$20,525	$29,819	$41,789
Health Insurance	$477		$1,390				$993
Christmas Bonus	$264	$330	$418			$382	$541
T-Shirt W/Logo	$30	$30	$30	$30	$30	$30	$30
Total Cost To Nursery	$31,462	$26,866	$35,379	$19,358	$20,555	$30,231	$43,353
Overtime Hours		55	55	55	55	55	
Total Hours	2080	2135	2135	2135	2135	2135	2080
Holidays Hours Paid	48	48	48			48	48
Vacation Hours Paid	40	40	40			40	40
Sick Hours Paid	32	32	32			32	32
Personal Hours Paid	36	36	36	36	36	36	36
Break Hours Paid	125	125	125	125	125	125	125
Total Nonwork Hours	281	281	281	161	161	281	281
Hours Actually Worked	1799	1854	1854	1974	1974	1854	1799
Actual Hourly Cost	$17.49	$14.49	$19.08	$9.81	$10.41	$16.31	$24.10
Actual Hourly Rate	$13.22	$11.00	$13.94	$8.00	$8.50	$12.73	$18.03
Burden Rate	$4.27	$3.49	$5.14	$1.81	$1.91	$3.58	$6.07
Burden %	32.29%	31.74%	36.89%	22.58%	22.50%	28.09%	33.66%

Business consultants

Have you thought about hiring a business consultant? If you're in the nursery business, the answer is probably no. Most old-style nursery owners operated under the logic that it was an insult to ask for help. Fortunately, the newer generation of nursery owners realizes that outside advice and perspective can be very helpful. So what are the signs of a nursery that needs a business consultant? There could be numerous signs, including eroding profits, mix-ups and customer complaints resulting from organizational problems, production inefficiencies, an overall decline in business, difficulty hiring and keeping good employees, poor cash flow, or problems managing growth.

If you're like me you've heard plenty of consultant jokes, and some of them are no doubt well deserved. But I hope to change the way you look at business consultants. Business consultants are really business doctors; they examine the symptoms of the patient (your nursery), diagnose the problem, and suggest or implement a treatment. Good business consultants have studied in, managed, or in many cases owned their own businesses. Just as with doctors, some consultants finished at the top of their class and some at the bottom; nevertheless, all are doctors, or in this case, consultants.

As you would when choosing a doctor, check out the business consultant's references carefully before making a financial commitment. Also be sure to select a business consultant who matches the needs of your business and think about the areas you feel need to be improved before you began interviewing consultants. You will have to decide if you want someone who has worked in the nursery business before or someone with an outside perspective.

Nurseries usually need a business consultant after it is well established. Systems begin to break down or become inefficient at or near the level of one million dollars in gross sales. Just as you would not run to the doctor with every cold, so would you not waste time and money going to a business consultant with minor problems. The opposite is also true, of course, and if you wait until your nursery is comatose, no one short of a consulting priest who administers last rites is going to be of any help.

What should you expect when you hire business consultants? First of all, plan to spend lots of money, anywhere between $100 and $200 per hour for good business consultants. I know this sounds high, but remember that unlike nursery owners, they have no product to sell other than their time and knowledge. A good business consultant should be able to save you at least double their consulting fee in the first year—assuming you actually implement their recommended changes.

The hiring of business consultants presents a classic paradox since the time when they are most needed is the time when the nursery has the least money. The lack of immediate funds often becomes the justification for putting off such a decision, even when you know it's needed. Try looking at the choice to hire consultants in a different way: if your nursery is strapped for cash and has been so for a while, how could you afford to wait any longer?

Our experience with business consultants has been fascinating. Actually, I could throw in a few more adjectives such as stressful, humbling, mentally taxing, enlightening, disheartening, fast-paced, and exhaustive. That being said, I'd do it all over again tomorrow. I'll add that if you have low self-esteem or an over-inflated ego, forego the consultants. In a session with a consultant, expect a lot of questions about your business, your goals, and your view of your business's problems. Many consulting firms offer an initial examination session at a nominal charge. In this session, the consultant will determine if further work is warranted and, possibly, will give you an approximation of how long the process will take along with a price for the entire service. The consultant will next want to examine your business records from sales to delivery to production, staffing, accounting, and order processing. In most cases, good consultants will point out problems that you didn't even know were problems.

The quality of the consultant you hire will determine the final step. Many consultants simply leave you with a report of changes that they recommend but I prefer consultants who work with you to not only fully understand the changes but to also begin actually implementing them. While the first option may be less expensive, how many nursery owners actually have time to completely implement structural changes to their business given their current workload? You should also not assume that you will be finished when the consultant leaves your business. Just as you would with a doctor, you may have questions as you begin to implement the recommendations. Of course, regular checkups are essential to remaining healthy.

Pricing

One area where the nursery industry has consistently done a poor job is in the pricing of plants. While most other industries have priced their products well in relation to their actual costs and inflation, the nursery industry, and most other agricultural fields, have not followed suit. This failing is partly because most agricultural commodities receive government price supports, so consumers don't realize their true market value. There remains a great need for education about the value of a plant in both the wholesale and retail nursery businesses. Recall the old story of the nurseryman who was confronted about selling 1-gallon azaleas for $1.50 each when his cost of production was $3. The nurseryman acknowledged the discrepancy but replied that $1.50 was all that the market would bear; however, he made up the difference by selling in volume. This humorous tale well indicates how little nursery owners understand their actual costs, as well as how the prices of agricultural products have not kept pace with the cost of other items in our lives.

Despite the ludicrous nature of the above example, many large chain stores strive to achieve exactly that, the selling of plants for less than what was paid for them. These large chains use a plant as a "loss leader" in the hopes that the customer will purchase other items on which money can be made. Regardless of the motivation behind the loss leader strategy, it is not a good idea to try it with your own nursery stock.

Pricing strategies are certainly based on the market that you choose to serve. If your niche is to sell wholesale to mass marketers, your pricing range is limited by the accepted norm in this very competitive and price-sensitive segment of the industry. The more people who sell the same product, the more price sensitive that particular product becomes.

Conversely, if you decide to sell specialty plants that are not widely available, your plants are far less price sensitive, though you won't have the advantage of a large, ready-made market. In the case of some very rare plants, the cost of production can even be disregarded because prices can be set strictly by how much supply and demand there is. Pricing decisions will be based on how many plants you have and on what you can price them for, at the same time ensuring that you sell the desired number of them. Having a small number of a rare item and setting its price low would be an illogical pricing decision.

Two good strategies exist for pricing, both of which are rarely used by nursery owners. These strategies involve knowing your cost of production and understanding supply and demand. Instead of employing these strategies to set prices, nursery owners most often visit nearby competing nurseries to check their prices. They then return to their own nursery and set their prices simply by undercutting their competitors. I have never understood wanting to make less money than a competitor; surely it is more logical to get more money than a competitor for the same product. Nurseries should consider adopting the old pricing rule of thumb, which is that if 20 percent of your customers complain about the prices being too high then you have set them about right.

Retail sellers quickly learn about price barriers or "price points," as they are often called. Every item has a price point at which customers feel they are not getting good value. That is the point where sales will diminish. Some common price points in the nursery industry are $1, $5, $10, $15, and $20. This means that if you set a price at $4.00, you are not taking full advantage of the price point. In theory, you could go up to $4.99 without suffering any loss in sales. Check with your local or state university's agricultural economist for help in determining price points in your region. You could also gather your own information by doing some pricing experiments at your own nursery.

In determining the selling price of your plants, you will need to know your cost of production (we will discuss this next), which is the sum of overhead costs and direct costs. Then simply add your desired profit to that figure. Most nursery owners have never heard about adding profit as a part of product pricing; my own first encounter with this idea was when my business consultants discussed it with me. No longer should you think of profit as "what's left" at the end of the year. That extra money left over is in excess of your budgeted profit and is called "super profit." The difference between these two concepts is important: profit is budgeted, super profit is not. A typical profit for a nursery business should be between 15 and 25 percent—before your CPA tries to reduce your tax burden, that is.

Now that you understand profit, the next most important factor in determining pricing is the cost of production. More ways of doing this exist than there are folks to do the calculations. One basic method is to determine your expenses for the year. Take your overhead expenses (overhead includes your rent, mortgage, light bills, office salaries, phone bills, copier paper, and so on) and divide it by the number of usable square feet that you have under production. If your overhead expenses are $400,000 and you have 40,000 square feet in production, then your overhead cost per square foot of growing area per year is $10. You can break this down further into a cost per week by simply dividing this figure by 52, which makes your cost per square foot $0.19 per week or $0.027 per square foot per day. According to figures from Will Carlson (1999) of Michigan State, a successful greenhouse usually has overhead costs between $0.023 and $0.033 per square foot per day. These costs are obviously for greenhouses that are kept full and for crops that are sold when they become ready. You still pay the same overhead if your greenhouses are kept only half full, but you are paying for the unused space. In effect, your overhead costs per square foot are doubled. Be sure that when figuring costs you take out unusable production space such as walkways. Carlson states that the standard figure for losses in greenhouse plant production are between 2 and 3 percent, which should be included when you calculate your true production costs.

Another factor to include in your production cost equation is the crop turnover rate. Do your crops sell in a timely manner? If you crop is ready in three months but it takes you six additional months to sell it, then the cost to produce the plants has risen dramatically. If our cost from the example above is $0.19 per square foot per week but the crop takes six extra months to sell, we have added $0.19 for a period of 26 weeks, which is $4.94, to the cost of each square foot of crop. If we grow four plants per square foot, then our cost per plant has risen by $1.24 each. Often the profit margin is lost just by holding onto the plant for too long. This brings us to the concept of turnover rate.

Turnover is the number of times an entire crop is sold over the course of the year. For example, a crop that can be produced in three months should be turned over four times during the course of a year. Turnover, of course, varies with the time required for the crop to mature. Ideal turnover ratios are hard to determine, since the production times of nursery crops vary widely, but the key is, once you have determined your turnover rate, that you work to constantly improve it. To determine your current turnover rate, divide your annual sales by the retail value of your inventory. If your sales are $1,000,000 and you have an end-of-year inventory of 333,000, then you have a turnover ratio of three ($1,000,000 divided by $333,000 is 3). This would be considered a good turnover rate for most crops; one to five is a normal turnover rate for most nursery crops. If your turnover ratio is too low, then your plants are not selling fast enough. You may then need to look at your product mix, the size of your inventory, or ways to improve your sales.

Once you have determined your overhead cost per square foot, factoring in your turnover rate, you will need to add the direct cost of production for each item. If plant A has a direct cost of $5 per plant (this includes the cost of the liner, potting mix, pot, fertilizer, water, and pesticide) and you can fit four, trade-gallon plants into one square foot of greenhouse space (which results in a cost of $20 per square foot per year), then you have a direct production cost of $20 per square foot for this crop. Next add this amount to your overhead cost per square foot. If crop A requires one year of production time, the overhead cost is $10 per square foot. In this case your total production cost per four plants is $30 per year or $7.50 per plant. To make money, you will need to then use your markup percentage of 20 percent × cost to earn $36 per square feet or approximately $9 per plant to be profitable.

Let's examine another example using the direct cost of production to determine the cost of a flat of smaller plants. Assume you can fit nine, square, quart plants per square foot and that direct costs are $1 per plant. Using the same overhead costs from the earlier example, the cost per square foot per year is $10 or $0.19 per week. If this plant takes four weeks to ready for sale, then the cost of producing nine plants is $9 (direct cost) plus $0.76 (overhead cost), which is $9.76 (total production cost). The cost per plant is therefore $1.08. Using our 20 percent markup figure, we would need to sell these plants at $1.30 each to make the desired profit.

You can further refine the actual costs of individual crops with better record keeping. By carefully monitoring the labor costs per crop, you may be able to break out your labor costs from the overhead expense category and apply the actual labor costs directly to the cost of each crop. Designating how long each employee spent working with each crop would require a lot of record keeping.

Similarly, you could break down other expenses, such as shipping, by cost per crop to get a more accurate idea of the actual production cost of each item.

There is a much simpler method of determining your average selling price, though if you have a wide range of plant prices and sizes, it will not give you the production cost of each plant but a good, overall cost analysis instead. Take the total money that you spent (overhead plus direct costs) from the prior year's profit and loss statement (P & L), which in our example is $400,000. Into that number, divide the total number of plants sold during that year, say 50,000 plants. The average per plant cost to produce and deliver these plants was $8.00. Add our 20 percent profit to that $8.00, which brings our average selling price to $9.60 each. If you use this formula, are you going to be priced higher than most of your competitors? Probably yes—unless you can explain this simple system to them as well, though most nursery owners still boast using sales, not profit figures.

You will also need to develop a pricing markup strategy if you purchase plants for resale. Markup in the nursery industry typically averages three times cost, but it could range slightly lower or higher, depending on how fast you can turn the crop around or how big a loss you expect on the crop. Some retailers will make price adjustments and often use a reduced multiplier on already expensive items, figuring that the increased dollar profit per plant will make up for a smaller sales volume. The industry norm among retailers is to have a 50 percent gross profit (Pearson 2000).

Sales

Having produced and priced the plants, you now want to be paid for them. Among the first things is to determine is how you would like to be paid. Every nursery would, of course, rather receive payment when the items are sold or delivered, but this is not always possible. Typically, retail nurseries require payment up front, while wholesalers usually operate on a net-30 payment schedule. Payment options are ever changing, as even wholesale nurseries are adding a credit card payment option. What methods of payment will you accept, checks, cash, credit, debit cards, and purchase orders? Whatever method of payment you accept, be sure to let your customers know up front, as this will impact the number and amount of their purchases. As with all purchases in all industries, people are willing to spend more money if they don't have to pay immediately.

Retail nurseries typically deal in cash, checks, and credit and debit cards. It is amazing that some nurseries still don't accept credit cards. Credit cards typically charge a fee, which is a percentage of each transaction. The fees usually range between 1 and 5 percent, with 2 to 3 percent being the typical amount. When you are ready to accept credit cards, shop around at different banks for the best rate. Rates are based on criteria such as your past credit history, the average value of each transaction, and whether you actually see the credit cards or simply have access to the numbers by phone or fax. If you sell plants via mail order and see only the credit card numbers, the banks will charge you a slightly higher rate because the number of defaults are higher.

There is no question that credit cards offer an advantage to nurseries, especially since the money is available to the nursery almost as soon as the cards are charged. The owner of the credit card also wins, as there is no facing the bill for at least 30 days. This is the primary reason that most customers will spend much more money if credit cards are accepted. Many nurseries still do not accept credit cards because of the percentage that they are charged by the bank. I find this a shortsighted approach as accepting credit cards provides such a convenience to your customers and also increases your sales. If the profit-margin percentage on your plant is so small that you couldn't absorb a 2 to 3 percent credit card charge, you need to examine your pricing. On a $10 plant, a 3 percent charge would be a whopping 30 cents. Would it not be better for your nursery to raise the price of the plant $0.30 and accept credit cards?

Very few nurseries still process credit cards manually because of the increase in time and labor that is necessary. Only when electronic means are unavailable is manual processing still used. Banks vary on how much they charge for the electronic swipers, just as the swipers themselves vary in cost depending on the quality and speed of the processed transactions. Most banks charge upwards of $700 for these swipers, which the nursery will usually purchase. In some cases, the banks will give you the credit card processing equipment and simply build the cost of the equipment into a higher percentage for your charges.

Extending credit is quite different from accepting credit cards, since the nursery is strictly responsible for the collection of receivable monies. As soon as you begin to accept orders on credit, you will need to develop a new system of accounting to monitor billing and accounts receivable. "Accounts receivable" is an accounting term that designates money owed to a business from a customer who purchased items on credit. Typically, wholesale nurseries are the only ones that deal with accounts receivable on a large scale. Retailers will rarely need to extend credit and usually only to government agencies and botanical gardens whose purchasing systems are set up on purchase orders.

Many wholesalers operate primarily by extending credit. Proceed with caution, however, as this single practice has caused many a nursery to close shop. Make sure that prospective customers fill out credit applications and then thoroughly investigate their references. Most nurseries ask for the name of the customer's bank, the customer's account numbers, no fewer than three credit references from the trade, and a personal guarantee of debt. A personal guarantee involves getting the signature of the corporation's owner or officer to guarantee that there will be someone who is personally liable for the debt in case the corporation is unable to pay. Unfortunately, many corporations in the past have tried to use the corporate shield to avoid financial obligations that may later arise.

The worst culprits in the industry in terms of credit risk seem to be nurseries that operate on very narrow profit margins and landscape businesses that are poorly run and who have trouble collecting money from their own clients. If you decide to extend credit to these purchasers, you should develop a system that tracks late or early payment charges and a system that monitors and follows up on delinquent payments. Fortunately, most widely used accounting programs have an automatic program to track delinquent accounts.

The standard payment terms for nursery-extended credit is known as "net 30," which means that the customer owes the amount of the invoice 30 days after the date of the invoice. Many businesses also offer 2–10, which means that a 2 percent discount is given if the invoice is paid within ten days. Remember to add finance charges to late payments as you are at that point acting as a lending institution. If your bank is charging 10 percent on your loans, you would most certainly charge your customer this rate or slightly more. Your CPA will help you figure out an interest schedule for late payments.

It is critical that, should you choose to accept purchase orders, that you actually obtain a hard copy of the purchase orders, not just a purchase order number. The purchase order itself is considered a legal contract, whereas a purchase order number will probably not be enough in the case of a dispute. In an amazing number of cases, an employee of an institution will place orders without a supervisor's permission using only a purchase order number. A supervisor who later decides to rescind a written purchase order will be out of luck because once you have a signed copy of the purchase order, you have a binding contract. I strongly recommend getting credit references on anyone to whom you plan to extend credit under a purchase order system. Even a number of government agencies have a terrible track record of paying bills on time—surprise!

When custom-grown plant orders are prebooked in larger than normal amounts or ordered for delivery at a much later date than usual, it is accepted practice to require a prepayment percentage of the order as a deposit against default. This amount typically ranges from 10 to 50 percent. Prepayments are especially advisable when doing business with companies with which you do not have a long-standing relationship.

Mail-order nurseries face a different dilemma regarding payment. When orders begin to arrive for plants in the winter, it is often a month or two in advance of the actual shipping season. Two divergent theories exist on when and how to charge the customer for these orders. The first theory is to charge for, and reserve, the plants when the order is received. The plants are then held by the nursery and shipped when the customers are ready or when planting time has arrived in their hardiness zone. This system is actually more advantageous for gardeners in colder climates because the plants are purchased by the customer when they are ordered, but held and looked after by the nursery until the time of delivery.

Some customers do not like to have their checks cashed and credit cards charged when they place their orders but the nursery has few options unless it is heavily capitalized. You can always ask customers to give you the date they would like to have their credit cards charged and they will then receive what plants are available at that time. Not many other retail businesses would accept an order without payment and hold the item for months until the customer was ready for the product. The other option is to charge customers only when the plants are shipped. This is more advantageous to gardeners in warmer zones who might order three months later than a customer in the north but who request an earlier delivery date because they have better weather earlier in the season. Gardeners who send their orders in earlier are at a disadvantage if their local weather conditions mean they cannot accept their orders as early.

Whether to offer discounts on plants is a very individual decision. There is no question that discounting of plants—or any purchase—will increase sales volume, but does it make sense for your operation? In making this decision, take a look at your mission statement. If your goal is to sell large numbers of plants and you have a large growing area, then quantity discounts will certainly encourage an increase in sales and consequently the need for increased production. If your growing area is limited, however, and if production already can't keep up with demand, then why offer discounts?

Retailers will often be asked by landscapers and others in related fields for a "trade discount." Giving discounts can be a double-edged sword as what you will soon discover is that every homeowner who purchases more than one kind of plant, whether for their own garden or for a neighbor's, will come to expect a discount. Many people will quickly take advantage of your trade discounts, and their expectation of discounts on ridiculously tiny orders will kill your profit margins.

Retailers without the ability to say no to trade discount requests soon find themselves with a growing pseudo-wholesale business, although such was never their intent. Similarly, wholesalers who offer trade discounts find themselves selling to more demanding and costly retail customers who tend to buy less. If you choose to offer discounts, consider basing them on purchase volume. Many nurseries would, for example, offer a 5 percent discount on annual purchases over $1,000, 6 percent on $2,500, 8 percent on $5,000, and 10 percent on purchases of $10,000 or more. By setting high target levels for discounts, you will weed out many of these annoying "pseudo-businesses" and make the economics of discounts for large purchases work for you. Also, by linking the discounts to annual purchases, you will not exclude legitimate purchasers who don't only buy large quantities at one time.

Another way to weed out homeowners who try to purchase plants under the guise of being a legitimate business is to require some type of business license or certification. Many states require licenses or certifications as a way of determining which customers should be paying sales taxes on purchases.

Obviously nurseries and suppliers must be careful not to discourage legitimate start-up businesses by refusing to sell to them. When our business was quite small, I found a number of wholesalers that were unwilling to provide me with a catalog or sell to me because my business was at an awkward stage between a large hobby and a small nursery. What I quickly discovered is that it made a big difference when I acted like a business. This is often easier to do on the phone than it is in person. For example, it would be easier for the owner of a small nursery to call in an order to a supplier and have a conversation such as this: "Good morning, sales department please. This is Joe from Joe's Nursery and I need to place an order for delivery. How does your delivery schedule look for our area? We prefer to charge this to our credit card please." The idea is that if you want to be a business, you must act like a business and at least appear as though you have done this before.

Smaller retail and mail-order nurseries often feel the need to offer bonus or gift plants. Offers like these may be popular with your beginning gardeners, but if you are selling to more advanced gardeners, the bonus plants most often become compost. Sending a bonus plant is, to me, a way of telling customers that what you are selling them is somehow not worth what you are charging and so you will make it up to them with an extra plant. I doubt this practice is standard in any other industry, except perhaps as an inducement to try a new product.

Among the most important sales tools that emerged toward the end of the 1990s is the point of sales (POS) system. Point of sales systems are simply mechanisms to capture and track information about your customers and their preferences, an exercise that computers have made both more feasible and usable than in the past. Most POS information is captured in the retail environment through the use of bar code scanners. It will only be a matter of time before all nurseries and garden centers of any size are using bar codes. The customer's name would be entered into the computer along with the scanned bar codes of the purchases. This information goes into a database for that customer that contains demographic information (such as age and income) as well as purchasing preferences and buying habits. Information like this will help the nursery to better analyze its customers so that it, in turn, can determine what to buy or grow and how to target that customer with specific advertising and sales strategies. Bar code scanners also allow for the speedier checkout of your customers.

Internal nursery communications

Communication around the nursery is of utmost importance. If you don't have the ability to reach staff members when they are needed, you and your staff will waste a tremendous amount of time trying to track each other down. If your phone system doesn't allow for paging between your key employees, then you should invest in a two-way radio system. Just as it is with phone systems, the technology is advancing so rapidly that it is impossible for me to make specific recommendations. However, I will say that as far as radios are concerned, the old adage "you get what you pay for" is right on the mark.

Two-way radios vary with their output wattage, which regulates how far they will transmit and through what kinds of structures. Be sure to examine what type of batteries and rechargers are required, as well as their costs. Most of the better radios require an FCC license to operate, which is another added expense.

Planning for emergencies and disasters

Although most nursery owners put planning for emergencies at the bottom of their priority list, there is no question that adequate planning can help make a disaster much easier to recover from. Having the correct insurance coverage is a major start in the recovery process, as we will discuss later. There are several types of emergencies, those involving plants, those involving facilities, and those involving employees.

A backup power supply is key in dealing successfully with crop emergencies. Like a backup water supply, a generator is not a luxury but a necessity. Generators are usually gasoline powered, but less expensive tractor-mounted units can also be used. Be sure in either case that you have an adequate fuel supply on hand that is also easily accessible. The generating equipment should be properly maintained and tested at regular intervals.

When you lose power, you of course lose the ability to heat and cool greenhouses and irrigate your crops. When we had a rash of hurricanes move through North Carolina in 1996, many nurseries lost plants in the days following the storm as several days before power was restored in the area the sun had begun to shine again and the plants dried out. Where heating and cooling outages can cause the decline and death of plants, alarm systems are also essential in notifying you of problems. But remember that most phone systems, computers, storage coolers, and other such equipment will also be down during an electrical outage. It is essential that you work with an electrician to install generators with enough capacity to handle your critical needs during a disaster.

In addition to natural disasters, which are impossible to prevent, there are an amazing number of preventable disasters. Fires are the most common preventable disasters as they are often started through poor housekeeping, improper wiring, accidents, and acts of arson. At the very least, contact your local fire department regarding the proper storage of flammable materials, the number of fire extinguishers and smoke alarms that you need, and where to properly locate them. Be sure that rags used with combustible materials are disposed of outside of any storage area, and consider hiring a licensed electrician to inspect your operation for correct and up-to-date wiring.

Have you considered the possibility of a burglary at your nursery? It may sound strange, but some people actually believe that there may be something valuable in a nursery office. You will need to consider taking precautions to reduce the incidences of break-ins and fires in your nursery facilities; these can be done primarily through common sense preparation and care. For example, you should take the simple step of regularly backing up all computer records in your office and then taking a backup copy of the valuable files offsite, say to your home. Other critical information that should be stored in a fireproof storage area includes your insurance and accounting information, legal contracts, and personnel files. Taking such precautions will allow you a much easier recovery from this and other disasters.

If you lease your nursery facilities, make sure that the agreement you have with your landlord clarifies what happens if a disaster strikes and you are unable to continue running your business. Are you still liable for your lease payments or will they be temporarily suspended? How long does the landlord have to get the facilities back in shape so that you can use them again? It is also imperative that you carry an adequate renter's insurance policy and that you update it every year as your nursery grows.

Emergencies might also strike and injure your employees, and you will need to plan for those. Keep information regarding the location and phone number of emergency personnel, as well as the nearest medical facilities, prominently posted. First-aid kits should also be placed at regular intervals around your nursery. To lessen the impact that a disaster can have on your employees, instruct them how to act in the event of an emergency. I recommend including information on emergency procedures in the employment manual and beside the time clock.

Chapter 14

The Catalog

Often there is no better way for nurseries to promote themselves than through a catalog, and yet the quality of catalogs I have seen ranges from good to extremely poor. I continually hear nursery owners say that their catalogs are used as an availability list and that their customers already know which plants they are looking for. I concede that if you offer only a limited selection of basic "commodity" plants, then that may be the case, but it is certainly not true for most nurseries. How else would a customer know, for example, that a new and improved selection of an old standby that costs 10 or 20 percent more is worthy of the higher price? However, nothing does more to sell a nursery's plants than a catalog. (This is not true for garden centers, however, since they don't produce their own plants but purchase them from availability lists, making catalogs almost impossible to assemble.) A good catalog should list, in a logical order, the items you have for sale and include descriptions of those items and their prices. In addition, a catalog should say something about your nursery, contain contact information, and explain the terms of doing business.

What makes a good catalog?

How do you know what makes a good catalog? For starters, find one that appeals to you and analyze it to determine what you like about it. Next, decide how you are going to make your catalog appealing but also unique so that it stands out in a crowd. More than likely, some key factors such as good descriptions, good pictures, and good organization will allow you to make sense of it and find the particular items you're searching for.

Whether you operate a wholesale, retail, or mail-order nursery, the goal of the catalog should be to convince customers that they should purchase the products you offer. A customer is enticed by a good description of the plant, information on its culture, and, of course, color pictures. You've heard it before and you are hearing it again: color sells! The more high-quality color photos you use, the more of each plant you will sell.

Your catalog should also be easy to use. Some are so disorganized or use such illogical methods of organization that customers cannot find what they want or how to order it. Catalogs that use a bizarre array of confusing symbols, constantly sending the reader back to the symbol reference charts, never fail to amaze me. If you want to tell customers that the plant needs full sun or that it attracts hummingbirds, then say it.

Good descriptions are sadly lacking in many of today's catalogs. Often they are simply recopied from one catalog to the next, and with inaccurate information and minimal or worthless descriptions such as "red flrs, summer, 6 ft. tall." What does this really tell you about the plant? The answer is, of course, nothing! By reading most catalogs, you can tell that the people writing them have never actually seen the plants they are describing. We like to write our catalog while looking at the plant or, at the very least, a good photo of it. One of our typical descriptions would read:

> *Arisaema sikokianum* (Japanese Cobra Lily) $25.00
> Part Sun to Light Shade * Zone 4–8 * 15" tall * Origin: Japan
>   *A. sikokianum* is considered the most stunningly beautiful member of the genus *Arisaema* . . . make that the entire plant kingdom! From an underground tuber in early spring (early April in North Carolina), the dark pitcher and two, five-lobed leaves emerge on a 1' tall fleshy stalk. After flowering, the foliage remains attractive until it goes dormant in late summer. *A. sikokianum* prefers a dry, well-drained site in the garden.

There is a fine line between a good description and too much description, and between too much fluff and no fluff. You will simply have to determine what works best for you, though I always advocate too much rather than too little. Some catalogs simply list prices, hardiness zones, and flower color, and this lack of enthusiasm speaks volumes to customers. I have gone through a myriad of catalogs listing dozens of cultivars with which I was unfamiliar; if there had been even a modicum of description and a personal endorsement, I would have ordered at least three times the amount that I did.

Specialty catalogs are often written by plant geeks who can't relate well to the average customer. After writing our catalog, I always like to give it to a non-plant person and ask for comments. I ask my catalog critics two questions: how easy is it to use, and without knowing the plants, can you picture what they look like from the written descriptions? I recommend you leave your ego behind and ask for suggestions on how to make the catalog easy to use.

Some of you may be thinking you're not equipped to write a catalog, which is possibly quite true. Did you know about professional garden writers? There are hundreds of people in the Garden Writers Association (GWA) whose job it is to do just what you need. Perhaps by placing a simple ad or making a few phone calls you could secure a professional writer. As you would with all job applicants, request a portfolio from the candidates; anyone can walk in off the street and call themselves a garden writer. Local colleges with horticulture programs may also have viable candidates to help you with writing the catalog. Don't try to tackle something for which you don't have a talent, as the results will be less than satisfactory.

I like to begin each Plant Delights catalog with a personal message or brief introduction. Part of the catalog's function is to establish a personal relationship between your nursery and your customers. Some nursery owners write about the trials and tribulations of their family or pets, while others describe their plants or the goings-on at the nursery. The key is to write something that your customers will want to read and that will establish a personal bond between you and your customer. For example, it could talk a little bit about your nursery, when was it founded, who the officers are, and what your mission is. Does your catalog clearly explain how to transact business? What methods of payment do you accept? Do you ship plants, or will they have to be picked up at the nursery? We devote several pages at the beginning of our catalog to sections such as ordering, shipping, guarantees, and so on, each topic receiving an explanation and the headings always in boldface. Critical components that are too often omitted from or hard to find in most catalogs are contact numbers, such as phone and fax numbers, and e-mail addresses. I like contact numbers to appear, at a minimum, on every other page, often at the bottom; spending as much as ten minutes looking through a catalog, as I have done, just to find the phone number is unacceptable!

Be sure to thoroughly explain how a customer is to do business with your nursery. I have seen dozens of catalogs filled with wonderful plants, but when I tried to decipher the charges and the ordering and shipping information, I found it so difficult to understand that I never got around to sending in my order. Make sure it is clear what your guarantees are and what the size and price of your plants are. Is there a way for a customer to check on the availability of each item? Can the curious customer visit the nursery, and if so when and how? It is a good idea for catalog writers to order from other catalogs so they will see how easy ordering can be for a customer.

If your catalog is not clearly organized it will be pretty useless to your potential customer. Remember that data is of no use unless it can be processed into usable information. You can organize a catalog in many ways: by including a list of deer-resistant plants if you are in a deer-prone area; by listing plants by flower color or season of bloom if you are promoting color; or by color-coding the flowering plants if you are marketing primarily to landscape designers, who love catalogs that use the standard Royal Horticultural Society color charts. Whichever method of organization you use, I recommend that you supplement it with a cross-index.

If your catalog is organized into plant groups (for example, groups of trees, shrubs, annuals, perennials, and bulbs), an index of both Latin and common names would make the catalog much more useful. A customer who is looking for a plant by its Latin name would find an index of common names useless, and obviously the reverse is also true. Similarly, customers who want a groundcover would find an alphabetical listing helpful only if it were cross-referenced. A plant listing that a customer cannot find is a waste of your money and catalog space—and you have wasted the customer's time trying to locate it. As you can see, when you decide how to organize your catalog, you should think like your target customers; after all, your catalog is the guide to your nursery, so make it both complete and understandable.

The catalog cover

The first thing that customers see and remember about your catalog is the cover, and yet it is often given the least thought. No matter how great the information is inside your catalog, if your customer doesn't open the catalog or isn't inspired to keep it at hand, how much good is it? If you think a cover doesn't matter, stop at a bookstore and study the covers on a selection of magazines; you will soon realize that no part of the magazine receives more thought, time, and money than the cover. A memorable catalog cover is a great way to not only build name recognition for your nursery but also to keep your catalog at the top of a customer's heap.

Excite the customer! A catalog cover from Plant Delights Nursery.

Look at different catalogs: what would make you remember one over another? Are there particular catalogs that you use again and again? Can you name the catalogs that you use regularly and describe their covers? I'll bet you can remember only a few catalog covers, so what is it about these few covers that attracts your attention and draws you back to them?

What thought do you want to have associated with your nursery and how will you convey that through the catalog cover? I think having identical covers every year is a mistake, though it is understandable since it's one less thing to think about changing every year. What if your favorite magazine used the same cover each issue? I prefer a different catalog cover for each catalog, one that nevertheless continues to reflect the personality or theme of the nursery. It is amazing, but customers remember certain covers and the years during which they appeared. When customers call, they will actually refer to the plants that were listed the year we had a particular cover.

We at Plant Delights wanted to relay the image of a fun-loving nursery while also doing something that was completely distinctive, so we opted for a cartoon format. After all, where do most people turn first in their daily newspapers? (No, not the obituary section!) Our catalog covers feature cartoon parodies of current events or situations that most people know something about. We tried to create a cover that would not only be memorable to customers but would also become a collector's item. Think about those catalogs you keep for years and

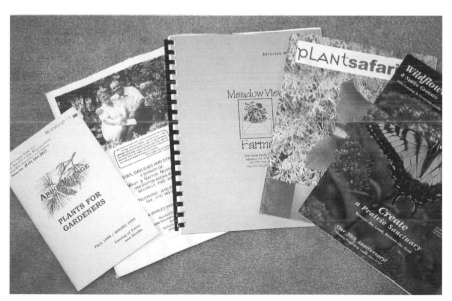

Appeal to your market. Other mail-order covers that appeal to different audiences.

those you throw away as soon as they arrive—no doubt the cover had something to do with your choices. Since you now realize that catalog cover art is a critical component of your catalog, consider hiring a professional artist, photographer, or graphic designer to help with the cover.

Selecting the items to feature in the catalog

When you begin selecting what to feature in your catalog, refer back to your mission statement to help determine if a potential listing will fit within your nursery focus. You will want to offer enough items to make it worth the customer's time looking through your catalog, but not so many that the customer is confused and loses interest. I've received catalogs that are so extensive that it literally takes weeks for me to finish going through their offerings. I usually put these epic catalogs off to the side until I have more time, which may take months—if I ever get around to reading them again at all. Most customers are not persistent enough to stick with these massive catalogs long enough to actually get an order together.

Specialty nurseries may list 500 to 1000 cultivars of a particular plant genus. While a few collectors are driven to collect every plant with a name, are there really that many plants of a particular genus that are truly distinctive, or are you simply selling differing plant names? I contend that if you have trouble writing distinctive descriptions for each plant cultivar, then you've got too many similar cultivars. In reality, massive collector lists leave most customers so confused that they will actually order less, if they order at all.

For the long-term success of your nursery, be sure that the plants you offer in your catalog are going to make good garden specimens in your market area. If you consistently offer plants that are quick and easy to produce but don't grow well in your region of sales, you are doing yourself a long-term disservice in the name of short-term profit.

What is often overlooked in selecting offerings is the process of costing out the catalog. Let's say that to cover expenses (overhead costs plus direct costs plus desired profit) the nursery must produce sales of $1,000,000. If your catalog has 96 pages, then each page must generate $10,416. Unfortunately, all pages will not contain sellable plants. Let's allocate 20 pages to text that contains a welcome, the instructions, the table of contents, the indexes, and so on. This means that 76 pages of plants must generate the same $1,000,000, which equates to $13,158 per page. Assuming that you can display and describe ten plants per page, each plant must generate $1,315 in sales.

If at the end of the season you find that certain plants do not pay for their space in the catalog, you must decide whether to continue to offer these plants. I am certainly not saying that you should drop all plants that do not reach a set economic threshold, but you will need to consider which of these plants to continue offering and which to drop. Keep in mind that when you are introducing a new plant to the market, it could take three to five years for the plant to catch on, in which case you may have to suffer a few years of low sales. A particular plant may be a poor seller but is desired by one or more of your good customers in marginally economic quantities. You will have to decide if the plant is worth offering as a way of keeping a good customer happy.

Plant nomenclature

Nomenclature may seem like a small thing to a nursery owner, but a catalog without good nomenclature can certainly hurt sales and also credibility. To understand why, again try to think like a customer: would you order from a clothes catalog that was filled with misspellings or incorrect names on the catalog items? Many nursery customers will immediately discard catalogs that are filled with nomenclature errors as they will assume that the nursery not only grows its plants with the same inattention to detail but that it also does not understand the plants it grows.

Years ago I received a catalog from a regional tree and shrub wholesaler. I was very impressed with the selections but was appalled and distracted by hundreds of simple misspellings. After first discarding the catalog I later retrieved it, red pen in hand, and corrected all the spelling errors. I mailed the catalog back to the nursery owner with a note telling him I liked his catalog offerings and that I hoped my corrections would help him be more successful. Nearly ten years later I met this nurseryman at a trade show; he introduced himself saying that he had been furious with my comments and that it was only years later when he realized that they were indeed a favor. He ended our conversation with a thank you, and the nursery has since become among the top regional growers.

Botanical or horticultural nomenclature can be quite intimidating to those who are just starting in the nursery business. You will quickly learn, however, that listing plants using only common names is a nightmare. Not only do common names vary from region to region but the same common name may also apply to several different plants. Whether you like it or not, you will have to learn a bit of Latin, and I strongly recommend using both botanical and common names wherever possible. Books such as Stearn's (1992) *Botanical Latin* will be very helpful in explaining many of these seemingly meaningless words.

The Latin names of plants are used so that each plant will have only one unique name that can be used around the world. Deciphering Latin plant names is actually quite simple once you understand a few basic rules. In the binomial plant nomenclature system, the first name of the plant is the genus (which is always capitalized), while the second is the species (which is always lowercased).

Where a plant of a species is selected for a particular quality that makes it different from the norm, it is given a cultivar (meaning *cultivated variety*) name, and this third name is always capitalized and enclosed with single quotes; an example of such a name is *Veronica repens* 'Sunshine'. When a cultivar is not a selection of a single species but a hybrid of two or more species, the genus name is followed immediately by the cultivar name. There is no species given, since more than one species contributed to the plant's origin. An example of a hybrid is *Veronica* 'Royal Candles'.

Another exception to the third name being the cultivar name occurs when a species of plant has several naturally occurring but distinct forms, varieties, or subspecies, usually from different native ranges. These are referred to as varieties (var.), subspecies (subsp.), or forms (forma or f.). In these cases, the plant has two lower case names after the genus: *Amsonia ciliata* var. *filifolia* and *Agave parryi* subsp. *huachucensis*.

Although most cultivars are propagated by vegetative asexual means such as cuttings, divisions, or grafts, some cultivars are still grown from seed. The most common examples would be annuals and some perennials such as aquilegias or columbines, where the parent plants are hybridized until they reproduce relatively true as a seed strain. Individuals within a seed-grown cultivar are fairly similar but there is always a small degree of genetic variation; however, they still are valid cultivars. When cultivars are completely identical and are propagated vegetatively from cuttings or divisions, the selections are called clones, which distinguishes them from seed-grown cultivars. Cloned plants are absolutely identical, even down to their genes. In short, all clones are cultivars but not all cultivars are clones.

Plant nomenclature is governed by two publications, *The International Code of Botanical Nomenclature* (ICBN) (Greuter et al. 1994) and *The International Code of Nomenclature for Cultivated Plants 1995* (ICNCP) (Trehane et al. 1995). Although it is the purpose of these codes to add stability to the naming of plants and to enhance the communication about plants for gardeners around the world, they are constantly changing in an attempt to address ongoing issues regarding plant names. While botanists and taxonomists are more concerned with the ICBN, it is the ICNCP that is of greater interest to horticulturists and nursery owners.

Since January 1, 1959, all new cultivar names must be composed of words in a modern language. In other words, no "Latinized" names are legitimate after this date. Cultivar names such as 'Variegata', 'Pendula', or 'Robusta' are no longer valid unless they were officially published prior to 1959. Cultivar names published after 1959 would more likely be 'Silver Stripe', 'Cascading Falls', or 'Whiskey Barrel'.

The Latin words that make up a plant's name all have meaning, though some meanings are more obvious than others. Most species names denote plant characteristics: *hirsutus* means hairy; *bilobus* means "having two lobes"; *axillaris* pertains to the leaf axils; *asteroides* means like a star or aster; *crispatus* means crinkly or curled; *decapetalus* means having ten petals; and *conspicuus* means "easily seen" or "showy." Other plant species names pertain to where the plant was discovered. *Bonariensis*, for example, refers to Buenos Aires, *balcanicus* to the Balkans, *sibiricus* to Siberia, and *novae-angliae* to New England. Most remaining names are derived from the person for whom the plant was named, such as *Hosta sieboldiana*, which is named after Von Siebold; *Buddleia forrestii*, named after George Forrest; *Arisaema wilsonii* after E. H. Wilson; and *Hosta yingeri* after Barry Yinger. A good reference to the meaning of plant names is the *Gardener's Latin* (Neal 1992).

Unfortunately, plant names are often less permanent than we would like. Plants sometimes have their names changed by people called taxonomists, although I have heard them called much worse. It certainly seems like the sole purpose of a taxonomist (a high-dollar botanist) is to give headaches to garden writers and nursery owners by changing plant names; I call it job security.

It seems that as soon as we learn a plant name it gets changed. In reality there are very few nomenclature changes and even good reasons behind what seems to be madness. A taxonomist may discover through research that another taxonomist had previously published a different name for the same plant prior to the adoption of the currently accepted name. (This problem is most commonly encountered when taxonomists in different countries fail to communicate between institutions in other countries.) According to the ICNCP, the first validly published name must take precedence. A typical example is the genus known today as *Hosta*, which was formerly known as *Funkia*. Through research, it was discovered that the same plant was earlier named *Hosta*. Therefore, the name was changed from *Funkia* to *Hosta*, thank goodness. Interestingly, the International Botanical Congress adopted an appeal provision in 1950 (called the Committee for Spermatophyta or CS) that, if approved, will allow the conservation of the later published but more popular name for economically important plants.

Another reason that plant names may be changed is because of the two divisions of taxonomists, the lumpers and the splitters. Lumpers believe that a species range is large and that many different looking populations of individual plants can comprise the same large species. Lumpers often take several known species that look superficially different and combine them all into one single species. This is what happened with the popular ornamental grasses, *Muhlenbergia capillaris* and *M. filipes*. While the two species look similar, one flowers three months before the other, and the species was resplit several decades later. Splitters, on the other hand, believe that minute differences between plant populations warrant designating a new species or genus. This was the case with the genus *Chrysanthemum*, which in the 1960s was split into *Argyranthemum, Dendran-*

thema, *Leucanthemum*, and *Ajania* based on small variances. Mother Nature, not being one to cater to our often myopic perspectives, has not provided clear dividing lines; the task of taxonomists is often, therefore, one of guesswork and opinions.

Within this framework of genus or species name changes, the cultivar name always stays the same. The only exception is when a plant is moved into a genus that already has a plant with the same cultivar name. Luckily, having to change a cultivar name is very rare.

A third reason for a plant name change arises when it is determined that plants in the trade were simply misidentified. While technically this is not a name change, the effects on your catalog will be the same. A name change could obviously be the result of a mistake in the genus, species, or cultivar name. There is no good method of verifying plant names without having to do quite a bit of work. If you have doubts about the identity of a plant that you are growing, I encourage you to make an effort to verify its accuracy through the use of area botanical gardens, local experts, and the Internet.

It is interesting that there is no final review board for name changes in horticultural taxonomy. When a particular taxonomist publishes a plant name change in an official botanical publication, these name changes become "accepted" only if other taxonomists begin to use them. The idea is that the published work of bad taxonomists simply gets ignored. As you can imagine, without a publication that lists all proposed plant name changes, the current system for accepting a new plant name creates a giant mess for horticulturists, especially for catalog writers who don't know what to believe.

The rapidly developing field of genetic fingerprinting promises to have a dramatic impact on the field of plant taxonomy and to add a plethora of future name changes. Genetic fingerprinting allows taxonomists to compare the genetic makeup of one plant to other related plants. In the past, plants were classified based primarily on floral and seed characteristics, and now there is this additional tool in determining the relationships among plants. Genetic analysis has revealed that some plants within the same genera are actually unrelated.

In determining when to change a plant name in your catalog and on your labels, I think it is better to adopt a cautious approach. I don't hesitate correcting the name of a misidentified plant, but I am very careful with other changes. Since the entire purpose of horticulture nomenclature is to communicate accurately, I suggest that you continue to use the more commonly recognized Latin name until the horticulture community accepts a new name as the industry standard. Nursery growers who change labels every time taxonomists change a name only confuse their workers and customers.

Principle 5 of the ICNCP holds that "Each taxonomic group of cultivated plants with a particular circumscription can bear only one accepted epithet, the earliest that is in accordance with the Rules." Principle 6 of the Code deals with cultivar epithets. Epithets must be "universally available in all countries for use by any person to denote a particular cultivar." This means that plant cultivars with valid names cannot be renamed once they have been published or established in the trade. No matter how unmarketable a name the breeder gives the plant or how unpronounceable that name is, it cannot be changed for those reasons. A good example is *Dianthus* 'Feuerhexe', which in the United States is sold as *Dianthus* 'Firewitch'. While 'Firewitch' is easier to pronounce, it is not a valid cultivar name for this plant; it is simply an English translation of the German 'Feuerhexe'. Firewitch dianthus should only be used as a common name for *Dianthus* 'Feuerhexe'. Preamble 9 states that "The only proper reasons for changing a name are either a more profound knowledge of the facts resulting from adequate taxonomic study or the necessity of giving up a nomenclature that is contrary to the Rules."

While I will address the legalities of trademarks in the next chapter, I should mention here how they affect plant nomenclature. Principle 6 further states, "In some countries, plants are marketed using trademarks. Such marks are assigned to a person or some corporate body and are not therefore universally available for any person to use; consequently, they cannot be considered cultivar epithets." What should be a very straightforward system of naming plants has now been muddied, nearly beyond hope, by the incorrect use of trademarks. In an attempt to keep plants as a sales exclusive, many larger nurseries began adding trademarks (TM) or registered trademarks (R) to the end of the cultivar name. This is both an improper and unenforceable use of the trademark, not to mention a nightmare of confusion for catalog writers! Every plant has only one valid cultivar name (which is designated in single quotes) that must remain free for everyone to use and cannot be trademarked. Trademark names are intended to designate only the origin of a plant or a brand of plants.

Finally, Article 17 of the ICNCP deals with actual cultivar names. Subsection 17.9, which is pertinent to the issue of trademark, holds that "To be established, a new cultivar epithet published on or after 1 January 1959 must be a word or words in a modern language." Now that we understand the basis for naming plants, let's look at how the improper use of trademarks has made a mockery of the spirit of the Code.

When nurseries finally realized that trademarking cultivar names was a violation of the Code, they began giving their new plant introductions nonsensical cultivar names that do not adhere to the Code, at least not unless you have a slick lawyer interpreting it. These nonsensical names often contain the first few letters of the name of the nursery and end with a series of extraneous letters. Nurseries then market the plants under their "good" selling name, which is then trademarked. Confusion results, as labels and advertisements often refer to these plants only with the trademarked names. The misled public soon thinks that the trademark name is actually the cultivar name.

Trademark names do not have to be associated with only one product. For example, a nursery may sell 100 different plants under the same trademark name, but only one at a particular time. If the owner of the trademark runs out of the cultivar that it is currently selling as such, it can legally substitute another cultivar and sell it under the same trademark name. In other words, there could be ten different cultivars sold over time that have the same trademark name. Cultivar names, on the other hand, can be associated with one and only one plant until the end of time. Article 11 of the ICNCP draws attention to *Rosa* 'Korlanum', which is marketed under three different trademark names, Surrey, Sommerwind, and Vente D'Été. In the case of *Loropetalum chinense* 'Hines Purpleleaf', a valid cultivar name, the same plant is marketed under at least four different trademark names by different nurseries. Are you confused yet?

The trend toward the improper and confusing use of trademarks, both by growers and marketers, has done an irreparable long-term disservice to the nursery industry by creating great confusion not only in the naming of plants but also in actually communicating about them. An otherwise wonderful book published in the late 1990s by a notable professor of horticulture contains references to a plant's marketing name rather than its correct horticultural name— no wonder trademark names trip up the rest of us!

Trademark names, as they are currently used, are highly confusing to the gardening public, in part because the public doesn't know to read the plant label. These labels should, according to trademark law and the Code, have the true cultivar name in single quotes. The best way to end the practice of intentionally confusing our horticultural language is for reputable nurseries and consumers to take a public stand against it. Short of this, it is going to be up to nursery catalog writers to identify plants by their one and only cultivar name and perhaps at the same time embarrass nurseries that persist in making up stupid, nonsensical names for new plants. For the long-term good of horticulture, I hope you will take up this cause!

How and when to print and mail a catalog

As a general rule, wholesale catalogs should be sent in late August and September, whereas retail catalogs that are sent so they arrive near the first of the year seem to be the most successful. Even within this broad scheme, getting the timing right is critical. When to send a catalog depends on the market. Wholesalers who cater to landscape installers find that their work tends to pick up in the fall, as does the garden center market. Many nursery retailers also prefer to order their plants in the fall for spring delivery. If a wholesale catalog arrives too early in the summer, no one will pay it much attention, but if it arrives too late in the fall, most customers will have already placed their orders, and sales will only pick up when other wholesalers run short on inventory.

No matter when you time your catalog's arrival, it is critical that wholesalers develop a way for updated availability lists to reach their customers throughout the season. Whether wholesalers send these lists via fax, e-mail, or other means, sending updated lists is critical to maintaining contact with your customers and to moving excess inventory.

Customers of retailers, especially mail-order retailers, tend to make most of their purchases in the spring. The primary exception to this trend is the nursery that offers bulb-type crops, which sell best in the fall. Most nurseries would prefer to increase fall sales and fall planting, but peak interest in purchasing plants will always be in the spring after a winter of rest and time away from the garden. This is not to say that fall ordering and planting is nonexistent, but it is a small fraction of the spring business. Retailers that issue their only retail catalog in the fall should follow it up again with some type of reminder in early spring.

I like to time retail mail-order catalogs so that they arrive after the Christmas holidays. In many households, catalogs that arrive before Christmas are often lost or forgotten in the holiday rush. Conversely, catalogs that arrive too late, usually in the midst of spring gardening season, are also often overlooked. Many mail-order customers actually allocate a certain budget each year for plants and they usually spend it on the first catalogs that arrive. Therefore, if your catalog arrives too late, many customers may have no money left.

Some retail mail-order nurseries, especially those that sell woody plants, prefer to ship in the fall and winter, issuing their catalogs in the fall. Although this strategy makes shipping easier, the volume of sales will be significantly less than what it would be if the catalog and shipping occurred during the spring season. There is little question that the customer would be better off with dormant plants that are shipped in the fall, but it's hard to fight human nature, especially the desire to garden in spring.

One interesting trick that many nurseries borrow from other industries is the issuance of several duplicate catalogs each year. The theory is that customers are more likely to order if they are deluged with catalogs, say four to six times a year, each one reminding them that they have not yet placed an order. Each catalog has the same content pages; only the cover changes with each mailing. My belief is that this practice wastes my time, and it certainly wastes paper. Perhaps when there were fewer catalogs being sent out, and certainly before the advent of on-line catalogs, this strategy might have worked, but I get very upset and frustrated when I take time to peruse a catalog only to find that I have already been there and done that! Better alternatives to mailing duplicate catalogs include sending a spring or fall update, an updated availability list, or a simple flyer or card reminding the customer that it's still a good time to order.

The next question to ask is whether to charge money for your catalogs. Most wholesalers give their catalogs away as part of the cost of doing business, whereas the trend in the retail mail-order industry has been to charge a few dollars. Virtually all the larger mail-order companies give away their catalogs for free, the premise being that this method attracts a larger customer base than it would otherwise as it includes those who are unwilling to pay for a catalog. The theory behind charging for a catalog is that you are culling those who would also be unlikely to spend money on plants but who wanted your catalog as reading material. While charging for your catalog does improve cash flow, it doesn't create the goodwill that comes with giving catalogs away for free. Conversely, the more you charge for your catalog, the more perceived value it has.

If you choose to charge for your catalog, be aware that you will not be charging your current customers but only potential new customers who request a catalog. Be sure to charge enough to make up for the time spent processing the checks, as labor costs can quickly eat up a small catalog charge.

We, like all retail mail-order nurseries, were faced with this dilemma in the early years of operation. We wanted to do something that would give our catalog value but without actually charging for it. We studied other nurseries and actually found several nurseries that refused to send out a catalog without the requisite $2 to $4 fee. I was never able to rationalize the economics of this, especially when the nursery would send the prospective customer a letter requesting payment before the catalog could be sent. This is a classic example of false economy where a business actually spends $2 to collect $1. Our solution was to request payment either in the form of postage stamps or a box of chocolates. Our in-house policy was that catalogs were actually free and would be sent to anyone, but when the catalog was promoted, our "catalog price" was stated as "ten stamps or a box of chocolates." Not only did this give the catalog value but it also allowed us not to have to cash small checks or purchase stamps for mailing the catalogs. An obvious side benefit was that our employees received an additional employment benefit as they enjoyed hundreds and hundreds of boxes of chocolates each season. No doubt there is a wide array of other creative solutions that have not yet been explored.

Catalog layout and design

Having made all the decisions about catalog content and when to publish, you are now faced with the job of laying out the catalog. Catalog layout focuses on what goes where and in what format. You may think this is not as critical as content but trust me, without good layout, customers can completely miss information that is right in front of them. Why do you think grocery-store vendors are so concerned about shelf space location and even offer incentives to have certain items placed on particular spots on the shelf? There is indeed a science in determining how the eye moves and, in turn, how we take in information.

I strongly recommend studying as many catalogs as possible to garner ideas from the best ones. Ideas are simply concepts, not exact formats or designs—and certainly not the text—as these are copyrighted. There is a fine line between plagiarism and the age-old concept of borrowing ideas.

The industry of graphic design has exploded as more and more people realized the value of this formerly overlooked skill. It is the job of a graphic designer to determine and arrange the catalog's size and format, determine the page margins, decide how to index the catalog and best use cross-reference charts, select font styles for the type, and so on. Something as simple as using the wrong font or printing the entire text in capital letters will make your catalog incredibly hard on the eyes and will cause your customer to overlook much of the text. Similarly, certain fonts may look artistically pretty but are virtually unreadable. While a good font can set the tone for your catalog, the wrong font can also be your biggest headache when it comes time to work with a printer. Be sure to ask potential printers to determine if your selection of fonts are compatible with their equipment before you begin to format your catalog.

Do-it-yourselfers with knowledge of desktop publishing now have the ability to create great, professional-looking catalogs. A wide range of desktop publishing programs allows small businesses that are computer-savvy to take on the task of laying out a catalog themselves.

Printing the catalog

One agonizing decision that has to be made is how many copies of the catalog to print. While you don't want to have catalogs left at the end of your season, you also don't want to run out of them too early. Unless you are a retail nursery, you aren't going to sell many plants if your customers don't have your catalog. However, catalog printing and mailing is very expensive, so don't send off more catalogs than you can afford.

Far too many nurseries simply assume that if they send out more catalogs or add color that they will make more money. There is little doubt that your sales will increase (after all, color does sell), but will the increase in sales be enough to cover your greatly increased expenses and still create a profit? If you keep accurate records over the years, the decision of how many copies to print becomes much easier. Using those records, look at the number you printed the previous year and multiply it by what your track record indicates will be your expected growth rate.

Keep in mind that any special events you intend to participate in during the season, such as presentations and trade shows, will necessitate printing extra catalogs. If you want to expand your potential customer base (you could do this by purchasing a mailing list), you may decide to print extra catalogs for this purpose. As with most purchases, price discounts increase in proportion to the quantity ordered. In the printing business, the per copy cost of printing a catalog drops dramatically as the size of the print run increases because many of the setup and related costs stay the same for a large and a small print run; only the amount of paper varies, but paper is relatively cheap.

A staggering number of smaller decisions have to be made when you move from the world of copy centers to that of printers. To begin with, you must determine the weight, size, finish, and quality of the paper you use, both for the catalog and the cover. The thicker the paper and the better the finish (gloss is a better finish than flat), the higher the cost. This higher cost must be balanced against the durability of the catalog and the perceived value of the items inside. In other words, while printing on low quality paper or even newsprint is much less expensive, the use of such paper translates into less perceived value for the plants inside. The type of paper you select, even if it is only significantly thicker, also affects the cost of mailing, since the thickness of the paper increases the weight of the catalog.

Will your catalog be in black and white or color? If you want a color catalog, what type of color process will you use, two color, four color, or more? The least expensive way to add color photos to a catalog is to place them on separate pages that are grouped together in one or two places inside the catalog. This is usually most economical on either a two- or four-color press. In order to print a full-color catalog where pictures appear on each page that contains a description of the plant, search out a printer with a Web-style press as it will be more economical. While it is often tempting to use paper with a background color other than white, this is usually a disaster as not only will the cost be higher, but readability will likely be reduced.

When printing pictures, you will need to pay close attention to how the photos are scanned. Scanning is the process by which slides and photos are transferred into an electronic format that can be reproduced in the catalog. There are many scanners to consider, from large-drum scanners to flatbed scanners. The higher quality (and more expensive) the scanner, the better the resolution of the resulting scans. If your intent is to sell more plants, the last thing you want is poorly scanned photos.

Be sure to get quotes from a number of printers as the printing industry has tremendous price variation for the same job. The type of printing equipment that is used will make a difference in the price of the job; generally, printers that use a two- or four-color press will be more competitive on smaller runs. Printers with large, Web-type presses will usually be more competitive on larger runs. Remember too, that the more detailed specifications you can give the printer, the less money will have to be built into the bid to cover anything you hadn't initially thought of.

More so than with any other business, I like to check the references of a printer. The most obvious area of inquiry is the quality of the printer's work; after all, if your catalog contains a lot of mistakes and must be reprinted, have you gained anything by saving a few dollars on the initial printing costs? Does the company always deliver the catalogs on time? If you are waiting for a catalog to take to a trade show or are hoping to target a particular mailing date, any delay in the catalog being completed on time will cost you plenty of money.

Once you select a printer you should sit down together to work out a schedule as well as a contract that spells out the printer's responsibilities. It is important to specify not only a date when the catalog will be printed but also a date for you to deliver specific items to the printer. Some nurseries include a penalty

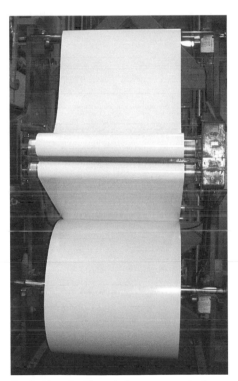

Really big rolls. The printing process starts with the selection of paper. Henry Wurst, Inc., North Carolina.

Roll the presses! The catalog printing process. Henry Wurst, Inc., North Carolina.

clause for a printer's late delivery, but while this may assure a timely completion, the printer will likely build in an added amount to his overall quote to cover this eventuality. Be aware that all printers, because of the nature of printing, have press overruns; if you order 10,000 catalogs, you could routinely expect overruns of 5 to 10 percent. As it is common practice for the customer to purchase these overruns, you should specify in your meeting with the printer that you will accept only a certain percentage of overruns.

Is it right? The color- and text-proofing stage is the last place to catch major errors. Henry Wurst, Inc., North Carolina.

Cutting it down to size. After printing, the trimmer makes the final cuts. Henry Wurst, Inc., North Carolina.

A stitch in time. Binding and stitching includes assembling the printed pages into a cohesive catalog. Henry Wurst, Inc., North Carolina.

In these electronic times, you will save a tremendous amount of money if all data transfers can be done electronically. The more manual work you require of your printer, the higher your printing costs will be.

Mailing the catalog

If you mail your catalog to a significant number of people (usually more than 200 recipients), you need to understand bulk mail and bulk mailers. Bulk mail refers to identical pieces of mail that are sent in large quantities to different addresses. The United States post office sets bulk rates, but these rates vary depending on a number of factors, including the size of the piece being sent and the type of addresses. Sending a catalog via bulk mail typically costs about 15 percent of first class postage. Although bulk mail doesn't usually get delivered quite as fast and some pieces get lost, the savings usually far outweigh these problems. If, for example, you mailed 100,000 catalogs at a bulk rate of $0.30 each, your postage bill would be $30,000. The same catalog mailed via first class would cost $2.00 each, for a total cost of $200,000.

While anyone can send bulk mail directly through the post office, the amount of regulations involved in trying to do so are comparable to attempting to understand the most complex botanical manual. Some nurseries still try to

Where's it going now? Automatically ink-jet addresses on the catalog to save time pasting on mailing labels. Henry Wurst, Inc., North Carolina.

Sort of. After addressing the catalogs, your bulk mailer will automatically sort them by destination for the best possible postage rate. Henry Wurst, Inc., North Carolina.

do their own bulk mailing by bringing in dozens of extra staff to print address labels, attach them to the catalogs, sort the catalogs by zip codes, bind them into bundles of a specified size with rubber bands of a specified size, and put these bundles into approved bags. The reason for these complicated rules is that the post office doesn't actually want to deal with individuals who are sending bulk mail; it prefers to direct their business to companies whose sole purpose is to do nothing but bulk mail for commercial customers. These companies are called bulk mailers and they are designed to accommodate all different types and sizes of mailings. Bulk mailers that deal with smaller bulk mailings (several hundred pieces) are often located in easily accessible areas such as malls, whereas those that deal with thousands to millions of pieces of mail are usually located in out-of-the-way places in an attempt to reduce overhead. Most larger printers have their own bulk mail capabilities, so be sure to ask about this service when you interview printers. Also discuss having addresses ink-jetted directly onto the catalog as this will save you from having to manually paste on address labels.

Bulk mailers operate on a very small markup and large volumes. They have to stay abreast of the ins and outs of the post office bulk mailing system, so despite their charges, they can save you a tremendous amount of money. Bulk mailers have an individual permit number that allows them to send bulk mail, so if you plan to use a bulk mailer, you must print this permit number on the back of your catalog. Bulk mailers are required to pay the post office for postage at the time of mailing and they will therefore usually require payment for postage before the piece is mailed; you will have to plan for this expense. They do not make money on the actual postage charge.

Bulk mailers stay in business by charging a fee for each service that they perform, and each service generally costs a few cents per piece. For example, they will address the catalog for you if you furnish them a mailing list on a disk, stripping your mailing address of duplicate addresses (a very cost-effective service), correcting addresses and zip codes, and adding special messages to catalogs being sent to a certain region. Bulk mailers are also very helpful in making sure the outside of your catalog fits postal regulations and in selecting the correct postal terms for your catalog such as "address correction requested." The wording that the post office requires for these procedures often changes, so be sure to ask your bulk mailer which terms or phrases will get the desired results. You may think this is insignificant, but if you put the wrong service wording on your mailed catalog you may be faced with thousands of dollars worth of service charges imposed by the post office.

Chapter 15

New Plants

With the bevy of new plants hitting the market each year, it sometimes seems as though there is a new-plant factory somewhere churning them all out. New plants actually come to market from plant enthusiasts, who find these plants as mutations or seedlings in their nurseries, discover them in the wild, or develop them through plant breeding. New plants can be either created hybrids or improved cultivars of a natural species.

Interestingly, it has been the amateur gardener who, throughout history, has developed far more new plants than nursery owners. Perhaps this is because nursery owners spend more time on the operation of the nursery than they do on developing new plants. In the 1990s, however, there was a dramatic shift in new plant development as more and more commercial nurseries took this on.

In developing a breeding program, nursery owners should always select plants that are unique and dramatically better than the industry standard. Plants that are only slight improvements don't generally gain widespread acceptance but instead clutter the market. It would be worthless, for example, to select a new cultivar of American holly that had a few more berries or was 1 foot taller. An American holly that had twice the number of berries or red foliage instead of green, however, would be a worthwhile selection.

It is, unfortunately, the natural tendency of inexperienced breeders to introduce every offspring that is only slightly different. It takes experienced breeders years or even a lifetime to develop distinctive breeding lines and produce a hybrid that is truly worthwhile and unique. As a breeder you must also learn to be ruthless when making selections. For example, in our hosta-breeding program, we will start with 20,000 seedlings and only pot about 2,000 plants. By the end of the first year we will keep only 500 plants from the current crop, and that number will drop to 200 by the following spring. Of this, most will be used in further breeding. It is likely that no more than one hosta plant in 50,000 to 100,000 will be worthy of introduction. Only when there has been no prior breeding work in a particular genus do random or first generation crosses yield plants that are truly worthy of introduction.

Most of the best new plants are actually discovered as mutations or sports on existing species or cultivars. For example, a white-edged branch that appears on a holly could be rooted; in most cases it will retain the new characteristics. Many folks visit nurseries and garden retailers looking for plant sports, a pastime that has gained the moniker "sport fishing." Assuming the mutation does not change the growth habit of the plant in an undesirable way, there is a much higher probability of getting a marketable plant from a sport than a seedling.

The number of new plants entering the market is dizzying with the United States and Japan leading the way, a distinction that was usurped from Europe in the 1990s. So how exactly does, and should, a new plant get to market, and how many plants do you need before offering a new plant? First look at the potential markets (which I describe later) and determine where your new plant fits in the grand scheme of gardening.

Ideally, new plants should be subjected to a trial period in varying climatic zones. Far too often new plants are put on the market without any idea of their performance in varying climates. Not only must nursery owners be concerned

A really good sport! *Hosta* 'Little Aurora' sported this curious maple-leaf pattern, which was patented as *Hosta* 'Tattoo' PP 11,603.

with a plant's unique, marketable qualities, its stable genetics, and its good performance, but they must also screen the plants for bad performance. For example, invasive plants that invade functioning, natural ecosystems and displace native plants are bad performers, not just quick multipliers that spread into a
disturbed area, which is often a good trait. The difficult part of a good screening
process is that it may take years to predict invasive potential, which differs from
one ecological region to another. Regardless, it is critical that nurseries perform
some type of screening before selling a new species that hasn't previously been
grown in their region. If you get involved in introducing new species to cultiva-
tion, you should contact the ANLA office to acquire a copy of the set of principles and code of conduct governing invasive species.

New plants must also undergo trials for genetic stability as particular patterns or characteristics often change with age and culture. This is especially true
with hostas, which take on their mature characteristics in their fifth season after first flowering. Most other perennials are quicker to take on stable adult characteristics, although woody plants can take much longer.

Our nursery has been fortunate to work with several breeders to trial and
evaluate their new plants. Although we stress to breeders that they need to be
patient, it is extremely difficult when they think they have just created or found
the greatest plant they have ever seen. Years of trialing and production obstacles
must usually be overcome before a new plant is ready to hit the market. If you
are interested in trialing plants, you will need to develop a good relationship
with breeders or companies that market the new plants.

Any breeder or owner (or the owner's agent) of a new plant should only send
out trial plants with great commercial potential under a trial agreement. Such
an agreement should stipulate that the plant is only for trialing purposes and
that the person or nursery performing the trial cannot sell, distribute, market,
propagate, breed with, or sleep with the plant—trialing only! A trial agreement
is critical, as is trust in the person performing the trials. If a plant is sold, stolen,
or distributed in violation of the trial agreement, the right to patent it is still lost.

If it is determined that the plant has commercial appeal, you must next determine the level of that appeal. I classify plants into three categories, "BIO" or
collector plants, good nursery plants, and mass market plants. BIO (meaning
botanical interest only) or collector plants are usually bizarre plants that appeal to
relatively small specialty groups of people. It is rarely feasible to protect these
plants through the use of a plant patent. If you find or develop one of these
plants, I suggest you offer the plant yourself, work out a voluntary royalty that
you propose to a nursery that specializes in such plants (it could, of course, propose one to you), or trade your rare plant for other plants you might want. Sales
of plants in this category are usually quite small, from dozens to hundreds.

Figure 13. Sample Trial Agreement

Trial Agreement

Between: _____ Owner, Owner's Representative

and

Between: _____ Representative of Test Site

It is hereby agreed that owner/representative grants permission to the representative of the test site to carry out trials of the following material, adhering to the conditions below:

Plants listed: _____. _____

1. All propagating material, plants, or other reproductive material and all rights thereto belong to the owner.
2. Without written permission, the tester must not propagate or allow propagation of the cultivar(s) listed above except to distribute to other secure test sites.
3. Sports which are found on tested cultivars belong to the owner and are covered by the same conditions.
4. Without written permission, the tester must not give or share the above plants with anyone, except under written trial agreement.
5. The tester must not offer for sale the above cultivar(s) without written permission of the owner.
6. The tester agrees to apprise the owner of the results of trialing and keep him or her apprised of agreed upon further trialing and patent royalty procedures, as agreed by both parties in writing.
7. The above cultivar(s) or parts thereof may not be used in any breeding program without the written permission of the owner.
8. The owner has the right to cancel this agreement at any time, and all plant material covered by the agreement will either be destroyed or returned to the owner.

Test Representative: Owner:

_____   _____

SIGNED   SIGNED

_____   _____

PRINT NAME   PRINT NAME:

Address: Address:

_____   _____

_____   _____

Date: _____   Date: _____

The second group of newly created plants is that which has appeal in mainstream nurseries, at both the retail and wholesale level. For plants that marginally fit this category, there is little economic feasibility in protecting them with a patent. However, plants at the upper end of this range have quite high prospects for good market penetration, and the cost of a plant patent and its associated enforcement costs may be warranted. You may choose to offer non-protected plants in this category yourself and to share them with other nurseries that have shared with you. The number of plants you'd be selling would be larger than those in the collector category.

I regard the final group of new plants as mass-market plants. Good mass-market plants are actually quite rare, and many breeders may work for a lifetime without developing even one. Mass-market plants must possess certain features depending on whether they fit a utilitarian niche or are an "impulse" plant. Impulse plants must have a "wow" factor that makes a potential customer want to purchase one. The other group of mass-market plants are those that fit a wide utilitarian niche, such as a groundcover or a low foundation shrub. All mass-market plants must be fast and easy for a nursery to produce, must ship well, should not require much maintenance once in the stores, and must, of course,

Only a mother could love this botanical curiosity. *Farfugium* 'Ryuto' is an example of a classic BIO plant. You'll never see this at a mass merchant. Plant Delights Nursery.

It's a biggie! *Vinca minor* 'Illumination' is an attractive mass-market plant. Plant Delights Nursery.

look good in a standard size container. Finally, they should be relatively insect and disease resistant.

Mass-market plants are produced by the millions and offer the introducer the best chance for sizeable returns from patent protection. Among my favorite stories is of a small grower who contacted us regarding a cultivar of a ground cover that she had developed. Her initial plan was to sell the plant over her Web site and allow us to offer the plant through our catalog. After one look at the plant, we advised her to put a hold on all plans and arranged trialing using our standard trial agreement. Once we determined that the plant had mass-market appeal, we called in a horticultural marketing and distribution firm to help with the patent and the subsequent licensing of growers. A series of propagators were then licensed to produce the plants. Before the plants were even launched, over one million had been ordered. This type of success story is far too rare in the world of horticulture.

It is always a gamble as you proceed with a new plant. If you hold it back too long, another plant that is as good or better than yours may hit the market, making your plant virtually worthless. Conversely, introducing a plant before the market is ready will not maximize its potential. I encourage you to seek the advice of someone who is experienced in plant marketing.

Plant names

The naming of plants is also a critical component in the success of any new plant. As we discussed in the last chapter, cultivar names must adhere to the ICNCP. Furthermore, plant names should in some way describe the plant and also be marketable to the general public. Unfortunately, commemorating a person by naming a plant after them often detracts from the marketability of the plant, unless the person is a national personality. A good marketing firm can be of great help in arriving at an appropriate name.

We were able to use the naming of new plants as part of the marketing plan for Plant Delights. Since we were involved in an active hosta breeding program, we decided to sacrifice a few early introductions in the name of marketing. While some of our earlier hybrids were very attractive garden plants, they didn't have the large-scale commercial appeal. We therefore used "catchy" cultivar names that were sure to attract attention and make us stand out as new players in a crowded field. Some of our early hosta names included *Hosta* 'Elvis Lives', *H.* 'White Wall Tire', *H.* 'Redneck Heaven', and *H.* 'Out House Delight'. Amazingly, we managed to establish a cult following that purchased our hybrids because of their unusual names.

While it is not necessary to register the name of your new plant, it is a good idea to do so. The ANLA can be helpful in directing you to the proper registration authority that will register your new plant. The list of registration authorities for each genus is listed in the ICNCP (Trehane et al. 1995). Some genera such as hostas, iris, and daylilies have their own registration authority; most others are registered through a central registrar. There is usually a nominal registration fee of a few dollars to cover the cost of data entry and paperwork. Registration provides no means of protections for your plant, however, but in the case of disputes over its correct name or origin, an official registration can help to establish precedent.

Patents, trademarks, and breeders' rights

With the increasing use of patents and trademarks in the nursery industry, it is essential that both plant breeders and nursery owners who propagate their own plants understand the legalities involved. The majority of nursery owners have no clue how to adhere to a patent and know even less when it comes to trademarks and yet it is essential to pay them close attention to avoid costly litigation as well as embarrassment.

Plant patents are the only legal means of protecting plants that are your property or introduction from being propagated or sold without your authorization. The inventor of a plant or the agent may apply to the U.S. Patent and Trademark Office (USPTO) for a plant patent. The cost to the government for a United States patent is generally less than $1,000, but your total cost will be more, depending on how much of the work you do yourself (which I do not recommend) and how much you ask the patent agent or patent attorney to do. Although anyone can file a patent, it is usually best to hire a patent agent or patent attorney, the former being far less expensive but equally as adept as the latter, at least for most plants.

Spending the extra money for a patent attorney is always advisable if you anticipate potential problems, such as when a competing nursery has a similar plant or if there may be a patent challenge. Also, patent attorneys are more help in getting the attention of nurseries that violate your patent, a transgression that is unfortunately quite prevalent. Amazingly, a few large nurseries thumb their noses at patented plants and will intentionally violate patent rights, so you will need to be prepared for this eventuality when you get your patent.

The patent application requires that you describe your new variety and explain how it is different from similar existing varieties. You will have to sign documents saying that your plant has not been offered for documented sale more than 12 months prior to your application filing date. Also, the plant must have been developed or discovered in a cultivated area and not in the wild.

Once a patent is issued for a plant, it can only be propagated by those licensed by the patent owner or the owner's agent. The right to control propagation of the patented plant remains in effect for the 20-year life of the patent, which begins with the original date that the patent application was filed. The plant should not be sold until the patent application has been filed, and although there is a grace period of 12 months, it is risky to sell the plant prior to filing a patent application. Additionally, you need to be very discreet in the publicity of potential, patent-worthy plants. Patent law states that if the plant is publicly sold or converted to public use, the right to patent may be lost. In other words, by simply displaying the plant in public, publishing photos in public, or writing articles about a new plant before the applications for patents are filed, you could invalidate your chance of obtaining a patent.

If a new plant is sold after the application is filed but before the patent is granted, the name of the plant must end with "PPAF," which means "Plant Patent Applied For." PPAF tells other nurseries that while the patent has not been granted, it has indeed been filed. Putting PPAF on a plant without intending to patent it is a serious violation of federal patent law and is punishable by a monumental fine. If other nurseries propagate and sell a PPAF plant, they will be liable to the patent owner if and when the patent is approved. Since customers often purchase plants from you intending to propagate them, PPAF must always be indicated by the nursery selling the plants, even though the patent may not be filed until the end of the 12-month grace period.

You will next have to decide whether to keep the rights to your plant or sell them to a large nursery. As a plant breeder, I recommend that you retain all patent rights to your plants and never sign them away. Unless you are truly desperate for cash, the long-term royalties of a mass-market plant will usually far exceed any up-front payment, as long as the plant is truly distinctive and marketable, of course. The only exception would be if another nursery infringed on your patent. While you would legally be in the right, it may cost you a great deal in legal expenses to prevail if the infringer is a larger nursery with deep pockets and few ethics.

The licensing of patented plants is handled in different ways depending on the owner of the patent. Most nurseries put a marketing or legal firm in charge of issuing licenses and collecting royalty payments. The marketing firm works to establish a market by promoting the plant to the public, to growers, or both. Next, they establish a royalty fee per plant sold and then become responsible for collecting, monitoring, and distributing the royalty fee.

Your licensing attorney or agent will be responsible for enforcing the patent against any violators. While most violations are truly accidental or result from a lack of knowledge, the licensing agent or attorney must be able and prepared to defend a patent when the violation is willful. This is the most expensive part of administering a patent. In the case of a willful violation, you or your agent could be faced with tremendous legal costs. Defending a patent involves everything from sending required legal correspondence to violators to doing genetic testing for use as evidence, and when large nurseries are pitted against each other, legal expenses in defending a patent can reach into the six figures.

Royalties are divided between the owner of the plant and the marketing firm according to a predetermined percentage. Royalties are set by the patent owner and patent agent and can vary with the size of the container in which the plant is sold. The percentage paid to the marketing firm, which may depend on the responsibilities they undertake, must be enough for it to promote the plant as well as administer the bookkeeping. I always prefer this type of incentive-based royalty percentage, as it compels the marketing firm to keep pushing sales volume. Royalty fees for marketing firms may range from 5 to more than 50 percent depending on how much work and level of involvement is required; the average fee ranges from 25 to 30 percent of the royalty amount.

Some believe that the owner of the patent should do all the propagation and sales. However, this is not the best way to maximize revenues from a patent, as sales from even the largest single nursery represent but a tiny drop in the proverbial horticultural bucket. Conversely, allowing a patented plant to be licensed to virtually everyone often makes larger nurseries reluctant to sign up because they fear competition and anticipate that others will benefit from the marketing dollars they spend to promote the patented item.

The smart owner of a plant patent often licenses a number of liner producers to ensure widespread distribution, which is where patents will pay large dividends. In the past, many nurseries used patents to restrict the propagation of a proprietary plant to the nursery that held the patent. Fortunately, the new trend is for patent owners to license as many growers and propagators as is feasible to produce and sell the plant. Of course, the fewer people who are licensed, the easier it will be to collect royalty payments. The perfect scenario, in other words, is the one large grower who sells to virtually everyone.

To grow a patented plant, you will either need to become a licensed propagator or find a grower who produces licensed liners. Many different strategies are employed by patent owners in licensing other growers depending on the owner's release strategy. Typically, licensing someone to produce a patented plant involves a propagation contract between the owner or agent of the patent and the propagator. Most contracts include clauses that cover an established royalty fee per plant, the payment schedule, the growing of plants in a certain manner, and the agreement that all sports or plants derived from the patented variety belong to the owner of the patent. Nurseries are usually charged a licensing or signing fee, which tends to weed out the small growers as the time and paperwork required far exceeds the revenues generated. (Remember, too, that the more producers you license, the more paperwork it takes to manage the royalties.) The licensing and collecting of royalties is a complex process, and it is rarely economical for nurseries to do their own policing.

Many patented plants are released via a wholesale nursery as their first point of release. I regard this as a mistake because it means bypassing mail order as a first-line retail offering. What you will need to consider is how to give the plant "perceived value," which is the value that is set by the initial offering. With new plants, it is always best to choose one or more national mail-order nurseries for a first-year retail exclusive. If mail-order nurseries offer a new plant for $50, instead of selling your liners for $2, you could perhaps charge $3, $5, or even $10. The initial retail value of $50 makes the $10 liner price look like a good deal. If, however, you set the initial wholesale price at $10 without an initial offering to establish a market value, growers would rightly balk at the higher wholesale price.

Royalty amounts on patented plants vary widely. Most often, royalties in the first couple of years are at their highest, after which they drop as the plant becomes more of a commodity. A typical royalty on a herbaceous plant may be as low as $0.02 or as high as several dollars per plant. Woody plants generally have a higher royalty, from $0.10 to several dollars. Royalties are often based on the size of the plant sold, so liners could have a royalty of $0.05, while gallon pots may have a royalty of $1 each.

Royalties are usually collected either annually or semiannually depending on the marketing season for the plants. Plants that are sold in large numbers on a year-round basis should probably have royalty payments due semiannually, while a yearly royalty payment on many shrub plants would probably make more sense. You or your agent will send a declaration of sales form to each of your licensed growers, who will then return it with their declared sales. You or your agent will then send an invoice for the amount owed based on their sales figures.

The ANLA annually updates its *Plant Patent Directory*, a list of all plants on which patents are still in effect. For some bizarre reason, this directory lists some plants by scientific name and others by common name, making it more difficult to use. Plant patent information and a list of patents granted in the preceding two months can also be gleaned from USPTO's Web site.

The ANLA also administers the National Association of Plant Patent Owners (NAPPO). NAPPO, founded in 1939, is a trade association dedicated to promoting the development, protection, production, and distribution of new and improved plant varieties. NAPPO's mission is primarily educational in that it promotes and lobbies for better plant patent systems. Active membership is available only to those who own a plant patent or a federally-registered plant trademark, although allied interests are allowed as associate members.

The United States is the only country that has a system for plant patents. While it had this system in about 1930, European Plant Breeders' Rights followed in 1964. As of 2000, almost all other major countries offer protection through plant breeders' rights that echo the European system. Most Asian Plant Breeders' Rights programs are very similar to the European system, differing primarily in the length of time that a plant can be on the market before a breeder files for PBR. All countries that offer plant protection are members of the Union for Protected Varieties (UPOV), an organization that meets every ten years with the mission of harmonizing plant breeders' rights and standards worldwide.

Keep in mind that United States patents will not protect your plant in overseas markets. If the plant has high commercial appeal in Europe, Japan, Canada, Australia, or New Zealand, you may want to consider obtaining Plant Breeder's Rights (PBR) as well. Don't kid yourself that your plant will not find its way to Europe; many keen nursery owners from around the world scour the United States plant catalogs looking for new plants in order to stay ahead of competitors in their own country. I have seen plants introduced in the United States one year and appear on the European wholesale market the following year. This is especially true if the plant is rapidly reproducible from tissue culture.

European Plant Breeders' Rights are different from United States plant patents in that under the European system, plants must first be tested for distinctiveness and genetic stability (called a DWS test). Any plant submitted for PBR must identify a single reference plant that will remain such for the life of the rights. The actual cost of a PBR in 2002 is approximately U.S. $1,500 plus the cost of an agent to handle the process. You will first have to pay the application fee for a PBR, and one year later you will pay the test and issuance fee. As with patents granted in the United States, a PBR is good for 20 years from the date the application is filed. However, unlike United States patents, PBRs charge a yearly maintenance fee that, in 2002, was approximately U.S. $300. An additional difference is that a breeder under the European system who comes up with a new cultivar that is derived (meaning it is either a sport or is hybridized) from an already protected cultivar may not market the new cultivar without the permission of the PBR owner.

The PBR system, in contrast to the patent system in the United States, offers full disclosure of applications. In other words, you can find out which plants have been submitted for PBR and follow the process. For some bizarre reason, the USPTO does not allow others to know if a patent application has been filed. PBR patents do not allow patent holders to restrict the propagation of their protected cultivar, whereas a United States patent does. Any nursery that wants to propagate a PBR-protected plant need only show that a particular market is not being met by current licensees.

Prior to the institution of Canada's PBR system in 1998, a cooperative had been developed called the Canadian Ornamental Plant Foundation (COPF).

COPF members were one of two types, growers or breeders. Breeders would submit a cultivar to the COPF program, usually for a minimal $50 fee. Grower members would benefit by having access to new cultivars and being able to propagate COPF-registered plants if they paid a voluntary royalty payment to the COPF system. To cover administrative costs, 10 to 15 percent of the royalty payment would be retained by COPF. The COPF system operates by growers policing each other and then publishing a list of violators. Today, the COPF system is still used when the grower doesn't want to incur the fees required to obtain a Canadian PBR.

Trademarks for legal protection

Although we discussed trademarks as they relate to nomenclature in the last chapter, we need to also consider their legal standing and how they impact a nursery's ability to grow and propagate these plants. Properly used, trademarks are a useful marketing tool, so it is a shame that a lot of people don't realize how to use them properly.

Most nurseries think that trademarks offer some form of protection similar to that offered by patents, but this is simply not the case. A trademark has no effect on the ability of another nursery to propagate or sell a particular plant under its valid cultivar name. Keep in mind that a plant has only one valid cultivar name that is available for everyone to use and that cannot be trademarked.

Trademarking an item can be as simple as writing *TM* after a name. To obtain a more sound legal footing, you should register the trademark with the USPTO so that it becomes a Registered Trademark (written as *R*). Registering costs about $250, although if the process is handled by a lawyer it will cost more. Trademarks are owned by an individual or company and cannot be affixed to an individual item, but they are registered for use on a particular group of items, such as plants. If they are used correctly, trademarks are valid for ten years and can be renewed indefinitely for additional ten-year periods. Although a trademark is granted, it may not be enforceable unless it is used correctly, which is rarely the case in the horticulture industry. To find out if a particular trademark has been federally registered, you can go to the USPTO Web site. Having access to this Web site offers tremendous savings as you used to need a trademark lawyer to do this type of research.

Trademarks are designed to promote a plant's origin through the use of a brand name. For example, if a series of rose cultivars was trademarked by Joe's Nursery as the Joe Blow™ series of roses, you could not sell Joe's Nursery's roses as part of the Joe Blow™ series without purchasing the plants from a licensed grower or without paying the owner of the trademark. You could, however, propagate and sell any of the Joe Blow™ roses by their cultivar name, as long as they were not patented.

Patents expire after 20 years (it used to be 17 years), so nursery owners can legally propagate and sell a formerly patented cultivar after that time. To further complicate matters, some nursery owners began to trademark as well as patent their new introductions. In other words, they could get the 20-year protection that the plant patent provides and add a further measure of protection by trademarking a second name for each plant, which they would then use to market to the public. Once the patent expired, others could propagate the plant but could not sell it under the trademark name. A classic example is Monrovia's *Limemound*™ *spirea*. At the end of the patent period, everyone could propagate *Spirea* 'Monhub' PP5834, but no one could legally sell the plant as *Limemound*™ *spirea*, assuming, of course, that the trademark had been legally used.

No one is quite sure why trademarks entered the horticulture arena but most nursery owners agree that it was first devised as a marketing tool to sell good plants that had bad cultivar names. Some larger nurseries soon realized that they were rather adept at coming up with good plant names but they wanted to keep these names to themselves and not allow other nurseries to use them. Unfortunately, some nursery owners then intentionally began giving their new plants nonsensical cultivar names that do not adhere to the spirit of the ICNCP. Since cultivar names are for public use and cannot be protected, other nurseries that propagated the plant after the patents expired could only sell it under the nonsensical cultivar name. These nursery owners added to the confusion by marketing the plant under its good, trademarked name while everyone else was forced to use the nonsensical cultivar name. The cultivar name, if it was even included in the ads and tags, would be printed in much smaller print compared to the "marketing name," and soon the public was associating a particular plant with that nursery's own trademarked name.

Using trademarks as a pseudo-cultivar name for a particular plant violates the spirit of the nomenclature code and, in many cases, the intent of the trademark. The trademark code states that if a trademark name becomes the common use or generic name, then the trademark becomes invalidated. Lawyers have advised nurseries to write the cultivar name in single quotes, as required by the ICNCP, followed by the trademark name that is not enclosed in single quotes. In addition, if the owner of the trademark does not enforce the mark's proper use, the mark becomes invalidated. This means that when the trademark is used in the trade as the generic name of a particular cultivar, a lack of enforcement against violators invalidates it. Most trademarks used in the horticulture industry are therefore completely invalid.

Chapter 16

Purchasing and Leasing

If your nursery is small and you are not very busy, it may be easy to remember what you have ordered, from whom, and when it is due to arrive. I say this with tongue planted firmly in cheek, as I cannot count the number of suppliers who have relayed stories about sending plants to a customer who had forgotten that the plants were on order, even to the point of arguing heatedly about receiving unordered plants.

Equipment purchasing procedure

All nurseries should develop a simple purchase order system. A purchase order is simply a piece of paper that details an order for a product that you intend to purchase. It is a legally binding document, so do not use one lightly. I like to make sure that the vendors I order from get a copy of the purchase order, and even when orders are placed over the phone, the vendor always receives a copy confirming the order. Purchase-order forms can be printed in bulk by a commercial printer or simply designed on a computer using a word processing program. Some of the more sophisticated nursery database programs have a purchase order integrated into the inventory database. At Plant Delights we create a blank table on the computer, which is then filled in with each order.

Each purchase order is assigned a purchase order or PO number. We chose a numbering system that begins with the year in which the order was sent to the vendor. Other details to be included are the number of each item ordered, the date ordered, the agreed upon price, how the order was sent to the supplier (by fax, mail, or e-mail), delivery information such as date, type, cost, and location, and the method and time of payment. I like to keep purchase orders together in an alphabetically arranged, loose-leaf binder. This way orders can be pulled out and matched with receiving tickets when purchased items arrive. By matching a copy of the packing invoice with a copy of the purchase order, the accounts payable department (meaning the person who writes the checks) will know for sure that the plants they are asked to pay for have actually arrived. It is critical that payments for delivered items be made in a timely manner.

Handling purchases sounds easy until you start dealing with back orders, items that are shipped at the wrong time, and in the wrong amount. The next thing that happens is that incorrect invoices begin to arrive—all of a sudden, you have a complete mess with invoices that are virtually impossible to reconcile. You can see why nurseries must have an accurate paper trail that allows you to make sense of things when problems occur.

Most nursery owners designate certain staff members to make purchases for the nursery. You put a great deal of trust in any member of staff you allow to make purchases for your business, so choose carefully. Small items are usually paid for out of cash-flow receipts—in other words, out of your bank account, either by cash or checks, although business credit cards are also becoming more

Figure 14. Sample Purchase Order

200_ Purchase Order

Your Nursery
Mailing and Shipping Address
1234 Sunnysideofthe Street
City, State Zip

TO:

PO# 0	Ship To: address above attn:	Requested by:

Terms.	Ship Via: BEST WAY	FOB:

ORDER DATE	QTY	UNIT	DESCRIPTION/ITEM	PRICE	TOTAL	REQUESTED DELIVERY DATE

	Shipping Charges	
	TOTAL	

page 1 of 1

Phone (000)000-0000
Fax (000) 000-0000
email purchasing@123456.com

and more popular. Most companies that offer business credit cards issue them in the business's name with different credit limits assigned to each card. It is often advisable to establish credit accounts with many of your regular suppliers to make purchasing easier.

When it comes to more expensive purchases, it is usually a good idea to first accept bids. Bids are requests for price quotations from prospective vendors. If you need a large number of any item, you will often get a better price if you send out what is known as a "request for quotation" to several vendors. Vendors, realizing you are soliciting prices from many of them, will often be willing to offer price breaks when given the opportunity to quote against competitors. In a request for quotation, be sure to spell out exactly how many of each item you will need, the size, the quality standard, and the date of delivery. This way, all the bidders are quoting on exactly the same criteria.

Purchasing plants

Do you know where to purchase plants? What sounds like an easy question is usually anything but easy. Although there are a wide array of plant suppliers around the country and the world, you still have to find them. Attending trade shows, networking, and obtaining personal references are all great ways of finding potential suppliers. At the same time, you will quickly learn which suppliers have a good reputation and which do not, and don't forget to use simple sleuthing techniques, such as checking the back of nursery tags at area retailers. More and more people now use the Internet, so the means of locating plants has changed dramatically. Regional publications that detail inventories from nurseries in the area are also very useful, and at the very least, you should use the regularly updated inventories that some nurseries are publishing and then posting online or sending to their customers via fax.

An obvious way of finding good plant sources is through attending state and regional trade shows, where you can see the plants you will be purchasing. Equally as important is the opportunity you have to talk with the other growers and establish long-term relationships. Don't be afraid to ask hard questions of the growers. One interesting thing I have found is that while growers may know how to produce the plants, some don't have much of a handle on getting the correct names on the plants they sell; the number of misnamed plants in nurseries is phenomenal. If you are trying to establish your nursery as one that actually sells correctly named plants, you will quickly learn that you cannot always depend on your supplier. You will have to do your own homework to verify that the plants you purchase for later resale are actually true to type.

The next wave of plant locator services will come from the business-to-business (or B to B) Internet sites. These sites are those where businesses list their inventories with a Web company that will compile the inventories into a database of plants, sizes, and prices. The customer will then order from the site, and the site owners will forward that order to the nursery that grows the requested plants. These B to B sites will make money either by skimming a percentage off the transaction amount from the seller or buyer or by getting a rebate from the seller.

It will be interesting to watch how the "old style" nurseries accept this new technology. One factor that will certainly have to change before B to B sites can function properly is that a nursery's listed inventory will have to be accurate and up-to-date. I hope I'm wrong, but I think B to B acceptance is a long way away for most plant producers. Perhaps a clever B to B site owner will provide computers and a bar code inventory program to nurseries that have a problem keeping up-to-date with their inventories; perhaps a staff person will be provided as well. It is unfortunate that such an investment would likely be necessary for B to B technology to work on a large scale.

Purchasing plants from overseas

If you have trouble finding the plants you need within the United States, there is always the possibility of importing them. To do this you will need an import permit from the USDA's Animal Plant Health Inspection Service (APHIS). There are basically three types of import permits. The Import Permit for Plants and Plant Products (permit Q-37) allows you to import virtually any plant, plant part, or seed that does not have some type of United States government restriction imposed on it. Once issued, a Q-37 permit is valid for seven years. At the time of writing, there was no fee for acquiring this permit.

A Post Entry Quarantine Permit (a 7 CFR 319.37 permit) allows you to import plants of specific genera. They must be held for two years and be regularly inspected by USDA agents for specific pests. During this time, propagation and distribution is prohibited, except as authorized by the USDA inspector. If the inspector recommends a specific treatment, including destruction of the plant material, you must comply. Again, there is no fee for a post entry permit.

The third type of permit is called a General Permit or PPQ-622. This permit is anything but "general," as it allows importation of regulated CITES plants into the country. CITES, which stands for Convention on International Trade in Endangered Species of Wild Fauna and Flora, is the regulating document that governs the importation and exportation of endangered species. It costs $75 to obtain this permit.

CITES plants are divided into Appendix I, II, and III plants. Appendix I plants are those that are currently threatened with extinction. They can be imported into the United States but must have two additional CITES permits, one that is issued by the country of origin (there is an exception for plants that are artificially propagated), and the other, which is known as permit 3-200, that is issued by the U.S. Fish and Wildlife Service. These latter permits are $25 and usually require about 60 days to process if approved. The permit application is available online. CITES import permits will be granted only if the permit will not endanger the plant's survival, if the purpose for importation is not primarily commercial, and if the importer has the ability to care for the plant. A CITES import permit is valid for one year.

Appendix II and III plants are those not currently threatened with extinction but, if not regulated, have been determined to be at risk. Appendix II and III plants do not require a CITES import permit but do require an export permit or certificate of artificial propagation from the country of origin. Appendix III plants are those that are only restricted from a particular country of origin.

If you have questions regarding which plants can be legally imported, contact the U.S. Fish and Wildlife Service's office of management. Importing the wrong plants, or even the right plants, without the proper permit will not only result in their confiscation but also a number of other regulatory headaches, including hefty fines. To apply for permits, you will need to contact APHIS. It will take several months from the time of application before you receive the permit, so don't wait until you are ready to import to send in application forms.

With very few exceptions, all plants imported into the United States must be free from soil, meaning they must be bare root. Approved packing materials in which these plants can be packed include ground peat moss, sphagnum moss, wood shavings, sawdust, vermiculite, and a few others. Seeds are regulated, but less so than plants, and all imported seed must be free from pulp and other flower parts that could harbor insects. The list of prohibited seed is available from the APHIS Web site. Any plant shipment entering the United States must include an alphabetical list by Latin name of all plants included in the shipment. Labels must be on each plant or packet of plants, and a copy of your import permit must be in the box.

You will also need a phytosanitary certificate from the country of origin when you import plants and seed into the United States. A phytosanitary certificate, according to the International Plant Protection Convention (IPPC), is an acknowledgment between participating countries that the inspectors in the country of origin have inspected the shipment and found that it is free of dangerous pests and otherwise meets the import regulations of the country of destination. The intended purpose of these certificates is to expedite the shipment of plants and seed from country to country. For many years, phytosanitary certificates were used primarily for exporting plants and importing large shipments, but the USDA has the authority to require phytosanitary certificates for all seed and plant imports as well. While this regulation has gone unenforced by the USDA, changes in international agreements may again result in the enforcement of this regulation. Be sure to check with the USDA regarding current requirements before importing plants or seed.

A number of ways exist to get plants into the United States. The easiest way is to use a standard commercial carrier such as the United States Postal Service (USPS), United Parcel Service (UPS), Fed Ex, or DHL. These carriers make transportation easy since they will drop the packages off at both customs and agricultural inspections, pick them up again, and then send them to your nursery. Unfortunately, many of these companies are hopelessly confused about their own policies for shipping plants. For years we shipped plants with one carrier, only to suddenly be refused; they told us they did not ship plants overseas and had never done so. Despite making numerous phone calls, I have never gotten a logical explanation for this unexpected refusal, so be prepared for a morass of confusion on the part of most shippers.

The other shipping option is to send plants via airfreight, which are commercial airlines that carry freight as well as passengers. While it may be cheaper to ship plants this way, airfreight companies will only drop the packages at U.S. Customs, meaning that you will have to hire a bonded customs broker to move the package from customs to agricultural inspections and then to reship the package to you. Customs brokers are at best a mixed bag; those we have used have ranged from wonderful to beyond our worst nightmares.

Many larger plant exporters, especially in countries such as the Netherlands, will hire a United States inspector to fly to Holland and pre-inspect the plants after they have been harvested and cleaned but before they are shipped. These shipments are known as precleared shipments and usually require less hassle when entering the United States. Most large bulb and perennial companies use this method of importation.

If you follow the proper steps, you can make the overseas trek yourself to bring back plants. First, make sure that it is possible to take plants out of the country that you are visiting. It is illegal to remove plants from a number of places such as India and several countries in South America without permission from the government. Other countries allow plants to be taken from their country but only if they are inspected by officials of that country. Remember to check with the country's ministry or department of agriculture to make sure you are not violating any laws before you depart with plants.

When dealing with large shipments it is always best to ship the plants into the United States instead of bringing them in on your person. However, it is possible to hand-carry small quantities of plants and seed through customs and agricultural inspections after an overseas trip, but if the inspection station is very busy or closed, you may be required to leave the items and hire a bonded customs broker to move the shipment through the inspection system. If you have the plants in a box with the waybill filled out from a major carrier, the agricultural inspectors will usually drop the package back into their delivery system. Be sure to call ahead to your port of entry and verify that this procedure is still in place. I also recommend confirming which ports have active inspection services (see Appendix 2) and their hours of operation before embarking on a trip, as inspection services are not available at all international airports at all times.

I have mentioned both customs and agricultural inspections, so I had best describe the role of both. United States Customs, the first stop of any shipment of plants into the United States, is a branch of the U.S. Treasury Department, whose mission it is to collect taxes owed on purchases. Shipments should be clearly labeled on the outside of the box as to its contents or it will be parked at the Customs office. Customs agents assess any taxes due on the shipment; fortunately, most plants have little or no tariff. You can find a list of customs tariffs on plants by following the traveler information links at the Customs Web site. Amazingly, there seems to be little cooperation between this first stop and the next one.

The second stop for plants entering the United States is at the USDA's APHIS. There are 12 to 15 ports in the United States through which plants may enter, each of which has an official USDA inspection station that is usually staffed by botanists and entomologists who make sure that all your plants are both legal and free from any pests not already in the United States. While they are not legally allowed to stop plants that have the latter problem, the enforcement of this aspect is misunderstood by a large number of the inspectors who mistakenly overstep their authority in this regard. If the inspectors are unsure of the pests involved or see pest damage, they may fumigate the plants with gas. Unfortunately, while this is very effective in killing most pests, it is also equally as effective in killing most plants.

Most agricultural inspectors have a botanical background, meaning that they are often oblivious to the world of horticulture. In other words, they understand how to identify plants but often have no clue regarding growing plants. They don't seem to realize that plants shipped bare root need special treatment and that they need it quickly. Granted, these inspectors have a big job, but many nursery owners, including myself, believe that some inspectors want to exercise authority just for the sake of it, completely forgetting that they work for us, the taxpayer. At the same time, however, I have dealt with a few inspectors who were very helpful, especially those in the Raleigh area. Sadly, they are in the minority.

It would be wonderful if you could choose the port of entry for your plants, but plants shipped into the United States arrive at the closest port to your home destination. Forget trying to specify otherwise. Flights from certain countries are routed to specific entry ports. The worst port is "Lost Angeles," with New

Jersey following close behind. Shipments coming through San Francisco and Seattle have posed no problems. Over the years, these latter two ports have appeared to be the most helpful; they actually seem to care about your plants. Miami also has a better than normal track record, probably because they deal with more plant shipments as a result of Florida's large foliage plant industry.

It is very important that you work with your overseas shipper to get as many t's crossed and i's dotted as possible. The more accurately the work is done on the shipper's end, the better the chance is that the plants will arrive in a satisfactory condition. However, even when we have laid out in great detail the necessary shipping format, dealing with certain Third World countries is truly a nightmare. Many crucial aspects are often overlooked (for example, permits were not placed where the inspectors could easily find them), causing enormous problems in getting the plants into the United States alive.

Once you receive your plants from abroad, you now have the fun task of paying for them. While some foreign nurseries prefer payment in advance, I advise against doing this if at all possible. Should there be a dispute, it will be virtually impossible to recover your money unless you are dealing with a very reputable firm. At the very least, pay only a partial deposit. In my experience, probably 50 percent of the foreign purchases by Plant Delights have resulted in problems that ranged from rotting and diseased plants to misnamed plants, no plants at all, and delivery nightmares.

The easiest ways to pay for overseas shipments are by credit cards or bank wire transfers. Wire transfers are easily accomplished once you have the vendor's name, bank name, account number, and routing number. Once you provide these numbers to your bank, the electronic transfer of money from your account into the foreign account is completed. This payment method is particularly useful in the countries where credit cards are not accepted and whose corrupt governments make other means of payment (such as checks and cash) unfeasible.

Receiving shipments

You may think it silly to discuss how to receive shipments, but you don't need to be in business long to realize that having a procedure in place to receive shipments will not only eliminate confusion but will also save you money.

First of all, forget the idea that you can schedule all shipments to arrive on time and in good condition; this is simply not reality. I can't tell you the number of mornings I have been awakened at five o'clock in the morning by the sound of a diesel truck in my driveway. Then there are the deliveries where, after the truck has pulled away, you find your prize flowerbed has been run over, the corner of a greenhouse destroyed, or your neighbor's mailbox leveled. Yes, I've seen it all!

Receiving freight begins with the communications you have with the vendor.

You should specify what shipment methods you require, what is necessary to promptly unload or receive the shipment, and an approximate shipping cost. I once ordered perennials from a broker who was purchasing them from a nursery on the West Coast, and although the plants arrived in good condition, the freight bill, which arrived a week later, was three times the cost of the plants. Also evaluate the types of delivery you are set up to receive. Can the UPS truck reach your property? Do you have enough room for a tractor-trailer? Shippers such as UPS, Fed Ex, or DHL may work well for small shipments, but a common carrier (one that uses tractor-trailers) is the most economical when you have larger shipments. If you can accommodate a common carrier, what size will the trailer be, 40 feet or 53 feet? The last thing you want is a tractor-trailer 53 feet long wedged into a tight spot, the driver unable to move forward. Large delivery vehicles need a tremendous amount of room in which to maneuver, far more than most nursery owners realize.

I have found that truck drivers have very different driving skills so I make them stop at our nursery entrance and look at where they will drop the freight. Driving a tractor-trailer on the road is the easy part, and it is only the best drivers who are able to maneuver into the tight spots without getting stuck or running over or damaging something. Many drivers will tell you that they cannot make a particular maneuver out of simple laziness. However, it is virtually useless to argue with most truck drivers, though I have found it useful to use a line like "the last two female drivers didn't have any problem backing into this area" with some male drivers.

Freight can arrive on several types of tractor-trailer bodies, including flat floors, dump bodies, and walking floors, so you will need to specify which you prefer before your shipment is loaded. Supplies that cannot be dumped are delivered on flat-floor beds, which necessitates freight being carried to the back of the truck and unloaded there. If the items to be delivered are on pallets, most trucks come equipped with a pallet jack for moving items from the front of the truck to the back. For items that can be dumped from the truck, your choice will be between a dump-body and walking-floor trailer. As you can imagine, dump bodies work by raising the trailer body until the items inside slide to the back of the truck and out. Dump bodies do a good job except where the land is uneven, as the height of the risen body makes the truck prone to turn over. If you have uneven land, request a walking-floor body. The floor of the truck in this style of trailer moves backward using hydraulics, which is how the items inside the truck are moved to the back of the truck and then onto the ground. Walking-floor trailers are becoming more common in the delivery of mulches and potting soils.

Most tractor-trailer companies allow you one to two hours to unload the trailer, though this varies with the shipper. You will therefore need to have either a crew or the necessary equipment on hand to unload the shipment when it arrives. Since deliveries rarely arrive when they are scheduled, planning for a delivery is made that much more difficult. Based on my years in the nursery business, I estimate that 5 percent of the tractor-trailer shipments actually arrived at or near the scheduled time. Remember to inquire about what you will need to unload the shipment and how long you will be given to unload before being charged extra. Do not expect the driver to assist in unloading; I am always pleasantly surprised when one offers to help.

If you receive freight via common carriers, it is essential that you familiarize yourself with Article II of the Uniform Commercial Code (the UCC), which codifies the rules for shipping and receiving freight via these carriers. Most freight is shipped free on board (known as "f.o.b.") to a particular location, meaning that the seller's responsibility ends when the freight is delivered to that destination. If you are in Florida and the seller is in New York, your freight can either be shipped f.o.b New York or f.o.b Florida. If it is shipped f.o.b New York, the freight becomes your property in New York when it is placed on the truck by the shipper for delivery to you, the consignee. Shipments that are shipped f.o.b Florida means that the seller retains ownership until the truck delivers the product to your nursery in Florida.

You will need to know the f.o.b. destination since that determines how and when payment is made for shipping and who makes it. In most instances, the freight will be shipped f.o.b the seller's home city and state. Since most freight companies are independent and do not actually work for the vendor nursery, plan to pay for the delivery when the truck arrives. The vendor can usually give you the cost of delivery in advance. If the freight is shipped f.o.b the consignee's location, the payment is the responsibility of the seller and you will have no financial responsibility to pay the shipper when the freight is delivered.

The important point to remember is that if the freight is shipped f.o.b the seller's location, then the freight becomes your property the moment the freight leaves the seller's location. Should the delivery arrive at the wrong time or on the wrong day, the freight is already your property. If something happens to the freight before you can take the delivery, you will have difficulty getting restitution from the seller, and your claim will most likely be with the trucking company. In other words, when the delivery truck arrives at eight o'clock on Friday night, you should think twice before sending it away until Monday morning as the plants are already your property.

Once the freight arrives, you should always inspect the deliveries and note any damages or problems on the bill of lading (the list of contents as provided by the shipping company). You have the right to inspect and open all boxes before accepting the shipment. I like to have the truck driver sign any notes that I make regarding the condition of any damaged freight. Although inspection is critical, you still have up to nine months to file a claim with the shipper for damaged or missing freight. The shipper has 30 days in which to acknowledge your claim and 120 days to settle the claim. As with any dispute, the more documentation, including photographs, that are available, the better chance there is for a satisfactory resolution.

Regardless of the delivery method, I recommend keeping a logbook to document each arriving shipment, making note of information such as receipt dates and times. Having a centralized location for the documentation of received items becomes critical as your nursery grows larger or when employees who are waiting for particular shipments are absent or busy with other projects when the shipments arrive. I have always found it best to designate one person as the official freight receiver; having more than one person assigned to this task can cause inconsistency and inevitably leads to confusion.

Another important step in the receiving process is checking the bill of lading against your purchase order to make sure that all items ordered have actually arrived. It is startling how often too few, or in some cases too many, items are shipped. Once the paperwork is reconciled, a copy of all bills of lading or receivers, as well as purchase orders, should be given to the accounts payable department. This is critical for your accounts payable department. Without something that tells the bill payer that the items were actually received, there is no way to tell if the invoice is correct or if the items have even been received.

Purchasing equipment

When, where, and how to purchase equipment are among the biggest decisions that any nursery will face. If large equipment purchases are not handled correctly, they can adversely affect cash flow, which in turn will have an impact on the viability of the business.

You must first determine how often you will be using the equipment that you plan to purchase and the projected payback time. A variety of costs associated with any piece of equipment, including operator salary, fuel, repairs, maintenance, the useful life of the equipment, and salvage price, must all be considered.

Since labor is the largest nursery expense, most equipment is purchased as a means of saving labor costs. To determine the labor savings that will be attained from new equipment, you will need to do a calculation. For example, let's say you are currently potting plants manually at the rate of 500 pots per person per day for a total of 200,000 pots per year. The potting machine that you have selected would increase the rate to 2500 pots per person per day. If you manually pot your plants, you will need 400 days of potting, assuming you are working eight-hour days. With an actual employee cost of $10 per hour or $80 per day, labor burden costs total $32,000 a year. Using the potting machine that produced 2500 pots per employee day, you would reduce the number of days needed to 80 (200,000 pots a year divided by 2500 pots per day equals 80 days). By then multiplying $80 per employee (8 hours × $10 per hour) by 80 employee days, you will see that labor costs drop to $6,400. If potting machine costs $20,000, add that to the cost of using the machine, which is $6,400. The yearly total cost to pot plants using a machine is $26,400 compared to $32,000 when potting is done manually. Not all machines will pay off in one year. Nurseries typically look for a payback within three years on new equipment.

The easiest and most common method of purchasing equipment is the outright purchase of equipment from current cash-flow receipts. What this means is that if you have enough cash flow during the course of the year, then you buy the equipment and pay for it along with your regular bills. This will, of course, require well-planned budgeting to ensure that your surplus funds are not going to be needed later in the calendar year for regular budgeted expenses. Nursery owners will frequently save these equipment purchases until the fall when they have completed most of their yearly purchases so they can assess how much money remains.

If your cash flow does not allow you to write a check for the equipment, you could finance the equipment with a bank or lending institution. Using this method, you would borrow money from the bank based on the cost of the equipment. Most banks will ask you to put down a deposit from 10 to 20 percent to insure that you have a stake in the equipment as well. Typically, equipment is financed for five years. While it may be difficult for your nursery to come up with $10,000 in cash, it should be much easier to pay $2,000 or more in interest each year.

Keep in mind that the cost of this equipment can be deducted over time from your taxes through depreciation. Depreciation is simply the value of the asset that you will use each year. For example, if you purchase a $10,000 potting machine that is predicted to last ten years and have no residual value at that the end of ten years, you will use up $1,000 of its value each year. Tax laws do not allow businesses to deduct the entire cost of equipment in one year despite the fact that the money was all paid in a particular year. Tax rules also determine the minimum number of years over which you can deduct the cost of your purchase from your taxes. Your accountant will be of help in explaining the tax ramifications of equipment purchases and depreciation.

Owning versus leasing equipment

When you are ready to purchase equipment, you will have to decide who will hold title to the asset. Most accountants and business consultants prefer that you own the asset personally or that your private leasing corporation own it and then lease it back to your business. Purchasing and owning equipment, buildings, and land personally, then leasing them back to your nursery has become a popular way to gain extra tax savings on income. Many people have even set up a separate leasing business as an LLC that actually owns the assets. This arrangement would add an extra measure of protection against lawsuit-related losses because the equipment is not actually owned by your nursery.

Virtually anything can be leased, from buildings that are constructed on your property according to your specifications to all kinds of equipment. If you purchased a tractor for $10,000, for example, you could lease it to your nursery for $400 per month. At the end of the second year, you have almost paid for the tractor. Your rent doesn't end, however, but instead continues for as long as the tractor remains in operating condition.

Outside leasing of land and equipment

If the equipment you need will be sitting still during most of each week and used only occasionally, it may be advantageous, from both a cost and tax standpoint, to lease the equipment from an outside vendor. A long-term lease may be the best answer for equipment that you will be using for a long period but not indefinitely, especially if the resale price at the end of your use period will be low.

Nursery owners who don't have property themselves or don't have enough could lease land from another individual or business. However, as nurseries can't just pick up and move at a moment's notice, be sure that you have a leasing agreement with the landlord that has been drawn up by a lawyer. The agreement should include the amount of the rent, the duration of the lease, the means by which the landlord can end the lease, and the criteria by which the rent amount can be changed. Will the landlord have to justify the rent increase or can it be increased at will?

For all leased property, you will need to clearly specify the area to be leased and the rights you have as a lessee. What responsibilities will you have for things such as paying taxes and utility bills? What type of notice must you give if you decide to move, and how will disputes be settled if a problem arises with the land or buildings being leased? A good, comprehensive lease is something you don't want to have to spend time or money on but it's better to be prepared than be caught unaware.

Chapter 17

Follow the Money

No matter how many great plants you produce, unless you have the ability to follow the money, you're not going to stay in business very long. Many nursery owners think they are in the nursery business as a higher calling, which is great; however, the bills still have to be paid. A good understanding of cash flow, financing, and proper accounting procedures are essential to remaining in business.

If you don't follow any of my other advice, hire a certified public accountant (CPA) to help with your books and taxes. There are plenty of places to skimp in a business, but this is not one of them. No sensible business owner would try to do his or her own taxes, and nursery owners should be no exception. A good CPA will actually save you money by knowing the ins and outs of tax law. Tax laws are constantly changing, and your own time is better spent keeping up-to-date on other aspects of your business. While you should certainly get recommendations from other businesses, I also recommend that you interview CPAs as you would a new employee. After all, this is the person who will share your most intimate business ideas and financial details.

Some CPAs have an understanding of the nursery business while others don't have a clue. The seasonal nature of the nursery business is very difficult for some accountants to comprehend, so choose your accountant carefully. Our first CPA firm had little experience in the nursery business, and although they did adequate accounting work, they told us that we could not afford to build more greenhouses at a time when expansion was critical. The job of CPAs is to analyze your business data primarily as it relates to taxes, so despite their tremendous benefits, do not look to CPAs to help you run your business efficiently or profitably. This is why business consultants are the perfect complement to your CPA, though in some cases the two will have divergent opinions on the same problem.

Accounting

Among your first accounting decisions will be whether to operate on a cash or accrual system. The system you choose determines how and when you will deduct expenses and whether or not you will be able to deduct weather-related losses. Nurseries that operate on a cash basis must report income when it is actually received, and those that operate on an accrual basis must report income when it is billed or earned, rather than when payment is received. Similarly, nurseries that operate on an accrual accounting must deduct capital expenses such as equipment when they are received and not when they are paid for. Virtually all small and medium-sized nurseries operate on a cash basis. The IRS is moving to force all nurseries to switch to an accrual system, but this has so far been kept at bay. As of 2002, only nurseries with gross sales over five million dollars were required to use an accrual accounting system, but I recommend you seek advice from your accountant on this matter.

With accountants come account codes. Account codes are designations between you and your accountant that track expenditures for tax purposes and monitor costs of operating your business. Nursery owners, together with their accountants, will formulate codes that are pertinent to their particular nursery. As you spend or take in money, you will assign a code from your list to each monetary transaction. These codes are then plugged into your balance sheet. Before there were computers, the codes were tracked on a manual spreadsheet. Computers have made the job quite a bit easier.

After having received your month-end financial data, your CPA will prepare a monthly balance sheet or profit and loss (P & L) statement. The P & L statement, which is prepared using standard accounting procedures, provides you with a snapshot of the business at a single point in time, usually at the end of each month. While your CPA will use the P & L statements to monitor cash flow and tax liabilities, you will use the P & L to monitor the financial operation of your business.

The first part of the P & L summarizes your income for the month and the second details your expenses. Although the P & L allows you to make historical comparisons, it is not an indication of how much money you have in the bank. These statements do not include income or expenses from the sale or purchase of capital expenses, such as vehicles and equipment, and they also do not include money due or paid on loans. What P & L statements do show under expenses is depreciation, which is an asset's reduction in value over time. However, in determining your monthly cash flow, depreciation is meaningless since it is not actually a monthly expenditure of funds. Most nurseries like to compare gross or net sales figures, but that comparison says little about the true profitability of the nursery. What matters, of course, is the bottom line or profit. Net income is gross or total income less any plant refunds you make. While early e-commerce sites tried to rewrite the rules of simple economics, most of these businesses, built like a house of cards, have come crashing down.

If you use a CPA—and I hope you do—your P & L expenses will be broken down into two groups, direct and overhead, the only two expense categories that show up on a P & L. Direct expenses are those that can be assigned to the cost of a particular product and they typically include the cost of plants purchased, irrigation supplies, shipping costs, chemicals, fertilizers, and production supplies such as pots, soil, and tags. These costs usually rise by a similar percentage as your sales. By subtracting the direct expenses from the net sales, you arrive at a figure known as gross profit.

The second group of expenses on your revenue or expense report includes your overhead or fixed expenses. This group covers everything not included in direct expenses, such as salaries, rent, phone bills, electric bills, taxes, and insurance. Often, these fixed costs stay the same for a given range of sales. Rent and insurance, for example, do not usually increase as sales increase. Salaries, on the other hand, typically increase in proportion to sales. To lower the percentage of net sales that direct costs contribute, you must increase income. In other words, if you pay $50,000 in rent on $500,000 in sales, your rent is 10 percent of your net sales, so by increasing your sales to $1,000,000, the same dollar amount of rent would amount to only 5 percent of your net sales.

Overhead or operating expenses are next subtracted from the gross profit, which gives you the net profit. This is the amount that you as the owner or stockholder get to split with the government in the form of taxes. Most nurseries aim for a net profit of 15 to 25 percent as anything above this range results in a tax burden that is astronomical, whereas anything below may make the business appear not financially sound enough to qualify for bank loans. If at the end of the year there is too much profit, your CPA might suggest disbursing extra income as bonuses or prepaying expenses for the upcoming year.

Let's now look at an actual P & L statement for a fictional mail-order nursery (see figure 15), beginning with part 1. Column A represents the type of expense, fixed or variable; column B is an itemized list of income and expense categories; column C details the income and expense amounts in each category from the most recent year (assume that is 2001); column D is the percentage of the income and expense total from the most recent year; column E is the budgeted amount of income and expenses for the upcoming year; column F is the budgeted percentage of the total; and column G is the budgeted cost per plant for the upcoming year. Column H in part 2 of the chart details summaries used in projecting growth and setting prices for the upcoming season.

I have filled in the figures for 2001 and am projecting growth at a 20 percent rate for the following year. The items in the first three lines at the top of the chart represent the section detailing sales income, which includes plant sales, income received for shipping, and refunds. You can see that for 2001, plant sales are 93.1 percent of the income, while income for shipping is 9 percent. Deducted from total income is the refunds amount, which comprises 2 percent of net sales.

The next section reflects direct expenses, which are those expenses directly attributable to the production and delivery of plants. These include expenses such as pesticides, seed, plants, fertilizer, irrigation, nursery and shipping salaries (but not office salaries), shipping expenses, greenhouse fuel, and royalties. When you subtract these direct expenses from the net sales, you are left with the gross profit. For 2001, the gross profit is 45.6 percent.

The third section of figures represents the overhead expenses. These are the expenses that are not directly attributable to the cost of producing a plant. Do you notice how many there are? The ability to control this group of expenses is what makes or breaks a nursery. You will notice that for 2001, the net profit was a meager $29,723 or 2.1 percent.

The final section is classified as other income and expense. Some like to include these as overhead, but many accountants prefer to break these out separately since they aren't a true cost of production. Included here are nominal expenses such as filling the employee drink machine and interest paid and earned. Adding this amount (which is known as "other income") to the operating income from the first section on sales, we arrive at a net profit of $30,726.

Obviously, this net profit is far below our target goals of 15 to 25 percent, so the profit for 2002 will have to be increased. After analyzing these figures, the nursery owner can make two initial moves. First, the nursery can raise plant prices by 7 percent and shipping charges by 11 percent. These changes in income are entered into the spreadsheet's budget column. Next, the nursery owner looks at each expense and determines a projected amount of expenditure. For each variable expense (which is designated in the left-most column with a "V"), an increase of 20 percent is figured using the targeted projection. For fixed costs (which are designated in the left-most column with an "F"), there is no increase since a sales increase would not cause a fixed cost to increase. In a few other cases, the fixed figures can be adjusted to reflect a known increase or decrease from the prior year. After plugging in these numbers, the nursery owner's net income or profit for the upcoming year rises to $233,102 or 9.9 percent. This is still far below the 15 to 25 percent that the nursery should be making, so the owner will need to adjust pricing again or decrease overhead costs for the following year as well.

At the end of the sample P & L statement (column H), I have made several calculations based on the budget numbers in columns C, D, and E. To get the average current selling price, divide the number of plants sold in 2001 (you should get this figure from the inventory system) into the total income of 2001, which is $1,445,659 divided by 110,000 plants. The average selling price for 2001 is $13.14. To calculate the average cost to produce each plant in 2001, take the direct expenses ($786,417), add it to the overhead expenses ($629,518), and divide that number by the number of plants sold (110,000). The average cost to produce each plant sold that year was $12.87. In other words, the profit made on each plant sold in 2001 was $0.27.

Figure 15. Profit and Loss Statement

PART 1

A	B	C	D	E	F	G
		2001 INCOME	% TOTAL	BUDGET 2002	% TOTAL	COST/PLANT
	Sales					
	Plant Sales	$1,345,202	93.1%	$1,727,239	92.6%	
	Shipping Charges Income	$ 129,462	9.0%	$ 172,443	9.2%	
	Refunds	$ (29,005)	-2.0%	$ (34,807)	-1.9%	
	Total Income	**$1,445,659**	**100.0%**	**$1,864,876**	**100.0%**	
	Direct Expenses					
V	Chemicals/Pesticides	$ 6,992	0.5%	$ 8,400	0.5%	$0.06
V	IPM-Beneficials	$ 932	0.1%	$ 1,100	0.1%	$0.01
V	Seeds	$ 1,350	0.1%	$ 1,600	0.1%	$0.01
V	Plants	$ 247,808	17.1%	$ 297,400	15.9%	$2.25
V	Fertilizer	$ 7,382	0.5%	$ 8,900	0.5%	$0.07
V	Nursery Production Material	$ 40,565	2.8%	$ 48,700	2.6%	$0.37
V	Nursery Operating Supplies	$ 2,223	0.2%	$ 2,700	0.1%	$0.02
F	Lease—Nursery Equipment	$ 8,000	0.6%	$ 8,000	0.4%	$0.06
V	Supplies—Irrigation	$ 7,044	0.5%	$ 8,500	0.5%	$0.06
V	Royalties & Commissions	$ 4,479	0.3%	$ 5,400	0.3%	$0.04
V	Salaries—Nursery	$ 251,416	17.4%	$ 301,700	16.2%	$2.29
V	Salaries—Shipping	$ 95,627	6.6%	$ 114,800	6.2%	$0.87
F	Fuel—Greenhouses	$ 17,320	1.2%	$ 17,000	0.9%	$0.13
V	Lab Supplies	$ 1,350	0.1%	$ 1,600	0.1%	$0.01
V	Supplies—Shipping	$ 8,710	0.6%	$ 10,500	0.6%	$0.08
V	Order Shipping—Freight	$ 85,219	5.9%	$ 102,300	5.5%	$0.78
	Total Direct Expenses	**$ 786,417**	**54.4%**	**$ 938,600**	**50.3%**	**Total Direct Cost/Plant $7.11**
	Gross Profit	**$ 659,241**	**45.6%**	**$ 926,276**	**49.7%**	**Avg. Gross Profit/Plant $7.02**
F	Salaries—Office	$ 166,623	11.5%	$ 166,600	8.9%	$1.26
V	Payroll Taxes	$ 45,311	3.1%	$ 52,500	2.8%	$0.40
F	Lease—Office Equipment	$ 7,733	0.5%	$ 7,700	0.4%	$0.06
F	Rent	$ 43,250	3.0%	$ 60,000	3.2%	$0.45
F	Depreciation	$ 23,962	1.7%	$ 24,000	1.3%	$0.18
F	Telephone	$ 4,728	0.3%	$ 4,700	0.3%	$0.04
F	Telephone—Cellular	$ 1,261	0.1%	$ 1,300	0.1%	$0.01
F	Telephone—Long Dist.	$ 1,648	0.1%	$ 2,250	0.1%	$0.02

V= variable, F = fixed

(continued)

A	B		C	D	E	F	G
			2001 INCOME	% TOTAL	BUDGET 2002	% TOTAL	COST/PLANT
F	Supplies—Office		$ 10,306	0.7%	$ 10,300	0.6%	$0.08
F	Supplies—Janitorial		$ 1,665	0.1%	$ 1,700	0.1%	$0.01
F	Internet Connection Fee		$ 779	0.1%	$ 800	0.0%	$0.01
F	Catalog Preparation		$ 5,000	0.3%	$ 5,000	0.3%	$0.04
V	Printing—Catalog		$ 120,067	8.3%	$ 148,507	8.0%	$1.13
F	Printing—Miscellaneous		$ 4,000	0.3%	$ 4,000	0.2%	$0.03
F	Web Site		$ 8,644	0.6%	$ 8,600	0.5%	$0.07
F	Advertising—Nursery		$ 1,000	0.1%	$ 1,000	0.1%	$0.01
F	Advertising—Employment		$ 500	0.0%	$ 500	0.0%	$0.00
F	Postage—General		$ 6,948	0.5%	$ 7,650	0.4%	$0.06
F	Postage—Catalogs		$ 34,937	2.4%	$ 41,924	2.2%	$0.32
F	Repairs & Maintenance		$ 33,480	2.3%	$ 33,500	1.8%	$0.25
F	Safety Materials		$ 737	0.1%	$ 700	0.0%	$0.01
F	Simple IRA—Employees		$ 8,745	0.6%	$ 8,700	0.5%	$0.07
F	Dues & Subscriptions		$ 5,261	0.4%	$ 5,300	0.3%	$0.04
F	Staff Registrations/ Meeting Expense		$ 570	0.0%	$ 600	0.0%	$0.00
F	Supplies—Open House		$ 630	0.0%	$ 600	0.0%	$0.00
F	Hospitality—On Site		$ 392	0.0%	$ 500	0.0%	$0.00
F	Professional Fees		$ 8,175	0.6%	$ 8,200	0.4%	$0.06
F	Insurance—Liability		$ 5,806	0.4%	$ 5,800	0.3%	$0.04
F	Insurance—Worker's Comp.		$ 9,533	0.7%	$ 9,600	0.5%	$0.07
F	Insurance—Health		$ 14,207	1.0%	$ 14,207	0.8%	$0.11
F	Taxes & License		$ 2,856	0.2%	$ 2,900	0.2%	$0.02
F	Meals & Entertainment		$ 2,226	0.2%	$ 2,200	0.1%	$0.02
V	Bank Fees—Credit Cards		$ 27,378	1.9%	$ 32,900	1.8%	$0.25
V	Bank Fees—Other		$ 2,005	0.1%	$ 2,406	0.1%	$0.02
F	Travel—Airfare		$ 6,788	0.5%	$ 5,000	0.3%	$0.04
F	Travel—Lodging		$ 4,376	0.3%	$ 4,400	0.2%	$0.03
F	Travel—Fuel + Car Rental		$ 1,890	0.1%	$ 1,900	0.1%	$0.01
F	Travel—Food		$ 300	0.0%	$ 300	0.0%	$0.00
F	Mileage Reimbursement		$ 2,586	0.2%	$ 2,600	0.1%	$0.02
F	Medical Treatment		$ 243	0.0%	$ 200	0.0%	$0.00
F	Vehicle Maintenance Expense		$ 1,875	0.1%	$ 1,900	0.1%	$0.01
F	Slides—Film Processing		$ 1,098	0.1%	$ 1,100	0.1%	$0.01
	Total Gen. & Admin Exp.		$ 629,518	43.5%	$ 694,544	37.2%	Overhead Cost/Plant $5.26
	Operating Income		$ 29,723	2.1%	$ 231,732	12.4%	Profit/Plant $1.76

PART 1 continued

A	B	C	D	E	F	
		2001 INCOME	% TOTAL	BUDGET 2002	% TOTAL	
	Other Income & Expense					
V	Drink Money Income	$ 1,755	0.1%	$ 1,755	0.1%	
V	Soft Drink Cost	$ (2,565)	-0.2%	$ (2,481)	-0.1%	
V	Drinks/Snacks	$ (810)	-0.1%	$ (726)	0.0%	
V	Interest Income	$ 2,707	0.2%	$ 2,707	0.1%	
V	Interest Expense	$ (894)	-0.1%	$ (611)	0.0%	
	Interest	$ 1,813	0.1%	$ 2,096	0.1%	
	Total Other Income (Expense)	$ 1,002	0.1%	$ 1,370	0.1%	
	Net Income (Loss)	$ 30,726	2.1%	$ 233,101	12.5%	

	PART 2	H	
	Estimated Growth	20%	
	Plant Sales Last Year (Units)	110,000	
	Avg. Current Selling Price	$ 12.23	
	Avg. Current Plant Income	$ 13.14	
	Plant Sales Next Year (Units)	132,000	
	Avg. Projected Selling Price	$ 13.09	
	Avg. Projected Plant Income	$ 14.13	
	Avg. Cost Per Plant Old	$ 12.87	
	Avg. Cost Per Plant New	$ 12.37	

V= variable, F = fixed

Using the predictions for the upcoming year, the nursery owner can project that the income per plant will rise to $14.13. This figure is arrived at by dividing the projected total income ($1,864,876) by the number of projected plants sold (110,000 plants × 20 percent, which is 132,000). Based on the projected cost of production for 2002, the cost per plant actually drops to $12.37, resulting in a profit of $1.76 per plant.

In making use of a P & L statement, the key is to first understand and control your overhead costs and then to ensure that your pricing stays proportionate to your production costs. If you wonder how you are doing compared to the rest of your industry, you could pull your business credit report. Companies such as Dunn & Bradstreet allow you to pull your financial report, which has been compared with others in your industry, from their Web sites.

Cash flow

Cash can be a wonderful thing, as long as more is flowing in than flowing out; unfortunately, the tide is often going in the wrong direction. Tracking cash flow can make or break a business. Standard accounting reports make it difficult to monitor cash flow as they are designed only for tax-based accounting, so I recommend constructing your own cash-flow charts. The measure of positive cash flow is called liquidity. Put simply, liquidity is the ability of a business to pay its bills on time. Liquidity in a nursery business varies throughout the season, being highest in the peak sales season (which is usually in spring) and lowest in winter. You would ideally like to maintain a 2:1 liquidity ratio for as long as possible. A liquidity ratio can be computed by dividing current liabilities by current assets, both of which should be on your balance sheet (Battersby 1998).

When calculating the actual amount of working capital you have, subtract current liabilities from current assets, as this tells you the amount of cash you have on hand. The cash-flow charts I use break down each month into columns that include income from the nursery, income from capital expenses, nursery expenses, capital expenses, interest income or expenses, and any business disbursements to the nursery owners. From these expenses, deduct the depreciation expense (it appears on the P & L statement), as it is not an actual expense. Finally add money borrowed for the business and money paid back to the business. At the end of each month, you will know whether a positive or negative cash flow was generated and also how much of one. After a year of charting your cash flow, you will find it much easier to plan for the upcoming year.

I recommend planning expenses month by month for the first year you are in business. After you have a year or two under your belt, you can budget by the quarter. Among the best reasons to look at expenses by the quarter instead of by the month is that recurring income and expenditures can vary from one month to the next. For example, a rainy month may throw your income off from a prior year. In many cases it will be made up the following month, so don't get too frightened when one month doesn't meet projections. This same variation also occurs with expenses.

When budgeting for future years, predict a reasonable growth factor that you think your business will be able to sustain and multiply this factor by last year's sales figures. When you get the monthly accounting reports back from your accountant, you can compare your projected figures with your actual results. If your projections and actual outcome vary wildly, you will have some basis for modifying your projections to past seasons. Learning how to predict income and expenses will prove to be an invaluable tool in monitoring and predicting cash flow. Don't get too concerned with month-by-month figures; concentrate instead on quarterly comparisons.

Once you are aware of recurring cash-flow shortages in your business, you can work on how to even out these low points. Festivals, holiday sales, open houses, and tours are all valuable ways to bring in money during normally off-peak sales periods. If August is a low cash flow month, try scheduling tour groups to your nursery during this time or plan a tour for your customers to other gardens and nurseries. If fall is a slow time, consider having fall sales, creating fall festivals, or some other type of holiday-related open house. You will be amazed at the cash that can be generated from a festival or special event.

Financing

Every nursery will eventually need a method of financing. Most often it is the owners who provide financing, thus acting as their own banks. Before you begin your nursery, you will need to take a realistic look at how much money you are willing to invest each year, how much of a return you need, and how long you are willing to wait for a return on your money. Some small nurseries have owners who are financially secure and are willing to operate their nurseries as a break-even proposition. There is certainly nothing wrong with operating a nursery that doesn't make money—it's done all the time. Just be sure that you are realistic about your financial needs before you begin.

For a prospective nursery owner or even the owner of an existing small nursery, borrowing money is at best difficult and at worst impossible. Not only is the nursery business one that deals with perishable commodities but it is also often one of very low net-profit margins. Unless you are working with a small-town bank that is willing to gamble, or unless you have a good track record with other related businesses, you will have a difficult time obtaining financing for a start-up nursery.

You will need to borrow money for three primary reasons: to start up a nursery, to make capital improvements, and to cover operating expenses during cash flow shortages. The most difficult financing to obtain is that for starting a new nursery, as lending institutions will want to see a sound, peer-reviewed business plan. While attitudes of banks toward small businesses change with the state of the economy, a lender's search for a solid investment remains constant. You will impress a lender by knowing exactly how much money you need, what you will use it for, and when you will repay the loan.

Most lending institutions struggle to understand the seasonal nature of the nursery industry. At best, most nurseries have six months of positive cash flow, meaning that income exceeds expenses, and six months of negative cash flow, where income is less than expenses. In reality, many nurseries have only four months of positive cash flow. Both types of income streams tend to make financial institutions nervous and unwilling to loan start-up money.

If you decide to borrow money for a start-up nursery, I strongly urge you to seek out an agricultural lender who may be more in tune with agricultural businesses. Such lenders could be a local farm credit association or a bank with an agricultural lending specialty. The best way to find out which bank is easiest to work with would be to consult with farmers and other nursery owners in your region. Farm credit associations are farmer-owned lending institutions, first established thanks to the Federal Farm Loan Act of 1916. Their primary purpose is to help farmers secure needed financing. I also recommend going to the SBA. Not only does it make loans but it is a great resource for figuring out how to prepare a loan proposal. You can find this information at the SBA's Web site by following the "starting your business," "startup kit," and "finding the money you need" links.

The first time my wife and I visited a bank we were seeking a small start-up loan for our business. "Come on in," said the loan officer, which turned out to be the last positive comment we heard during the visit. The officer wanted first to see two years of financial statements and then to know exactly how profitable our business was. The business was very small at the time, having just started, and both my wife and I were still working other jobs. I wanted to tell the loan officer that if the business were actually profitable, then I wouldn't be in need of a loan. After a few minutes of discussion about the need for a positive track record and the risky nature of our business, we gave up—at least on the idea of getting a loan. We realized we were going to have to make the finances work without any help from the bank.

You might think the chances of a fledgling nursery getting a bank loan are as good as those of the ocean freezing over and I would not necessarily disagree with that. However, if you do go to the trouble of applying for a loan then, you should increase your chances of success by being very well prepared. Make sure you have a good understanding of your nursery's finances. Although everyone wants to know how much it costs to start a nursery, as with any other business, there are no black and white answers, particularly since costs are based on the size and type of the nursery. Among the best, most detailed studies that I recommend you read is by Badenhop et al, which provides some concrete figures from 1984 and offers technical data that is usually impossible to find elsewhere (1987). It is also a good idea to know exactly how much money you need and how long it will take you to pay it back.

As I mentioned earlier, it is quite typical for nurseries to start up without borrowing money. One factor to keep in mind, however, is that the more money you are able to secure for your start-up, the less time it will take to reach a larger sales volume. Conversely, the less money you have for starting a nursery, the longer it will take to reach the same sales volume. The up-front costs for infrastructure are merely a drop in the proverbial bucket compared to the unforeseen costs that we will cover in later chapters.

When they give start-up loans, lending institutions demand profit projections, a financial statement, and some collateral or other guarantee against default. You are much more likely to be successful if you keep good financial records and start your nursery without borrowing money; the time you will have to spend building a solid financial foundation and making long-term business relationships is just too burdensome. A business history, however small, will more likely establish a track record for when you apply for operating lines of credit. Also, work to establish a personal relationship with your lender. Ask lots of questions and continually seek advice. Financial institutions are like conscientious business owners who want to learn how to do things right.

Once your nursery is in operation, the most important type of funding is an operating loan. Cash flow in the nursery business is only positive during about half the year, and although few nursery owners ever discuss operating loans or lines of credit openly, few of them do not have one in place. Lines of credit are usually used for large recurring seasonal expenses, such as purchasing a large quantity of plants, printing a catalog, or hiring a large labor crew for seasonal needs. Most lines of credit must be paid off at some point during the year, but there are many different variations on this theme depending on the lender.

My wife and I put off the idea of obtaining operating capital for years until one day a car pulled up along the road in front of our nursery. "Is this a nursery business?" the gentleman asked. Since we were a mail-order business, I replied that the answer depended on who he was and why he was asking. Rolling his window down further, our visitor explained that he was with the local farm credit office and he wondered if we would like to borrow any money. Needless to say, we invited him inside and began what would be a wonderful relationship and our first line of credit.

Most nurseries require lines of credit during the winter months and occasionally during the summer. Wholesale nurseries usually don't have much money coming in until late spring, while mail-order nurseries usually start having decent cash flow around February. Retail garden centers often get a big cash-flow boost around Christmas, but that drops off again until the first few warm days of spring. It will take a fair bit of practice to learn how best to balance plant and other purchases to coincide with a positive cash flow, as well as how to manage your line of credit.

Once the lender agrees to extend you a line of credit, you will next negotiate the terms of the loan. Don't think your lender's first offer is etched in stone. The initial offer is based on a lending formula that is used by that particular lender. You will be able to negotiate interest rates, which are often set as a percentage plus an established index rate, such as the prime or the London Interbank Offered Rate (LIBOR). Prime is the interest rate on corporate loans charged by more than 75 percent of the 30 largest banks in the United States, and LIBOR is an international money market index rate set by London banks. If you have not had experience borrowing large amounts of money, it can be a terrifying experience.

Keep in mind that interest rates are more negotiable as the size of your loan rises. Since the lender must make money, the larger the amount they will be lending, the lower the percentage they can afford to offer. You can also negotiate, within a narrow range, the amount of the loan, the repayment terms, and the collateral for the loan. Collateral is simply an exchange of value between you and the lender. If the lender agrees to lend you money, you promise something of value in case you default. Ideally, you would choose as collateral something you can stand to lose. The lender of course, will prefer something it can sell in case you default on the loan. Examples of commonly used collateral include the nursery land, a house or structure, equipment, or the product inventory.

It is always advantageous for the nursery owner to use the business's inventory of plants as collateral. If you keep an adequate inventory, it should be quite simple to determine its value. This is a commonly accepted practice, especially with local farm credit institutions. If your inventory isn't large enough to qualify for the line of credit you will need, you may need to put up other collateral such as your land, house, vehicle, and greenhouses. Although this may make the lending institution feel better, it will do nothing but add an extra level of anxiety to your already adequate stress level. Typically, financial institutions lend only a percentage of the value of the collateral. If you use inventory as collateral, expect to get between 40 and 60 percent of its value. Equipment will get you a loan of between 70 and 80 percent of its value, and real estate will produce a loan between 80 and 90 percent (Broome 1995).

If your nursery does not yet have enough of a track record to qualify for a loan, you always have the option of using credit cards. While this is not advisable as a long-term loan strategy, credit cards may be a lifesaver when you are getting started and managing your way through cash-flow shortages. Many nurseries, including mine, used this technique before we were able to establish a line of credit. For example, if you are expecting a delivery with payment terms of net 30, wait until the bill is due and then call the company and put the purchase on a credit card. Depending on the billing cycle, this may give you another 30 days to pay for the purchase; if you can stand the high interest rates, you can have an even longer period. Credit card companies give out more cards than anyone can possibly use, which means that some folks have perfected the technique of transferring balances between cards to extend payment deadlines even further. Again, this practice should only be used as a last resort, and only to help with cash-flow shortfalls, not to cover income shortfalls. Credit card misuse can ruin your financial future if you aren't careful.

Capital loans are loans that cover the cost of capital expenses. Capital expenses are for things that become assets of the business, including land, buildings, greenhouses, vehicles, and equipment. These are items that must be depreciated for income tax purposes. Loans for capital expenses are similar to lines of credit except they are for a specific term of years, usually coinciding with the depreciation schedule of the item being purchased. Collateral for capital expenses is often the item itself. It is usually not a good idea to tie up a line of credit for a long-term capital expense because of the loan's yearly payoff terms and because the line of credit may be needed elsewhere in your operation. Again, shop around at different financial institutions as rates on capital loans vary dramatically.

Internal controls

Another important factor to consider when you attempt to follow the money within your company is the type of internal controls you have in place. The American Institute of Certified Public Accountants believes that trusted employees are responsible for a significant amount of embezzlement activity as they are easily able to take advantage of inadequate internal cash controls. Great —all you needed about now was something else to worry about!

So what do you do? First, you should have any employee who handles large amounts of money bonded, which means acquiring an insurance policy against employee theft. Keep your ear open for employees who talk about cheating or taking advantage of others. Trust me, employees who would cheat someone else, even the government, would certainly cheat their employer. A frightening study done by the Josephson Institute of Ethics (1998) found, after surveying more than 20,000 people, that 47 percent of high-school students admitted stealing from a store within the past year, 70 percent admitted to cheating on an exam within the previous 12 months, and, according to *American Nurseryman*, more than 33 percent said they would lie on a job application (1993). Are you worried yet?

The second thing I recommend is to work with your CPA to develop a series of checks and balances on the money coming into and going out of your company. For example, you could create a check register as well as backup systems to monitor outgoing and incoming checks, and you could institute a policy of not letting cash remain undeposited. Another good policy is to have someone else assume the duties of any employee who handles funds during that person's vacation. It is often embezzling employees who never want to take a vacation for fear of having their scams discovered.

Chapter 18

Administrative Stuff

While many nursery owners embrace technology in the production phases of their nursery, these same owners tend to run in the opposite direction at the thought of office technology. Whether that technology is the phone or a computer, it is this part of the business that is truly a weak link in most nurseries. In today's marketplace, it is the technology of communications, as well as the ability to keep good records, that separates the successful nursery from the unsuccessful nursery.

Office technology and customer communications

The bane of most nursery owners' existence is still the telephone. Unfortunately, it is also the lifeline of the business. Customers are well aware of the array of communications technology and they expect vendors to be so equipped. No longer is it acceptable for a customer to leave a voice message and wait days for an answer. I know of many nurseries whose reputation is based primarily on their inability to answer the telephone or their unwillingness to return phone calls. I find it quite fascinating that nursery owners think that whatever it is they are involved in is more important than talking to customers, especially if it is about their orders.

How you handle your telephone calls is greatly influenced by your mission statement and, in particular, by your customer profile. Obviously a small nursery cannot afford to have a secretary answering calls and relaying messages. Phone inquiries are generally about either plants or orders. As a general rule, customers who are lazy require more of your time on the phone as they request information that can easily be found elsewhere with a modicum of effort. Other customers are just lonely and want someone to talk with.

It is impossible for small nurseries to spend as much time with customers as they require and still get any work done. Our nursery receives quite a few questions from people who want us to recommend a plant for a particular spot or, in some cases, to design their entire garden. It would be easy to spend hours doing this, and it is possible that some large orders might result. You must, however, refer to your mission statement and customer profile; if extensive customer support is not part of your business, do not let yourself get sidetracked. Nevertheless, it is always a good idea to provide the customer with alternative means of obtaining information, such as providing the names of local landscape designers or the contact details of their county extension service. I recommend you provide as much information as possible in your catalog, advertisements, or Web site, as this allows those who are willing to search for the information to help themselves.

Among the most important employees you will ever hire is the one who answers the telephone. When hiring someone for this position, be aware that a good phone voice and manner is of utmost importance. Some employees who seem perfect in person may be terrible on the phone. Just as your catalog is the first printed impression that customers have of your nursery, the telephone is the first voice contact for many. For a large number of nurseries, it will also be the last contact; a customer greeted by a receptionist who is doing a bad job likely won't call back. Think about how other businesses answer your phone calls. Is the voice cheery, or does the person at the other end seem to be saying, "I'm having a bad day, so don't bother me"? People who answer the phone must speak clearly, and they should also always answer with the name of the business as well as their own name. By immediately getting onto a first-name basis, your employee has immediately personalized the relationship with the customer.

Nursery owners who are a one-person operation should use a high-quality cordless or comparable phone. Answering machines are a poor substitute during regular business hours, although they may be the only option when no one is at the nursery. If you are going to use an answering machine, be sure to have an upbeat, concise message and tell the customer when you will return the call. There is nothing worse than a generic message that doesn't even tell callers if they have the right number.

Telephone systems are becoming more advanced, and at the same time, competition in the market has caused prices to drop. Phone systems work along the same lines as networked computers. They are linked together and allow for communications between several phone extensions while also handling incoming and outgoing calls. These systems are available in a range of sizes, models, and prices to suit any sized business.

As technological advances continue, you will have to make sure that you do not miss out on those innovations that can improve your nursery's efficiency. Only a few years ago, fax machines were seen as a luxury, but now they are essential to doing business as they allow orders to be sent inexpensively from any part of the world at any time of day or night. Of course, nursery owners who keep their fax machine in their home are advised to use a switch to turn off the ringer at night—assuming they like to sleep. Many customers, especially overseas customers in different time zones, will send faxes at the most inopportune times.

Just as the fax machine was once considered a luxury, so was e-mail. A startling number of nursery owners tell me that they simply don't have time for e-mail. What they are saying is that they do not have time to talk with their customers, even with a method that is much more efficient than either phone or fax. Just because e-mail doesn't seem as personal as a phone call, do not assume that customers will tolerate a delay in receiving a response. In fact, e-mail seems to have made customers even more impatient about expecting a response. I recommend you designate one person to be in charge of receiving and answering e-mail messages, as well as forwarding to the proper person those messages requiring special attention. While it may be tempting, the nursery owner should never be the one who has the first-line responsibility of getting e-mail, as this is not an efficient use of the owner's time.

Computers

Nursery owners are often the last ones to employ computer technology. It has become increasingly difficult, however, to stay profitable in the nursery business without a good computer system. Computers are now used to maintain customer mailing lists, record and track inventory, monitor sales and cash flow, record sales history, schedule and track deliveries, as well as schedule propagation and other production processes. Certainly, with the rapid advances in computer technology, it won't be long before everyone is using computers to schedule and track irrigation, monitor weather and related alarm systems, and close down the office at the end of the day. Every week, it seems, there are more and more things that computers can do more efficiently than employees.

A crucial first step toward a well-developed administrative system is to establish a good working relationship with a computer consultant. Typically, an in-house staff member is designated as your systems administrator, the person other employees go to when they have computer questions or problems. The systems administrator is often able to solve minor computer problems without you having to hire a costly consultant, but where this is not possible, it is the systems administrator who decides when outside consultants are needed and who makes such contact.

Computer consultants come in three varieties, software consultants, hardware consultants, and programmers. It is difficult to find one who is qualified in all three areas of specialization. You can easily find computer consultants by asking nearby businesses for recommendations or by visiting local computer stores to ask for references. Good computer consultants of any kind who can be contacted when needed are worth more than their weight in gold.

Software consultants can help you in both selecting the programs that will work best for your business and in installing those programs on your computers.

If the program you need doesn't exist, these consultants can recommend a programmer if they cannot handle the project themselves. Software consultants also train employees to properly use the programs. I hesitate to recommend specific programs, as changes in the software industry and in the software itself are so rapid that any suggestions would be immediately out-of-date. Basic programs you will need include an accounting program, a word processing program, a desktop publishing program, an Internet and e-mail program, and a relational database, one that integrates more than one set of data.

The most important program will likely be the database. A database is simply a filing system of all your records that is stored on a computer and that is also searchable. Ideally, you would have what is known as a relational database, one in which, for example, your orders database communicates with your customer database, inventory database, financial database, purchase order database, and so on. Off-the-shelf relational databases are becoming more and more common. The database you use should also be able to print reports. How will you track sales unless your database can assemble information on such vital information as sales figures and month by month sales charts? Since the nursery industry is still very young in its use of databases, there is nothing even approaching an industry standard. If your software consultant can't find what you need, attend a state or regional nursery show, where you will find programs that have already been custom written for nurseries. These programs will more than likely be the best match for your needs.

With regard to the other three software programs you will need, I recommend purchasing an accounting program that can communicate directly with your CPA's system. The same recommendation holds true for your word processing system, although most computers these days can talk to each other regardless of the word processing program used. Word processing systems simply allow you to type, format, print, and then save documents onto the computer's hard drive. A desktop publishing program is one that allows you to self-publish catalogs or, at the very least, to lay out the catalog or prepare advertisements. These are not the simplest programs to master, so you may want to visit a computer store where you can trial these programs prior to purchasing them. If you plan to be working with a commercial printer, be sure to ask which desktop publishing program they use, as your choice must be compatible.

The next kind of computer consultant you should know about is the hardware consultant, the person who builds and sells computers. If you want a computer to talk to another computer or want it to have more memory or a different drive, you will need a hardware consultant. By the time you hire a hardware consultant, you will have chosen whether to use a PC or a Mac. While progress has been made for the two types of computers to communicate with each other, they remain the technological version of the Hatfields and the McCoys. Generally, most commercial printing firms and graphic designers use Macs, and almost everyone else uses PCs.

A good hardware consultant should be able to recommend the proper speed and memory of a computer that will suit your needs, as well as when to replace outdated and slower machines. With the increasing processing speed of computers, it is rare for a computer more than three years old to be economical to operate. Throwing away anything at a nursery is difficult—just wait until you start tossing out old but still functioning computers. Hardware consultants also set up computer networks, backup systems, printers, and modems.

Although it would seem to be a foregone conclusion that all computers at a nursery should be networked, many people remain behind the times in this regard. Being networked simply means that the computers are all linked to each other so that data entered on each computer can be shared between all the others at the nursery. The cost of moving data between computers manually is not an effective use of anyone's time. I once hired a new employee who was shocked that we didn't have to save every file to a disk and then reinstall every update on each of the other computers manually.

Most nurseries will never need the assistance of the third kind of computer consultant, the computer programmer, which is probably a good thing. Software consultants often do some programming, although large-scale programming projects usually require someone who is more specialized. Working with computer programmers can be a very time-consuming project; fortunately it is unnecessary in most cases if there is a suitable off-the-shelf program. Since each type of nursery business is specialized, however, you might not be able to find one that fits your operation.

You may decide to have a custom program written specifically for your business. This is a long, expensive, and time-consuming process that requires a great deal of dedication, both by the nursery and the computer programmer. In the long run, custom programs can pay great dividends, but the trials and tribulations of dealing with most computer programmers makes the rest of the nursery business look easy. Be sure you have a computer programmer you can depend on for both programming and long-term support. In other words, ask a lot of hard, in-depth questions to get a thorough understanding of what is involved.

Plant Delights Nursery needed a relational database that catered to a production-oriented, mail-order nursery. Only after five agonizing years and thousands of man-hours did we finally complete (and I use that word loosely) a program with the desired results. Even so, the program is still not without minor bugs. Working with a computer programmer to develop such a program is only economical if the programmer sells the program to other users to recoup the development costs or if the nursery owner underwrites the entire project, which can easily top $100,000.

A discussion of computers is not complete without mentioning the Internet. The Internet is an extremely valuable tool, but as with any tool, it is only valuable when it is used correctly. Tools such as e-mail have revolutionized the breadth of communication that was possible just a few years earlier. Unnecessary e-mail, however, can slow work down instead of speeding it up. It is very important that each employee who is entrusted with Internet access understand a clear policy that you will develop regarding its use and misuse. Avoiding the possibility of misuse by not making the Internet accessible is not a wise business move as it takes away one of the most incredible tools at your disposal.

Creating a paper trail

Processing orders is a challenge far removed from growing the plants themselves. Nurseries that spend too much time on growing plants and not enough on systems to deliver the plants and manage information about the order will not be favorites with customers. With a good paperwork system in place, including a working paper trail, it becomes much easier to manage the flow of relevant information regarding your plants and orders. Order processing involves all the steps it takes to manage an order, such as recording the order, processing the shipping information, confirming the order with the customer, managing inventory, processing back orders, obtaining payment information, and doing any necessary follow-up.

Your office system must also provide a tracking system to deal with orders that don't fit into the normal flow. No matter how much we would like all orders to fit into a specified pattern, the reality is that a percentage of them will simply not fit into any standard model you set. For example, there's that order for 100 of an item, where half will not be ready for a few weeks or a month. Many nurseries lose large amounts of money simply because their paper trail doesn't allow them to handle unusual orders. Similarly, you should develop a means of handling problems or disputes over the order. For example, if the shipment contains a wrong item or a miscount of the proper item, how will your paperwork system allow you to solve the problem and track the replacement plants?

The first stage in any order processing is the means by which an order is received. Since sales in retail establishments are done primarily on a walk-in basis, order processing is mostly applicable to wholesale and mail-order nurseries. The most common methods of receiving an order are via phone, fax, or e-mail, and as the way businesses communicate changes, so too will the way in which orders are received. Once an order is received it should be recorded by the nursery in a standard format that you have developed. If you kept each order in its original form as sent by the customer, there would be no consistency in format, readability, or retrieval ability for later storage. Having consistent records is a key ingredient to providing good customer service.

Most nurseries enter incoming orders into a computer database. Once the order is entered, a pull ticket is printed and given an order number. This number becomes the reference for both the nursery and the customer when questions arise regarding the order. After comparing the plants on the order with the available inventory and by using the requested ship date (which is the date the shipment is scheduled to depart), the nursery prints a pull ticket. It is never advisable to pull orders using the original paperwork, as it may get lost or damaged, particularly in a nursery setting. When there is no backup reference copy, orders are often lost. With an accurate plant inventory in your database and a good production schedule, a competent computer program will automatically compare the order quantity with the inventory and print the pull ticket according to the preprogrammed parameters you have set in your program. If this part of the process is not computerized, an employee will have to go over each order manually to determine which plants are available for the customer by the requested delivery date.

It is at this point in the order processing that a nursery employee should confirm with the customer which items will be delivered and when. Most nurseries now do this via fax or e-mail; only a few still use postal mail. Confirmation of orders should be done as soon as possible after the order has arrived so that the customer has time to find items you are unable to supply from other vendors. Little is more frustrating than expecting an item to be delivered and then finding out too late that not only is it unavailable from your original source but from all your other sources as well.

After the availability of the ordered items has been confirmed, the pull tickets are organized by dates and passed along to the staff who will assemble the orders. A major difference between selling live plants as opposed to widgets is that plants may be available but not sellable. Obviously, this causes problems in pulling orders. For example, a heavy rain or a caterpillar attack that has stripped the foliage from a plant the day before an order was to be pulled will render a plant that had been beautiful completely unsellable. You will need to develop a method for handling and recording the problems that arise in pulling orders. Some nurseries make use of back orders, which is a system that alerts the nursery when the items are finally available. The nursery then checks with the customer to see if the plants are still wanted.

Once the orders are pulled and confirmed, the paperwork must go to the person who will handle the delivery or shipping of the order. The shipping manager determines the best and most economical way to ship something. In wholesale nurseries, the shipping manager has to develop a system of combining shipments to several nurseries in one vehicle while also coordinating delivery times with each nursery that is to receive plants. This coordination needs to occur under the watchful eye of a very detail-oriented shipping manager. It won't take too many botched deliveries to accelerate the learning curve in this part of the nursery's operation.

Once you have a good handle on the actual shipping, you must set up a system to pass these shipping costs along to the customer. You will often be able to "predict" shipping costs and so quote the customer a precise shipping cost at the time the order is placed. Other times, however, you will have to bill the customer for shipping after the delivery. Many nurseries that use outside, independent trucking carriers will actually have the shipping company bill the customer directly when the truck arrives with the plants.

I have mentioned inventory several times, so let's explore that aspect of a nursery. Inventory is simply the amount of each item you have in stock. A good, usable inventory, however, contains much more information, such as the size of the container and the readiness of the crop to be sold. Computers and scanners have dramatically improved the monitoring of a crop's availability. I recommend doing at least one annual inventory of your nursery stock. When to do the inventory depends on your type of business. Typically, fall is a prime time as you prepare for the spring sales season. Some nurseries do a second, late spring inventory to capture information regarding "winter losses" and to help gather information that is pertinent to decisions regarding the summer production.

Most inventories are still done as manual counts. Obviously, the more organized way in which you grow your plants, the faster the count will proceed. I always recommend using teams of two or three for inventory counts as accurate counts are amazingly difficult to obtain. At our nursery, we always follow up an inventory count with a secondary check. A different group of counters will go behind each original group and do a random recount of about one-third of the items. If major discrepancies are found, then the entire block or greenhouse will be recounted. Although it is difficult to get an accurate count, you will not be as good as you could be in filling your customers' needs if you don't have good information.

Once you have taken inventory, you must enter the data into your computerized order processing system. If you use a bar code tag, hand scanners can upload the information as the count is taken. Without bar codes, it will be necessary to manually enter the data into the computer.

Having received and processed the order, be sure that you have properly processed the payment information. The most complex process is when you have extended credit to a customer. I suggest you devise a system that tracks delinquent payments and calculates late payment charges, as well as a method of follow-up invoicing to those who have not paid. Most computer databases allow you to "flag" an order so that a standard monthly query will reveal delinquent payments. More and more nurseries are accepting credit cards for payment as a way of reducing the complexity of processing an order. Regardless of the payment method, it is critical that the payment information be clearly recorded or posted in the database with the appropriate order.

Based on the number of nurseries from which we purchase, I can tell you that many nurseries are unable to send accurate invoices, track payments, and make timely and proper deliveries. If you had a choice between doing business with a nursery that has an accurate order processing system and one that doesn't, which would you choose? I trust it is now clear that growing the plants that comprise your nursery's inventory is only a small fraction of the important work you will be doing.

Chapter 19

The Joy of Government

You have no doubt heard the saying that the only sure things in life are death and taxes. I think we need to add government regulation to that list. In the name of fairness to all—except the business owner—our government keeps adding a seemingly endless amount of taxes and regulations that further complicate our lives. Since many of the existing laws will impact your business, you might as well know about them ahead of time.

Sales taxes

Most states impose a sales tax. In some states, the tax on agricultural products is waived if nurseries actually produce their own plants. Often those that produce 50 percent of the products they sell will qualify for the waiver. Be aware, however, that goods sold by nurseries other than agricultural products are usually subject to the normal tax rate. Where the tax is applicable, the nursery is required to collect the tax on sales and remit it to the proper tax authority. Large businesses must remit sales tax payments monthly, whereas smaller nurseries may be allowed to make quarterly payments.

Products that wholesalers sell to other nurseries for later resale to the end consumer are often not subject to sales tax. In most cases you will need a tax exemption certificate from the governing body in your region, which is usually the state's department of revenue. Keep the sales tax exemption certificates for each of your customers on file.

As with any government program, there are numerous gray areas that are open to interpretation. Many states try to collect sales tax from nurseries that are selling at shows rather than in their home states. There is an ongoing battle regarding whether mail-order nurseries are required to collect local sales taxes for each county into which they ship. As you can imagine, it would be a nightmare for mail-order businesses to have to track each local tax, but when has our government been remotely concerned with making things easy for small businesses? The courts have so far ruled that nurseries do not have to charge local taxes, but be sure to keep an eye out for any new decisions because this issue can change at any time.

Wholesale nurseries have also been brought into the tax fray. In 2001, an out-of-state nursery delivering plants to a customer in New Jersey was stopped for nonpayment of New Jersey's corporate and sales and use taxes. Even though the company was not located in New Jersey and sold no plants in that state, the delivery truck was seized and only released after payment of $15,000 (*ANLA Update* March 2001). Such ludicrous laws are on the books in several states, so I recommend you investigate the tax laws of a particular state before you ship plants into it. This is what happens when lawmakers become greedy and forget that their purpose is to serve people.

Unemployment tax

As if sales tax wasn't enough, you will also have to deal with the Federal Unemployment Tax Act (FUTA), which is usually made as a quarterly payment. The joint federal and state tax was designed to temporarily support workers who lost their job through no fault of their own. It has unfortunately become among the most disgusting taxes for anyone who has put forth the effort to start their own business, as it facilitates those who leech off your success when they claim unemployment compensation after they've been fired for doing a bad job. FUTA is usually around 0.8 percent of your payroll according to the Employment and Training Administration.

The state unemployment tax varies from state to state and even varies for different industries within a particular state. The idea is that you will pay a percentage of your payroll (usually from 1 to 6 percent) into a "reserve fund" based on the size of your workforce. The money is held by the state and then, in theory, used to compensate laid-off workers. In reality, workers who are fired or quit are almost always allowed to also draw from this fund despite protests from the employers.

States have two basic methods for computing the taxes you will pay. Nearly two-thirds of the states use a reserve ratio method, while the other third uses a benefit ratio formula. Reserve ratio rates are based on the size of your workforce and are calculated by dividing the size of your reserve by the three-year average of your taxable wages. This reserve ratio is then compared to a table to determine what rate you will pay. Most states require a reserve equal to about 6 to 10 percent of the annual average taxable wages. For help with state unemployment taxes, you could contact groups such as The Unemployment Tax Advisory Difference. (See Appendix 1.)

The benefit ratio plan compares the benefits charged against your account with the size of your workforce. All the benefits your state has paid out against your company, usually over the preceding three years, are totaled and then divided by your nursery's taxable wages during the same period. The resulting percentage is your benefit ratio.

Government regulation

The government also imposes enough regulations to put many people out of business. Among the most feared of federal agencies is the Department of Labor's (DOL) Occupational Safety and Health Administration (OSHA). The purpose of The OSHA Act of 1970 is to protect your workers from workplace hazards that may result in death or serious harm. OSHA has a mind-boggling list of regulations, so complex that most nursery owners could read the Act and still not have any idea how many regulations they are violating. If you don't have a copy of the ANLA's OSHA Compliance Manual, then I recommend you get one at once.

OSHA regulations extend from mandates about what type of ladders you use to how you open and close filing cabinets. In the 1990s there was a push to add even more regulations to our industry, especially in the area of ergonomics. Fortunately, the poorly thought-out ergonomics law was quickly repealed. Most but not all OSHA inspections arise from complaints by employees, so if you take good care of your employees you'll likely avoid an OSHA inspection. I can only hope that you never have a close encounter of the OSHA kind.

Renee Reback (2000) offers a great example of what you can expect from an OSHA inspection. Reback writes about a nursery owner who was visited by two inspectors with the DOL's Employment Standards Administration (ESA) Wage and Hour Division for a health and safety inspection.

> After spending two days reviewing the owner's books and visiting his fields, the inspectors indicated they found no serious health and safety problems, adding that the operation was 'the best-looking nursery we've been to.' Despite these positive comments, the owner, who asked to remain anonymous, received notice of $6,500 in proposed penalties. Of that, $1,400 was levied because the portable toilets had muddy floors. The nursery owner had contracted to have the toilets cleaned every Tuesday, but this hadn't yet occurred for the week of the inspectors' visit.

I could go on with more of this story, but you no doubt see the absurd nature of such penalties.

Attempts at creating a friendlier government that began in the mid 1990s have resulted in responsibilities being placed on federal enforcement agencies as well as businesses. Under the Small Business Regulatory Enforcement Fairness Act of 1996 (SBREFA), an oversight Regional Fairness Board was established to handle business complaints concerning excessive enforcement action by a federal agency. If you feel that you have been unfairly treated by the DOL, don't hesitate to contact the Board at 888.734.3247, the DOL Office of Small Business Programs at 202.219.9148, or your local DOL Regional Office.

Nurseries with less than 250 employees can also contact their state's OSHA consultation service, which can be found on OSHA's Web site at the "programs" link. This free, confidential service works with nurseries to identify and solve potential problems under an advisory instead of regulatory basis. You will be required to resolve in a timely manner any problems that are found by the OSHA inspection team.

Most nursery owners are unaware that the Federal Trade Commission (FTC) governs many aspects of how they do business. All nursery owners should obtain from the ANLA office a copy of the FTC's *Guides for the Nursery Industry*. The regulations are also printed in the Federal Register, the official daily publication for rules, proposed rules, and notices of federal agencies and organizations. This fascinating guide defines accepted practices in the nursery industry, offers guidelines on how to adopt those practices, and defines everything from lining-out stock to the term "nursery-propagated" as it is legally understood.

The guide also defines deceptive business practices. Deceptive practices include telling customers that plants will thrive without fertilizer or will flower for longer periods than is true, selling an old plant under a new name, telling customers that the plant is only available in small numbers when that is not the case, or promoting plants as rare when they are not. Additionally, the guide covers digging plants from the wild without disclosing such to your customers as well as nursery owners who promote plants to be of a particular size or maturity and then deliver plants that do not conform to the advertised standards.

Other federal regulations that you should be aware of are the Americans with Disabilities Act (ADA), the Family Medical Leave Act (FMLA), the Civil Rights Act (CRA), the Age Discrimination in Employment Act (ADEA), and the Fair Labor Standards Act (FLSA). If you have 15 or more employees, the 1990 Americans with Disabilities Act (ADA) regulates everything from whether you are allowed to have stairs to hiring the handicapped. If you are a fan of government regulation, wait until you see some of the bizarre definitions of "handicap" put forth by our representatives. With everything from alcoholism to near-sightedness being classified as a disability, quite a number of lawsuits by businesses have already been filed to challenge the unintended consequences of this poorly written law. You can find more about ADA at the Department of Justice's Web site.

The FMLA of 1993 applies to nurseries with 50 or more employees. If an employee or an employee's family member has a medical emergency, the employer must allow them 12 weeks off from work and hold their job open until they return. Again, you can find more information at the Department of Labor's Web site. The CRA, administered by the Equal Employment Opportunity Commission, prohibits discrimination in employment based on race, color, religion, sex, national origin, or handicap. (See Appendix 1.) Then there is the ADEA, which prohibits discrimination in certain protected age groups, and finally the Equal Pay Provision of the FLSA, which prohibits employers from paying men and women different rates for the same job.

Government often seems to forget that businesses exist to make money, not to create jobs. The creation of jobs is certainly a positive consequence of a prospering business, but it is my view that a business that is doing well would be stupid not to try and care for its employees; it does not need government to tell it that. If our government looked out for the rights of businesses as well as it does for the rights of employees, we'd all be in fine shape.

Chapter 20

Insurance

The last thing that folks think about when starting a business is insurance. Insurance is not a dirty word but is an absolute necessity when venturing into this or any business. The types of insurance you should consider includes life and disability insurance, health insurance, liability insurance, property insurance, and crop insurance.

Life or disability insurance

Why is life or disability insurance important to a nursery owner? The most obvious reason is that it offers the owner's family financial support in case the owner dies or cannot continue to operate the nursery. I recommend a minimum coverage of at least twice the amount of any outstanding loans or lines of credit that would be in force at the time of an untimely demise.

It is typical for owners of smaller nurseries to take a small salary, which means they have little money invested in either the social security system or a private retirement program. If the small business owner dies, life insurance is often the only support available to the surviving family members. The same reasoning holds true for disability insurance.

Health insurance

Health or medical insurance that covers medical bills in times of accident and illness is of equal importance to the nursery owner. Again, it is typically those owners of small nurseries who fail to invest in medical insurance. Most state nursery associations have selected an insurance firm they recommend to member nurseries, which is a good place to start looking for a good agent. In most cases, even one-person businesses qualify for group insurance rates. While the government does not require nurseries to provide medical insurance, there are government regulations that must be followed if you decide to offer this as a benefit. I recommend you thoroughly investigate this issue with your insurance agent.

It is becoming increasingly necessary for nurseries to offer medical insurance programs as a way to compete for good employees. You can arrange any number of payment options, from the nursery paying a percentage of the premiums to the entire premium in some rare cases. There are almost as many different insurance plans as there are insurance companies.

Liability and homeowner's insurance

All businesses should carry liability insurance, especially if customers will be visiting your nursery. Given today's litigious society, and considering the number of ruts and ditches on a nursery's property, I wouldn't recommend going without a good liability policy. Most agents recommend an inexpensive personal umbrella policy in addition to a good homeowner's policy. Consult your insurance agent for help.

Homeowner's insurance is a necessity for the coverage of a nursery's facilities and equipment in case of disaster. Among the easiest things to forget is the updating of your insurance every year as the value of your facilities grows. In just a few years you could add three new computers and two new potting buildings. Without updating your insurance every year, and ensuring that you have replacement value coverage, you will be hard pressed to recover from a disaster such as a fire or flood.

Crop insurance

Most horticultural crops are completely subject to the weather. Although it may be disastrous for a nursery to be hit by a hailstorm during a busy season, crop insurance is usually so expensive that purchasing it is not economical. There may be particular types of insurance, especially for floods, that are affordable. The in-

Dorothy . . . what happened to Dorothy? Just when you least expect them, disasters like this tornado can strike your nursery. Hoffman Nursery, North Carolina.

surance industry is undergoing many changes regarding crop insurance, so be sure and check with your state nursery association for the latest developments.

Workers' compensation insurance

Workers' compensation insurance is required in most states when you exceed a specified number of employees, although in some states it is required for even one full- or part-time worker. It is a state-regulated insurance and so is different in each state. You can find the requirements for your state by going to the SBA Web site, which has links to all the state's sites. Premiums for this type of insurance are paid by the employer on a regular basis (sometimes yearly) and cover employees who suffer from an injury received on the job. Rates are based both on payroll amount and the worker's occupation. For example, landscapers in most states pay a much higher rate than nursery workers because of the increased likelihood of injuries. The more injuries that the insurance pays for, the higher the rate of premiums.

Be sure to find out if your workers' compensation insurance agent is putting you in an insurance category known as assigned risk. Assigned risk is a high-risk, catch-all category used especially by insurance agents who don't specialize in assessing risk. These agents have other specialties and simply write workers' compensation insurance as a convenience. Assigned risk offers you no benefits but instead costs you quite a bit more in premiums. If you have lots of accidents and claims, you may have no choice but to be placed in the assigned risk category. If not, and if your agent writes only assigned risk policies, find another agent.

Chapter 21

Employees: *The "E" Word*

Employees can be the best part of your business and the worst, all in the same day. Good employees are a joy to have on staff, and if they have the appropriate skills, they can help your business explore new opportunities that you couldn't begin to attempt on your own. Bad employees, however, can cause problems beyond your worst nightmares. Did you know that 20 percent of all lawsuits are employment disputes (Kristen 1998)? Employer to employee relationships can be classified into three categories: hiring, the ongoing relationship, and termination (Swartz 1995). Having employees is often what drives small nurseries out of business, not because the employees are inherently bad but because nursery owners are ill equipped to handle the employment relationship.

Hiring

Many people who started their nurseries as backyard operations never had any intention of hiring employees and actually convinced themselves that they would never need any. Even with the best of these intentions, it won't take long before the backyard nursery owner is using part-time help. Then, before you know it, part-time help becomes more than part time and you have your first full time employee. If you don't make plans for this inevitability, you will find yourself unprepared, stretched too thin, and unable to satisfy your customers' needs.

Smaller nurseries can often get by in the early years with hiring teenagers, stay-at-home parents, retirees, friends, and neighbors. The need for labor in the nursery business is often seasonal, and other options may include using temporary services or even migrant workers who may be finishing jobs at nearby nurseries or farms. The biggest challenge for small businesses, however, is hiring the first full-time employee. When hiring full-time employees, look for people with whom you can work as well as those who have skills that will help the business. Hiring skills that you, as the business owner, do not possess will make the employee even more valuable to your business.

Before hiring your first employee, develop an employment application form. I recommend you consult ANLA as you are doing this because as there are many questions regarding personal information that are illegal to include on employment application forms. For example, you cannot ask about marital status, religious affiliation, plans to start or add to a family, and much more. Since more than one third of the respondents to a Josephson Institute survey said they would lie on a resume or employment application to get a job (*American Nurseryman* 1993), I recommend you make the applicant sign the application form asserting that all statements are true. It is easier to dismiss an employee later should a conflict arise about the information they provided.

Checking references as well as doing criminal background checks will sometimes yield surprising results. Always contact former employers, even though it is often difficult to get them to tell you much more beyond the verification of employment. Most state laws do not require the employer to disclose anything about the employee, although there is an exception for matters of safety. Similarly, an employer can discuss an employee's embezzlement or other criminal acts and not be found liable for defamation provided those statements are true. However, fear of being sued by a disgruntled former employee has led many employers to say nothing about a former employee, which I think is an absolutely disgusting development. I have hired more than one sorry employee simply because I could not get a straight answer from a former employer. In some states, employers face potential legal action when they fail to divulge a problem after being asked about a former employee who later causes harm to the new employer. While you may not wish to volunteer information about a former employee, try to find a way (even by refusing to answer certain questions) to communicate with a prospective new employer about any potential problems. Most of all, be honest.

Many employers use one of several preemployment screening tools. These questionnaires are designed to highlight any potential problems such as a lack of integrity, work ethic, values, and so on that would not turn up during a typical interview process. Sykes (2001) has noted that the two most common preemployment screening tools are the Lousig-Nont Phase II Profile and the Stanton Survey.

Be aware that you are not only hiring the employee but also the baggage that comes with each employee. If you hire someone who is constantly late to work, don't kid yourself that you can change this pattern. Similarly, if you hire a person who had disagreements with management at their previous job or whose family members are constantly sick, don't expect this to change. Once you have employees, part of your job will be to counsel, advise, console, motivate, and discipline.

As you can see, hiring a good employee is not as simple as it seems. As business owners, our first reaction is to hire the applicant we like as opposed to the one with the best track record of success. Obviously we would prefer that the one we like best also be the best applicant, but this is often not the case.

The ongoing relationship

Now that you have employees, you will next have to set about managing and keeping them, at least the good ones. It is rare that employees leave for more money; this is simply the excuse you will hear. Entire books are written on how to treat employees well, but the most important things to remember are that employees need to be given encouragement as well as proper direction, and they need to be rewarded when they perform well. Whenever possible, devise incentive-based programs for your employees as they work wonders on morale and loyalty.

Supervision is among the toughest tasks for many nursery owners, as they would rather avoid this often unpleasant task. Supervising ranges from instructing employees on the technical aspects of a task to doing evaluations and issuing reprimands. In reality, even nursery owners who don't mind supervising employees are poorly trained (if they are trained at all) to be good supervisors. Although I was fortunate to have had a number of supervisory classes in my earlier career, I still believe that nothing is as good as practical experience.

While some employees seem magically to know what to do, how to do it, and when to do it, don't expect every employee to have this rare combination of personality and skill. As a supervisor, you will have to train your employees in your own methods, thought processes, and expectations. I take the approach that if an employee makes a mistake then I did not do an adequate job of training or supervising. But if I correct the employee and the same mistake is made again, guess who gets the blame?

Be conscious of what type of employee will best suit your management style. There is an increasing trend toward personality typing of prospective employees, and companies that handle this type of personnel evaluation proliferated in the 1990s. After having your own personality profiled, you can get to work on potential employees. Do you want employees who don't think independently but will blindly follow your lead, or do you want those who will think for themselves? Some business owners are overly controlling and possessive and feel threatened by employees who have too many of their own ideas. Waterman (1993) noted that many managers were surprised that surveyed employees "often put more value on responsibility than on pay increases. Responsibility can be very fulfilling for an employee and represents an increase in status." In a 1986 study by Ken Kovach, employees and supervisors were asked to rate from one to ten the importance (one being the most important) of various factors in what they want from their job (McCartney 1994).

JOB PRIORITY	EMPLOYEE	SUPERVISOR
Help on personal problems	10	9
Interesting work	1	5
High wages	5	1
Job security	4	2
Personal loyalty of supervisor	8	7
Tactful disciplining	9	6
Full appreciation of work done	2	8
Feeling of being in on things	3	10
Good working conditions	7	4
Promotion in the company	6	3

Based on these results, you need to carefully examine your own prejudices and ego in both selecting and keeping employees.

A number of personality profile indicators have been created. One of the most common indicators, which is adopted loosely from the Myers-Briggs survey, reveals whether the prospective employee is an introvert or an extravert. Introverts get recharged from being alone, whereas extraverts are stimulated by being around other people. There are also a number of different ways in which individuals make decisions; rarely do they mirror your own decision-making process. Sensing individuals make decisions based on the facts, whereas intuitive people prefer to make them based on speculation. Feeling individuals make decisions based on emotions, and thinkers tend to use logic. If you want an employee who can handle repetitive production chores well, you should hire someone who is not an idea person, as this personality type would be bored too quickly. If you know what type of employee you are looking for, you can bring out many of their personality traits in the interview process.

Employees are also profiled according to how they would deal with various situations that may arise on the job. Perceivers are more flexible and spontaneous, whereas judgers prefer their schedule to be rigid and planned. It is important to realize that all employees do not think or process information in the same way as the owner. While it is easy to get frustrated with employees who don't think "correctly," just remember that all personality types have a place in the business team; it is simply up to you to correctly use their talents.

Termination

Terminating an employee is often the most traumatic part of the nursery owner's relationship with an employee because of the nature of conflict required. Any experienced employer will tell you that it is critical to eliminate a problem employee before the situation worsens. Delays often dampen workplace moral and can lead to other employees being drawn into problems they should not be involved in. Be sure to document any problems you have with an employee and keep these records in your personnel file for that employee. Should legal action ever occur, accurate documentation plays a key role in you prevailing, and this includes keeping accurate records of any communication you have with the employee. I recommend you read Perry's (1993) article on how to avoid many of the pitfalls that can occur when trying to terminate an employee.

Establishing nursery positions

As your staff grows, you will need to establish positions that have job descriptions attached to them outlining the assigned tasks and responsibilities. It is always advisable to write job descriptions before applicants are interviewed. Be sure to list all the essential duties of a particular job, but also include a statement that management can change job duties at any time. Such a statement allows you to resolve potential conflicts with employees who have a "that is not my job" attitude and may also work in your favor during possible future litigation. Nurseries set up positions in a variety of ways based on their size. The most common positions are those of laborer, nursery worker, grower, plant pathologist, propagator, horticulturist, production manager, section manager, nursery manager, shipping manager, facilities manager, equipment operator, general manager, office manager, and secretary.

Laborers are often the most versatile of staff as they perform a variety of tasks around the nursery. They are also often the lowest paid even though they have a great impact on profitability by making your business more efficient day-to-day. The quality of laborers depends on the rate of employment in your area; in a tighter job market, it is more difficult to attract the better workers to a nursery operation. Nursery workers are usually the next level above a laborer in that they usually have either some nursery experience or training.

A grower is responsible for taking care of the crops you are growing. In other words, this person controls the quality of the plants you produce. Obviously this is a key position and one that must be filled with great care. It is also a position that will require large amounts of overtime, especially during the growing season. Duties assigned to a grower could include plant monitoring, pesticide application, pruning, fertilizing, lighting, irrigation, and climatic monitoring in the growing area.

Another crucial employee is the plant pathologist, the person who maintains the quality of the crops you produce. In smaller operations, the grower may actually serve as your pathologist until the nursery's size permits a separate position. The job of a plant pathologist is to scout for, prevent, and control any pest problems that occur in your nursery. People who fit this position well are detail oriented and often have a true curiosity about plants and diseases. They must also be flexible enough with their schedule that they can attend to problems as they occur. Except for in the larger operations, this person is responsible for all pesticide applications.

A propagator is the person responsible for making sure that plants are timely propagated and in adequate quantities. Obviously this is an important job because plants cannot be sold unless they are propagated. This employee will work very closely with your grower. If you purchase all your stock from other nurseries, you can do away with this position.

If your nursery features a large variety of plants or if you need to answer plant-related questions from consumers, you may consider hiring a horticulturist. Good horticulturists can be indispensable both because of the help they give customers and the information they provide to the rest of your production staff on a plant's growing peculiarities and needs. Obviously this person needs to have good communication skills and the ability to make complex explanations understandable.

A nursery business makes use of many kinds of managers. A production manager or grower can function as a propagator in smaller operations, but in the larger nurseries the production manager is in charge of all potting operations and the placing of plants in the growing area. This employee is also often in charge of inventory control. Production managers work closely with or supervise both the propagator and the grower. A fast-paced, detail-oriented person with good leadership skills will make the best production manager.

In larger operations, it is the section manager who is in charge of the growing areas. Depending on the size of the operation, section managers may actually perform the growing duties. In the largest of operations, they may serve only as a coordinating and supervising manager for the growers. The nursery manager is the employee who makes sure that all aspects of the nursery are running properly and efficiently. Not all businesses are large enough to justify such a person. An ideal nursery manager should be able to make good decisions, manage employees efficiently, and keep a close watch on all aspects of the nursery. This is the person who must troubleshoot problems as they arise, which means that this is not a 40-hour per week job. You will want hire someone who makes logical, fact-based decisions and who can juggle many problems at once.

A shipping manager or supervisor is an important component in both wholesale and mail-order businesses. Although the duties will vary with each business, the primary tasks of getting the plants to the customer and keeping the paper trail in order remain the same. This position calls for a very detail-oriented person with good people skills. In the spring shipping season, this employee's hours will be excessive, so it is essential you hire an energetic person with few personal commitments outside the nursery during that season. I confess to having worn out far more than our share of shipping managers.

A facilities manager is a position that is often needed long before it is actually filled. This employee makes sure that everything functions as it should, from irrigation systems to tractors to heaters. I advise you to hire someone with as broad a range of fix-it experience as possible. Even though this employee will rarely generate any income, it won't take too many occasions of having to hire and pay outside contractors to do repairs and construction work before you will see the economic benefits of a facilities manager. Owners of smaller nurseries should consider hiring local farmers to help with these types of chores.

As your business grows, you may need to examine the need for an equipment operator or mechanic in addition to your facilities manager. Such an employee takes care of chores from mowing the grass to grading slopes, from operating tractors to doing mechanical repairs. Obviously, the more versatile the employee is, the easier it becomes to justify filling this position.

The final managerial position is that of the general manager. The owner usually holds this position, but that is only until the nursery reaches such a size that the owner can no longer function well in this role and needs to delegate the running of the business to someone else. In most nurseries, the general manager is concerned with the overall operation of the nursery, from the growing of plants to the running of the office. The extent of duties depends on the individual nursery and on the role the owner desires to take on.

The office staff is an obviously critical component of any business, especially a nursery's. As we discussed in chapter 18, a nursery can produce the best plants in the world, but unless the administrative tasks such as keeping track of paperwork are done properly, that won't matter. Office staff, including secretaries and customer service representatives, should be detail oriented and possess the ability to multi-task otherwise the tasks of delivering the plants and getting paid will become overwhelming. While your office staff doesn't produce a single plant, be sure that you understand and appreciate their value to your business.

Employee handling and organization

Once you have decided on which positions to have in your nursery, you should organize them into a flow chart. A flow chart is simply a sketch of who reports to whom (see figure 16). I have seen small nurseries in complete disarray (and some have even lost key employees) because of a confusion in the chain of command. Such confusion is particularly prevalent in nurseries in which both spouses work or where the business is owned by more than one partner, mostly because of an unclear delineation of authority and responsibility. An employee who is told what to do by several conflicting voices will not be a happy or long-term employee.

Figure 16. A Sample Organizational Flow Chart

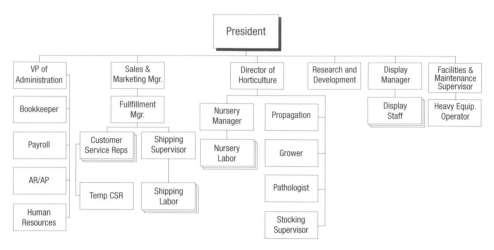

As the number of employees grows, so does the need to establish an employee handbook that spells out the rules under which your business operates. Such rules would cover performance evaluations, raises, vacations, sick days, retirement or insurance benefits, grievance measures, and a number of other employment related issues. To reduce potential lawsuits, all employee manuals should have a prominent disclaimer in the front saying that "policies are subject to change with or without prior notice." (Kristen 1998). Trade associations such as ANLA have sample manuals that serve as models. Another resource is the older established nursery; many of them have extensive employee manuals and are glad to help you get started with your own.

Keep in mind that although employee handbooks are quite beneficial, if all employees are not subject to the same rules or treated the same way under these rules then they could be just as detrimental. An inconsistent application of the rules can land employers in court facing disgruntled employees.

Once you have decided to hire employees, you will have to determine how many to hire and when. Employees can be grouped into two basic groups, those who produce the crops you sell, and those who comprise the support staff. Both types are essential—without a crop to sell, you won't stay in business for long, but without staff to deliver them in a way that satisfies customers, they are of little use. There isn't a good guide regarding the optimal percentage of producers and nonproducers, as each type of nursery varies tremendously. Retail nurseries that buy and resell would obviously need fewer producers than would a large wholesale nursery. However, it is important to keep track of the percentages of each category of employee you hire and to monitor any dramatic changes.

Another decision you'll have to make is how to accommodate your seasonal labor needs. Most nurseries need employees from early spring through fall, and although most maintain a skeleton staff during the winter months, they are not able to retain many full-time employees during the low cash flow months of winter. In the southern areas of the United States, nurseries struggle to keep full-time employees during the hot summer months.

Every nursery must come up with its own methods of handling these staffing issues. Nursery owners don't take long to realize that they need to do something to hold onto well-trained employees as it is always financially advantageous to keep qualified help rather than spend the time and money training new workers. Some owners set up areas where work can be accomplished during the winter, and using good scheduling, they postpone some jobs until the normally slow winter months. Other nurseries make use of migrant or full-time workers from south of the border. These workers go back to their home country during the winter months and return to their jobs in the United States with the warm weather in spring. Their absence in the winter also means that you are not forced to deplete your cash-flow reserves during those months.

Another way of handling seasonal labor is to implement job-sharing programs with other employers whose seasonal work needs complement your own. At Plant Delights, one employee helps with our shipping during the spring and early fall, but during the summer he works at a nearby swimming pool, and in the late fall and winter he takes a job with a Christmas-tree lot. The recreation industry makes use of seasonal employees in both the winter and summer months, so nurseries could look there to fill their own seasonal labor needs. We have also had good luck with parents who are willing to work in the spring and fall but who take the summers and winters off when their kids are home from school. With a little coordination, you will be able to find good employees and ensure their continued employment during your low cash-flow seasons.

Where it is not possible to use seasonal labor, nurseries will "lay off" employees during the winter months. Under this arrangement, nursery workers apply for unemployment benefits during the time they are laid off at a rate that is usually slightly higher than half their regular salary. As this lay-off period typically occurs around the holiday season, many employees take a part-time winter job elsewhere. At a specified time, the workers drop off the unemployment rolls and return to work. All nurseries pay unemployment premiums on their workers, and the more the unemployment fund is used by the nursery's employees, the higher its premiums rise to a set amount. I recommend you work with your accountant to determine what are the most economical options for your particular operation.

Since many nurseries are family-run businesses, you will often face family-related issues that complicate the already difficult task of running a business. The dysfunction that exists in some family units will only be exaggerated in a business setting, so if a child is spoiled at home, you can expect temper tantrums in the family-owned workplace when they do not get their own way. Likewise, women employees who are part of a male-dominated family may not be given the respect that they deserve even when their business-related ideas are actually better than the men's. If there is a problem of sibling rivalry, you may be faced with the challenge of getting everyone to pull together for the benefit of the business instead of behaving as though it were every kid for himself.

Occasionally a family member or relative must be fired. How will this impact your relationship with your family outside the business? I think most people in the nursery business have hired family members only to wish later that they had not. When decisions involving firing or disciplining an employee become a family as well as a business decision, the owner is put in a truly no-win situation. It is critical that these and other potential conflicts be considered before the nursery owner gets in too deep to retreat.

Migrant or guest-worker labor

If you thought hiring family members was difficult, wait until you try hiring migrant labor or guest workers. According to the Migrant and Seasonal Agricultural Worker Protection Act (MSWPA), which you can find on the Department of Labor's Web site, migrant workers are defined as those workers, usually United States citizens, whose seasonal employment requires them to be absent from their permanent residence overnight. Guest workers are foreign citizens who are issued temporary work visas to enter the United States for a particular seasonal job, usually one that is related to agriculture.

When the United States economy is strong and there is a reduction in work ethic, especially in labor jobs, the agriculture industry is often faced with a tremendous shortage of workers. As I travel around the country, I hear horror stories of nurseries and landscapers losing hundreds of thousands of dollars in guaranteed sales solely as the result of inadequate labor. Most guest workers and migrant laborers are willing to work hard and for long hours, but the difficulty for the nursery owner lies in finding and keeping them. The nursery industry has turned primarily to labor from foreign lands but has been thwarted by a quagmire of governmental bureaucracy. The government's lack of initiative in providing a workable guest-worker program and its inability to patrol national borders means that small businesses are the ones that suffer. Nurseries become so desperate for workers that they will often hire just about anyone, only to have to worry later that the government will discover that their workers are illegal.

Every employee hired since November 1986 must complete an Immigration and Naturalization Service form (an INS I-9 form) at the time of hiring, which the employer must keep on file. The I-9 form verifies that the employee is legally eligible to work in the United States. As an employer, you must examine documents that prove the applicant's ability to legally work within three business days of the date employment begins. Twenty-nine documents can be used by the prospective employee to do this verification. These documents are broken down into three groups, A, B, and C. You must examine at least one document from group A, or one each from groups B and C. It is critical that you photocopy each document that you examine and keep these on file attached to the I-9 form. A number of other important regulations are contained in the INS Handbook for Employers (Form M-274), which is available from the INS.

The most common identification used from the A list is called a Permanent Resident Card (Form I-551), commonly known as a green card. The green card establishes the ability to work based on the holder's permanent residence status. Unfortunately, a large majority of these green cards are forgeries. A nursery owner who is proved to knowingly or unknowingly hire illegal workers is liable and can be jailed. Conversely, if you investigate because you think a green card is a forgery, this too is illegal since you are violating the individual's rights (one of which must be the right to be a criminal).

Other forms of identification are also often forgeries. Plant Delights once had a worker from outside the United States who was using the social security number of a vagrant. We were made aware of this only when the Social Security Administration called to check on a verification of employment for the true owner of the number. The social security number had either been stolen or sold to an illegal alien. My best advice is to call the INS with any questions you have, which, if nothing else, throws the issue back in their laps. The INS has field offices in virtually every state, which are listed on its Web site. Nursery owners often joke over drinks about how many illegal workers they are using and how they couldn't stay in business without them. Having known a prominent nursery owner who spent time in a federal prison for hiring illegal aliens, I do not consider this a joking matter. If you think that hiring alien workers will simply get you a slap on the wrist or that the government will look the other way, you are wrong and should now be frightened to death.

Pay rates

When you first hire employees, it is essential that you obtain a copy of the federal wage and hour law from the DOL. This provision of the 1938 FLSA regulates everything from overtime to child labor, the minimum wage, migrant labor, record keeping, and details on how time cards are to be calculated. Enforcement falls to the Wage and Hour Division of the DOL's Employment Standards Administration. The DOL's Web site is a well-written and easily understandable site that can answer a lot of questions. A great publication that helps to explain some of the complexities of this law is Atterbury's (1997) *Wage and Hour Summary* published by the ANLA.

How do you determine how much you will pay an employee? The local or national job market dictates much of your decision. Just as plant prices are cheaper in certain parts of the country, so too are labor prices, which may make it tough to bring a national, high-quality candidate to a nursery in an economically depressed region of the country. Many of the industry trade publications publish yearly salary comparisons for a variety of nursery jobs in each region of the country. Among the best is the annual wage and salary survey published each October by *Grower Talks*. By regularly looking at various salary compensation packages, you will know if what you are offering your employees is reasonable in your area. Remember that there are many hidden costs when you hire an employee, which we discussed earlier, so it is essential that you are aware of the total costs when hiring employees. *American Nurseryman* also publishes a salary survey every year that gives you a measuring stick in comparing yourself to others in the industry. As a national average, most nurseries spend between 27 and 35 percent of their gross expenses on payroll. Retailers, on the other hand, average between 46 and 61 percent (Greenridge 2000).

All employees expect yearly raises, although this is beginning to change. After the 2000–2001 dot-com bust, where excessive salaries were commonplace, bottom lines again became more meaningful. Businesses that had to offer competitive salaries can again work to hold down increases until salaries are back in line with the work performed. Employees need to know, through some sort of evaluation program, if they are doing well, and then they need to be rewarded for their work. Salary increases are another reason why businesses must continue to grow rather than remain the same size. No matter how hard you work to control increases in expenses, you will find salaries the toughest expense to contain, and the cost of your products will have to rise to cover your increasing labor costs. The best way to keep salary increases in line is through the increased efficiency of your employees and a reduction in the growth rate of your staff size. Although there is no magic formula, salary increases are typically based on performance and are related to the national "cost of living increases," which are estimates of inflation. While pay rates are certainly important to most employees, we have seen that many other factors are just as important in keeping a good employee and ensuring their job satisfaction.

If the business cannot afford large raises, consider that most employees are interested in opportunities for advancement. In small nurseries, there is little chance to move up unless the business continues to grow, so be aware that you will probably not be able to keep a star employee for long without expanding your business. On the other hand, some employees find a comfort level with small businesses that they cannot find with larger companies, and if the business grows, even some of your best employees may be unwilling or unable to adapt to the new needs of the business. Often the toughest part of being an owner is to recognize when employees are not willing to progress with the business and are actually holding the business back.

Payroll

How often are you going to pay your employees, weekly, every two weeks, twice a month, or monthly? Weekly and monthly payrolls are rarely chosen options, as a weekly payroll requires quite a lot more labor, and a monthly payroll, while it saves on paperwork, is not attractive to employees who have difficulty managing money for an entire month. Payroll that is done twice a month (on the 15th and at the end of the month) is a good compromise between saving paperwork and making it easy on employees and has therefore become the most common payroll schedule in the nursery industry. Your accountant will obviously be of help in making these decisions.

Many nursery owners who have never operated a business before are unfamiliar with common business practices such as paying payroll taxes. Every time you pay an employee you must calculate the amount of the employee's money that you will withhold from their pay. This withheld money goes to pay that employee's state and federal taxes, the amount being based on the number of exemptions claimed on the individual employee's federal W-4 forms and state withholding forms. The government provides the tax tables reflecting the amount of money to be withheld.

For each employee you hire, you will have to withhold and match their social security taxes (at the time of writing this was 7.65 percent of a salary up to $57,600, plus an additional 1.45 percent up to $135,000). These taxes, which are authorized under the Federal Insurance Contributions Act and known as FICA taxes, include money for social security and Medicare. Social security is the government's retirement program, and Medicare is its medical insurance program. The employer must deposit these payments each month using a federal tax identification number that is issued by the government. This number must be applied for and assigned before you are allowed to legally pay any employee. These forms can be received by calling the IRS, your CPA, or a business attorney. Each state has different regulations regarding how and when monies are deposited for the state's withholding program, and I recommend you contact your state nursery association or revenue department for help. Making timely deposits is essential, as late penalties can be astronomical, enough to put a small business out of business.

When you set up your business, even if it is a sole proprietorship, you will have to file a federal tax return form with the IRS stating that you are an agricultural employer. Most businesses file a form 941, but agriculture employers use a 943 form. Again, contact your accountant or local IRS office to set this up correctly. Those who file once every quarter (the 941 filers) or once a year (the 943 filers) must fill out and submit a report to the government detailing monies paid to employees and the funds withheld. The government uses the information on this form to make sure that the payments you have made during the year balance with the salaries you paid.

I strongly recommend hiring a CPA or payroll service to handle your payroll checks. Unless you have an accountant on staff, the quirks of payroll and payroll taxes are very time consuming, both to handle and to update according to the latest changes in regulations. It is possible to have the payroll data entered at your nursery office and electronically transferred to the company handling your payroll.

Given such a complex payroll system, it is easy to see why many nurseries like to transact business in cash. There is no question that a majority of small, backyard nurseries continue to pay—and always will pay—employees in cash. Cash payments are much easier on the employer and the employees also keep far more of their money. However, paying employee salaries in cash without the proper deductions is not only illegal but also deprives the workers of money that would otherwise be paid into the social security system on their behalf. The IRS is becoming more sophisticated every year at catching tax cheaters, and the penalties are quite severe.

Overtime

As a general rule, the labor laws concerning overtime (which is calculated as one-and-a-half-times the normal pay rate for any hours over 40 per week) are complex. While the FLSA exempts most agricultural workers from overtime pay, numerous exceptions exist. For example, non-salaried employees who answer the phone, work at the computer, load trucks, or sell plants are entitled to overtime. The law on overtime is so difficult to comply with that this is where most federal labor violations occur. I strongly suggest consulting the DOL Web site, an ANLA labor consultant, and your CPA on this matter.

Independent contractors

For many years, the nursery industry began hiring workers as independent contractors instead of as employees. Business owners realized that they could hire self-employed independent contractors and not be responsible for any of the costs we discussed earlier, such as unemployment taxes. This trend escalated through the mid-1990s until the IRS, which was being deprived of tax revenues, began cracking down on nurseries and other businesses that sought to avoid their tax burdens by misclassifying workers as independent contractors. These workers were in fact employees but were paid as though they were independent contractors. Many businesses that violated this law were faced with stiff fines and penalties for improperly classifying their employees as contractors.

The IRS set forth a series of distinctions between an employee and an independent contractor as a way to reduce the confusion. Independent contractors work on their own schedule, with their own tools, are not directly supervised by employees of the nursery, and are paid by the job rather than at regular intervals. If, for example, you were building an office and needed Sheetrock work completed, you would hire an independent contractor. To see how these rules apply to nursery owners, contact the IRS for a copy of their publication 1779. Just remember that despite the temptation of potential savings, it is better that you don't mess with the IRS.

Chapter 22

Real Nursery Owners Don't Do Marketing

Without question, the most overlooked and least understood part of the nursery business is marketing. Because many nurseries are already producing all the plants that they can sell, the owners see no need for marketing. As new nurseries enter the market, they emulate the ones that are already there and again pay little attention to marketing. Granted, some nurseries succeed in spite of a lack of marketing, but this is generally only in good economic times or in areas where there is a lack of competition.

What many nurseries fail to realize is that marketing involves not only selling more products but also selling them for a higher price. The key to marketing, which is also overlooked, is to give your products "perceived value." If you sell specialty or new plants, marketing becomes even more important since you will have to familiarize your customers with the product before you convince them to purchase it.

Before implementing a marketing program, determine what you will be marketing and to which audience. This may sound simplistic but are you going to market plant selection, quality, and service, or will you instead market a particular person in your organization? Your mission statement should help provide guidance with these issues. I strongly believe in marketing individuals within your organization, ideally one of the company's owners or officers. Think about every time you pass by a Wendy's restaurant—do any of you not imagine the founder, Dave Thomas? You too want someone who is a visible figure associated with your brand, which is your nursery.

Much of this type of marketing is termed "branding," which means giving your commodities a recognizable name or logo throughout your customer base. Branding is the new catchword in nursery advertising, and the big fallacy is thinking that nurseries can create branding quickly and easily just by spending lots of money. In most cases this is not the case as branding involves getting your customers to rely on your company for dependable service, quality products, and assistance with solving problems. There is no question that with enough advertising dollars, brands will become part of your customers' short-term consciousness, but what gives a nursery true market preference as well as staying power is the consistent, long-term branding that results from the combination of good advertising and publicity with a quality product and good service. Make no mistake about it, consistently promoting your brand is necessary in achieving success.

There are many types of marketing, but I like to divide them into two major groups, marketing off the nursery site and marketing on the site. Obviously it is the off-site marketing that must be effective, for that is what will get the customers to come to the nursery where the on-site marketing can be used. I further divide off-site marketing into two categories, publicity and advertising. Publicity is typically the more effective of the two and certainly the less expensive, if not free. Advertising is more often relied upon, however, as unlike publicity, it can happen overnight. In the mid-1990s, after we ran some test ads in a national magazine that resulted in less than two dozen responses to each, we were fortunate that the same magazine decided to do a feature story on our nursery. The feature story brought 1,600 requests for our catalog. It's pretty obvious which form of marketing works best—but only if you have done something worthy of the publicity.

Unconventional advertisements

Some gardening magazines have a new plant issue each spring. Nurseries are allowed to send information and photos of new plants to be featured in that issue, and although the magazines do not have room for all the plants, if your plant is chosen, it is a great chance to get some wonderful free publicity. Magazines also have source lists for the plants featured in their articles. These lists came about after readers complained that the plants being written about were unavailable for purchase. If you ship plants via mail order, you should send copies of your catalog to the magazine editors for reference when writing articles.

You may decide that you would like to be the featured story in a magazine since this is the type of advertising that offers the greatest benefit to your business. Depending on the size of the magazine or newspaper, catalog requests resulting from the story can number from a few dozen to several thousand. Before you allow your nursery to be profiled in a well-known publication, be sure you can adequately handle the requests that will follow. There is nothing worse than starting off on the wrong foot with a potential new customer.

Press releases

An excellent way to get publicity is through press releases. These are worthy news items that you write and send to the media in the hopes that they will run them as a story. While this type of publicity is incredibly effective, it is not the easiest to obtain. First, realize that magazine, television, radio, and newspaper editors and producers are very busy and have little time for the majority of the "junk mail" that they receive. What you must do is to catch their interest with a concise, newsworthy story that stands out from everything else they receive.

To prepare a good press release, look at the type of stories that are being run and see if your story warrants the editor's time. Stories that look like advertisements are wastebasket material, as are stories that don't have a unique angle or community interest. If you write a story about a giant sale on petunias, then you aren't going to hear from the editor. If you donate thousands of petunias to a shelter for abused children that will be planted by volunteers, that story stands a much better chance of getting an editor interested. Be sure your story outline is written concisely so that it grabs the reader's attention in the first sentence; you may not have another chance. I recommend sending the story with at least six months of lead time so that the editor or publisher has time to appreciate what you have written.

All editors and producers have deadlines, so don't pester them about a story idea at those times. Most of all, stay on friendly terms with the editor or producer. Constantly asking when and if your story will run will get the wrong results. Similarly, offering the editor or producer a discount or free gift will appear to be a bribe and will generally end any relationship. Although the editorial and advertising sections of the paper operate very independently, mentioning that you are an advertiser of the station or paper is also an ethical no-no, as you come across as trying to bully your way into the editorial section.

Networking

The key strategy for any business obtaining good publicity is networking. Networking is simply the process of developing relationships with others who will help to spread the word about your business. Networking is similar to the premise on which many pyramid-scheme businesses are based, namely that it's not what you sell but how many people are selling products for you. In other words, you want every person who knows about your business to tell another and so on. No business operates in a vacuum, and the more people who are aware of your nursery, the more business will come your way. Networking can be as simple as speaking to groups, staying in touch with university research and extension personnel as well as botanic gardens and arboreta, or as diverse as traveling to other related businesses and attending trade shows and symposiums.

In addition to promoting your business, networking is advantageous in that it allows you to learn about new products that may benefit other parts of your business. Let's say that Joe's Nursery has developed a new transplanter. How would you find out what Joe is doing without networking? Joe's Nursery may have a surplus of a plant that is in short supply at your nursery. To keep abreast of the changes and happenings in the nursery industry, it is essential that you read as many of the trade magazines as possible. Although each has a slightly different focus, I consider the following to be invaluable: *Grower Talks, American Nurseryman, Nursery Manager Pro, GMPro, Nursery Retailer, Garden Center Merchandising and Management,* and *Garden Center Products and Supplies.* Most of these are free to growers and are fully supported by advertisers. More and more regional trade newspapers are emerging that are also quite useful.

If you want to learn more about the business end of the nursery industry there is no better group to join that the ANLA. Their annual meetings are invaluable for meeting and listening to other successful nursery owners as well as leaders from other industries. The annual meetings of the Perennial Plant Association (PPA) is a must if you are growing perennials. One great benefit of these meetings is the chance to talk with both workers and business owners. Another of my absolute favorites is the International Plant Propagators Society (IPPS), whose stated mission is to share information. Just like ANLA and PPA, IPPS provides an incredible opportunity to network with a virtual Who's Who in the nursery industry.

Specialized plant associations are a superb way to network and become better known by your peers and prospective customers interested in a selected groups of plants. There are more plant associations than anyone can ever participate in, so I recommend you select areas of specialty for your business. Most national groups have annual conventions, which are often great resources of information. For example, if a nursery owner were looking to purchase a reliable selection of Louisiana iris cultivars, I would recommend heading to the Louisiana Iris Society. Conversely, those looking to sell quality Louisiana irises would make sure that they were well known and active in that society. Since one of the specialties of Plant Delights is hostas, we wouldn't dare miss a meeting of the American Hosta Society. When garden writers are looking for experts in a particular field, they call the applicable society for help, so this is one way you can be discovered and get free exposure as an expert.

I have long touted the benefits of becoming an "expert" as a tremendous source of publicity. Experts are simply folks with an extensive knowledge of a particular subject. Have you ever noticed that when you mention a particular subject or group of plants that you are consistently told to talk to a particular person? This is marketing at its finest. It will take a good bit of study and dedication, but anyone can become an expert on a particular subject. If you experiment with many different potting soils, you can become an expert; if you grow a wide variety of camellias, you can become an expert. The key is to become associated with one or more specialties.

Should there be no society devoted to your particular specialty, consider starting one. I know this may sound like a radical idea, but this is truly a win-win situation. If you are a local retailer specializing in hostas, a local society that encourages growing and collecting hostas would certainly be of benefit to you, and no doubt others.

While modern communication technologies make it possible to network from home, there is no substitute for traveling to visit other gardeners, plant collectors, nurseries, and so on. By doing this, you can develop personal relationships that will greatly enhance your ability to get valuable information as well as new plants. Nursery owners continually decry their inability to leave their nurseries to travel, but this doesn't hold water. Yes, trips are very time-consuming and difficult to fit in with business pressures, but this means you must do a better job of delegating and scheduling. Carefully planned and thought-out travel will generally be an economically advantageous venture. Whether you find a new plant or a new money-saving technique, the payoff is almost always there.

Botanic gardens and arboreta are all too often overlooked as networking venues. Be sure that these institutions, both local and nationwide, are aware of your interests and specialties because they very often refer customers to your nursery. Conversely, you must be willing to give back to these institutions, usually by offering financial or labor support or by sharing plants. Many botanic gardens and arboreta also maintain libraries in which your catalogs can be displayed.

While networking is incredibly valuable to an existing nursery business, it is more valuable before the business is even started. Since nurseries are often second careers, you can start networking long before you ever open your business. If you make strong connections, both with your industry peers and with the public, starting your business will be much smoother. You will also see where the gaps are in the local nursery market and, therefore, where you might find a niche market. In an ideal world, you would be working in a similar or related business so that in addition to gaining personal contacts, you would also be acquiring the skills required in your own business.

Garden writing

There is probably no better way to get known than to become a garden writer. You will need a talent for writing, and if you don't have one, you will have to hire an employee who does. The focus of your nursery would determine whether you write for a local, regional, or national paper, magazine, or newsletter. Trade groups such as the Garden Writers Association (GWA) are invaluable associations to join should you decide to move into this arena.

If you will be retailing in a small region, perhaps a local paper would be an appropriate venue for your writing. Small local papers often have a very small budget for writers, but they are usually glad to have articles contributed for free. Since the printed word is considered gospel, you will quickly become an expert in the region. If the local paper is hesitant, try convincing them that paid advertisements from garden-related businesses will quickly follow once readership by gardeners increases. As we all know, paid ads drive virtually all publications, so when you are starting out, consider taking out some of the ads yourself. Larger newspapers do pay for garden columns (rates vary dramatically with the size of the newspaper's circulation), but remember that it is the publicity that is the main benefit.

If your nursery focus is wholesale, a state or national trade journal would be a better outlet for establishing your name and reputation. Don't be afraid to become better known outside of your sales region, as this too will greatly help your publicity efforts. For those whose nurseries have a national sales scope, writing for magazines is worth considering as they are always looking for good writers; however, know that breaking in on your own is tough. By attending meetings of GWA and networking, you may break in quite quickly. Retail gardening magazines typically pay quite well, depending, of course, on their circulation. Nursery trade magazines either don't pay at all or offer a nominal fee. A number of other writing venues exist, from garden-club newsletters to arboretum and botanic garden publications, all of which are often in need of good writers.

Radio and television

Radio stations have an ever-increasing need for garden experts. It may take considerable networking to get an "in" with a radio station, but perseverance will pay off. As with print media, radio personalities are definitely thought of as experts. Radio stations will often invite guests on a show for a one-time event, particularly if the guest has an engaging personality and interesting story to tell. Many weekly gardening shows use both paid and volunteer gardening experts. In addition, there is a new trend whereby nursery owners pay for the privilege of being a guest on a radio show.

Television is another great media for nursery exposure. A local story that features your business would be ideal, so try to determine what will make you interesting to the station. What kind of event or unique nature of your business will make you newsworthy? It's often much easier to get a public television station to go for such ideas than a local affiliate or network. You could also become a contributor on a television station. Both local access channels and local network affiliates look for experts with a good knowledge of the subject matter, but more importantly they want someone with a good public persona. Learn to be witty and charming.

Public speaking

As gardening increases in popularity, so do the number of garden clubs and gardening symposiums. There will always be a shortage of both new and good horticultural speakers, so if you have the knowledge and ability to become a public speaker, it will do wonders for your business. The best way to become good is to practice on small groups until you become comfortable. Then begin networking with those on the speakers' circuit when you feel ready to move to the next level. While you are primarily looking to publicize your business, you should always charge for your talks. Without question, the more a speaker charges, the more importance and validity is given to what he or she is saying. By networking with other speakers you will be able to determine the current rates. In 2002, rates for beginners were around $200 per talk plus expenses, while the top tier speakers charge $1,000 or more.

Internet—caught in the web

It is almost frightening how the Internet has changed the face of all businesses, and the nursery business is no exception. Marketing techniques are changing right before our eyes because of the worldwide nature of the Internet. Among the first things to determine is how to make the Internet help your business. Businesses most commonly use the Internet by establishing their presence via a Web site. Web sites are essentially advertisements that are posted electronically on the Internet. They can be as simple as a single page containing contact information, directions, and hours of operation or as complex as an electronic nursery catalog that features pictures and even online ordering.

Retail mail-order nurseries should have an online catalog with electronic ordering capabilities. If you are a large wholesaler, perhaps the Internet could best serve your business by listing online inventory that is accessible only to qualified customers or by promoting those retail nurseries that purchase your plants. Be careful not to let the lure of Internet money and potential customers divert you from the core of your business as laid out in your mission statement, which happens far too often. What may seem like a profitable change in the mission of your business because of the Internet may in fact be the trading of short-term profits for the undermining of the entire structure on which your nursery was started.

No form of communication has seen its audience increase at such as rate as the Internet. It would be silly for me to quote figures on the number of people using the Internet since they would be outdated in no time. I can tell you that as a mail-order nursery, Plant Delights saw its sales over the Internet for the first five years soar from 1.5 percent of total sales (which includes sales through the printed catalog and on-site open houses) to 6.5 percent to 13 percent to 21 percent and finally to 40 percent in our sixth year of Internet sales. Within the same five years, more than 25,000 catalog requests per year were generated solely from our Web site. The cost of putting a catalog on the net is much lower than conventional printing, and the same holds true for building a large photographic library on a Web site. An additional advantage is that you can list currently available stock from your ready-to-sell inventories.

Now that Web-building software is widely available, anyone with a knowledge of computers can build a Web site. However, not everyone so inclined can build a good Web site. Unlike a bad Web site, a good Web site can be quickly operated, is easily navigated, and provides information that is of interest to the customer. Web sites usually range between two extremes, those that are too simple and offer no reason for the customer to visit, and those that are so complex and filled with so many graphics that the customer cannot easily maneuver around it. I recommend you spend plenty of time on the Internet looking at other Web sites, not just those in the nursery industry, to get an idea of what you like about some sites and why they appeal to you. Web sites are more attractive to consumers if they offer something in addition to the chance to purchase items online. Make use of the educational opportunities a Web site offers as well as the opportunities that exist for sharing creative ideas on the Internet. The more time consumers spend on your site, the greater the chance they will become customers.

If you get serious about constructing a Web site that offers more than basic information, consider hiring a professional Web designer. There are thousands of these professionals; simply enter "Web site designer" into your favorite search engine and take your pick. In choosing a Web designer, study the sites that each company has designed and talk with their clients. I also advocate talking with others in the nursery and other industries and gathering recommendations from those whose site you would like to emulate. Some Web designers are inexpensive and good, while others are expensive and bad. Price does not always seem to be a reflection of the quality of the finished product.

It is the job of the Web designer to formulate the layout of your site so that information is not only available but also laid out in a logical format. What seems simple on the site is actually among the most complex parts of assembling a Web site. The designer will also be responsible for updating the site with changes, formatting reports so that you can track the progress of the site, arranging keywords so that your site will be found by search engines, and quite a bit more.

Despite what some nursery owners think, Web sites don't just happen. In the late 1990s I received a call from the owner of a well-known mail-order nursery. She had just visited our Web site, and after asking quite a few questions, she finally got around to asking how many hits our site was attracting. When I replied that the hits were in the millions, the nursery owner became silent. Only after a few moments was she able to resume our conversation by telling me that their site only got 50 hits per month. She went on to explain that her staff had designed the site and that they had done so inexpensively.

If you choose to sell online, be sure that you or your Web designer chooses a good "shopping cart." A shopping cart is a program that allows your customers to check out at the end of their online ordering. As with everything else, there are good and bad shopping cart programs. Web sites are not like mystical baseball fields; if you build them, folks will not automatically come. With the number of Web sites in the millions, you must advertise and promote your Web site in order for it to stand out and promote your nursery. Promoting your Web site means that you advertise it everywhere, on every key chain, scratchpad, matchbook, and ink pen that you give away. It must be visible on your catalog, printed on your stationery, added to every e-mail, mentioned in every article about your nursery, plastered on the side of your vehicles—everywhere.

Web sites can be made more useful if reciprocal links are incorporated in them. Links are a method of connecting your Web site to other, related Web sites so that you are not lost in cyberspace. Visitors who might visit a nursery that sold complementary items would then be directed to your site. To secure a link, simply e-mail the business to which you wish to link and indicate your desire for a reciprocal link. You are more likely to receive positive responses when it is clear that the link will benefit both businesses.

You or your Web designer must also choose a Web host. A Web host is an Internet service provider that allows your site to reside within their computer system. When choosing a Web host, be sure it is capable of hosting a site of your size and potential commercial volume and check with other business sites to determine their reliability. Web hosts that are inexpensive but often out of service are not a good value.

Conventional advertisements

Most nursery owners who have tried retail magazine advertisements consistently find these the least effective means of advertising for their money. These ads are quite expensive, and the return of prospective customers is quite low. Having said this, I believe it is still a good way for a young mail-order nursery to develop an initial national customer base. An ad will have to be placed a number of times before it pays off. Studies have shown that most customers must see that advertisement at least three times before they will consciously recognize it and seven times before they are likely to respond. You can often get a better return on money spent with specialty journals and society publications. These, of course, are only of benefit if you are growing the specialty crops that appeal to the readers of these publications.

Retail nurseries rely on newspaper and phone book advertisements. They are often afraid not to if a competitor is advertising in the same publication. I cannot go into detailed advertising strategies, but I can state that the key is to make your advertisement look appealing and different. If it blends in with the other ads in the magazine, the chance of getting the attention of a prospective customer dims.

Most retailers spend between 3 and 5 percent of gross sales on advertising. In the face of heavy competition or when the store is new, that rate may actually double. Plenty of complex formulas help determine if your advertising is actually working, but to make things simple, divide the money you are spending on the advertisement by the percentage of gross profit. In other words, if your standard cost of goods is 50 percent of gross profit and your advertisement costs $1,000, you would need to sell $2,000 above your normal sales for the ad to break even. If you figure on an advertising budget of 10 percent, then you would hope that a $1,000 ad would generate $10,000 in sales.

It is always helpful to know and understand your customers as a means of obtaining better target advertising. Things as simple as in-store surveys can be helpful in determining why a customer came to your store, where they came from, whether they came because of an ad, and what their reactions to your selection and service are. Some garden centers use maps on which customers put dots or pins indicating where they live. It won't take long to determine where your customer base lives, and armed with this knowledge, you will be better able to target your advertising to existing customers or to advertise in areas where you want to build a larger customer base.

Trade magazines provide the best outlet for wholesale nurseries wanting to place conventional advertisements. These ads are considerably less expensive than comparable ones placed in retail magazines and appear to be much more effective. Most nursery associations have some type of publication that accepts advertising. Regional and national availability locators (lists that lay out which plants are available where) are also emerging, both in printed form and over the Internet. I have always liked the idea of "fax trees" in which all participating growers in a particular state or region are hooked up to one central fax number. When a customer sends a fax to a central number looking for a list of plants, it is automatically refaxed to all participating nurseries so that there is less work on everyone's part. Any nursery can then respond to a customer's fax.

Trade shows
Trade shows are the most common venue for wholesale nurseries to market their materials. They can be statewide, regional, or national in scope and they offer nursery staff the chance to meet customers and display the new items they will be introducing to the market. There are large differences in attendance num-

bers among the trade shows. Be sure to carefully research the best trade shows in the region where you do or would like to do business, since participating in a trade show is an expensive venture, both in terms of the time spent traveling to and attending the show as well as in setup costs.

Direct mail

A commonly used method of advertising is that of direct mail. Those unsolicited mailings we have all received at one time or another advertising a product or service is the result of direct mail marketing. Virtually every time you make a purchase, all sorts of information about you and that transaction is captured in a computer database. Certain businesses collect and compile that information and then sell it to new businesses.

How does a retail or mail-order nursery go about developing a mailing list? As a nursery owner, you can call a mail-order list seller and order a list of names that fits your specifications. For example, if you have a retail nursery or garden center, you could order a list of customers who had purchased lawn and garden products at least twice in the last six months and who had an annual family income of more than $100,000. You can also request lists of customers in particular zip codes as well as those who have recently purchased new houses in a particular region. The possibilities are endless. Many businesses use direct mail to build their initial list and then abandon it for higher return options. As a general rule, direct-mail lists usually result in 1 to 2 percent customer response rate. By comparison, nursery owners who develop their list using more of a word-of-mouth and referral strategy have response rates from 20 to 50 percent.

Mail-order nurseries often swap or sell lists to each other. Nurseries of similar size with complementary product lines commonly exchange mailing labels for a one-time use. If yours is the smaller nursery, it is also fairly common to purchase names from a larger nursery. Most large mail-order nurseries sell their lists, so a small nursery could order the names of all customers who had ordered more than $200 worth of plants during the last year. These lists usually yield more than the 2 percent response rate of direct-mail lists. Nursery owners can also borrow or purchase the mailing lists of groups such as the GWA, the group of writers, speakers, and others who use public outlets to promote gardening.

Once you develop a mailing list, which is undoubtedly among the most valuable assets of any nursery, you will need to maintain it. Not only is the list helpful in keeping track of customers but it also is valuable to companies that rent mailing lists. What makes a good mailing list? First, a list should define and thereby target particular groups of customers. You will need to set up your customer database so that customers without an order history within the given parameters become deactivated. Second, a mailing list is more valuable if it is kept "tight," meaning that it is composed only of active customers. What nurseries consider as an active customer varies widely from one nursery to another. Most mail-order nurseries drop customers from their mailing list if they do not make a purchase for two or three years. There is the exception for those who are worth keeping on the list even if they never make a purchase. Garden writers are an exception, and others could include radio personalities, botanical gardens, libraries, extension service offices, and even gardening gurus in your region, anyone who might network with potential customers. Some of the larger mail-order nurseries seem to keep all customers on their mailing list forever, and I continue to receive catalogs from several large mail-order nurseries that I have never purchased anything from.

Chapter 23

Service With a Smile

Assuming that you are generating business, how do you plan to keep that business and satisfy your customers? While certain industries are very well aware of the importance of satisfying customers, the nursery industry is notorious for lagging far behind in this area.

As your nursery grows, you should designate someone as the customer service manager, whose job it is to handle all customer problems. As most readers can attest, there is nothing more annoying than having a valid complaint only to be sent to a seemingly endless stream of people, none of who is able to resolve your problem. Once you have designated such an individual, provide them with the knowledge—and the authority—to resolve problems when they occur. In small operations the owner can serve as the customer service manager, but it is very easy for the owner to remain in this position for too long. As owner, your top priority must be to the smooth and efficient operation of the business, which means that customer service is forced to take a back seat, creating an obvious problem.

The customer service manager doesn't have to answer technical, plant-related problems but does need to know how and where to get that information promptly. Too often, owners keep the answers to themselves, which causes a virtual bottleneck when there is a long line of staff and customers waiting for one decision after another. In situations of such congestion, no one wins, neither your customers nor your staff.

All businesses will have to deal with upset customers. Good communication and telephone skills can go a long way to satisfy customers, even those who are upset. Someone who not only has a pleasant voice but is also willing to listen instead of being confrontational can work wonders with angry customers. Whoever is in charge of answering the phone must be well trained in phone etiquette and customer relations.

While there is certainly an art of dealing with upset customers, you should also realize that there are simply some bad customers. I like to divide bad customers into two groups, those who don't know any better, and those who enjoy being difficult or intend to take advantage of a business. Most of us have never been trained to be good customers and need a bit of guidance. Plant Delights was possibly the first nursery to publish its expectations of good customer behavior (Avent 1996). Customers need to understand that there are always more of them than there are of you and that patience is a virtue. In addition, it is worth reminding some of them of the old adage that you can catch more flies with honey than with vinegar.

Habitually bad customers are another issue. While I realize that most customer service books and speakers will tell you to bend over backward for even these customers, I disagree. No amount of business or other financial reward can make it worthwhile dealing with a truly bad customer. In reality, bad customers simply move from nursery to nursery taking advantage of whomever they can for as much as they can. When nursery owners get together to compare "bad customer" lists, the amount of duplication is amazing.

Customer service "experts" tell you that if you upset even one bad customer, that person will tell others who in turn will tell others and so on. While I agree that this may occasionally happen, good customers, when hearing these tales, will likely consider the source. In reality, bad customers are often difficult to get along with in other aspects of their lives, and if they have friends who discontinue purchasing from you, they are probably bad customer wannabes who you would rather not deal with. I do not believe that good customers will give up on a nursery based on the complaints of a constant whiner. Granted, some businesses out there want every customer regardless of how much trouble they may be. I therefore recommend that you offer your bad customer list at no charge to those businesses.

As soon as you open your nursery, you will need to establish a guarantee or refund policy for your products. Guarantees are obviously more difficult in our industry than in many others since we are dealing with a highly perishable and living commodity. In the past, nurseries promised to deliver healthy plants to customers, but increased competition in the form of large companies with deep pockets has meant that extended guarantees have become a way of doing business, even if they force smaller companies out of business. When large mass marketers got into the nursery business in a big way, they tried to place living plants on the same level as widgets, which, if broken, could be replaced as though they were potentially defective. Owners of smaller nurseries felt that they had no choice but to offer similar guarantees, and before long, the industry standard was to offer some kind of long-term guarantee. I think this is quite appalling and part of the larger societal trend away from personal responsibility. The last time I checked, pets and children weren't guaranteed, so why have we made such a mockery of the nursery business by offering guarantees on living plants? Granted, we should work to help customers keep plants alive and to learn from their mistakes, but offering guarantees means we have gone from the sensible warranties (such as trueness to name, freedom from insects and disease, and good health) to ridiculous promises involving the replacement of plants for any period after they have left the nursery. Some nurseries offer guarantees of up to one year! I haven't seen a plant anywhere I couldn't kill within a couple of weeks without too much effort.

Chapter 24

The End Is Near: Closing, Selling, or Willing Away Your Nursery

You've finally had it—it's time to retire, change careers, or cash in before moving on. How do you go about disposing of a nursery and for how much? You could just close the doors and walk away, but after expending all that work on building a business, you would probably think it a shame not to get something back.

Assuming that you haven't gone hog-wild with pesticides and created a new Superfund site, the best way to get rid of a nursery is to sell the land for development. Nursery owners most often choose this route because their nurseries are usually located just outside a town on what was relatively inexpensive land when the nursery was started. As the city expands outward, the value of the land increases until it surpasses the value of the crops being produced.

If you are considering selling your land for development, make sure that the zoning rules say the land is suitable for development. Failing that, find out if the land can be rezoned because a developer's contract will be contingent on the approval of rezoning for development purposes. If rezoning is successful, your selling price is probably not going to be related to the value of your nursery stock but rather to the value of the adjacent land. One larger, aging nursery near us was demolished several years ago to make way for a Wal-Mart and a K-Mart, and I'm sure that the nursery had never even come close to producing the amount of income that resulted from the sale of the land.

The prospect of selling your nursery as a nursery is more complex. Quite a bit of the value of a nursery depends on how it was constructed. If construction was done on a shoestring budget with homemade greenhouses, temporary irrigation, and other such shoddy work, the infrastructure of the nursery will not have much value. A nursery that was well constructed with quality material and workmanship and that has been properly maintained will have far more value.

Other decisions you'll have to make include what and how much of a thing you are willing to sell. Will you sell your inventory, equipment, mailing list, corporate identity, and telephone number? Be sure to spell this all out clearly in any contract to sell the nursery. Also keep in mind that a profitable nursery has much more value than one that is less profitable or stagnant in its growth. The better the records and inventory you have kept, the easier it will be to justify your sales figure. Most nurseries do a terrible job of keeping records, so make sure that doesn't become a problem for you when you try to sell.

Every nursery owner has a different formula for determining the nursery's value. Some former nursery owners I have spoken with used formulas that seemed more complex than the IRS code. Interestingly, after talking with many nursery owners around the country, I have noticed that virtually all these complex formulas looked almost identical to the nursery's best year's gross income (assuming, of course, that the nursery was set up to be an asset and not a liability to a prospective purchaser).

One exception to using the best year's gross income occurs when an independent nursery is purchased by a larger chain. Having had conversations with many former nursery owners in this situation, I found that the purchasing price far exceeded the best year's gross. In fact, most figures I gathered show that prices ranged from two to three times the best year's gross (though this would certainly vary if the nursery had a large income but was not profitable). Another commonly used formula relates more to net profit, with a figure that represents six times the average of the last five years of net profit being used for a base selling price. Regardless of which formula is used, these are figures that would make any nursery owner sit up and listen.

How do you go about completing the transaction? For example, will you be paid cash by the acquiring owners? Unless you are selling to a developer, a nursery chain, or a large corporation, the answer probably is no. It will be difficult for a prospective nursery owner to obtain financing to purchase an existing nursery of any size. Most lending institutions do not understand the nursery business and are unlikely to take the time necessary to do so (Steingold 1998). More than likely, you will have to agree to finance the nursery purchase yourself. If you do this, it is essential that you get a large down payment in case of later problems. The monthly payments you receive will be stretched out over a period that fits the purchaser's ability to pay you from projected seasonal profits. If you allow a buyer an extended payment schedule, it is crucial that you do an extensive background check on the purchaser's payment and credit history.

Although I don't have any concrete figures, I know of many nursery sales in which the new owners defaulted on payments after running the business into the ground. The original owner then had to take over the business again to keep from losing everything on which they had planned to retire. Sure, you get the property back and you can sue the new owners for defaulting on their payments, but if they have no money, a court judgment in your favor is worthless. Most problems with purchasers who default seem to involve individual owners rather than large corporate purchasers, as these latter don't usually purchase using owner financing.

When you sell your nursery, you will often be offered an employment contract by the new owner, especially if you are well known by the public and are an integral part of the business. These contracts allow the new owner to own not only the facilities that you have built but also to draw on your name and personality. In addition, the employment contract requires that you stay on with the business in some capacity, either advisory or managerial. These contracts typically meet with disaster because independent-thinking owners struggle to switch to a new paradigm in which they find themselves working under a boss whose business philosophy will probably be different. Conflicts that result in disastrous outcomes are actually quite common in the nursery industry.

Nursery buyers typically require that the original sellers sign noncompete agreements to prevent them from starting up a competing nursery after selling off the old one. Since many customers are loyal not just to the business but to the business owner as well, it would be easy for an owner to steal away the very customer base that made the business attractive for the purchasers in the first place. The typical noncompete agreement is for a period of about five years and is usually valid only in a limited region of the country. Most court decisions have ruled that much longer and more extensive agreements are simply too restrictive. Some states will not even enforce noncompete agreements. You probably can't imagine getting out of the nursery business and then diving back in, but the nursery industry is strange in that way. Nurseries often become a part of your psyche, and many owners find it difficult to get out and stay out of the business.

In rarer situations usually restricted to smaller nurseries, the owner will simply close down the nursery and sell off the nursery's assets. This is usually done where the nursery owner doesn't want to deal with the problems associated with financing new owners in the hope that they will keep the business running in a profitable manner. Nursery owners sometimes do this when the nursery is located around the owner's home or on family property that the owner doesn't wish to sell.

Selling off the assets of a nursery is often a complicated process. The nursery stock is probably the easiest asset to dispose of because often your customers, either wholesale or retail, will buy your plants, usually at a greatly discounted price. In most cases, it is much easier to offer a package deal to one or two buyers. In trying to maximize profit, a retailer in our area actually held a three-year-long "going out of business sale." After the first couple of months, the nursery became the butt of jokes in the region and customers quit stopping by to look for bargains.

Nursery equipment is most often sold at nursery auctions, which are quite popular in the industry, and a few auction firms that specialize in nursery auctions regularly advertise in trade journals. Nursery structures such as green-houses are truly of little value. Usually the cost associated with purchasing and moving them equals the cost of new materials. That doesn't mean that you shouldn't try to sell your greenhouse structures; just don't be disappointed when you fail to get what you think is a good price. You could get lucky and find yourself selling to a potential new nursery owner who regards them as a bargain. I'd be happy to have someone come and remove the greenhouses for free to keep me from having to hire a bulldozer and truck to demolish them, particularly as metal greenhouses are a mess to demolish and remove.

If you are in mail order or retail, your mailing list is among your greatest assets, especially if you have done a good job in capturing data about each of your customers. Mailing lists can have a value of up to several dollars per active customer. Your options here include renting names to mailing list firms or other nurseries or actually selling the customer list to a single nursery. I have known nurseries to bring in good, six-figure incomes from selling their mailing lists.

Among the interesting phenomena you will experience when closing a retail or mail-order nursery is a backlash from angry customers. Some customers will be very upset and feel that you have deserted them; they will likely want you to reopen your business. You have worked hard to establish customer loyalty, so it is only natural that the sword cuts both ways when you decide to close your business. It is therefore always advisable to use a post office box for your mail, particularly if you are in the mail-order business. If your mail-order business has been mentioned in books and periodicals, it will continue to receive catalog requests for years after you have closed the business. You will be faced with the monumental task and expense of returning all the nursery's mail, much of which will be catalog requests with funds enclosed, if you keep the same address.

If your nursery is still running or will be sold, you need to examine how it, or the money from its sale, will be passed along to your heirs. Leaving the business to your heirs means that you need to be aware of the infamous estate or "death tax." Not only does the government tax the property that you own through sales and property taxes while you are still alive, but it also taxes their value again when, upon your death, the property goes to your heirs. This tax, which was first instituted in 1916, has increased in percentage through the years to become an incredible burden today. Nurseries appreciate in value as a result both of the amount of business they transact and of the value of the land on which it is located. This appreciation is known as capital gains and refers to the amount of the original cost of the land or the nursery and the improvements subtracted from the current value.

As of 2002, there is an exemption of $675,000 for the deceased owner's heirs. The remaining value of the nursery is taxed at a rate of between 37 and 55 percent, with values over three million being taxed at the 55 percent rate. If the value of the nursery when the owner dies is five million dollars, subtract the original cost of the land from that five million. For example, the land could have cost $100,000, and an additional $100,000 could have been spent on improvements. After subtracting the $675,000 exemption from the total value, the tax on the remaining value of the estate would be almost 2.3 million dollars—and this is just the tax, excluding your legal fees! (Sturdivant 2000; Giardina 2000). If you think this is fair, then you are probably very well off, have plenty of tax loopholes to make use of, haven't started your business yet, or aren't yet dead. Although good financial planners can help to reduce this burden, it is a shame that they have to be employed to help the family keep what they have worked so hard to attain.

While some forces in Congress are trying to repeal this anti-small-business tax, at this time it is unfortunately still in place. This death tax is a prime reason that businesses do not survive from one generation to the next. In fact, according to the handbook on the 1995 White House Conference on Small Business, more than 70 percent of businesses do not survive the second generation, and a whopping 87 percent do not survive into the third generation, all because of the death tax. Surely this is not what the Founding Fathers of our country intended from our government.

Epilogue

So are you still psyched about getting into the nursery business? If so, then you are at least better prepared to face what lies ahead. If you decide against getting into the nursery business, perhaps you have saved yourself some headaches, money, and time. At the very least, you no doubt have a much greater appreciation of what goes on behind the scenes when you walk into a nursery to purchase a plant—and you'll know that what on the surface appears to be a giant profit usually isn't.

Despite what you may have concluded about me from reading this book, I love the nursery business. There are few other careers where competitors are so friendly and so willing to share information, even secrets, with you. Most of all, those of us already in the industry genuinely want newcomers to succeed. Established, well-run nurseries in particular want start-ups to have a clear understanding of costs and pricing. If you start a nursery and then figure out a way to produce, market, and ship plants more cheaply than your competitors, then more power to you. No one wins, however, if you unknowingly underprice your products and then go out of business.

I, like most others in the nursery trade, wouldn't trade this business and lifestyle for anything. Granted, I'm not saying this during one of those months with low cash flow, or just after all my key employees have quit, or after two heaters have burned out on the coldest night of the year, or after root rot has wiped out an entire greenhouse of my most valuable crop. Perhaps you should talk to me again next week.

Appendix I.

Helpful Sources of Information

All Web sites listed below were current at the time of writing but may have changed since.

American Institute of Certified Public
  Accountants
1211 Avenue of the Americas
New York, New York 10036
Phone: 212.596.6200
www.aicpa.org

American Nursery and Landscape
  Association (ANLA)
1000 Vermont Avenue N.W., Suite 300
Washington, D.C. 20005-4914
Phone: 202.789.2900
www.ANLA.org

American Nurseryman
American Nurseryman Publishing
  Company
77 W. Washington Street, Suite 2100
Chicago, Illinois 60602
Phone: 312.782.5505
www.amerinursery.com

Employment and Training
  Administration
www.doleta.gov

Environmental Protection Agency
  (EPA)
1200 Pennsylvania Avenue N.W.
Washington, D.C. 20460
www.epa.gov

Equal Employment Opportunity
  Commission
1801 L Street N.W.
Washington, D.C. 20507
Phone: 800.669.4000
www.eeoc.gov

The Federal Register Online
www.access.gpo.gov/su_docs/aces/aces
  140.html

Federal Trade Commission (FTC)
600 Pennsylvania Avenue N.W.
Washington, D.C. 20580
Phone: 202.326.2222
www.ftc.gov

*Garden Center Merchandising and
  Management*
Branch-Smith Publishing Company
120 St. Louis Avenue
Fort Worth, Texas 76104
Phone: 817.882.4120
www.greenbeam.com

Garden Center Products and Supplies
Branch-Smith Publishing Company
120 St. Louis Avenue
Fort Worth, Texas 76104
Phone: 817.882.4120
www.greenbeam.com

Garden Writers Association
10210 Leatherleaf Court
Manassas, Virginia 20111
Phone: 703.257.1032
www.gwaa.org

Gempler's *Alert*
Gempler's Inc.
P.O. Box 270
Belleville, Wisconsin 53508
Phone: 800.882.8473
www.gemplersalert.com

Greenhouse Grower
Meister Publishing Company
37733 Euclid Avenue
Willoughby, Ohio 44094
Phone: 440.942.2000
www.greenhousegrower.com

Greenhouse Management and Production
Branch-Smith Publishing Company
120 St. Louis Avenue
Fort Worth, Texas 76104
Phone: 817.882.4121
www.greenbeam.com

Grower Talks
Ball Publishing Company
335 N. River Street
P.O. Box 9
Batavia, Illinois 60510
Phone: 630.208.9080
www.growertalks.com

Immigration and Naturalization Service
(INS)
HQPDI
425 I Street N.W., Room 4370r
Washington, D.C. 20536
www.ins.gov

Integrated Pest Management for
Floriculture and Nurseries
University of California
Agriculture and Natural Resources
Communication Services
6701 San Pablo Avenue
Oakland, California 94608
Phone: 800.994.8849

International Plant Propagators Society
(IPPS)
www.ipps.org

IR-4 Project Headquarters Center for
Minor Crop Pest Management
Technology Center of New Jersey
Rutgers, The State University of New
Jersey
681 U.S. Highway #1 South
North Brunswick, New Jersey 08902-3390
Phone: 732.932.9575
www.cook.rutgers.edu/~ir4/

National Association of Plant Patent
Owners (NAPPO)
1250 I Street N.W. Suite 500
Washington, D.C. 20005
Phone: 202.789.2900
www.anla.org/industry/patents/index.htm

National Bark and Soil Producers
Association
10210 Leatherleaf Court
Manassas, Virginia 20111
Phone: 703.257.0111
www.nbspa.org

Nursery Management and Production
Branch-Smith Publishing Company
120 St. Louis Avenue
Fort Worth, Texas 76104
Phone: 817.882.4120
www.greenbeam.com

Nursery Retailer
Brantwood Publishing
Phone: 727.786.9771
www.nurseryretailer.com

Occupational Safety and Health
Administration (OSHA)
200 Constitution Avenue N.W.
Washington, D.C. 20210
Phone: 202.693.1999
www.osha.gov; www.osha.gov/
oshprogs/consult.html

Perennial Plant Association (PPA)
3383 Schirtzinger Road
Hilliard, Ohio 43026
Phone: 614.771.8431
www.perennialplant.org

Pinkerton Services Group
13950 Ballentyne Corporate Place
Charlotte, North Carolina 28277
Phone: 800.528.5745
www.pinkertons.com

Reid London House
153 W. Ohio Street # 400
Chicago, Illinois 60610
Phone: 312.938.9200

Royal Horticultural Society
Mail-Order Department
RHS Garden Wisley
Woking, Surrey, GU23 6QB
U.K.
Phone: 0044.483.212357
www.rhs.org.uk/

Small Business Administration (SBA)
200 North College Street, Suite A-2015
Charlotte, North Carolina 28202
Phone: 800.827.5722
www.sba.gov; www.sba.gov/hotlist/
license
www.sbaonline.sba.gov/starting/
finding.html

Southern Nursery Association (SNA)
1827 Powers Ferry Road, Bldg. 4, Suite 100
Atlanta, Georgia 30339
Phone: 770.953.3311
www.sna.org

The Unemployment Tax Advisory
Difference
www.uchelp.com

U.S. Department of Agriculture Animal
and Plant Health Inspection Service
(USDA-APHIS)
4700 River Road, Unit 133
Riverdale, Maryland 20737
Phone: 877.770.5990
www.aphis.usda.gov

U.S. Department of Customs
Customs Headquarters
1300 Pennsylvania Avenue N.W,
Room 6.3D
Washington, D.C. 20229
Phone: 202.927.0400
www.customs.gov
www.customs.gov/travel/travel.htm

U.S. Department of Justice (DOJ)
950 Pennsylvania Avenue N.W.
Washington, D.C. 20530-0001
Phone: 202.353.1555
www.usdoj.gov.

U.S. Department of Labor (DOL)
200 Constitution Avenue N.W.
Washington, D.C. 20210
Phone: 202.219.5000
www.dol.gov

U.S. Fish and Wildlife (USFW)
1849 C Street N.W.
Washington, D.C. 20240
Phone: 800.358.2104
www.fws.gov

U.S. Patent and Trademark Office (USPTO)
Crystal Plaza 3
Washington, D.C. 20231
Phone: 800.786.9199
www.uspto.gov

Appendix II.

Designated Ports of Entry for Plants

All ports listed have an active USDA Animal Plant Health Inspection Service and Plant Protection and Quarantine (PPQ) system.

ARIZONA
Plant Inspection Station
North Grand Avenue, Room 2214
Nogales, Arizona 85621
Phone: 520.287.4783
Fax: 520.287.6941

CALIFORNIA
Los Angeles Inspection Station/Cargo
11840 S. La Cienega Blvd.
Hawthorne, California 90250
Phone: 310.725.1910
Fax: 310.725.1913

Plant Inspection Station
P.O. Box 434419
San Diego, California 92143-4419
Phone: 619.661.3316
Fax: 619.661.3047

Plant Inspection Station
389 Oyster Point Blvd., Suite 2
South San Francisco, California 94080
Phone: 650.876.9093
Fax: 650.876.9008

FLORIDA
Plant Inspection Station
P.O. Box 59-2136
Miami, Florida 33159
Phone: 305.526.2825
Fax: 305.871.4205

Plant Inspection Station
9317 Tradeport Drive
Orlando, Florida 32827
Phone: 407.648.6856
Fax: 407.648.6859

HAWAII
Honolulu Inspection Station
Honolulu International Airport
300 Rodgers Blvd., No. 57
Honolulu, Hawaii 96819-1897
Phone: 808.861.8494
Fax: 808.861.8500

LOUISIANA
Plant Inspection Station
P.O. Box 20114
New Orleans, Louisiana 70141-0114
Phone: 504.464.0430
Fax: 504.465.0968

NEW JERSEY
Hoboken, New Jersey (Port of New York)
Frances Krim Memorial Inspection
   Station
2500 Brunswick Avenue (Building G)
Linden, New Jersey 07036
Phone: 908.862.2012
Fax: 908.862.2095

NEW YORK
JFK International Airport
Plant Inspection Station
Building 77, Room 127
Jamaica, New York 11430
Phone: 718.553.1732
Fax: 718.553.0060

PUERTO RICO
P.O. Box 37521
San Juan, Puerto Rico 00937
Phone: 787.253.4699
Fax: 787.253.7837

TEXAS
Plant Inspection Station
P.O. Drawer Box 393
100 Los Indios Boulevard
Los Indios, Texas 78567
Phone: 956.399.2085
Fax: 956.399.4001

Appendix III.

State and Regional Nursery Associations

(Reprinted with permission. The American Nursery and Landscape Association 2002)

CANADA

Atlantic Provinces Nursery Trades Association
Ms. Tanya Morrison
130 Bluewater Road
Bedford, Nova Scotia B4B 1G7
Phone: 902.835.7387
Fax: 902.835.5498

BC Landscape and Nursery Association
Ms. Jane Stock, Executive Director
5830 176 A Street, Suite 101
Surrey, British Columbia V3S 4E3
Phone: 604.574.7772
Fax: 604.574.7773

Canadian Nursery Landscape Association
Mr. Chris Andrews, Executive Director
7856 Fifth Line S
RR4 Station Main
Milton, Ontario L9T 2X8
Phone: 905.875.1399; 888.446.3499
Fax: 905.875.1840
www.canadanursery.com

Landscape Alberta Nursery Trades Association
Mr. Nigel Bowles, Executive Director
10215 176th Street
Edmonton, Alberta T5S 1M1
Phone: 780.489.1991; 800.378.3198
Fax: 780.444.2152

Landscape Manitoba
Ms. Evelyn Mackenzie-Reid, Executive Administrator
808 Muriel Street
Winnipeg, Manitoba R2Y 0Y3
Phone: 204.889.5981
www.canadanursery.com/lm

Landscape Ontario Horticultural Trades Association
Mr. Tony Di Giovanni, Executive Director
7856 5th Line S
RR 4 Station Main
Milton, Ontario L9T 2X8
Phone: 905.875.1805
Fax: 905.875.3942

New Brunswick Horticultural Trades Association
Mr. James Landry
P.O. Box 711
Saint John, New Brunswick E2L 4B3
Phone: 506.636.6243
Fax: 506.847.0097

Saskatchewan Nursery Trades
  Association
Mr. Tim VanDuyvendyk
685 Reid Road
Saskatoon, SASK S7N 3J4
Phone: 306.249.0151

UNITED STATES

Alabama Nurserymen's Association
Ms. Linda H.Van Dyke, Executive
  Secretary
369 S College Street
P.O. Box 9
Auburn, Alabama 36831-0009
Phone: 334.821.5148
Fax: 334.821.9111
www.alna.org

Alaska Horticulture Association
Mr. Wayne Vandre
c/o Alaska Cooperative Extension
2221 E Northern Lights Blvd, No.18
Anchorage, Alaska 99508-4143
Phone: 907.279.6575

Arizona Nursery Association
Ms. Cheryl Goar, CAE Executive Director
1430 W Broadway Road, Suite A-180
Tempe, Arizona 85282-1199
Phone: 480.966.1610
Fax: 480.966.0923
www.azna.or

Arkansas Green Industry Association
Ms. Anne H. Borg, Executive Director
P.O. Box 21715
Little Rock, Arkansas 72221-1715
Phone: 501.225.0029
Fax: 501.224.0988
www.argia.org

California Association of Nurserymen
Ms. Elaine Thompson, Executive Director
3947 Lennane Suite 150
Sacramento, California 95834-1957
Phone: 916.928.3900; 800.748.6214
Fax: 916.567.0505
www.can-online.org

Colorado Nursery Association
Ms. Sharon R. Harris
5290 E Yale Circle Suite 204
Denver, Colorado 80222-6933
Phone: 303.758.6672; 888.758.6672
Fax: 303.758.6805
www.colorado-nursery-assn.org/
  sys-tmpl/door/

Connecticut Nursery and Landscape
  Association
Mr. Robert V. Heffernan, Executive
  Director
P.O. Box 414
Botsford, Connecticut 06404-0414
Phone: 203.445.0110; 800.562.0610
Fax: 203.261.5429
www.flowersplantsinct.com/cnla/
  cnlaindex.htm

Delaware Nursery & Landscape
  Association
Ms. Valann Budischak, Executive Director
P.O. Box 897
Hockessin, Delaware 19707-0897
Phone: 888.448.1203
Fax: 888.448.1203

Florida Nurserymen & Growers
  Association
Mr. Ben Bolusky, Executive Vice President
1533 Park Center Drive
Orlando, Florida 32835-5705
Phone: 407.295.7994; 800.375.FNGA
Fax: 407.295.1619
www.fnga.org

Georgia Green Industry Association
Ms. Sherry Loudermilk, Executive
  Director
Hwy 5 N
P.O. Box 369
Epworth, Georgia 30541-0369
Phone: 706.632.0100
Fax: 706.632.0300
www.ggia.org

Idaho Nursery Association
Ms. Ann Bates, Executive Director
P.O. Box 2065
Idaho Falls, Idaho 83403-2065
Phone: 208.522.7307; 800.INA.GROW
Fax: 208.529.0832
www.inagrow.org

Illinois Nurserymen's Association
Mr. David Bender
1717 S Fifth St
Springfield, Illinois 62703-3116
Phone: 217.525.6222
Fax: 217.525.6257
www.ina-online.org

Indiana Nursery and Landscape
  Association
Ms. Paula Williams, Executive Director
233 McCrea Street, Suite 200
Indianapolis, Indiana 46225
Phone: 317.955.0628
Fax: 317.955.3163
www.inla1.org/index.html

Iowa Nursery and Landscape
  Association
Ms. Sarah Woody Bibens, Executive
  Director
1210 Frederick Avenue
St. Joseph, Missouri 64501
Phone: 816.233.1481
Fax: 816.233.4774
www.iowanla.org

Kansas Association of Nurserymen
Ms. Mary Odgers, Executive Secretary
411 Poplar
Wamego, Kansas 66547-1446
Phone: 785.456.2066

Kentucky Nursery and Landscape
  Association
Ms. Betsie Taylor, Executive Director
350 Village Drive
Frankfort, Kentucky 40601
Phone: 502.848.0055; 800.735.9791
Fax: 502.848.0032
www.knla.org

Louisiana Nursery and Landscape
  Association
Allen D. Owings, Executive Director
P.O. Box 25100
Baton Rouge, Louisiana 70894-5100
Phone: 225.578.2222
Fax: 225.578.0773
www.lnla.org

Maine Landscape & Nursery
  Association
Ms. Edith Ellis, Executive Secretary
RR 2 Box 1584
Turner, Maine 04282-9658
Phone: 207.225.3767
Fax: 207.225.3768
www.melna.org

Maryland Nursery & Landscape
  Association
Ms. Nancy Akehurst
P.O. Box 18989
Baltimore, Maryland 21206-0089
Phone: 410.254.3302
Fax: 410.882.0535
www.mdnurserymen.org

Massachusetts Nursery & Landscape Association
Ms. Rena M. Sumner, Executive Director
1270 Whateley Road
P.O. Box 387
Conway, Massachusetts 01341-9772
Phone: 413.369.4731
Fax: 413.369.4962
www.mnla.com

Michigan Nursery & Landscape Association
Ms. Amy E. Frankmann, Executive Director
2149 Commons Parkway
Okemos, Michigan 48864-3987
Phone: 517.381.0437; 800.879.6652
Fax: 517.381.0638
www.mnla.org

Minnesota Nursery & Landscape Association
Mr. Bob Fitch, Executive Director
2151 Hamline Avenue N, Suite 109
P.O. Box 130307
St. Paul, Minnesota 55113-4226
Phone: 651.633.4987; 888.886.6652
Fax: 651.633.4986
www.mnlandscape.org

Mississippi Nurserymen's Association
David Tatum, Executive Secretary and Treasurer
246 Dorman Hall
P.O. Box 5385
Miss. State, Mississippi 39762-5385
Phone: 662.325.1682
Fax: 662.325.8379
www.msnla.org

Missouri Landscape and Nursery Association
Ms. Sarah Woody Bibens, Executive Director
1210 Frederick Avenue
St. Joseph, Missouri 64501
Phone: 816.233.1481
Fax: 816.233.4774
www.mlna.org

Montana Association of Nurserymen
Ms. Robin L. Childers, Executive Director
P.O. Box 4553
Missoula, Montana 59806-4553
Phone: 406.721.7334
Fax: 406.721.7016
www.plantingmontana.com

Nebraska Nursery and Landscape Association
Ms. Sarah Woody Bibens, Executive Director
1210 Frederick Avenue
St. Joseph, Missouri 64501
Phone: 816.233.1481
Fax: 816.233.4774
www.nnla.org

Nevada Landscape Association
Ms. Debra Rae Drew, Executive Director
P.O. Box 7431
Reno, Nevada 89510-7431
Phone: 775.673.0404; 800.645.9794
Fax: 775.673.5828
www.nevadanla.com

New England Nursery Association
Ms. M. Virginia Wood, Executive Director
8D Pleasant Street
South Natick, Massachusetts 01760
Phone: 508.653.3112
Fax: 508.653.4112
www.NEnsyAssn.org

New Hampshire Plant Growers
  Association
Mr. Chris Robarge
56 Leavitt Road
Hampton, New Hampshire 03842-3938
Phone: 603.862.1074

New Jersey Nursery & Landscape
  Association
Mr. S. Howard Davis, Executive Director
605 Farnsworth Avenue
Bordentown, New Jersey 08505-2028
Phone: 609.291.7070; 800.314.4836
Fax: 609.291.1121
www.gardennj.net

New Mexico Association of Nursery
  Industries
Ms. Linda McClean
P.O. Box 30003, Department 3Q
Las Cruces, New Mexico 88003-8003
Phone: 505.646.1902
Fax: 505.646.6041

New York State Nursery and Landscape
  Association
Mr. Mark Rupprecht
2115 Downer Street
P.O. Box 657
Baldwinsville, New York 13027-9702
Phone: 315.635.5008; 800.647.0384
Fax: 315.635.4874
www.nysnla.org

North Carolina Association of
  Nurserymen
Mr. Ronald E. Gelvin, Executive Director
968 Trinity Road
Raleigh, North Carolina 27607
Phone: 919.816.9119
Fax: 919.816.9118
www.ncan.com

North Dakota Nursery & Greenhouse
  Association
Ms. Mary Holm
P.O. Box 34
Neche, North Dakota 58265
Phone: 701.886.7673

Ohio Nursery & Landscape Association
Mr. William Stalter, Executive Director
72 Dorchester Square
Westerville, Ohio 43081-3350
Phone: 614.899.1195; 800.825.5062
Fax: 614.899.9489
www.onla.org

Oklahoma State Nurserymen's
  Association
Mr. Carroll Emberton, Executive Director
400 N Portland Street
Oklahoma City, Oklahoma 73107-6110
Phone: 405.942.5276
Fax: 405.945.3382
www.oknurserymen.org

Oregon Association of Nurserymen
Mr. John J. Aguirre
2780 SE Harrison Street, Suite 102
Milwaukie, Oregon 97222-7584
Phone: 503.653.8733; 800.342.6401
Fax: 503.653.1528
www.nurseryguide.com

Pennsylvania Landscape and Nursery
  Association
Ms. Michele Corbin, Legislative Director
1707 S Cameron Street
Harrisburg, Pennsylvania 17104-3148
Phone: 717.238.1673; 800.898.3411
Fax: 717.238.1675
www.plna.com

Rhode Island Nursery & Landscape
    Association
Mr. Kenneth A. Lagerquist, Executive
    Secretary
64 Bittersweet Drive
Seekonk, Massachusetts 02771-1103
Phone: 508.761.9260
Fax: 508.761.9260
www.uri.edu/research/sustland/rina.ht
    ml

South Carolina Nursery & Landscape
    Association
Ms. Donna Shealy Foster, Executive
    Secretary
332 Sunward Path
Inman, South Carolina 29349-8266
Phone: 864.592.3868
Fax: 864.592.3857
www.scnla.com

South Dakota Nursery and Landscape
    Association
Ms. Julie Hoffman, Executive Director
East River Nursery
5659 Dakota South
Huron, South Dakota 57350-6550
Phone: 605.352.4414
Fax: 605.352.8836

Southern Nursery Association
Mr. Danny Summers, Executive Vice
    President
1827 Powers Ferry Road, Bldg 4, Suite
    100
Atlanta, Georgia 30339
Phone:770.953.3311
Fax: 770.953.4411
www.sna.org

Tennessee Nursery & Landscape
    Association Inc.
Mr. Roger Spivey, Executive Vice
    President
115 Lyon Street
P.O. Box 57
McMinnville, Tennessee 37110-2545
Phone: 931.473.3951
Fax: 931.473.5883
www.tnla.com

Texas Nursery & Landscape Association
Mr. Eddy D. Edmondson, President
7730 South IH-35
Austin, Texas 78745-6698
Phone: 512.280.5182; 800.880.0343
Fax: 512.280.3012
www.txnla.org

Utah Nursery & Landscape Association
Ms. Diane Jones, Executive Director
P.O. Box 526314
Salt Lake City, Utah 84152-6314
Phone: 801.484.4426
Fax: 801.463.0026
www.utahgreen.org

Vermont Association of Professional
    Horticulturists
Ms. Jane Lavanway, Executive Director
P.O. Box 396
Jonesville, Vermont 05466-0396
Phone: 802.865.5979
Fax: 802.865.5967

Virginia Nursery & Landscape
    Association Inc.
Mr. Jeffrey B. Miller, Executive Director
383 Coal Hollow Road
Christiansburg, Virginia 24073-6721
Phone: 540.382.0943; 800.476.0055
Fax: 540.382.2716
www.VNLA.org

Washington State Nursery & Landscape
  Association
Ms. Marianne Pratt, Executive Director
P.O. Box 670
Sumner, Washington 98390-0120
Phone: 253.863.4482; 800.672.7711
Fax: 253.863.6732
www.wsnla.org

Western Nursery & Landscape
  Association
Ms. Sarah Woody Bibens, Executive
  Director
1210 Frederick Avenue
St. Joseph, Missouri 64501
Phone: 816.233.1481
Fax: 816.233.4774
www.wnla.org

West Virginia Nursery & Landscape
  Association
Mr. Bradford C. Bearce, Executive
  Director
1517 Kingwood Pike
Morgantown, West Virginia 26508
Phone: 304.292.2440; 800.221.9862
Fax: 304.292.2488
www.wvnla.org

Wisconsin Nursery Association Inc.
Mr. Joe Phillips, Executive Director
9910 W Layton
Greenfield, Wisconsin 53228-3347
Phone: 414.529.4705
Fax: 414.529.4722
www.wislf.org

Conversion Chart

(Reprinted with permission. Bilderback 2001)

MULTIPLY	BY	TO OBTAIN
Acres	43,560	square feet
Acres	4,047	square meters
Acres	4,840	square yards
Acre feet	12	cubic feet
Acre feet	6,272,640	acre inches
Acre feet	43,560	cubic feet
Acre feet	325,872	gallons
Acre inches	3,630	cubic feet
Acre inches	6,272,640	cubic inches
Acre inches	27,154	gallons
Centimeters	.03281	feet
Centimeters	.3937	inches
Centimeters	.01	meters
Cubic feet	28,316.84	cubic centimeters
Cubic feet	1,728	cubic inches
Cubic feet	.03704	cubic yards
Cubic feet	7.481	gallons
Cubic feet	51.42	pints (dry)
Cubic feet	59.84	pints (liquid)
Cubic inches	.0005787	cubic feet
Cubic inches	.00001639	cubic meters
Cubic inches	.00002143	cubic yards
Cubic inches	.004329	gallons
Cubic inches	.5541	ounces (fluid)
Cubic inches	.02976	pints (dry)
Cubic inches	.03463	pints (fluid)
Cubic inches	.01488	quarts (dry)
Cubic inches	.01732	quarts (fluid)
Cubic yards	27	cubic feet
Cubic yards	46,656	cubic inches

MULTIPLY	BY	TO OBTAIN
Cubic yards	.7646	cubic meters
Cubic yards	202	gallons
Cubic yards	1,616	pints (fluid)
Cubic yards	807.9	quarts (fluid)
Cups (dry)	.5	pints (dry)
Cups (dry)	.25	quarts (dry)
Cups (dry)	16	tablespoons (dry)
Cups (dry)	48	teaspoons (dry)
Feet	30.48	centimeters
Feet	.3048	meters
Feet per second	.6818	miles per hour
Gallons	.1337	cubic feet
Gallons	231	cubic inches
Gallons	3.785	liters
Gallons	8	pints (fluid)
Gallons	4	quarts (fluid)
Gallons per minute	.134	cubic feet per minute
Gallons per minute	.002228	cubic feet per second
Grams	.002205	pounds
Inches	2.54	centimeters
Inches	.08333	feet
Liters	1,000	cubic centimeters
Liters	.03531	cubic feet
Liters	.001308	cubic yards
Liters	.2642	gallons (fluid)
Liters	2.113	pints (fluid)
Liters	1.057	quarts (fluid)
Meters	1.0936	yards
Mils	.001	inches
Milligrams per liter	1	parts per million (ppm)
Ounces (fluid)	.0078125	gallons
Ounces (fluid)	.02957	liters
Ounces (fluid)	2	tablespoons (fluid)
Ounces (fluid)	6	teaspoons (fluid)
Parts per million (ppm)	.013	ounces per 100 gallons
Parts per million (ppm)	.0083	pounds per 1000 gallons
Pints (fluid)	.0167	cubic feet
Pints (fluid)	28.875	cubic inches
Pints (fluid)	.125	gallons (fluid)

MULTIPLY	BY	TO OBTAIN
Pints (fluid)	.4732	liters (fluid)
Pints (fluid)	16	ounces (fluid)
Pints (fluid)	.5	quarts (fluid)
Pounds	16	ounces
Pounds of water	.01602	cubic feet
Pounds of water	.1198	gallons
Quarts (dry)	.0389	cubic feet
Quarts (dry)	67.20	cubic inches
Quarts (dry)	2	pints (dry)
Quarts (fluid)	.0334	cubic feet
Quarts (fluid)	.25	gallons (fluid)
Quarts (fluid)	.9463	liters (fluid)
Quarts (fluid)	32	ounces (fluid)
Quarts (fluid)	2	pints (fluid)
Square feet	.00002296	acres
Square feet	144	square inches
Square feet	.0929	square meters
Square meters	.000247	acres
Square meters	10.764	square feet
Square miles	640	acres
Square yards	.0002066	acres
Square yards	9	square feet
Square yards	.8361	square meters
Tablespoons (dry)	.0625	cups (dry)
Tablespoons (dry)	.333	ounces (dry)
Tablespoons (dry)	3	teaspoons (dry)
Tablespoons (fluid)	.0625	cups (fluid)
Tablespoons (fluid)	15	milliliters (fluid)
Tablespoons (fluid)	.5	ounces (fluid)
Teaspoons (dry)	.111	ounces (dry)
Teaspoons (dry)	.333	tablespoons (dry)
Teaspoons (fluid)	.0208	cups (fluid)
Teaspoons (fluid)	5	milliliters (fluid)
Teaspoons (fluid)	.1666	ounces (fluid)
Temperature C +17.8	1.8	temperature F
Temperature F -32	.55	temperature C
Yards	3	feet
Yards	36	inches
Yards	.9144	meters

Bibliography

Acme Engineering. 1993. *The Greenhouse Climate Control Handbook.* Acme Engineering and Manufacturing Corporation.

American Institute of Certified Public Accountants, *CPA Client Bulletin.*

American Nurseryman. 1993. Employers Beware. (January 1).

American Nursery and Landscape Association (ANLA).1989. *Interviewing and Hiring Employees.*

———. 1990. *Legal Status of Horticulture.*

———. 1991. *Uniform Charts of Accounts.*

———. 1992a. *Americans With Disabilities Act.*

———. 1992b. *Integrated Pest Management for Nursery Growers.*

———. 1993. *Establishing and Operating a Garden Center.*

———. 1994a. *Guides for the Nursery Industry.*

———. 1994b. *Federal OSHA Compliance Manual.*

———. 1996a. *American Standards for Nursery Stock.*

———. 1996b. *Federal/State Quarantine Summaries.*

———. 1997. *Directory of Plant Patents.*

———. 1998. *Operating Cost Study.*

———. 2000. *Grapevine Study.*

———. 2001. *ANLA Update.*

Arkin, J. 1992. Freight facts. *American Nurseryman.* (February 15).

Atterbury, Fred. 1997. Wage and hour summary. *ANLA.*

Avent, T. 1996. How to be a good customer. Plant Delights Nursery Catalog.

Badenhop, M. B., T. D. Phillips, and F. B. Perry. 1985. Costs of establishing and operating field nurseries differentiated by size of firm and species of plant in USDA climatic Zones 7 and 8. Southern Cooperative Series Bulletin 311 for Southern Regional Research Project S-103, Department of Research Information, Alabama Agricultural Experiment Station, Auburn University, Auburn, Alabama.

———. 1987. Costs of establishing and operating a small and large size container nursery in USDA climatic Zones 7 and 8. Southern Cooperative Series Bulletin 327 for Southern Regional Research Project S-103, Department of Research Information, Alabama Agricultural Experiment Station Auburn University, Auburn, Alabama.

Baker, J. 1996. *Urban Integrated Pest Management.* North Carolina Cooperative Extension Service College of Agriculture and Life Sciences: North Carolina State University. Retrieved 2002. http://ipm.ncsu.edu/urban/cropsci/cp5pesta/phototox.html

Bartok, J., Jr. 2000. Make the best use of space. *GMPro.* (December).

Battersby, M. 1998. Ratios: Accounting gear that every grower needs. *Grower Talks.* (May).

Bilderback, T. 2001. *Nuts and Bolts of the Nursery Industry: A Reference and Resource Manual 2001.* Raleigh, North Carolina: North Carolina Association of Nurserymen.

Bilderback, T., and D. Bir. 2001. Nutrient and chemical capacity factors for water, mid-season substrates, and plant tissue for woody ornamental nursery container crops: suggested ranges and limits. In *Nuts and Bolts of the Nursery Industry: A Reference and Resource Manual 2001*. Raleigh, North Carolina: North Carolina Association of Nurserymen.

Both, A. J. 2000. It's cold out! So why ventilate? *Grower Talks*. (December).

Broome, T., Jr. 1995. Common objections from bank loan officers and how to overcome them. *Greenhouse Management and Production*. (March).

Brumfield, R. 1993. The price is right. *GMPro*. (August).

———. 1998. How to decide what equipment to buy. *GMPro*. (September).

Bush, E. 2001. Cyclic irrigation. *GMPro*. (January).

Carlson, W. 1999. Make the next millennium profitable. *Greenhouse Grower*. (November).

Cherim, M. 1998. *Green Good Methods Manual: The Original Bio-Control Primer*. Nottingham, New Hampshire: The Green Spot Limited Publishing Division.

Childs, K., R. Beeson, Jr., and J. Haydu. 2000. Alternative irrigation. *American Nurseryman*. (October 1).

Cohen, L. 1993. Perennials for sale, Part II. *American Nurseryman*. (April 1).

Dole, J., and H. Wilkins. 1999. *Floriculture: Principles and Species*. New Jersey: Prentice Hall.

Faulkner, M. 1999. How to know your marketing plan worked. *Grower Talks*. (April).

Flemmer, W. 1990. Rewarding careers in the nursery industry. ANLA.

Gerber, M. E. 1986. *The E-myth: Why Most Businesses Don't Work and What To Do About It*. Cambridge, Massachusetts: Ballinger Publishing.

Giardina, B. 2000. Estate. *Garden Center Merchandising and Management*. (September).

Goria, V. 1996. Making your mark. *American Nurseryman*. (October 1).

Greenridge, C. 2000. Planning profitable programs. *Nursery Retailer*. (October/November).

Greuter W., F. R. Barrie, H. M. Burdet, W. G. Chaloner, V. Demoulin, D. L. Hawksworth, P. M. Joorgensen, D. H. Nicolson, P. C. Silva, and P. Trehane, eds. 1994. *International Code of Botanical Nomenclature*.

Grissell, E. 2001. *Insects and Gardens*. Portland, Oregon: Timber Press.

Haman, D. 2000. Irrigation 101. *American Nurseryman*. (October 1).

Hammer, A. 2000. IR-4: Your tax dollars at work. *Grower Talks*. (August).

Josephson Institute of Ethics. 1998. 1998 report card on the ethics of American youth. (October). Retrieved February 2002. http://www.jiethics.org

Kristen, D. 1998. Risky business. *American Nurseryman*. (February 1).

McCartney, M. 1994. Motivation through communication. *American Nurseryman*. (June 15).

McKay, A. 2000. Get the most for your automation buck. *GMPro*. (November).

Neal, B. 1992. *Gardener's Latin*. Chapel Hill, North Carolina: Algonquin Books.

Pasian, C. C., and R. K. Lindquist. 1998. Sticky traps: A useful tool for pest-scouting. Ohio State University Fact Sheet, HYG-1033-98. Retrieved February 2002. http://ohioline.osu.edu/hyg-fact/1000/1033.html

Pearson, B. 2000. So you want to own a store. *Garden Center Merchandising and Management*. (September).

———. 2000. Independents.com. *Greenbeam*. Retrieved February 2002. http://www.greenbeam.com/features/they122500.stm

Perry, P. 1993. Terminating employees. *American Nurseryman*. (January 15).

———. 1997. Using the media to your benefit. *American Nurseryman*. (May 15).

Rain Bird Corporation. 2001. Landscape irrigation products 2001 catalog. Glendora, California: Rain Bird International.

Reback, R. 2000. Standard compliance. *American Nurseryman.* (October 1).

Ross, F. 1993. Financing your business. *ANLA.*

Safley, C., and M. K. Wohlgenant. 1994. Factors influencing purchases of nursery products in North Carolina. ARE Report No. 8, Department of Agricultural and Resource Economics, North Carolina State University, Raleigh, North Carolina.

Short, T. 2001. How to control energy costs. *GMPro.* (April).

Singley, T. 1999. Mission Possible. *American Nurseryman.* (February 15).

Steingold, F. 1994. *The Employer's Legal Handbook.* 2d ed. Soquel, California: Nolo Press.

———. 1997. *The Legal Guide for Starting and Running a Small Business.* 3d ed. Soquel, California: Nolo Press.

———. 1998. Let's make a deal. *American Nurseryman.* (July 1).

Steponkus, P., G. Good, and S. Wiest. 1976. Root hardiness of woody plants. *American Nurseryman.* (September 15).

Stearn, W. 1992. *Botanical Latin,* 4th ed. Portland, Oregon: Timber Press.

Sturdivant, B. 2000. Can your heirs afford your nursery? *NMPro.* (August).

Swartz, J. 1995. Three phases of the employer-employee relationship. *The Public Garden.* (October).

Sykes, C. 2001. Taking the test. *Garden Center Merchandising and Management.* (March).

Trehane, P., et al. 1995. *International Code of Nomenclature for Cultivated Plants,* Quarterjack Publishing, U.K.

Uniform Commercial Code. 1992. The American Law Institute and the National Conference of Commissioners on Uniform State Laws. Retrieved February 2002. http://www.law.cornell.edu/uniform/ucc.html

U.S. Department of Agriculture. 1998. 1998 census of horticultural specialties. Retrieved February 2002. http://www.nass.usda.gov/census/census97/horticulture/horticulture.htm

U.S. Department of Agriculture. Plant protection and quarantine. Animal and Plant Health Inspection Service, Riverdale, Maryland. Retrieved February 2002. http://www.aphis.usda.gov/ppq/

U.S. Department of Labor. *Small Business Handbook.* Laws Regulations and Technical Assistance Services. Retrieved February 2002. http://www.dol.gov/asp/programs/handbook/main.htm

U.S. Environmental Protection Agency. 1993. The worker protection standard for agricultural pesticides: How to comply—what employers need to know. EPA Publication 735-B-93-001, Washington, D.C.

U.S. Internal Revenue Service 1999. Independent contractor or employee. IRS Publication 1779, Washington, D.C.

Vinchesi, B. 2000. A well-planned, properly installed system with the right parts will meet your watering needs. *Grounds Maintenance.* (June).

Vollmer, G. 1999. Calculating your production costs—in plain English. *Grower Talks.* (January).

Warren, S., K. Perry, and D. Bir. 1990. Overwintering container-grown nursery crops: Plant, air and medium thermal Response to Porous Row Covers. *Journal of Environmental Horticulture* 8 (4): 161–165.

Index

Note: Page numbers in *italic type* indicate photographs or illustrations. Page numbers in **boldface type** indicate tables.